KU-721-320

Christopher Columbus, Plaza de Colón

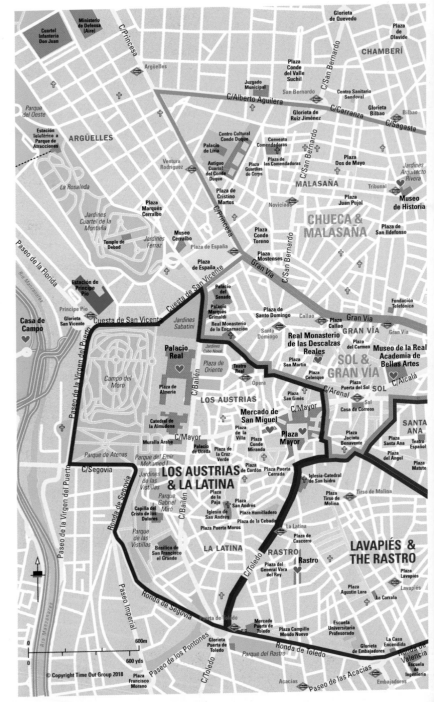

# Madrid

**timeout.com / madrid**

**72**

**143**

178

# Contents

# Introduction

Madrid has few residents who can call themselves *madrileño*, yet the presence of migrants from all over the country makes the capital what it is. Andalucía may be the birthplace of flamenco, but Madrid has the top-class venues, and sooner or later the best artists all make their way here; similarly, any aspiring *torero* must make his debut in Las Ventas bullring. The city may be far from the sea, but it has long boasted the best fish and seafood in Europe. Unable to provide its own produce, Madrid demands and pays for the choicest pickings.

In the euphoria of newly democratic Spain, when anything seemed possible, Madrid filled with artists, actors, musicians and filmmakers, creating the much-lauded Movida cultural movement. Since then, political infighting and the recession have taken their toll on this bouncy optimism, but the vital café and club society endures, and Madrid today offers a greater variety of nightlife than any other European city. Sure, there are challenges aplenty, but it is still possible to get caught up in that same uplifting swirl of energy that the city first experienced way back in the 1980s.

Paseo del Prado

## ABOUT THE GUIDE

This is one of a series of Time Out guidebooks to cities across the globe. Written by local experts, our guides are thoroughly researched and meticulously updated. They aim to be inspiring, irreverent, well-informed and trustworthy.

**Time Out Madrid** is divided into five sections: Discover, Explore, Experience, Understand and Plan.

**Discover** introduces the city and provides inspiration for your visit.

**Explore** is the main sightseeing section of the guide and includes detailed listings and reviews for sights and museums, restaurants ❿, tapas bars ❿, cafés and bars ❿, and shops and services ❿, all organised by area with a corresponding street map. To help navigation, each area of Madrid has been assigned its own colour.

**Experience** covers the cultural life of the city in depth, including festivals, film, LGBT, music, nightlife, theatre and more.

**Understand** provides in-depth background information that places Madrid in its historical and cultural context.

**Plan** offers practical visitor information, including accommodation options and details of public transport.

### Hearts

We use hearts ♥ to pick out venues, sights and experiences in the city that we particularly recommend. The very best of these are featured in the Top 20 (*see p10*) and receive extended coverage in the guide.

### Maps

A detachable fold-out map can be found on the inside back cover. There's also an overview map (*see p8*) and individual streets maps for each area of the city. The venues featured in the guide have been given a grid reference so that you can find them easily on the maps and on the ground.

### Prices

All our **restaurant listings** are marked with a euro symbol category from budget to blow-out (€-€€€€), indicating the price you should expect to pay for an average main course: € = under €10; €€ = €10-€20; €€€ = €20-€30; €€€€ = over €30.

A similar system is used in our **Accommodation** chapter based on the hotel's standard prices for one night in a double room: **Budget** = under €100; **Moderate** = €100-€150; **Expensive** = €150-€200; **Luxury** = over €200.

# Discover

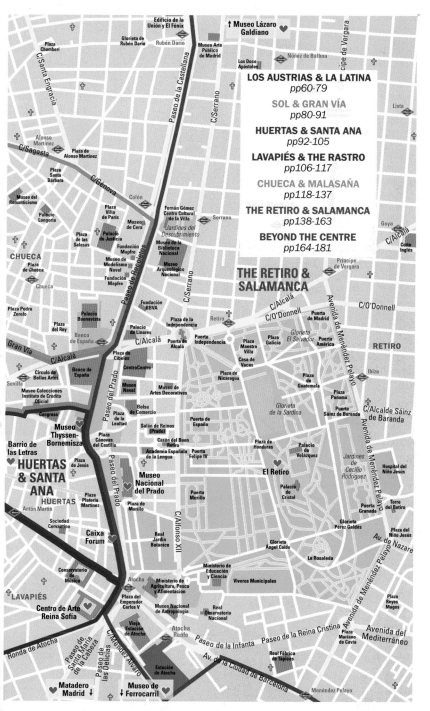

**LOS AUSTRIAS & LA LATINA**
*pp60-79*

**SOL & GRAN VÍA**
*pp80-91*

**HUERTAS & SANTA ANA**
*pp92-105*

**LAVAPIÉS & THE RASTRO**
*pp106-117*

**CHUECA & MALASAÑA**
*pp118-137*

**THE RETIRO & SALAMANCA**
*pp138-163*

**BEYOND THE CENTRE**
*pp164-181*

# Top 20

*From royal art to the Rastro market, we count down the city's finest*

# 01

**Museo Nacional del Prado** *p144*

This iconic gallery houses the greatest collection of religious art in the world, and is an essential stop on any Madrid circuit. The focus is on paintings from the 15th to the 17th centuries – most notably with the works of Velázquez – but fans of Goya, Hieronymous Bosch, Rubens and many other major artists will not leave disappointed.

# 02

## Museo Thyssen-Bornemisza *p96*

Home to an unparalleled private collection of art, this gallery offers an impressive number and range of significant artists and movements – from Tintoretto to Kandinsky, from Flemish old masters to cubism. It has the feel of a highly personal selection, which clearly displays the occasionally quirky tastes of the late Baron Hans-Heinrich Thyssen-Bornemisza and his wife.

# 03

### Plaza Mayor *p68*

The handsome, arcaded Plaza Mayor has been a hub of city life since the 15th century, when it was a market square. It was spectacularly overhauled according to a commission from Philip III (who is represented in the equestrian statue at its centre) in the 16th century, and it has had many impressive buildings added since.

# 04

### Palacio Real *p66*

The Royal Palace has an unfathomable 3,000 rooms, many of which are open to the public and are decorated with exquisite frescoes and reliefs, and filled with glorious statuary and paintings. Highlights include the throne room and the armoury, where you can see the same armour that El Cid wore into battle.

# 05

### Museo Nacional Centro de Arte Reina Sofía *p112*

Though it doesn't claim the same clout as the Prado or the Thyssen, the Reina Sofía boasts as its showpiece Picasso's *Guernica*, a vast outpouring of grief and rage at the horrors of war. Most other important Spanish artists are represented, too, and you'll see further works by Picasso, as well as art by Miró and Dalí.

# 06

### The Retiro *p143*

The Retiro in the early evening after the punishing temperatures of a hot summer's day is a sight not to be missed. Families and couples turn out to stroll arm in arm along the park's manicured pathways under its numerous trees or to take a boat for a turn on its pretty lake.

# 07

## The Rastro *p111*

Madrid's beloved flea market is less of a shopping experience and more of a Sunday tradition. Turn up early for any chance of a bargain, or simply stroll among the stalls soaking up the atmosphere, and make the most of the many nearby cafés that have sprung up to cater for the leisurely brunch crowd.

# 08

## CaixaForum Madrid *p273*

Housed in the former Mediodía Electric Power Station, and remodelled by architects Herzog & de Meuron to striking effect, this cutting-edge cultural centre runs a lively programme of events and exhibitions. Contemporary and traditional temporary art exhibitions are run alongside engaging and stimulating music and poetry events, as well as lectures, debates and workshops.

# 09

## Museo Lázaro Galdiano *p157*

This is a wonderfully eclectic private collection that includes not only 15,000 artworks (including a couple of typically eerie paintings by Goya, as well as work from Bosch, El Greco and Constable), but ancient jewellery, armour and weaponry, illuminated manuscripts, ceramics and furniture. The former home of businessman and art collector Lázaro Galdiano, the building itself is worth the trip uptown.

# 10

## Real Monasterio de las Descalzas Reales *p85*

The favoured convent of barefoot (*descalza*) novices from the aristocracy, and benefitting from royal patronage, the wildly baroque Descalzas Reales was bequeathed many great works of art over the years, including paintings by Titian and Breughel. Most of the art is on show to the public today, and a cloistered community of nuns still lives here.

# 11

## Museo de la Real Academia de Bellas Artes de San Fernando *p86*

Unjustly overlooked thanks to fierce competition from Madrid's major art museums, the Bellas Artes, as it is known, has a fantastic collection of paintings, mostly from the 15th to 17th centuries. These include 13 important works by Goya, as well as paintings by Velázquez, Rubens and Zurbarán. It also houses an engravings museum that has original plates used by Goya for his etchings.

# 12

## Barrio de las Letras *p102*

The area around Plaza Santa Ana and Calle Huertas is known as the 'District of Letters' for the playwrights, poets and men of words that once walked these streets. Quotes from their better-known works are inlaid in the pavements in bronze. Today, this is still the city's main theatre district, with the landmark Teatro Español and Teatro de la Zarzuela.

# 13

### Mercado de San Miguel *p72*

This elegant market, with a restored 19th-century wrought-iron facade, has been a huge success story since reopening in 2009 and was one of the first of a number of gastro markets to open all over Spain. It's a good place to pick up local delicacies to take home as souvenirs, or to just crawl the many tapas bars.

# 14

### San Isidro *p201*

There is no shortage of festivals in Madrid but none is more riotous than the Fiestas de San Isidro in mid May, celebrating the city's patron saint. There is a series of concerts, shows and performances in venues and squares all over the city, and families go on a pilgrimage to the Ermita de San Isidro in traditional *castizo* costume on the 15th.

# 15

### Parque El Capricho de la Alameda de Osuna *p170*

Outside the centre but accessible by metro, the Parque El Capricho is a real delight, with rose gardens, lakes and replica classical temples. It was the 18th-century country estate of the Duke and Duchess of Osuna, who had its theatrically designed gardens designed as a meeting place for the great artistic minds of the time, as well as more enlightened members of the aristocracy.

# 16

## Casa de Campo *p167*

This huge slice of parkland is close to the centre but feels like the countryside, providing a much-needed green lung to the city. In addition to its vast expanses of grass and network of wooded pathways, it has a boating lake lined with cafés, a zoo, swimming pools and a funfair. You can get here on the Teleférico de Madrid cable car.

# 17

## Museo de Historia *p123*

The History Museum lay virtually empty for many years, but has been superbly revamped to house a collection of paintings, scale models, furniture, interesting artefacts and old photos of Madrid. It now provides an informative and enjoyable introduction to the history of the city starting from the beginning of its importance in the 16th century.

# 18

## Matadero Madrid *p178*

This vibrant cultural centre is situated in the improbably handsome surroundings of a former slaughterhouse (*matadero*). As well as some of the most exciting artistic, cinematic and musical programming in the city, the rambling complex is a great place for lunch in its restaurant in the former boilerhouse, or for a drink under the stars in summer.

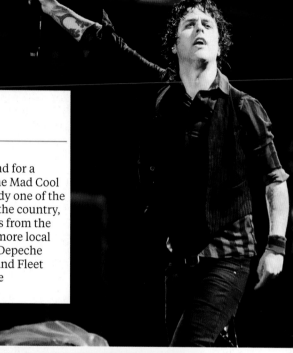

# 19

## Mad Cool *p203*

It has only been around for a couple of years, but the Mad Cool music festival is already one of the most talked-about in the country, and pulls in big names from the UK and US as well as more local acts. Massive Attack, Depeche Mode, Jack Johnson and Fleet Foxes all feature in the line-up for 2018.

# 20

## Museo del Ferrocarril de Madrid
*p181*

In a city of such grand attractions and with an abundance of high culture, the appeal of this modest little railway museum – with its interesting collection of old locomotives, clocks, models and train-related paraphernalia – is curiously enduring. Something of a sleeper hit, you might say.

# COME
# HERE, YOU

Get to know the Madrid attractions
with pulling power, and book them for
less with Time Out.

 **TIMEOUT.COM/
MADRID/ATTRACTIONS**

# Itineraries

*Make the most of every Madrid moment with a tailored travel plan*

## ESSENTIAL WEEKEND

**Budget** €340 for two (€325 with the Paseo del Arte ticket, *p99*)
**Getting around** Walking

## DAY 1

### Morning

Start the day in the **Puerta del Sol** (*see p82*), Madrid's official centre, by enjoying a coffee and a pastry in **La Mallorquina** (*see p90*) – something of a Madrid institution.

Head south-east down the Carrera de San Jerónimo until you reach the **Paseo del Prado** (*see p140*). Madrid's three world-famous art museums – the Thyssen, the Prado and the Reina Sofía – are all in the vicinity, but we don't suggest you try to tackle them all. The **Museo Nacional del Prado** (*see p144*), based on Spain's royal collections, is the absolute don't-miss. Buy a ticket from the machine outside to skip the queues, and head to the Goya rooms. Other highlights include Bosch's *Garden of Earthly Delights* and Velázquez's *Las Meninas*.

Museo Nacional del Prado

## Afternoon

**Estado Puro** (*see p101*), not far from the Prado, is a good bet if you're looking for local cuisine in a chic space. Then enjoy a post-meal stroll south down the Paseo, taking in the façade of the **CaixaForum** (*see p273*) on the right – its vertical garden is now one of the most photographed spots in town.

After a morning of culture, you might like to enjoy some of Madrid's green highlights; the restful **Jardín Botánico** (*see p152*) lies just off the Paseo del Prado, while the **Retiro** park (*see p143*), with its shady avenues, is reached via the pedestrianised **Cuesta de Moyano** (*see p142*), lined with high-quality second-hand book stalls.

CaixaForum Madrid

## Evening

After a few hours relaxing in the park, head north-west to the historic *barrio* of Los Austrias. In Madrid, afternoon shopping hours are 4pm to around 9pm, and in Plaza del Conde de Barajas, near the Plaza Mayor, you'll find **Taller Puntera** (*see p74*), Madrid's best shop for artisan leather products. After flexing the credit card, head round the corner to the **Mercado de San Miguel** (*see p72*) for some upmarket tapas – it's a great spot to witness *madrileños* doing what they do best: enjoying food and drink in sociable surroundings.

Taller Puntera

# DAY 2

## Morning

Environmentally minded mayor Manuela Carmena is changing the face of Madrid and nowhere is this more apparent than in **Gran Vía**, with its newly pedestrianised status. Strolling down here, you can now properly appreciate the grandiose architecture, little changed over the decades and beloved of various film directors. Head east until it merges with C/Alcalá, at the spectacular **Edificio Metrópolis** (*see p271*), and cross the road to the elegant **Círculo de Bellas Artes** (*see p87*) for coffee. Suitably fuelled, walk a couple of blocks south to the **Museo Thyssen-Bornemisza** (*see p96*) for a morning walking among artistic treasures from almost every major movement.

Gran Vía

Museo Nacional Centro de Arte Reina Sofía

## Afternoon

The area just south-west of here has seen a recent explosion in cool, independent bistros, particularly in the streets around C/Huertas. The best might just be **TriCiclo** (*see p101*), or – if it's full – its little sister **Tandem** (*see p101*), down the road. This was the favoured *barrio* of Madrid's men of letters during Spain's Golden Age of literature, and you might want to visit one of its quirky little sights, such as the **Sociedad Cervantina** printing press (*see p102*), where the first edition of *Don Quixote* was created. Alternatively, and depending on energy levels, you could walk down to the city's third art palace, the **Reina Sofía** (*see p112*).

MUSEO THYSSEN BORNEMISZA

Círculo de Bellas Artes

Sociedad Cervantina

Salmón Guru

## Evening

Bars and restaurants around the Reina Sofía are largely aimed at the sightseeing public, but if you head back up to C/ Huertas, you will eventually arrive at the elegant Plaza Santa Ana, ringed with café terraces. To walk in Hemingway's footsteps, have a beer at his old haunt, the **Cervecería Alemana** (*see p104*) and follow it up with a light supper at lively **Ana La Santa** (*see p100*) on the same square. The area also lays claim to Madrid's new, coolest cocktail joint, **Salmón Guru** (*see p105*), the ideal spot for the final nightcap.

# BUDGET BREAK

**Budget** €55 for two
**Getting around** Walking

## Morning

Malasaña was the focus of the post-Franco counter-cultural movement known as **La Movida Madrileña** (*see pp262-265*). Although the movement is well and truly over, the neighbourhood retains an atmospheric, grungy feel, with boho cafés and music-led bars. Soak up the vibe with a late breakfast at **Levadura Madre** (*see p136*) or **Lolina Vintage Café** (*see p136*).

After fuelling up for the day ahead, take a wander around the neighbourhood's laid-back streets. Some of Madrid's best small shops are to be found in this area, including **J&J Books & Coffee** (*see p137*) and espadrilles-specialist **Antigua Casa Crespo** (*see p137*). The area is home to the **Centro Cultural Conde Duque** (*see p130*) – both the building and the contemporary art museum within it (*see p132*) are worth a visit – and the newly renovated **Museo de Historia** (*see p123*), which, like all municipally run museums, is free to enter.

## Afternoon

Although there are plenty of good restaurants in Malasaña, to get a sense of the distinctness of Madrid's different neighbourhoods, cross over Calle de Fuencarral into Chueca for lunch. The famously gay *barrio* has several good, and chic, restaurants, but if money is an object, try the ineffable **Tienda de Vinos** (also known as El Comunista, *see p127*), for cheap and cheerful Spanish grub in an unbeatably old-school atmosphere.

After a leisurely lunch, you'll have time to explore more of Madrid's *barrios*. The city's compact size means that its central neighbourhoods are all within walking distance of each other. Head south of Gran Vía, through the Puerta del Sol, until you reach Lavapiés, the city's most multicultural *barrio*. It begins at the spruced-up **Plaza Tirso de Molina** (*see p108*).

Centro Cultural Conde Duque

## Evening

A stroll through Lavapiés brings you to Calle de Santa Isabel, home to Madrid's national film theatre in the art nouveau **Cine Doré** (*see p211*). The place has featured in films by Pedro Almodóvar, a key Movida figure, and its café is a lively meeting spot for film buffs before a cheap (€2.50) screening – perhaps of a silent movie, or a classic from the national archives.

On the same street as the Cine Doré lies one of Madrid's best tapas bars, **La Musa de Espronceda** (*see p115*), a great starting point for a Lavapiés bar crawl.

Antigua Casa Crespo

# FAMILY DAY OUT

**Budget** €340 for two adults, two children
**Getting around** Cable car, walking

## Morning

In Madrid, modes of transport can be as much fun for kids as the destinations themselves, and none provides as much exhilaration as the cable car, or **Teleférico** (*see p175*), to Casa de Campo park, a spine-tingling ride over the tree tops. Once there, the **Casa de Campo** (*see p167*) is a giant playground, with swimming pools, a zoo and playgrounds for little ones, but the main draw is the **Parque de Atracciones** funfair (*see p173*), which has some properly scary rides – along with some beautifully sedate ones.

Casa de Campo

## Afternoon

Unless you've organised a picnic, eating options are fairly poor in the park, but the return trip on the cable car brings you close to **Casa Mingo** (*see p175*), a huge, noisy and family-friendly place, where chicken and chips is the order of the day. Stroll it off afterwards via the **Plaza de Oriente** (*see p64*) and head for the **Palacio Real** (*see p66*), loved by kids for its spectacular collection of armour. From here it's a five- to ten-minute walk to **Chocolatería San Ginés** (*see p71*), for a much-needed energy boost in the form of *churros* dipped in hot chocolate.

## Evening

Fifty metres or so south of here is the stunning **Plaza Mayor** (*see p68*), a huge arcaded square where children can wander about, gazing at the human statues, buskers and hawkers until hunger strikes again. The square is a great place for parents to sip on a beer, meanwhile, but not really to eat – better to head south to any of the many tapas bars along C/Cava Baja or C/Cava Alta. Though *madrileños* wouldn't dream of eating before 9pm, most will be serving food well before that, and the earlier you go, the better chance of the little ones getting a seat.

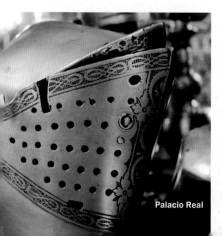

Palacio Real

Plaza Mayor

# When to Visit

*Madrid by season*

Being high up and on a plain, Madrid is exposed to some pretty fierce temperatures – *nueve meses de invierno, tres meses de infierno* (nine months of winter, three months of hell), as the saying goes – but has adapted to both these extremes with aplomb, with a cosy range of options in winter and an ever-increasing range of al fresco fun in summer. It's impossible to get bored in Madrid, and the packed cultural programme of festivals, concerts and exhibitions is spread throughout the year (see pp198-206).

### Spring

A Madrid spring can be unpredictable, weather-wise – bring clothes for all eventualities – but at its best will be warm, with blue skies. **Easter** week can be very busy (and hotel prices astronomical), and April normally sees some rain, though this rarely lasts long. The grand event of the season is the festival of **San Isidro** (see p201) in mid May, in which the entire city spills out on to the streets.

San Isidro

Real Jardín Botánico p152

MIA at Mad Cool

## Summer

It used to the be case that Madrid was deserted in summer and hotels were practically giving away rooms, but this has changed in recent years with rising visitor numbers and more of a focus on summer activities (along with a huge increase in hotel swimming pools). It's still a good time for accommodation bargains, however, with even five-star rooms going for a song. The summer kicks off with the month-long **Suma Flamenca** festival (*see p202*) in May and June, followed by the wonderful, all-encompassing **Veranos de la Villa** (*see p204*), with its concerts, theatre, fireworks and outdoor movies. New music festival **Mad Cool** (*see p203*) in July is a must for indie fans.

## Autumn

Autumn tends to be the time when the big-hitting exhibitions are launched, as *madrileños* trail back into town from their mountain retreats. The 'big three' art museums are good bets for this, but it's also worth checking the websites for the **Fundación Mapfre** (*see p156*) and the **CaixaForum** (*see p273*). The weather is mostly mild, and it's worth bringing an umbrella in October (though rain is far from guaranteed).

## Winter

Madrid does winter well, and its finest dishes are warming, hearty stews, best eaten in cosy, traditional restaurants such as **La Bola Taberna** (*see p87*) or **Casa Lucio** (*see p76*). The twinkling **Christmas market** in the Plaza Mayor is not be missed, and if you possibly can, try and catch the Three Kings' parade along C/ Alcalá for **Epiphany** on 5 January.

Plaza Mayor at Christmas

# Madrid Today

*Back from the brink*

Madrid is picking itself up and dusting itself off. Barraged by an almost decade-long economic crisis that saw crippling strikes, constant demonstrations, staggering unemployment and swingeing cuts to healthcare and education, the Spanish capital is finally emerging blinking from its foxhole, a little leaner, meaner and savvier. And a lot more outward-looking. Once mocked as a closed-minded provincial capital, the city has grown increasingly worldly since immigration took off in the '80s, but the crisis has driven Spaniards to look for opportunities beyond their borders like never before. An export boom has helped steer GDP back to pre-crisis levels, while Madrid has become more adept at attracting foreign tourists. In 2016, the capital welcomed more international than Spanish visitors for the first time.

Tourists have encountered a city even better equipped to cater to their needs and without the exorbitant prices of London or Paris. There is another side to the city, however. Unemployment has fallen from a jaw-dropping 26 per cent at the height of the crisis but remains persistently high at just over 18 per cent, and jobs are insecure, while wages are low. Nevertheless, with Spain now boasting the best-performing major economy in the EU, there's at least room for cautious optimism among long-suffering *madrileños*.

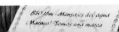

## Miracle granny

Spanish politics entered a new age after the mass protests of the '*indignados*' in 2011. This movement of the disaffected and those tired of austerity measures saw the occupation of the Puerta del Sol and ultimately gave rise to the popular Podemos party, a more youthful and left-wing political force than had been seen in Spain for quite some time. While Madrid has been the stage for many of these political changes, their real effect on the city is best personified by its new mayor, septuagenarian retired judge Manuela Carmena. Dubbed the 'miracle granny', the head of Ahora Madrid – a platform that includes Podemos and other leftist groups – became the capital's first non-People's Party (PP) mayor in 24 years when she took over from Ana Botella, wife of the former PP prime minister, José María Aznar, in 2015. She quickly got to work fulfilling election pledges such as stopping evictions, reducing inequality and, above all, listening to *madrileños*, boasting of having held 360 meetings with people from King Felipe to street musicians during her first 100 days in office.

The mass protests of the *indignados* in 2011 ushered in a new age for Madrid.

Manuela Carmena, the 'miracle granny' and retired judge, is head of Ahora Madrid.

A reluctant politician – she has repeatedly said she won't stand for re-election in 2019 – Carmena has sought to remain independent, distancing herself from Podemos and often finding herself criticised as much from the left as the right. *Madrileños* seem to like her lone ranger stance, however, especially the younger ones: 65 per cent of 18- to 34-year-olds back her, according to a poll in May 2017.

Part of Carmena's remit has been to get *madrileños* more involved in how their city is governed. In February 2017, residents were invited to vote on a variety of local issues for the first time. These ranged in scope from whether there should be a single ticket for the entire public transport system to plans to remodel the Plaza de España (*see p32* Squaring Up). Only 212,000 of the 2.7 million people eligible voted in the ballot, which City Hall predictably hailed a roaring success and the opposition branded a colossal waste of funds.

Whatever the case, the outcomes of the experiment will leave their mark. Among them are plans to semi-pedestrianise the main Gran Vía thoroughfare, introducing wider pavements, a dedicated bike path and fewer lanes for vehicles as part of a long-term plan to turn Madrid into a low-emissions city. Things are certainly looking a whole lot greener under Carmena, who has also steamed ahead with other environmental initiatives – notably controversial anti-pollution measures, originally drawn up by Botella, that include the banning of half the city's cars from roads on days when harmful nitrogen dioxide refuses to drop below recommended levels (so far it has only been put into practice once, in December 2016). She also plans to expand the city's cycle lane network and new BiciMad bike rental service.

But one of the most spectacular environmental changes has been taking place down by the river. In May 2016 City Hall began a project put forward by NGO Ecologistas en

## Things are certainly looking a whole lot greener under Carmena, Madrid's septuagenarian mayor

Work continues along the banks of the Manzanares. It is hoped that planting native trees, shrubs and plants will encourage more wildlife.

# Squaring Up

*The reinvention of Plaza de España*

For an illustrative example of the changes Mayor Manuela Carmena is introducing to the city, head to Plaza de España. In February 2017 she gave *madrileños* their first-ever vote on a city planning proposal when she asked them to pick the design to polish up the plaza. The winner – whittled down from close to 70 projects – was architects Lorenzo Fernández-Ordóñez and Fernando Porras-Isla's 'Welcome Mother Nature, Goodbye Mr Ford', which will spruce up the square by planting 1,000 new trees and further cover surrounding roads to create pedestrianised green 'corridors' linking the plaza with the Palacio Real's Sabatini Gardens and the Parque Oeste. A new esplanade will connect the square to Gran Vía, while a central clearing will provide a space for activities.

The enormous 117-metre (384-feet) Edificio España, which looms over the plaza, will also be getting a long-awaited makeover after a decade lying derelict. Built as a showpiece for the Franco regime in 1948-53 and shuttered in 2005, the 27-floor tower passed from the Santander bank to the Chinese-owned Wanda group – whose idea to demolish and partly rebuild it was rejected by City Hall – before finally arriving in the hands of Mallorcan hotel chain Riu, which plans to spend €400 million turning it into a 650-room hotel.

Scheduled to open in 2019, it won't be the only new hotel on the block. The boutique Dear Madrid on the corner with Gran Vía was the first new arrival in 2015, followed two years later by the five-star Barceló Torre Madrid in the plaza's other skyscraper, the Torre de Madrid. With the similarly exclusive VP Plaza de España adding to the square's luxury accommodation options in autumn 2017, Plaza de España is scrubbing up well.

Acción (Ecologists in Action) to raise seven of the ten dams controlling the flow of the city's Manzanares river – site of former PP mayor Alberto Ruiz Gallardón's grand Madrid Río project, which buried the M-30 ring road and built a riverside park ten kilometres long on top. The result has been an amazing explosion of life as water levels dropped, islands of sediment formed and vegetation grew to attract an abundance of urban wildlife – including ducks, herons, storks, egrets, cormorants and kingfishers above the surface, along with carp, barbel, pike, tench and even the odd escaped terrapin below. Work is now under way to bring nature back to the banks of a 1.3-kilometre (0.8-mile) stretch of river just above the Madrid Río park between the Los Franceses and Reina Victoria bridges, planting 16,831 native trees, shrubs and plants with the aim of encouraging more wildlife.

Elsewhere, Real Madrid's Bernabéu football stadium is set to get a €400-million makeover (that's the price of just over two Neymars), while city rivals Atlético Madrid have moved into their new home in La Peineta stadium (rechristened

Atlético Madrid's new home is La Peineta stadium (rechristened the Wanda Metropolitano).

the Wanda Metropolitano), finally putting one of the biggest white elephants left over from the city's three failed Olympics bids to good use. And don't hold your breath, but it looks like the long-delayed Operation Chamartín project, first put forward in 1993, looks like it might finally be moving ahead after Carmena, the Public Works Ministry and construction operators agreed on plans. Once it gets final approval by City Hall, the €6,000 million project to build 11,000 new homes and redevelop Chamartín train station as the centre of a flash new financial district to lure multinationals will hopefully get under way in 2019.

Madrid's financial district

### Not fade away

Big changes once again lie ahead. How much *madrileños* will embrace them, however, remains to be seen. Some have already expressed concerns about the effect unbridled tourism is having on the city centre, as locals find themselves priced out by landlords turning residential apartments into more lucrative occasional accommodation. Rents have risen by 14.6 per cent in just one year, according to the Bank of Spain. Perhaps such are the prices you have to pay for more wealth and jobs, but what if they come at the cost of the thing that makes the city so appealing in the first place? After all, it's the energy of the streets – the heaving terrace bars, honking car horns, hollering tradesman, hurrying waiters, hustling markets – that really define Madrid and seduce so many visitors. What if it all faded away?

Spain's capital has undoubtedly become more sensible, more efficient and tamer since the wild post-Franco Movida years – certainly no bad thing if you like getting your paperwork done or internet installed on time. But the question of how much further the city should or could tread this corporate path will continue to dog Carmena, her successors and *madrileños* themselves, as Madrid matures.

**Some locals have expressed concerns about the effect unbridled tourism is having on the city centre**

# Eating & Drinking

*From* cocido *to curry, it's all here*

Not so long ago dishes from Asturias were thought exotic here in the capital. But today, thanks in no small part to immigration, *madrileños* have become Spain's unlikely flag-bearers for culinary globalisation. Mexican, of course, has always been around, and Asian food now features strongly too. Add in Italian, French, Cuban, Middle Eastern, Thai and Japanese, and you start to wonder about the future of paella. Whereas the dining scene used to be all red-checked tablecloths or old-style elegance, now those who fancy chic and minimal have a place to go. Finally, vegetarians can smile too – the options are no longer limited to tortilla or green beans with the ham picked out.

## Capital mainstays

The famous *cocido madrileño* – a stew of various bits of meat, offal and vegetables served up in three courses – is still eaten religiously, particularly at weekends. The down-home *casas de comida* (eating houses) are packed daily with regulars who are perfectly happy with a plain *ensalada mixta* followed by a greasy pork chop and the ubiquitous *flan* for dessert. Even young hipsters are faithful to the less expensive classic *mesones* (old-style taverns), while the most upscale traditional places still require you to join a waiting list.

Most traditional *madrileño* cuisine is found in the area around Los Austrias and La Latina – particularly along C/Cava Baja, leading south from the Plaza Mayor. Chueca and Huertas are packed with stylish restaurants offering both international and Spanish cuisine (many of which offer great value at lunchtime). The city's most upmarket restaurants can be found in the Salamanca area.

❤ **Best restaurants**

**Ribeira do Miño** *p126*
Impossibly fresh seafood in a festive atmosphere.

**El Sobrino de Botín** *p70*
Madrid's best loved, and the world's oldest.

**TriCiclo** *p95*
The best of the new wave of creative bistros.

**In the know**
**Smoke signal**

Spain's tough anti-smoking laws mean that smoking is now banned in all restaurants, though there has been a marked increase in permit applications for open-air terraces as a result.

Cocido madrileño

## Timing and prices

Rule number one for visitors to Madrid: don't go out too early. *Madrileños* rarely eat lunch before 2pm. Consequently, dinner is usually eaten late as well – around 10pm, and even later in summer. It's advisable to book a table in most places for Friday and Saturday nights, and at other times if you're in a big group. Many restaurants close on Sunday evening and all day Monday. August is livelier than it used to be, but most restaurants still close for at least two weeks. Where possible, we've indicated this, but it's best to ring and check.

While the *menú del día* is aimed at workers looking for a cheap three-course lunch, the concept also works well for hungry tourists after a morning's sightseeing. It can be a great way to eat cheaply and well, and usually consists of a starter, main course, dessert, bread and wine. Dishes cost much less than they would do à la carte (although portions tend to be smaller) and the *menú del día* also provides a chance to sample upmarket places on a budget. Standard Spanish restaurants tend to offer typical *comida casera* (home cooking), though, so don't expect fireworks. The *menú del día* should not be confused with the *menú degustación*, a tasting menu.

By law, restaurants are obliged to declare on the menu if VAT (IVA) is included and if there's a cover charge. In practice, however, they almost never do, and there almost always is (strictly speaking cover charges are illegal, but are often disguised as a charge for bread). In bars it's customary to pay at the end, although different rules apply in touristy places or on outdoor terraces. Tipping is something of a grey area – around five per cent is a reasonable rule of thumb. In a bar you'd just leave the small change given back to you, while in restaurants, a couple of euros will suffice – though don't be shy about tipping more if you're impressed.

# Tapas Glossary

*A primer of the classics*

There are three basic sizes of *tapa* portion: a *pincho* (more or less a mouthful), a *tapa* (a saucerful or so) and a *ración* (a small plateful). Some bars offer *media raciones* (a half-*ración*). If there's something you like the look of that isn't identifiable on the menu or the list behind the bar, just point to it. Bread (*pan*) normally comes automatically, but if not, just ask. Most often, you let a tapas bill mount up and pay when you've finished, not when you order; it's usually about 25 per cent more expensive if you sit at a table rather than eat at the bar.

## Basics

**Bocadillo** sandwich in a roll or part of a baguette; **cazuelita** small hot casserole; **montados** canapé-style mixed tapas, often a slice of bread with a topping; **pincho/pinchito** small titbit on a toothpick, or mouthful-sized *tapa*; **pulga/pulguita** small filled roll; **ración** a portion (small plateful); **tabla** platter (of cheese, cold meats) **tosta** slice of toast with topping; **una de gambas, chorizo**... one portion of prawns, chorizo...; **por unidad** per item.

## Carne, aves y embutidos (meat, poultry & charcuterie)

**Albóndigas** meatballs; **alitas de pollo** chicken wings; **callos** tripe; **cecina** dry-cured beef; **chistorra** Navarrese sausage with paprika; **chorizo** spicy sausage, eaten cooked or cold; **criadillas** bulls' testicles; **flamenquines** ham and pork rolls in breadcrumbs; **longaniza, fuet** mild but chewy, often herby, salami-type sausages; **mollejas** sweetbreads; **morcilla** black, blood sausage; **oreja (de cerdo)** pig's ear; **pincho moruno** grilled meat brochette; **riñones al Jerez** kidneys cooked in sherry; **salchichón** fatty, soft, salami-type sausage; **San Jacobo** fried ham and cheese escalope; **sobrassada** soft Mallorcan paprika sausage; **torrezno** pork crackling; **zarajo** grilled sheep's intestine on a stick.

## Pescado y mariscos (fish & shellfish)

**Ahumados** smoked fish; **almejas** clams; **anchoas** salted conserved anchovies; **anguilas** eels; **angulas** elvers; **berberechos** cockles; **bienmesabe** marinated fried fish; **boquerones en vinagre/fritos** pickled/fried fresh anchovies; **calamares a la romana** squid rings fried in batter; **calamares en su tinta** squid cooked in their ink; **carabineiros** large red ocean prawns; **centollo** spider crab; **chanquetes** tiny fish, served deep-fried; **chipirones en su tinta** small Atlantic squid in their ink; **chopito** small cuttlefish; **cigalas** crayfish; **croqueta de bacalao** salt cod croquette; **fritura de pescado** flash-fried fish; **gambas al ajillo** prawns fried with garlic; **gambas en gabardina** prawns deep-fried in batter; **huevas** fish roe; **mojama** dried and salted tuna fish; **navajas** razor clams; **nécora** swimming crab; **percebes** goose-neck barnacles; **pulpo a feira/a la gallega** octopus with paprika and olive oil; **quisquillas** shrimps; **salpicón** cold chopped salad, often with some shellfish; **sepia** large squid; **soldaditos de pavía** strips of salt cod, fried in light batter; **tigres** mussels cooked with a spicy tomato and béchamel sauce; **zamburiñas** small scallops.

## Vegetales (vegetable tapas)

**Aceitunas**, **olivas (adobados, rellenos)** olives (pickled, stuffed); **almendras saladas** salted almonds; **pan con tomate** bread rubbed with fresh tomato and olive oil; **patatas bravas** deep-fried potatoes with hot pepper sauce; **perdiz de huerta** lettuce hearts; **pimientos de Padrón** fried, and occasionally hot small green peppers; **queso en aceite** cheese marinated in olive oil; **setas** wild mushrooms.

## Other tapas

**Caracoles** snails; **croquetas** potato croquettes (which may be made with chicken, ham, tuna, and so on); **empanada** flat pies, usually made with a tuna filling; **empanadilla** small fried pasties, usually with a tomato and tuna filling; **ensaladilla rusa** potato salad with onions, red peppers, usually tuna and other ingredients in mayonnaise, now a completely Spanish dish that's still called a Russian salad; **huevos rellenos** stuffed, cold hard-boiled eggs; **migas (con huevo frito)** fried breadcrumbs (with fried egg); **pisto manchego** ratatouille with meat (usually ham) and egg; **revuelto** scrambled eggs.

**Morcilla**

## Tapas tips

In their more fanciful moments, Spaniards will describe them as 'the world on a plate'. They will tell you that the eating of tapas is proof of the country's gregarious nature, its need to share and the importance it places on spending time in good company. Thanks to the *tapa*, it's possible to spend the whole night in a bar without requiring help to get home. This is the point so often missed by those outside the country, those who reproduce them for dinner parties or nibble them in expensive restaurants in London. For the Spanish, it's not about what you eat, it's about how you eat.

Tapas vary from region to region, and examples of most can be found in Madrid. Galician bars highlight octopus, prawns and seafood, served in ceramic bowls, traditionally with white Ribeiro wine. In Extremaduran bars you'll find *migas* (crumbs), fried and mixed with chorizo. Asturian bars specialise in *sidra* (cider), theatrically poured from

❤ **Best tapas bars**

**Casa Alberto** *p101*
Picture-perfect traditional bar with dishes to match.

**La Taberna de Antonio Sánchez** *p115*
Unchanged in decades, with tapas that won't break the bank.

**Taberna Matritum** *p77*
Modern creative tapas with an excellent wine list.

> **Thanks to the *tapa*, it's possible to spend the whole night in a bar without requiring help to get home**

La Taberna de Antonio Sánchez *p115*

# Grape Expectations

*Spanish wines are not to be sniffed at*

Madrid is an oenophile's playground, with none of the solemnity and hefty price tags attached to wine-drinking elsewhere. Everyone drinks it here, from builders to nuns. It so pervades daily life, in fact, that the Spanish Ministry of Agriculture categorises wine as food rather than an alcoholic beverage.

Wine-lovers around the globe have now caught on to the fact that Spanish labels are the best value for your euro. US wine tsar Robert Parker claims Spain is one of the hottest regions in Europe. The sad fact remains, however, that a lot of bars serve plonk. To taste the good stuff, get to a wine bar. Madrid has a number of cosy little *enotecas* where you can settle in at the bar and try different wines by the glass. **La Cruzada** (C/Amnistía 8, Los Austrias, 91 493 91 95), for example, offers a good selection of reasonably priced *vinos*. King Alfonso XII reportedly used to frequent this bar when he needed to escape the nearby royal palace for a tipple. Check out the lovely carvings of bare-breasted women on the bar, dating back to 1827. Other spots for quality wines include the new **La Fisna** (C/Amparo 91, Lavapiés, 91 539 56 15), **Casa González** (C/León 12, Huertas, 91 429 56 18) and **Entrevinos** (C/Ferraz 36, Argüelles, 91 548 31 14).

An entertaining way to dive into Spanish wine is to attend one of Madrid's wine-tasting classes, known as *cursos de cata*, which get you swirling, sniffing and sipping good wine. **Lavinia** (C/José Ortega y Gasset 16, Salamanca, 91 426 06 04, www.lavinia.es) is a good bet, and has an impressive collection.

Run by an enthusiastic and knowledgeable Kiwi, **Devour Madrid** (madridfoodtour.com) runs wine tours, and holds tastings and introductory classes in its own cellar. You might also visit the **Escuela de Cata** (C/Martires Concepcionistas 19, Salamanca, 91 402 67 04, www.torres.es) for professional classes covering everything from soil types to food pairing. Many of the city's best wine shops, such as **Reserva y Cata** (C/Conde de Xiquena 13, Chueca, 91 319 04 01) and **Bodegas Santa Cecilia** (C/Blasco de Garay 74, Chamberí, 91 445 52 83), also offer regular *cursos de cata* in Spanish.

above the head to separate out sediment, accompanied by blood sausage (*morcilla*) or blue cabrales cheese. Andalucían bars offer dry fino sherry with *mojama* (dry-cured tuna) or sardines. Madrid's own specialities are *patatas bravas*, offal (particularly *callos*, tripe), and snails in a hot sauce.

Tapas have become more sophisticated and consequently more expensive in recent times, and an evening's *tapeo* can cost more than a full meal in a restaurant.

## What to drink

A *café con leche* is a largeish milky coffee. An espresso is a *café solo*; the same with a dash of milk is *un cortado*, while *un americano* is black, diluted with twice the normal amount of water. A *carajillo* is usually a *solo* with a shot of coñac, and you can equally ask for a *carajillo de whisky, de ron* (rum), *de Bailey's* (pronounced 'bye-lees'), *de anís* or anything else you fancy.

La Taberna de Antonio Sánchez *p115*

### In the know
**High spirits**

Be warned: spirit measures in Spain are very generous. When ordering a gin and tonic (or vodka equivalent), it's customary for the barman to keep pouring the gin into the glass until the customer tells him or her to stop, meaning that you'll often end up with half gin, half tonic.

Decaffeinated coffee is *descafeinado*, and you will normally be asked if you want it from a sachet (*de sobre*) or the machine (*de máquina*). In summer, a great alternative is *café con hielo* – iced coffee.

Tea in bars is usually awful and, unless you specifically request otherwise, will often come as a glass of hot milk with a teabag on the side. Very popular, however, are herbal teas (*infusiones*), such as *menta* (mint) or *manzanilla* (camomile). Hot chocolate is also popular and comes thick as tar, all the better for dipping *churros*, deep-fried batter sticks.

Draught beer is served in *cañas*, a small measure that varies but is less than half a pint. Some places even serve *pintas* (pints), often in a *jarra*, a large, heavy glass with a handle – but be warned that Spanish lagers are usually strong. Spain produces some good-quality beers. In Madrid, the favourite is the local Mahou, with two basic varieties – green label Mahou Clásica and stronger red label Cinco Estrellas. San Miguel is less common, while Andalucían favourite Cruzcampo is growing in popularity. A darker Mahou beer (*negra*) is also available. Shandy is *clara*, and is made with bitter lemon. Imported beers are now common, too, and craft beers can be found in many bars around town.

All bars have a sturdy, cheap red wine (*tinto*) on offer, and usually there's a white (*blanco*) and a rosé as well (*rosado*). Madrid's traditional summer drink is *tinto de verano* (red in a tall glass over ice, with a slice of lemon and topped up with lemonade).

Low- and alcohol-free beers (Laiker, Buckler, Kaliber) have an important niche in the market; other favourites for non-alcohol drinkers are the Campari-like but booze-free Bitter Kas, and plain tonic (*una tónica*) with ice and lemon. Fresh orange juice, *zumo de naranja*, is often available. Mineral water (*agua mineral*) can be ordered anywhere, either sparkling (*con gas*) or still (*sin gas*).

❤ **Best cocktail bars**

**Hemingway** *p90*
Underground speakeasy-style, perfect for lovers.

**Museo Chicote** *p90*
Hemingway's former hangout, now with added DJs.

**Salmón Guru** *p105*
A clubby, comfortable vibe and top-notch cocktails.

**Museo Chicote**

# Food Glossary
*Understanding the menu*

## Basics
**Primer plato (entrante)** first course; **segundo plato** second or main course; **postre** dessert; **plato combinado** quick, one-course meal, with several ingredients served on the same plate; **aceite y vinagre** oil and vinegar; **agua** water (**con gas/sin gas** fizzy/still); **pan** bread; **vino** wine (**tinto** red, **blanco** white, **rosado** rosé); **cerveza** beer; **la cuenta** the bill; **servicio incluído** service included; **propina** tip.

## Cooking styles and techniques
**Adobado** marinated; **al ajillo** with olive oil and garlic; **al chilindrón** (usually chicken or lamb) cooked in a spicy tomato, pepper, ham, onion and garlic sauce; **a la marinera** (fish or shellfish) cooked with garlic, onions and white wine; **a la parrilla** charcoal-grilled; **al pil-pil** (Basque) flash-fried in sizzling oil and garlic; **a la plancha** grilled directly on a hot metal plate; **al vapor** steamed; **asado** (**al horno de leña**) roast (in a wood-fired oven); **crudo** raw; **en salsa** in a sauce or gravy; **escabechado, en escabeche** marinated in vinegar with bay leaves and garlic; **estofado** braised; **frito** fried; **guisado** stewed; **hervido** boiled; **(en) pepitoria** casserole dish, usually of chicken or game, with egg, wine and almonds; **relleno** stuffed.

## Sopas y potajes (soups and stews)
**Caldo (gallego)** broth of pork and greens; **fabada** rich Asturian stew of beans, chorizo and *morcilla* (black blood sausage); **gazpacho** cold soup, usually of tomatoes, red pepper and cucumber; **purrusalda** (Basque) soup of salt cod, leeks and potatoes; **sopa de ajo** garlic soup; **sopa castellana** garlic soup with poached egg and chickpeas; **sopa de fideos** noodle soup.

## Huevos (eggs)
**Huevos fritos** fried eggs (sometimes served with chorizo); **revuelto** scrambled eggs; **tortilla asturiana** omelette with tomato, tuna and onion; **tortilla francesa** plain omelette; **tortilla de patatas** Spanish potato omelette.

## Pescado y mariscos (fish & shellfish)
**Almejas** clams; **atún, bonito** tuna; **bacalao** salt cod; **besugo** sea bream; **bogavante** lobster; **caballa** mackerel; **calamares** squid; **camarones** small shrimps; **cangrejo, buey de mar** crab; **cangrejo de río** freshwater crayfish; **dorada** gilthead bream; **gambas** prawns; **kokotxas** (Basque) hake cheeks; **langosta** spiny lobster; **langostinos** langoustines; **lubina** sea bass; **mejillones** mussels; **mero** grouper; **merluza** hake; **ostras** oysters; **pescadilla** whiting; **pescaditos** whitebait; **pulpo** octopus; **rape** monkfish; **rodaballo** turbot; **salmonete** red mullet; **sardinas** sardines; **sepia** cuttlefish; **trucha** trout; **ventresca de bonito** tuna fillet; **vieiras** scallops.

## Carne, aves, caza y embutidos (meat, poultry, game & charcuterie)
**Bistec** steak; **buey, vacuno** (cuts: **solomillo, entrecot**) beef; **butifarra** Catalan sausage; **callos** tripe; **capón** capon; **cerdo** pork, pig; **chorizo** spicy sausage, served cooked or cold; **choto** kid; **chuletas, chuletones, chuletillas** chops; **cochinillo** roast suckling pig; **cocido** traditional stew of Madrid; **codillo** knuckle (normally ham); **codornices** quails; **conejo** rabbit; **cordero** lamb; **costillas** ribs; **estofado de ternera** beef stew; **faisán** pheasant; **gallina** chicken; **hígado** liver; **jabalí** wild boar; **jamón ibérico** cured ham from Iberian

Gazpacho

**Octopus and mussels**

pigs; **jamón serrano** cured ham; **jamón york** cooked ham; **lacón** gammon ham; **lechazo, cordero lechal** milk-fed baby lamb; **liebre** hare; **lomo (de cerdo)** loin of pork; **morcilla** black blood sausage; **pato** duck; **pavo** turkey; **perdiz** partridge; **pollo** chicken; **riñones** kidneys; **salchichas** frying sausages; **sesos** brains; **ternera** veal (in Spain it is slaughtered much later than most veal, so is more accurately young beef).

### Arroz y legumbres (rice & pulses)
**Alubias, judías** white beans; **arroz a banda** rice cooked in shellfish stock; **arroz negro** black rice cooked in squid ink; **fideuà** seafood dish similar to a paella, but made with noodles instead of rice; **fríjoles** red kidney beans; **garbanzos** chickpeas; **judiones** large haricot beans; **lentejas** lentils; **pochas (caparrones)** new-season kidney beans.

### Verduras (vegetables)
**Acelgas** Swiss chard; **alcachofas** artichokes; **berenjena** aubergine/eggplant; **calabacines** courgettes/zucchini; **cebolla** onion; **champiñones** mushrooms; **col** cabbage; **ensalada mixta** basic salad of lettuce, tomato and onion; **ensalada verde** green salad, without tomato; **espárragos** asparagus; **espinacas** spinach; **grelos** turnip leaves; **guisantes** peas; **habas** broad beans; **judías verdes** green beans; **lechuga** lettuce; **menestra** braised mixed vegetables; **patatas fritas** chips; **pepino** cucumber; **pimientos** sweet peppers; **pimientos de piquillo** slightly hot red peppers; **pisto** mixture of cooked vegetables, similar to ratatouille; **setas** oyster mushrooms; **tomate** tomato; **zanahoria** carrot.

### Fruta (fruit)
**Arándanos** cranberries, blueberries, redcurrants or blackcurrants; **cerezas** cherries; **ciruelas** plums; **fresas** strawberries; **higos** figs; **macedonia** fruit salad; **manzana** apple; **melocotón** peach; **melón** melon; **moras** blackberries; **naranja** orange; **pera** pear; **piña** pineapple; **plátano** banana; **sandía** watermelon; **uvas** grapes.

### Postres (desserts)
**Arroz con leche** rice pudding; **bizcocho** sponge cake; **brazo de gitano** swiss roll; **cuajada** junket (served with honey); **flan** crème caramel; **helado** ice-cream; **leche frita** custard fried in breadcrumbs; **membrillo** quince jelly (often served with cheese); **tarta** cake; **tarta de Santiago** sponge-like almond cake; **torrijas** sweet bread fritters.

### Quesos (cheeses)
**Burgos, villalón, requesón** white, cottage-like cheeses, often eaten as dessert; **cabrales** strong blue Asturian goat's cheese; **idiazábal** Basque sheep's milk cheese; **mahón** cow's milk cheese from Menorca; **manchego (tierno, añejo, semi, seco)** hard sheep's-milk cheese (young, mature, semi-soft, dry); **tetilla** soft cow's milk cheese; **torta del casar** tangy sheep's milk cheese from Extremadura.

# Shopping

*From high-street giants to hipster boutiques*

The high streets of Madrid have undeniably taken on the identikit look of most European capitals, albeit with Spanish chains – Zara, Mango, Bershka – proliferating; but get off those thoroughfares and what strikes you is the curious mix of the traditional and the new. Here the chains and international franchises rub shoulders with museum-piece, family-run businesses and ancient shops dedicated to just one product – espadrilles, maybe, or Spanish ceramics.

Visitors from cities with cutting-edge fashion scenes, such as London, New York and Berlin, are sometimes disappointed by Madrid's clothes shops; however, the scattering of independent boutiques that have opened around Malasaña, Conde Duque and Alonso Martínez is starting to raise consumer expectations.

Loewe, Calle de Serrano p163

## Where to shop

Madrid isn't a large city, and its main shopping areas break down into several distinctive zones, all conveniently within walking distance – or a short metro ride – of one another. A short walk from the Puerta del Sol, C/Preciados and C/Carmen are always bustling with shoppers, and offer a mix of chains and smaller stores selling cheap and mid-price clothes, shoes and accessories. Several branches of **El Corte Inglés** are in this area. Gran Vía itself is given over to the flagship stores of many a household name like **Zara**, the **Nike Store** and many more.

After battling through the crowds of dawdling shoppers on the Gran Vía, the tranquil area of Los Austrias comes as a welcome respite, with its musical instrument stores, bohemian gift shops and troves of decorative items. Chueca houses a host of hip independents, such as **Bunkha** (*see p137*), **Isolée** (*see p129*) and bookshop **Panta Rhei** (*see p129*), as well as the youth-orientated brands of C/Fuencarral (home to **Diesel** and **Puma**, as well as Spanish brand **Hoss Intropia**). Also on C/Fuencarral are branches of upmarket international cosmetics and skincare brands, such as **MAC** and **Kiehls**.

### ♥ Best bookshops

**J&J Books & Coffee** *p137*
Wide selection of English second-hand novels.

**Cuesta de Moyano** *p142*
First editions and rare finds.

**FNAC** *p49*
The latest blockbusters and plenty for kids.

**Ocho y Medio** *p177*
The cinephiles' choice.

## If you're all about labels, then Salamanca is the place to be

Madrid al Cubo *p109*

Cuesta de Moyano

💙 **Best for fashion**

**La Antigua** *p137*
Indie threads.

**Antigua Casa Crespo** *p137*
Rainbow-coloured
espadrilles.

**Custo Barcelona** *p129*
Bright, funky patterns.

**¡Oh, qué Luna!** *p163*
Silky, sexy underwear.

For shoes, head down C/Augusto Figueroa, and then continue north up C/Barquillo for the more refined fashion boutiques, most of which are squeezed into the area between C/Argensola and Plaza Santa Barbara.

West of here, the trendy triangle called triBall – just west of where C/Fuencarral meets Gran Vía – and the area around C/Conde Duque are now home to some of the city's most interesting boutiques.

If you're all about labels, then Salamanca is the place to be, in particular C/Serrano, where on the same block you will find **Loewe**, **Yves Saint Laurent** and **La Perla**, as well as smaller designer boutiques throughout the area. Lots of upmarket, specialist antique dealers can be found on and around C/Claudio Coello.

### High-street heavyweights

International chain stores are to be found on Gran Vía (with **H&M** at no.37, for example, or **Primark** at no.32) and C/Fuencarral. Global Spanish chains **Mango** (C/Fuencarral 70) and **Zara** (C/Fuencarral 126-128 and Gran Vía 34) are slightly cheaper here than in shops outside Spain. There's also a branch of **Topshop** (Puerta del Sol 6).

**In the know**
**Best foot first**

Spain is a major producer of footwear, with the Valencia and Alicante areas dominated by shoe factories. As a result, Madrid is a haven for the confirmed shoe addict. Head for C/Augusto Figueroa, in the heart of Chueca. Here you'll find a street packed with factory *muestrarios* (selling samples). For famous Spanish leather specialist **Loewe**, see *p163*.

FNAC *p49*

♥ **Best for crafts and gifts**

**Antigua Casa Talavera** *p90*
Hand-painted ceramics.

**Patrimonio Comunal Olivarero** *p129*
The finest olive oil.

**Popland** *p137*
Joyfully kitsch.

**Madrid al Cubo** *p105*
Souvenirs with a difference.

Spain's biggest retail concern has blown all the rest of the competition out of the water. **El Corte Inglés** (901 122 122, www.elcorteingles.es) is the solution when all else fails for some, but the first choice for many. You can get practically everything you need, be it clothes, household goods, books or multimedia products, and the store also offers a range of services from cutting keys to booking tickets. Most outlets also have well-stocked, if expensive, supermarkets and luxury food sections called the Club del Gourmet. Information points staffed by multilingual employees are a plus, as is the decent customer service, which is rare in Spain. The branches on C/Preciados specialise in film, music, electronics, books, fashion and

**In the know**
**Museum shops**

Madrid's 'Paseo del Arte' museums all have excellent bookshops and souvenir shops. The shop in **Reina Sofía** (see *p112*) is particularly good for books, while the **Prado** (see *p144* is great for a Hieronymous Bosch t-shirt or Goya notebook. The **CaixaForum** cultural centre (see *p273*) is great for quirky gifts and useful gadgets.

sports. The branch on the Plaza de Callao has homewares, toys and electronics.

The French giant **FNAC** (902 100 632, www.fnac.es) offers a huge range of CDs, DVDs, videos and books, plus computer hardware and software, all at competitive prices and under one roof. At the C/Preciados branch (no.28), among the CDs there are good world music and flamenco sections, and the helpful staff can look up titles on the database. There is a reasonable English-language book section, with recent paperbacks as well as classics. Downstairs there's a ticket booking service, a café and paper shop with a good range of foreign press and magazines, and the FNAC Forum, which hosts readings and film and record launches.

## Market day

Madrid's markets are a noisy, colourful way to stock up on cheap food – and to get close to the locals. They offer a vast range of fruit and veg, meat, fish, cheese, charcuterie and offal. Markets are usually open from around 9am to 2pm and 5 to 8pm during the week, and 9am to 2pm on Saturdays.

The city's biggest flea market, the **Rastro** (*see p108*) is an obligatory visit, but more for the atmosphere than the goods – you will almost certainly walk away empty-handed.

The Rastro *p108*

Some markets are now better known for their eating options than their fresh produce, including the atmospheric **Mercado de San Miguel** (*see p72*) in Los Austrias, with its gourmet specialists, and the **Mercado de San Antón** (*see p127*) gastro market in Chueca. To sample more delicacies, head along to **Magerit**, stand no.20/21 in **La Cebada** market in the Plaza de la Cebada in La Latina – it's an excellent place to buy cheese. For olives of all varieties, **Fillanas**, stalls no. 33-44 in the **Mercado de Chamberí** (www.mercadodechamberi.es, C/ Alonso Cano 10), is a good bet.

## Back to basics

Opening times are changing, as is the traditional August break. While smaller stores will still close for two or three hours at lunch and stay shut on Saturday afternoons, some mid-size and nearly all large outlets will remain open all day. If you have yet to get used to a 2pm lunch and can face the heat in the summer, head to the bigger stores in the early afternoon and you will miss the crowds. Pressure from large retailers brought about a relaxation of the laws on Sunday opening too, all amid much grumbling from small businesses, who find it very hard to compete with such timetables. As a result, large retailers can – and do – open every first Sunday of the month. As revenue from tourists becomes more vital to the shopkeepers of Madrid, August is no longer a month when the city closes down.

Sales are usually on through January and February, and then in July and August. Non-EU residents can claim refund cheques for purchases over the value of €90.16. The VAT can be reclaimed at the Global Blue (www.globalblue.com) offices in C/Claudio Coello, Western Union on Gran Vía, Exact Exchange in Puerta del Sol, and Barajas airport terminals 1, 2 and 4. Look out for the Tax-Free sticker in the window of participating outlets.

Mercado de San Miguel *p72*

**In the know**
**End of the line**

Spaniards do queue (although it may not look like it) – just ask '*¿Quién es el último/la última?*' ('Who's last in the queue?') before joining.

Karam gift shop, Calle Postas

# Explore

Plaza de Cibeles

# Getting Started

The old city, with its narrow medieval streets, contains Madrid's most atmospheric and well-defined *barrios*, as well as its best eating, drinking and nightlife options and many of its landmark buildings. Most visitors spend the bulk of their time here – whether enjoying the Habsburg and Bourbon splendour of Los Austrias, the laid-back tapas bars of La Latina, the alternative cultural scene of Lavapiés, or the heady nightlife and hip cafés of Malasaña and Chueca. The heart of the area is the Puerta del Sol, and much of old Madrid converges on this square. Plaza Mayor, the heart of Golden Age Madrid, lies south-west of here, along C/Mayor, while two art museums from Madrid's 'Golden Triangle' – the Reina Sofía and the Thyssen-Bornemisza – lie to the east, bordering the Paseo del Prado.

### An overview of the city

Madrid is a surprisingly walkable city and most neighbourhoods of interest lie within a 20-minute stroll of the Puerta del Sol. This is literally the centre of the city, in that all street numbers in Madrid count outwards from Sol and it contains *kilómetro cero* (marked by a plaque in the pavement), from which distances to the

## ♥ Best views

**Faro de Moncloa** *p169*
A trip in the glass lift up Madrid's former communications tower gives spectacular views.

**Teleférico de Madrid** *p175*
Take a ride on the city's cable car for a bird's-eye perspective of Madrid.

**Las Vistillas** *p64*
See incredible magenta sunsets from a *terraza* at Las Vistillas.

> Madrid is a surprisingly walkable city and most areas of interest lie within a 20-minute stroll of the Puerta del Sol

Puerta del Sol

rest of Spain are measured. Much of the old city is pedestrianised and, with the efforts of Mayor Manuela Carmena, this is gradually extending to include grand avenues such as the Gran Vía.

Seen from the air, or on a map, two of Madrid's main features immediately stand out: one is the immensely long Paseo de la Castellana, a north–south arterial avenue that slices Madrid in two and links the old city with its newer northern business districts. To the west of the Castellana are the grid-iron patterned streets of **Salamanca** (*see pp153-163*). The second unmissable feature is the cramped old city with its maze of rambling streets, sliced in two from east to west by the Gran Vía.

Neighbourhoods – defined here according to the overview map on *pp8-9* – mostly have quite distinct flavours, with marked differences both architecturally and in terms of the types of restaurants, bars and shops that dominate. In this

### ♥ Best art collections

**Museo Nacional Centro de Arte Reina Sofía** *p112*
Madrid's modern art gallery, famously home to Picasso's *Guernica*.

**Museo Nacional del Prado** *p144*
The world's biggest collection of Spanish art.

**Museo de la Real Academia de Bellas Artes de San Fernando** *p86*
Often overlooked, this gallery showcases significant works by Goya, among others.

**Museo Thyssen-Bornemisza** *p96*
Broad range of artwork from old masters to pop art.

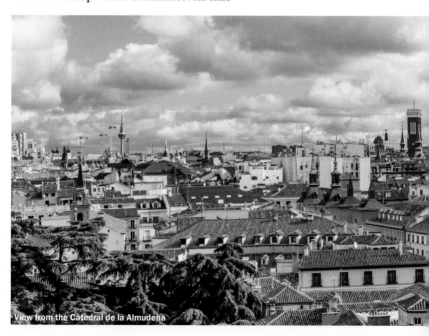

View from the Catedral de la Almudena

guide, we've split the old city into five districts. Just south-west of **Sol** (*pp80-91*), along C/Mayor, lies the Habsburg city (**Los Austrias**, *see pp62-74*), including Plaza Mayor, the heart of Golden Age Madrid, while south of the square is Madrid's most multicultural barrio, **Lavapiés** (*see pp108-117*). Plaza **Santa Ana and Huertas** (*see pp92-105*) are to the south-east. Running east from Sol is C/Alcalá, which connects the square with the Plaza de Cibeles, the junction with the Castellana that leads to modern Madrid. Just north of Sol, the historic but buzzing areas of **Chueca and Malasaña** (*see pp118-137*) border on the Gran Vía.

Finally, we've listed some of Madrid's outlying districts as **Beyond the Centre** (*see pp164-181*). Though the neighbourhoods themselves are not particularly exciting, they do contain a handful of the city's most inspiring attractions.

♥ **Best for children**

**Casa de Campo** *p167*
The vast and verdant Casa de Campo has a zoo, swimming pools and tennis courts.

**Parque de Atracciones** *p173*
Check out the rides at this funfair in the Casa de Campo with nippers in tow.

**Plaza de Oriente** *p64*
Let your children loose in the playground in this square while you watch from the sidelines with a stiff drink.

**The Retiro** *p143*
Messing about in boats is easily done at the leafy, shaded Retiro park.

## Getting around

While much of Madrid can be navigated on foot, the metro system is reasonably efficient and covers most areas of interest. It links with local train systems, but the maps can be quite baffling to follow – if in doubt, ask at the ticket office. The bus is useful for journeys up the Castellana, but otherwise it's probably simpler to stick to the metro. For more information on getting around and fares on public transport, *see p283*.

## Sights and museums

Madrid's most famous attractions are, of course, its world-class art museums: the **Prado** (*see p144*), the **Reina Sofía** (*see p112*) and the **Thyssen-Bornemisza** (*see p96*), but these have been joined in recent years by the **CaixaForum Madrid** (*see p273*), which has a limited permanent collection, but some of the best temporary programming in the city. Thanks to this spectacular quartet, some of the other collections are unjustly overlooked, such as the superb paintings spanning a range of eras and styles at the **Museo de la Real Academia de Bellas Artes de San Fernando** (*see p86*), or the collections within the many convents and monasteries, such as those at the **Real Monasterio de la de la Encarnación** (*see p87*) and the **Real Monasterio de las Descalzas Reales** (*see p85*). In the same area, you'll find the magnificent **Palacio Real** (*see p66*).

Though art is the principal player, Madrid also has a fine selection of thematic museums, such as history (**Museo de Historia**, *p123*); archaeology (**Museo Arqueológico Nacional**, *p158*); ships (**Museo Naval**, *p151*); clothing (**Museo del Traje**, *p172*); and trains (**Museo del Ferrocarril**, *p181*). It's worth putting aside some time for some of its kookier museums, however; something that Madrid excels in. A couple of the most charming are the **Museo Lázaro Galdiano** (*see p157*) and the **Museo del Romanticismo** (*see p124*).

Finally, when the weather is right (because Madrid can get blisteringly hot and bitterly cold), don't miss the two main parks – the vast **Casa de Campo** (*see p167*) and the elegant **Retiro** (*see p143*).

## Tourist information

The **Centros de Turismo** run by the city council, and the tourist office run by the regional authority (Comunidad de Madrid) provide similar basic information on Madrid and the surrounding region, plus free maps. The city also runs a phone information line for locals, 010, which can be useful to visitors. For details of this number plus more on Centros de Turismo, *see p295*. Tourist offices do not make hotel bookings but can advise on vacancies.

> **In the know**
> **Monday blues**
>
> Most museums are closed on Mondays, with the exception of the Reina Sofía, which closes on a Tuesday.

Calle Álvarez Gato

Plaza Mayor

Full information on what's on is in local papers and listings magazines (*see p290*). For useful websites, *see p297*.

## Tours

If you prefer to see the city independently, but need extra guidance, then the website www.madridenruta.com has a large number of suggested routes and guided maps you can print out.

### On foot and by bicycle

All the guides at **Carpetania Madrid** (91 531 40 18, www.carpetaniamadrid.com, 2-hr tours €9-€12) are art history specialists. As well as city routes, they offer expert guided tours around art exhibitions. With over 100 different itineraries (by bus and on foot) run by the tourist board, **Madrid En Ruta** (648 078 568, www.madridenruta.com, tickets on foot €5.90, by bike €6.90, under-5s free) offers tours focusing on architecture, literature and history. **MadWay to Madrid** (www.madwaytomadrid.com) has alternative and eco-friendly tours on foot or by bike, in English, Dutch, Spanish, French or Italian.

### By bus

Offering city tours and/or trips focused on bullfights, flamenco and so on, as well as tours of Toledo, Ávila, Segovia and other towns around Madrid, are **Juliá Travel** (91 559 96 05, http:juliatravel.com) and **Trapsatur** (91 542 66 66, www.trapsatur. com). **Madrid City Tour** (902 02 47 58) is a city-owned tour service with two routes. You can purchase tickets online, by phone, at the Madrid City Tour information office next to the Prado, at the tourist office, or through Juliá Travel (*see above*).

### By car

Zip around Madrid in a little yellow **GoCar** (91 559 45 35, www.gocartours.com/ locations/madrid, from €35 for 1hr), a computer-guided storytelling vehicle that allows you to sightsee at your own pace. The average tour is two to three hours.

### By Segway

Segway tour company, **Madsegs** (mobile 659 824 499, www.madsegs.com, €45), offers a two-wheeled way to see the city. Price includes a helmet, refreshments and photos.

---

**In the know**
**Paseo del Arte**

For information on the Paseo del Arte ticket, which gives cut-price entry to the Prado, Thyssen and Reina Sofía, *see p99* Paseo del Arte.

# Los Austrias & La Latina

The oldest part of the city, site of the Muslim town and of most of medieval Madrid, falls between Plaza de la Cebada, Plaza Mayor and the Palacio Real and was for centuries the seat of power. Even though most of the streets still follow their original medieval lines, this may not be immediately apparent today. Like several other parts of the Old City, this area has been smartened up over the past decade, and is now home to a slew of wine bars and expensive restaurants.

## ♥ Don't miss

**1 Plaza Mayor** *p68*
Grand arcaded square at the centre of Madrid life.

**2 Palacio Real** *p66*
Vast Bourbon palace, with 3,000 rooms.

**3 Mercado de San Miguel** *p72*
Gastronomic market in a century-old iron and glass structure.

**4 Basílica de San Francisco el Grande** *p74*
Domed church that forms a landmark of the city's skyline.

### In the know
### Getting around

The rambling streets of Madrid de Los Austrias are best explored on foot and have the Ópera metro station (L2, L5) at their heart. The district of La Latina is best reached by metro to the station of the same name (L5) and, again, is very easy to walk around.

PLAZA
M.AYOR

# LOS AUSTRIAS

Despite its ancient beginnings, the area spreading out from the **Palacio Real** has come to be known as the 'Madrid de los Austrias', after the Habsburgs, although in truth Philip II and his dynasty can scarcely claim responsibility for much of it. The greatest monument they *did* build, however, stands at the area's core: the **Plaza Mayor**, archetypal creation of Castilian Baroque (a style that's also known as 'Herreran', after its key architect).

To the west of the square, off C/Cava de San Miguel, lies one of the city's most successful openings, the **Mercado de San Miguel**, a refurbished food market that's become a favoured tapas-munching spot for tourists and upper-class *madrileños*. Just down from here is the peaceful **Plaza del Conde de Barajas**, home to the excellent Taller Puntera leather goods shop. To the east, leading on from the C/ Cava de San Miguel, is the **Arco de los Cuchilleros** (Knifemakers' Arch), which runs from the south-west corner of the square via a spectacular bank of steps leading down through C/Cuchilleros to the **Plaza de la Puerta Cerrada**, the walls of which are decorated with some engaging 1970s murals.

To the south-east of the square, at the **Plaza de la Provincia**, is another major work in the Herreran style: the squatly proportioned **Palacio de Santa Cruz**, which was the work of several architects between 1629 and 1643. Despite its grand appearance,

---

## ❤ Time to eat & drink

**Coffee with a view**
Café de Oriente *p71*

**Creative tapas**
Juanalaloca *p77*

**Slow-roast lamb**
El Sobrino de Botín *p70*

**Late-night munchies**
Chocolatería San Ginés *p71*

---

## ❤ Time to shop

**Religious kitsch**
Belloso *p73*

**Colourful meringues**
El Riojano *p73*

**Hand-stitched leather bags**
Taller Puntera *p74*

**Retro furniture and art**
Tiempos Modernos *p74*

---

# LOS AUSTRIAS & LA LATINA

## Restaurants

❶ La Botillería de Maxi
❷ Casa Ciriaco
❸ Casa Lucio
❹ Emma y Júlia
❺ El Estragón
❻ Julián de Tolosa
❼ La Musa Latina
❽ El Sobrino de Botín
❾ La Taberna del Alabardero
❿ Taberna Salamanca
⓫ El Viajero
⓬ Viuda de Vacas
⓭ Xentes

## Tapas

❶ El Almendro 13
❷ Bodegas Ricla
❸ Juanalaloca
❹ Mercado de San Miguel
❺ Taberna Matritum
❻ El Tempranillo
❼ La Torre del Oro
❽ Txirimiri

## Cafés & bars

❶ Almacén de Vinos (Casa Gerardo)
❷ El Anciano Rey de los Vinos
❸ Café del Nuncio
❹ Café de Oriente
❺ Café del Real
❻ Chocolatería San Ginés
❼ Delic
❽ La Fontanilla
❾ El Sainete
❿ El Ventorillo

## Shops & services

❶ Belloso
❷ El Flamenco Vive
❸ Mar de Letras
❹ El Riojano
❺ Stamp & Coin Market
❻ Taller Puntera
❼ Tiempos Modernos

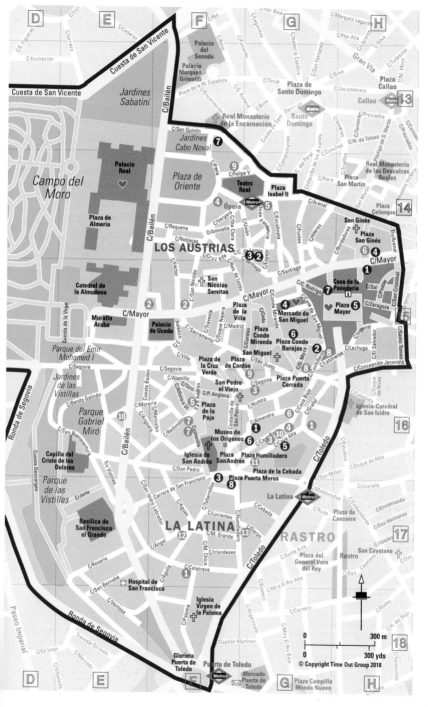

the palace was originally the court prison, with a dungeon so deep that prisoners had to rub their rags with lard and set them alight to stop themselves from going blind. These days the building has a somewhat more dignified role as the Foreign Ministry.

For centuries C/Mayor was Madrid's main thoroughfare. The cross-streets between Mayor and Arenal offer an odd mixture of bookbinders, picture-framers and Galician restaurants. Just above C/Mayor is the 12th-century **San Nicolás de los Servitas**, while just off it is the **Plaza de la Villa**, Madrid's oldest square and home to the city hall, the **Casa de la Villa**. In pre-Habsburg times, the square was also the preferred place of residence for the elite; one such residence, the **Torre de los Lujanes**, can still be seen there. Along with the **Casa de Cisneros**, also on the square, the buildings make up a compendium of the history of the city from provincial town to the imperial capital it was to become.

The western end of C/Mayor, near the **Palacio Real**, has several old palaces and runs out west into C/Bailén, connected southwards to a splendid 1930s concrete **viaduct** that offers views of the *sierra* and the Casa de Campo. The viaduct's notoriety as a suicide point has led the city authorities to place giant glass panels all along it, giving it a very strange look and feel – without doing much to deter the jumpers. If you continue down C/Segovia beneath the viaduct, you'll pass a forlorn fragment of the ninth-century **Muralla Árabe** (Arab wall), the only substantial relic of Madrid's Muslim founders. The area around it is a landscaped park known as the **Parque Emir Mohammed I**, with information plaques giving interesting historical information.

At the southern end of the viaduct are the hill and park of **Las Vistillas**. The park has more great views and is often used for neighbourhood events, concerts and dances during *fiestas* and in summer. Beyond the park are the river and the elegant arches of the **Puente de Segovia**, a bridge commissioned by Philip II from Juan de Herrera and completed in 1584 to make it easier for the king to get to El Escorial.

**Ópera**, the area between Plaza Mayor and the Palacio Real, is named after the **Teatro Real** opera house at its centre. As well as containing some of the city's most important buildings (the **cathedral** among them), this is one of the most elegant areas of Madrid. A tunnel whisks traffic under the stunning **Plaza de Oriente**, so named because it sits just east of the palace, making it one of the most pleasant spots for a coffee. Curiously, Madrid owes this stately square, which seems to complement the Palacio Real ideally, not to the Bourbon monarchs

but to Spain's 'non-king', Joseph Bonaparte, who initiated the clearing of the area during his brief reign (1808-13). After his departure it was largely neglected before being laid out in formal style in 1844. During the dictatorship, devotees from all over the country stormed the square for a glimpse of Franco, who addressed his rallies from the palace balcony.

At the square's centre is a fine equestrian statue of Philip IV that once stood in the courtyard of the Palacio del Buen Retiro. It was made in the 1640s by the Italian sculptor Pietro Tacca, who – on the insistence of the Count-Duke of Olivares – was required to create the first-ever monumental bronze statue featuring a rearing horse, rather than one with four feet on the ground. This remarkable feat was achieved with engineering assistance from Galileo.

On the esplanade between the cathedral and the palace, archaeological excavations unearthed the remains of the original Muslim fortress and of the foundations of Philip II's Alcázar, covered over by the building of the later Palacio Real. Some of the discoveries, including impressive Moorish arches, are open to public view. Behind the palace, the delightful **Campo del Moro** gardens run down towards the Manzanares and the Paseo de la Florida.

## Sights & museums

### Campo del Moro
*Paseo de la Virgen del Puerto (91 454 88 00). Metro Príncipe Pío.* **Open** *Oct-Mar 10am-6pm Mon-Sat; 9am-6pm Sun. Apr-Sept 10am-8pm daily.* **Map** *p62 D14.*

This vast garden was named after a Muslim leader in the Middle Ages, Ali Ben Yusut, who attempted to capture the fortress that is now the Palacio Real. Unfortunately, it is only accessible from the Paseo de la Virgen del Puerto side, requiring a fairly long walk down Cuesta de San Vicente or Cuesta de la Vega. As a reward, however, you will see two fine monumental fountains. Nearest the palace is Los Tritones, originally made in 1657 for the palace in Aranjuez (*see p191*); the other is Las Conchas, designed in the 18th century by Ventura Rodríguez. Both were moved here in the 1890s.

### Catedral de la Almudena
*C/Bailén 10 (91 542 22 00, www. catedraldelaalmudena.es). Metro Ópera.* **Open** *9am-8.30pm daily.* **Admission** *Cathedral free (suggested donation €1). Museum & dome €6; €4 reductions.* **Map** *p62 E15.*

# Saints and Sinners

*Madrid's church-going public are kept busy all year round*

If you're female and single, you might want to make a discreet pilgrimage to the **Ermita de San Antonio de la Florida** (*see p169*) if you happen to be in Madrid on 13 June. This is Anthony of Padua's feast day, a saint whose many attributes supposedly include the ability to rustle up boyfriends out of thin air – for Madrid girls at least. The tradition was perhaps started by young seamstresses, as the custom is to turn up at the church with a handful of pins. The girls queue up to drop the pins in the font, then stick their hand into the water. The test is whether the pins stick to their hand. If so, love is just around the corner. It's got to be worth a go.

The **Iglesia de San Antón** on C/Hortaleza, on the other hand, is dedicated to Saint Anthony of Egypt, who, like Saint Francis, had a way with animals. On 17 January, the people of Madrid commemorate this by bringing not only their pets, but also farm animals, to the church to be blessed. This causes something of a livestock bottleneck in the narrow, busy C/Hortaleza, as dogs, cats, rabbits, goats, donkeys and pigs wait to enter the church. Not far away, at the **Iglesia de Santa Pascual** on the Paseo de Recoletos, you might catch sight of a famous face slinking in or out. The church contains a figure of Saint Clare, who in recent times has been appointed the patron saint of television. Actors, actresses and stars of reality TV pop in to ask her to help them get the role that will finally make them a household name.

On 27 July, expect to see a very long queue of people if you are in the vicinity of the **Real Monasterio de la Encarnación** (*see p87*). The reliquary of this 17th-century convent contains a phial of blood purportedly belonging to Pantaleón, the doctor saint. On his feast day, the dubious contents of the phial miraculously liquefy, which augurs great things for those who witness the event. Yet more expectant queuing goes on every Friday outside the **Iglesia de Jesús de Medinaceli** on Plaza de Jesús. Inside the church is a statue of Jesus of Nazareth that had fallen into the hands of the Moors and was retrieved against all odds by Trinitarian monks in the 17th century. Kissing the foot of the statue is believed to be very auspicious. In fact, after announcing their engagement in 2003, one of the first things the then Prince Felipe and his wife-to-be Letizia did was turn up at the church to do just that.

They got married in the **Catedral de la Almudena** (*see p64*), named after a wooden figure now to be found in the crypt. When the Moors arrived in Madrid, they displaced the Visigoths, who before fleeing hid the statue in the wall of their fortress, along with two burning candles. A few centuries later, when the Christians regained power, the hiding place was discovered – and guess what? Those candles were still flickering away. This happy event has led to a public holiday on 9 November, something that has kept Almudena as everybody's favourite saint, with no further miracles required.

Catedral de la Almudena

# 💙 Palacio Real (Palacio de Oriente)

*Plaza de Oriente, C/Bailén (91 454 88 00). Metro Ópera.* **Open** *Oct-Mar 10am-6pm daily. Apr-Sept 10am-8pm daily.* **Admission** *€10; €5 reductions. Incl guided tour €14; €9 reductions; free under-4s. Free to EU citizens Oct-Mar 4-6pm & Apr-Sept 6-8pm Mon-Thur.* **Map** *p62 E14.*

Commissioned by Philip V after the earlier Alcázar was lost to a fire in 1734, the Royal Palace is rarely used by the royal family, and many of its 3,000 rooms are open to view. The architects principally responsible for the final design, which reflects the taste of the Spanish Bourbons, were Italian – Giambattista Sacchetti and Francesco Sabatini – with contributions by the Spaniard Ventura Rodríguez. Filippo Juvarra, Philip V's first choice, had planned a palace four times as large, but after his death the project became a little less ambitious. Completed in 1764, the late-Baroque palace is built almost entirely of granite and white Colmenar stone, and, surrounded as it is by majestic gardens, contributes to the splendour of the city.

Inside, you must keep to a fixed route, but are free to set your own pace rather than follow a tour. The entrance into the palace is awe-inspiring: you pass up a truly vast staircase and then through the main state rooms, the Hall of Halbardiers and Hall of Columns, all with soaring ceilings and frescoes by Corrado Giaquinto and Giambattista Tiepolo. In the grand Throne Room there are some fine 17th-century sculptures commissioned by Velázquez, which were saved from the earlier Alcázar. Other highlights are the extravagantly ornate private apartments of the palace's first resident, Charles III, again decorated by Italians. Particularly striking are the Gasparini Room, the king's dressing room, covered in mosaics and rococo stuccoes by Mattia Gasparini; and the Porcelain Room, its walls covered entirely in porcelain reliefs. A later addition is another giant: the State Dining Room, redesigned for King Alfonso XII in 1880 and still used for official banquets. There are also imposing collections of tapestries, table porcelain, gold and silver plates, and finally

clocks, a particular passion of the little-admired King Charles IV.

One of the highlights is the Real Armería (Royal Armoury), reached via a separate entrance off the palace courtyard, with a superb collection of ceremonial armour, much of it worn by Charles V and other Habsburgs. Look out, too, for the suits of armour worn by El Cid and his horse – displayed on life-size statues. On the other side of the courtyard, the Royal Pharmacy is also worth a visit. One of the oldest in Europe, it was wholly dedicated to attending to the many ailments of Spain's crowned heads over several centuries. In years to come, an opportunity to view the excavations of the older Alcázar and Muslim fortress beneath the palace will also form part of the visit. The palace is closed to the public when official receptions or ceremonies are due, so it's a good idea to check before visiting. On the first Wednesday of each month the Royal Guard stages a ceremonial Changing of the Guard in the courtyard, at noon. There are tours of the Palace throughout the day.

This is not Spain's most impressive cathedral, and it's something of a miracle that it exists at all. For centuries, Church and State could not agree on whether Madrid should have a cathedral; once they did, it took 110 years to complete it. Work began in 1883 on a neo-Gothic design by the Marqués de Cubas, but this scheme went off course after only the crypt was completed. Another architect, Fernando Chueca Goitia, took over in 1944, and introduced a neoclassical style. Although the cathedral has failed to win much affection over the years, it was finally finished in 1993 and visited by the Pope. The site once contained the church of Santa María de la Almudena, formerly the main mosque of Muslim Madrid (the name comes from the Arabic *al mudin*, 'the mill') until it was knocked down by liberal reformers in 1870. One of its more interesting pieces is the 13th-century polychromatic funerary chest of San Isidro. The admission ticket includes entrance to the cathedral museum, which displays paintings, sculptures, liturgical vestments, and a 13th-century manuscript describing the life of San Isidro, and access (via a steep flight of stairs) to the cathedral dome, which has panoramic views.

### Plaza de la Villa
*Metro Ópera or Sol.* **Map** *p62 G15.*

Madrid's oldest square, home to the city's main marketplace in Muslim and early medieval times, contains three noteworthy buildings. Dominant is the Casa de la Villa, or City Hall, designed in Castilian-Baroque style by Juan Gómez de Mora in 1630, although not completed until 1695. The façade was also altered by Juan de Villanueva in the 1780s. It contrasts nicely with the Casa de Cisneros, which was built as a palace by a relative of the great Cardinal Cisneros in 1537. Restored in 1910, it now also houses municipal offices. Opposite the Casa de la Villa is the simple Torre de los Lujanes, from the 1460s, where one of Madrid's aristocratic families once resided. It is believed that King Francis I of France was kept prisoner in the tower by Charles V after his capture in 1525.

### San Nicolás de los Servitas
*Plaza San Nicolás (91 559 40 64). Metro Ópera.* **Open** *8.30am-1.30pm, 5.30-8pm Mon; 8.30-9am, 6.30-8pm Tue-Sat; 10-10.30am, 6.30-8.30pm Sun.* **Map** *p62 F15.*

The oldest surviving church in Madrid stands a few minutes from Plaza de Oriente. Its 12th-century tower is one of two Mudéjar towers (*see also p76* San Pedro el Viejo), built by Muslim craftsmen living under Christian rule, in the city. Most of the rest of the church was rebuilt later, during the 15th and 16th centuries. There is no entry during mass.

**Top 20**

# ❤ Plaza Mayor

*Metro Sol.* **Map** *p62 H15.*

Plaza Mayor began life in the 15th century as a humble market square, then known as the Plaza del Arrabal ('Square outside the Walls'). In the 1560s, after Madrid was made capital of Spain by Philip II, architect Juan de Herrera drew up plans for it to be completely rebuilt, but the only part constructed immediately was the Casa de la Panadería ('the Bakery'). Finished under the direction of Diego Sillero in 1590, it's typical of the Herreran style, with grey slate roofs, spiky pinnacles and two towers that dominate the square. In the early 1990s, in a move unlikely to be contemplated in most other countries, this historic edifice was decorated with colourful psychedelic murals. The rest of the *plaza* was built by Juan Gómez de Mora for Philip III and completed in 1619, although large sections were destroyed by fire in 1790 and had to be rebuilt. Bullfights, carnivals and all the great ceremonies of imperial Madrid were held here. At its centre is a statue from 1616 of Philip III on horseback by Giambologna and Pietro Tacca, which stood originally in the Casa de Campo and was moved here in the 19th century.

The square is still an important hub, with most Madrid-wide celebrations, such as the Veranos de la Villa or San Isidro festivals, centred here, along with a traditional Christmas fair in December. Best enjoyed on quiet weekday mornings, Plaza Mayor has plenty of pavement cafés from which to contemplate its graceful architecture. On Sunday mornings the *plaza* bustles with a stamp and coin market. On the north side of the *plaza* is the city's main tourist office.

## Restaurants

### Casa Ciriaco €€€

*C/Mayor 84 (91 548 06 20). Metro Ópera or Sol.* **Open** *1-4pm, 8pm-12.30am Mon, Tue, Thur-Sun. Closed Aug.* **Map** *p62 F15* ❷
*Castilian*

Pick your way down the side of the open kitchen to a deep dining room hung with pictures of visiting royals and celebrities, along with rather grimmer photos of the 1906 bombing of the wedding procession for Alfonso XIII and his English wife Victoria Eugenie – which happened right outside the door. Undamaged and still going strong, Casa Ciriaco was a meeting place for the intelligentsia in pre-Civil War days and although it no longer attracts many thinkers, the Castilian fare is a taste of days gone by. *Gallina en pepitoria* (chicken in an almond and white wine sauce) is the speciality.

### ❤ El Sobrino de Botín €€€

*C/Cuchilleros 17 (91 366 42 17, 91 366 30 26, www.botin.es). Metro Sol.* **Open** *1-4pm, 8pm-midnight daily.* **Map** *p62 G15* ❽
*Castilian*

The world's oldest restaurant is still coming up with the goods after nearly 300 years. For all its popularity as a tourist destination, its nooks and crannies add up to an atmospheric – if cramped – dining spot over several floors. Ask for a table in the vaulted cellar for the full effect. Order the suckling pig or the lamb, which are roasted in a huge wood-fired oven. And yes, since you asked, Hemingway did come here.

### La Taberna del Alabardero €€€€

*C/Felipe V 6 (91 547 25 77, www.grupolezama. es). Metro Ópera.* **Open** *1-3pm, 9-11pm daily.* **Map** *p62 F14* ❾ *Spanish*

Father Lezama started up his traditional tavern back in 1974, when he put underprivileged boys to work as waiters in this converted 16th-century townhouse. With a quiet *terraza* on the street that runs along the north side of the Teatro Real, it's still one of the most popular post-theatre dining spots, serving up traditional tapas at the bar and Basque cuisine in the restaurant in the back. Lezama is now a very prosperous restaurateur – he has opened six more restaurants in Spain and one in Washington, DC. Some of those original boys are now shareholders.

## Tapas

### Bodegas Ricla

*C/Cuchilleros 6 (91 365 20 69). Metro Ópera.* **Open** *1-4pm, 7pm-midnight Mon, Wed, Thur; 1-4pm, 7pm-1am Fri, Sat; 1-5pm Sun.* **No cards.** **Map** *p62 G15* ❷

A tiny, bright and friendly mother-and-son operation, Bodegas Ricla does a great line in garlicky *boquerones* and an incongruous one in soft rock. Cheap but good wine and sherry are available by the litre, poured from tall clay urns, or there is vermouth on tap. Also worth trying are the *cecina* (thin slices of cured venison) and Cabrales cheese in cider.

### La Torre del Oro

*Plaza Mayor 26 (91 366 50 16). Metro Sol.* **Open** *11am-1am daily.* **Map** *p62 G15* ❼

It's smack on the Plaza Mayor, so don't expect any bargains, especially if you sit out in the square, but this Andalucían bar is the real deal, with bullfighting memorabilia and incomprehensible waiters. If you can understand and make yourself understood, ask for prawns or whitebait (*pescaítos*), and accompany them with a cold, dry *fino*.

El Sobrino de Botín

Café de Oriente

## Cafés & bars

### Café del Nuncio
*C/Nuncio 12 & C/Segovia 9 (91 366 08 53).
Metro La Latina.* **Open** *11am-1am daily.* **Map**
*p62 G16*

Split into two halves at either end of the
narrow Escalinata del Nuncio, the Café
del Nuncio is a classic, though a recent
renovation has ripped out a lot of its old-
school charm. The real joy of the place,
however, lies in the terrace outside on the
stepped slope dividing the two spaces; this
is one of the most picturesque streets in the
old city.

### ❤ Café de Oriente
*Plaza de Oriente 2 (91 541 39 74, www.
cafedeoriente.es). Metro Ópera.* **Open**
*8.30am-1am Mon-Sat; 9am-1am Sun.* **Map**
*p62 F14* 4

The belle époque interior is entirely fake
yet entirely convincing, making this one of
the most peaceful and elegant spots to flick
through the newspapers or recover from
the exertions of the Palacio Real opposite.
Despite its location, with tables outside on
the stunning Plaza de Oriente, the café seems
to be more popular with locals than tourists,
who are perhaps put off by its air of grandeur.

### Café del Real
*Plaza de Isabel II 2 (91 547 21 24). Metro
Ópera.* **Open** *9am-midnight Mon-Thur;
9am-1am Fri; 10am-1am Sat; 10am-11pm Sun.*
**No cards.** **Map** *p62 G14* 5

This likeable, cramped café with a lovely
façade is a good place for coffee and cake
(chocolate or carrot), though prices are a
tad on the high side. Head upstairs to a low-
beamed room with red leather chairs and old
opera posters, overlooking the *plaza*. The café
was a favourite haunt of intellectuals, artists
and actors in the 1980s, but it's popular with a
more varied crowd these days.

### ❤ Chocolatería San Ginés
*Pasadizo de San Ginés 5 (91 365 65 46). Metro
Ópera or Sol.* **Open** *24hrs daily.* **Map** *p62
H14* 6

Serving chocolate and *churros* (deep-fried
batter sticks) to the city night and day since
1894, this veritable institution has had to
introduce a ticketing system – pay before
you order – to deal with the 5am queues of
exhausted clubbers and chipper old ladies.
The lighting is a bit much if you fall into
the former category, but at least there are
tables outside.

### La Fontanilla
*Plaza Puerta Cerrada 13 (91 365 22 91). Metro
La Latina.* **Open** *1pm-2am Mon-Thur; noon-
2am Fri-Sun.* **Map** *p62 G15* 8

La Fontanilla claims to be not the biggest or
the best or the oldest, but the smallest Irish
pub in Madrid. There's no disputing this
singular claim, but the place does manage to
cram in a couple of wooden tables alongside
wide hatches opening on to the street. The
myriad beers racked up on the walls are
sadly not for sale, but there is Murphy's
and Guinness.

### El Sainete
*C/Segovia 8 (91 819 58 08, www.
cerveceraindependiente.com). Metro La
Latina.* **Open** *noon-midnight Mon-Thur;
noon-1am Fri, Sat; noon-11am Sun.* **Map** *p62
G16* 9

Opened in 2017 on the crest of the craft beer
wave, El Sainete matches an impressive range
of beers (20 on tap, regularly changing, and
something like 150 bottled beers from all
around the world), with an equally carefully
selected range of gourmet tapas. It also hosts
tastings in its various pared-down, bare
brick rooms.

# 💙 Mercado de San Miguel

*Plaza de San Miguel (www.mercadode sanmiguel.es). Metro Sol.* **Open** *10am-midnight Mon-Wed, Sun; 10am-2am Thur-Sat.* **Map** *p62 G15* ❹

One of Madrid's biggest success stories of recent times, the Mercado de San Miguel is the daily food market/tapas emporium in Plaza de San Miguel, immediately south-west of the Plaza Mayor, which reopened its polished-up glass doors in 2009 after a decade-long restoration.

The 1915 wrought-iron and glass structure, with boutique-style food stands inside, has created a culinary buzz in the city; the place is often heaving at lunchtimes and in the evening, and it continues in this vein until well after midnight (when you can nab bargain tapas). Some say it's lost some of its original soul and that it's overpriced, yet the slick operation – one of the few covered markets in the city – is always rammed with smart-looking

*madrileños* and tourists enjoying *pinchos de bacalao* (salt cod on bruschetta), oysters, tortillas, wine, sherry, vermouth and, just as important, conversation.

Have a wander round the market to check out the different options before you make your choices, and then take your tapas selection to one of the perches or tables in the centre. It's difficult to make a bad choice here with so many delicious options, but there are some essential don't-miss highlights.

An excellent starting point is also one of San Miguel's best-loved spots: **La Hora del Vermut** (lahoradelvermut.wordpress. com), which specialises in aperitifs – namely vermouth and sherry – and nibbles with which to accompany them. With 15 different types of *vermút*, it's an excellent place to initiate yourself in the quintessential *madrileño* tradition. Sherry – known in Spain simply as *vino de Jerez* – is also taken seriously here. Whichever tipple

you go for, be sure to accompany it with some *encurtidos* (pickles) to help lessen the alcoholic punch.

Once you've whet your appetite here, you'll want to move on to more solid fodder. Salt cod specialist **La Casa de Bacalao** (www.lacasadebacalao.es) just along from La Hora del Vermut, offers some of the market's most popular tapas: *pinchos* (small rounds of toast) topped with puréed *bacalao* in a range of different guises, such as with caviar. At around €1 per *pincho*, it's tempting to order several, but be sure to save room for the market's other temptations.

Two more stands not to be missed are upmarket **Lhardy**, on the opposite side to La Casa de Bacalao, and, a little way along, the oyster stand. A classic Spanish tortilla from Lhardy will set you back €8, but rest assured it's the real deal. The traditional food store also sells a tempting range of *empanadas*, quiches and meals.

Meanwhile, **Ostra Sorlut** (www.ostrasorlut.com) is a great spot in which to undertake the oyster rite of passage, or, if you're already an aficionado, to enjoy the slippery molluscs (€2-€3.50) in suitably salubrious surroundings, knocked back with a cold glass of white wine.

The **Carro de Croquetas** stand is a stall on wheels that's always to be found somewhere in the market – it sells Basque croquettes (filled with salt cod, mushroom, leek and so on, at €1.50 each), either ready to eat, or uncooked to take home.

Spanish tapas tend to be fairly heavy, with copious quantities of oil. For a lighter snack, there's **Sushimarket**, next to Lhardy; sushi is becoming more popular in the city as locals have steadily expanded their culinary horizons.

If you want to go in a distinctly unhealthy vein, however, head to the opposite corner. Here you'll find a little block of tempting bakeries, including the **Horno San Onofre**, offering artisanal ice-cream, with original flavours, such as cava and lemon, as well as meringues, sugared almonds and more.

Whichever option you go for, the market is an excellent place to people-watch and marvel at *madrileños* doing what they do best: enjoying food in a civilised fashion, and being social – as if it were a duty, a passion and a performance, all rolled into one.

## Shops & services

### ❤ Belloso

*C/Mayor 23 (629 328 644, www.belloso.es). Metro Sol.* **Open** *10am-1.30pm, 4.30-8pm Mon-Fri; 10am-1.30pm Sat.* **Map** *p62 H15* ❶ *Gifts & souvenirs*

This neighbourhood has an abundance of shops selling Catholic paraphernalia, but Belloso is one of the best. The gear on offer covers a huge range, including rosaries, crucifixes and statues of the Virgin.

### El Flamenco Vive

*C/Conde de Lemos 7 (91 547 39 17, www.elflamencovive.es). Metro Ópera.* **Open** *10am-2pm, 5-8.30pm Mon-Fri; 10am-2pm Sat.* **Map** *p62 G14* ❷ *Books & music*

Even if you harbour only a passing interest in flamenco, the brilliant range of CDs, guitars, books and other paraphernalia at this shop will lure you in.

### Mar de Letras

*C/Santiago 18 (91 541 71 09, www.lamardeletras.com). Metro Ópera.* **Open** *10.30am-2pm, 5-8.30pm Mon-Fri; 10.30am-2.30pm, 5-8.30pm Sat. Closed 2wks Aug.* **Map** *p62 G14* ❸ *Books & music*

Mar de Letras is a well-stocked bookshop specialising in kids' editions. Look out, too, for the English-language titles and educational toys.

### ❤ El Riojano

*C/Mayor 10 (91 366 44 82, www.confiteriaelriojano.com). Metro Sol.* **Open** *10am-2pm, 5-9pm daily.* **Map** *p62 H14* ❹ *Food & drink*

El Riojano has been in business since 1885, selling irresistible cakes, pastries, meringues and seasonal goodies. All are made in the traditional way, with meringues a particular speciality. Enjoy one with a coffee in the café out back.

### Stamp & Coin Market

*Plaza Mayor. Metro Sol.* **Open** *approx 9am-2pm Sun.* **Map** *p62 H15* ❺ *Market*

On Sunday mornings, an avid mass of stamp and coin collectors swarms over the Plaza Mayor, buying, selling and eyeing up one another's wares. Other traders sell old magazines, second-hand books, postcards, badges and ex-Soviet bloc military regalia. You can even get phone cards nowadays, along with just about anything else that someone, somewhere, considers collectable.

### ♥ Taller Puntera

*Plaza Conde de Barajas 4 (91 364 29 26, www. puntera.com). Metro Tirso de Molina.* **Open** *10am-2.30pm, 4-8.30pm Mon-Sat.* **Map** *p62 G15* ❻ *Fashion*

This lovely leather accessories shop/ workshop makes simple but stylish bags, satchels, rucksacks, wallets, notebooks and more, all in top-quality leather, and available in a range of tasteful colours. Each 'piece' has a story behind it, and you can personalise most of them (dependent on the kind of leather) by getting your name engraved for free. What's more, the staff are genuinely friendly and the prices are excellent for this level of workmanship. A gem.

### ♥ Tiempos Modernos

*C/Arrieta 17 (91 542 85 94, www.tiempos-modernos.com). Metro Ópera.* **Open** *11am-8pm Mon-Fri; 11am-2pm Sat. Closed 3wks Aug.* **Map** *p62 F13* ❼ *Antiques*

Tiempos Modernos deals in modern Spanish painting, and hosts temporary shows and exhibitions of photography and artwork. The main line of business, though, is the great range of 1940s, '50s and '60s furniture.

Taller Puntera

# LA LATINA

The **C/Cava Baja**, home to many of the most celebrated *mesones*, temples to Madrid's traditional cuisine, runs south from the Plaza Mayor and leads to the squares (**Plaza de San Andrés**, **Plaza del Humilladero** and **Plaza de la Paja**) that are prime territory for the traditional Sunday La Latina tapas bar crawl. **La Latina** takes its name from the nickname of Beatriz Galindo, teacher of Latin and confidante to Queen Isabella. At the end of the 15th century, she paid for a hospital to be built on the square that bears her name. Its site is now occupied by the **Teatro La Latina**, a stronghold of traditional Spanish entertainment. The district is relatively quiet except during its grand *fiestas*, around the time of **La Paloma** (*see p202* Fiestas) in August.

The area is mostly known for its wide range of restaurants and bars, but contains several important sights, such as the Mudéjar tower of the 14th-century **San Pedro el Viejo**; the lofty, neoclassical **Basílica de San Francisco el Grande**; the **Museo de los Orígenes**, and the church of **San Andrés**. Close to here is the **Plaza de la Cebada**, where, in former times, executions often took place; it's just a tumbril ride away from the former prison at the Palacio de Santa Cruz (*see p270*).

## Sights & museums

### ♥ Basílica de San Francisco el Grande

*Plaza de San Francisco (91 365 38 00). Metro La Latina.* **Open** *Sept-June 10.30am-12.30pm, 4-6pm Tue-Sat. July, Aug 10.30am-12.30pm, 5-7pm Tue-Sun. Last admission half hour before closing.* **Admission** *(guided tour only) €3; €2 reductions; free under-4s.* **Map** *p62 E17.*

This huge, multi-tiered church between Puerta de Toledo and the Palacio Real is difficult to miss. A monastery on the site, reputedly founded by St Francis of Assisi,

---

**In the know
La Latina Sundays**

La Latina remains a popular Sunday outing for *madrileños* of all stripes. The tradition is to start at El Rastro flea market, and then head to the tapas bars around Cava Baja, Plaza de la Paja, Plaza San Andrés and Calle Humilladero for an aperitif of vermouth and some tapas. The hedonistic, sociable affair continues all day long, with some bars resembling scenes normally associated with late-night antics.

Basílica de San Francisco el Grande

was knocked down in 1760; between 1761 and 1784 Francisco Cabezas and later Francesco Sabatini built this neoclassical church in its place. Most challenging was the construction of the spectacular dome, with a diameter of 33m (108ft). The dome was restored fairly recently, and work on the rest of the basilica has also now been completed. Inside there is an early Goya, *The Sermon of San Bernardino of Siena* (1781), and several frescoes by other artists.

### Museo de San Isidro (Casa de San Isidro)

*Plaza de San Andrés 2 (91 366 74 15, www. madrid.es/museosanisidro). Metro La Latina.* **Open** *mid Sept-mid June 9.30am-8pm Tue-Sun. Mid June-mid Sept 10am-7pm Tue-Sun.* **Admission** *free.* **Map** *p62 F16.*

Dedicated to the city's patron saint, the well-digger and labourer San Isidro, this museum sits on the spot where he supposedly lived and performed one of his most famous miracles: when his son, Illán, fell into a well, Isidro made the water rise and thus was able to rescue the unfortunate lad. The well – or *a* well, anyway – is preserved inside the house, as is the chapel built in 1663 on the spot where Isidro allegedly died. According to legend, he was originally buried here, too. This is, then,

a museum that deals in legends as much as in solid artefacts, and the current material on show is a little limited. More interesting are the finds from local archaeological digs, formerly kept in the Museo de Historia and now in the basement here. They include items from lower-Palaeolithic settlements in the area, as well as artefacts from the Roman villas along the Manzanares river, and from the Muslim era.

### San Andrés, Capilla del Obispo & Capilla de San Isidro

*Plaza de San Andrés 1 (91 365 48 71). Metro La Latina.* **Open** *9am-1pm, 6-8pm Mon-Sat; for services only Sun.* **Capilla del Obispo** *12.30pm-1.15pm, 6.30-8.30pm Mon-Sat; guided tours (€2) 10am-12.30pm Tue, 4-5.30pm Thur.* **Admission** *free.* **Map** *p62 F16.*

The large church of San Andrés dates from the 16th century, but was badly damaged in the Civil War in 1936 and later rebuilt in a relatively simple style. Attached to it (but with separate entrances) are two of Madrid's most historic early church buildings. The Capilla del Obispo (Bishop's Chapel, 1520-35), with its entrance on Plaza de la Paja, is the best-preserved Gothic building in the city.

It contains finely carved tombs and a 1550 altarpiece by Francisco Giralte. It reopened to the public (by guided tour only) in 2010, after being closed for restoration for some 40 years. Further towards Plaza de los Carros is the Capilla de San Isidro, built in 1642-69 by Pedro de la Torre to house the remains of the saint, which were later transferred to the Iglesia-Catedral de San Isidro.

### San Pedro el Viejo
*Costanilla de San Pedro (91 365 12 84). Metro La Latina.* **Open** *6-8pm daily (phone to check).* **Admission** *free.* **Map** *p62 F16.*

This impressive Mudéjar brick tower dates from the 14th century, although the rest of the church dates from much later, having been rebuilt during the 17th century.

## Restaurants

### La Botillería de Maxi €
*C/Cava Alta 4 (91 365 12 49, www. labotilleriademaxi.com). Metro La Latina.* **Open** *12.30-4pm, 8.30pm-12.30am Tue-Sat; 12.30-6pm Sun. Closed last 2wks Aug.* **No cards.** **Map** *p62 G16* ❶ *Spanish*

Fashionably scruffy young waiting staff and blaring flamenco in a no-frills classic setting make for an unpretentious blend of old and new. While the *callos a la madrileña* (tripe in a spicy sauce) is acknowledged as the best in town, there's no shame in going for the *pisto manchego* (aubergine, courgette, pepper and tomato stew) with fried eggs, or the partridge pâté or the *mojama* (air-dried tuna).

### Casa Lucio €€€
*C/Cava Baja 35 (91 365 82 17, www.casalucio. es). Metro La Latina.* **Open** *1-4pm, 8.30-11.30pm daily. Closed Aug.* **Map** *p62 G16* ❸ *Spanish*

A restaurant unsurpassed by any other in Madrid for its famous patrons: the former king Juan Carlos, Bill Clinton and Penélope Cruz among them. This is the place of historical rendezvous, where Aznar and Bush's wives did lunch back when alliances were in the making. It also knows how to cook up one cracking *solomillo* (beef). The key to Lucio's glory is the use of a coal-fired oven and the best olive oil. Another star dish is a starter of lightly fried eggs laid on top of a bed of crisp, thinly cut chips – Juan Carlos always orders it. Be sure to ask for a table on the first floor.

### Emma y Júlia €€
*C/Cava Baja 19 (91 366 10 23, www. emmayjulia.com). Metro La Latina.* **Open** *8pm-midnight Tue; 1.30-4.30pm, 8.30pm-midnight Wed, Thur; 1.30-4.30pm,*

*8.30pm-1am Fri, Sat; 1.30-4.30pm, 8.30-11.30pm Sun. Closed July.* **Map** *p62 G16* ❹ *Italian*

Smack in the middle of a street flanked with traditional restaurants and gourmet tapas bars is this popular Italian eaterie – a sound option when a big salad and pizza are in order (a whole range of gluten-free dishes, including pizzas, are available). The staff are friendly, the environment laid-back and the food solid. The breaded artichokes are divine, and the house red is good and cheap. It's often wise to reserve in advance.

### El Estragón €€
*Costanilla de San Andrés 10, Plaza de la Paja (91 365 89 82, www.elestragonvegetariano. com). Metro La Latina.* **Open** *1pm-midnight Mon-Thur, Sun; 1pm-1am Fri, Sat.* **Map** *p62 F16* ❺ *Vegetarian*

El Estragón's underlying concept appears to be 'vegetarian food for meat-eaters', and thus there is no shortage of soya 'meatballs', 'hamburgers' and so on. Where this place really excels, however, is in its straightforward vegetarian dishes, such as a fabulous towering heap of *risotto verde* containing every green vegetable you can think of, topped with stringy Emmental. It's a delightful spot, with terracotta tiles, blue-and-white gingham and views over Plaza de la Paja, where tables are set out in summer.

### Julián de Tolosa €€€€
*C/Cava Baja 18 (91 365 82 10, www.casajulian detolosa.com). Metro La Latina.* **Open** *1.30-4pm, 9pm-midnight.* **Map** *p62 G16* ❻ *Basque*

Probably the most modern restaurant in the *barrio*, this upscale Basque establishment is all smooth wood, glass and brick, housed in a 19th-century building. With a very limited, simple menu, the main attraction here is the grilled steak (*chuletón de buey*), a contender for the city's best. Try the smoky Idiazábal sheep's cheese, a speciality from the little Basque town of the same name. The maître d' will steer you through an excellent selection of more than 100 wines.

### La Musa Latina €
*Costanilla San Andrés 12 (91 354 02 55, www. grupolamusa.com). Metro La Latina.* **Open** *10am-1am Mon, Tue, Sat, Sun; 10am-1.30am Wed; 10am-2am Thur, Fri (kitchen open from 1pm).* **Map** *p62 F16* ❼ *Global*

A laid-back vibe, tasty tapas and stir-fries, and a great location on Plaza de la Paja all contribute towards making La Musa Latina into a tempting package. Try the fried green tomatoes and the prawn tempura with avocado. There are plenty of indulgent desserts – go for the chocolate brownie or the *dulce de leche* panna cotta. Waiters are super cool but friendly, and the diners well-heeled and hip (note the Junk Club downstairs). There is a sister restaurant in Malasaña, but this one is roomier. **Other locations** La Musa, C/Manuela Malasaña 18, Malasaña (91 448 75 58); Ojalá, C/San Andrés 1 (91 523 27 47); Cafetería HD, C/Guzman el Bueno 67 (91 544 23 82).

### Taberna Salamanca €€
*C/Cava Baja 31 (91 365 31 10). Metro La Latina.* **Open** *1-4pm, 8.30pm-midnight Tue-Thur; 1-4pm, 8.30pm-1am Fri, Sat; 1-4.30pm Sun. Closed mid July-mid Aug.* **No cards.** **Map** *p62 G16* ❿ *Spanish*

On a street crammed to the hilt with high-priced eateries, this is where the cool, young and more frugal set comes to eat. There are three lunch *menús* at €9.50 to choose from, offering the usual Spanish pickings – the *croquetas*, courgette tortilla and endives with Roquefort cheese are all pretty reliable choices. The staff are friendly and young, with a tendency to whack up the stereo.

### El Viajero €€
*Plaza de la Cebada 11 (mobile 620 638 159, www.elviajeromadrid.com). Metro La Latina.* **Open** *12.30pm-1.30am Wed, Thur; 12.30pm-2.30am Fri; 11am-2.30am Sat; 11am-12.30am Sun. Closed 3wks Jan & last 2wks Aug.* **Map** *p62 G16* ⓫ *Mediterranean*

La Latina scenesters in sideburns and retro couture still flock to this three-storey bar/restaurant famous for its rooftop *terraza*. The food, a mixed array of Mediterranean dishes and barbecued meats, is delicious, if a little expensive. The carpaccios are melt-in-the-mouth and the pastas, particularly the *taglioni marinera*, drip with flavour. Discriminating carnivores love El Viajero for the high-quality, hormone-free Argentine meat, while sweet-tooths rejoice over the scrumptious tiramisu.

### Viuda de Vacas €€
*C/Águila 2 (91 366 58 47, viudavacas. es). Metro La Latina.* **Open** *1.30-4.30pm, 9pm-midnight Mon-Wed, Fri, Sat; 1.30-4.30pm Sun. Closed July.* **Map** *p62 F17* ⓬ *Castilian*

Viuda de Vacas has moved from its location on Cava Alta, where Pedro Almodóvar filmed on several occasions, but the unpretentious authenticity has survived just about intact. Classic Castilian home cooking has been in the Canova family for three generations; the restaurant was established by the feisty grandmother (the widow of Señor

Vacas). Favourite dishes include the stuffed courgettes and the baked hake or sea bream.

### Xentes €€
*C/Humilladero 13 (91 366 42 66). Metro La Latina.* **Open** *1.30-4.30pm Mon, Sun; 1.30-4.30pm, 9pm-midnight Tue-Sat. Closed Aug.* **Map** *p62 G17* ⓭ *Spanish*

With the TV blaring and some half-hearted nautical decor, this is a rather strange setting for some of the best seafood in Madrid. But the Galician patrons at the bar happily gulp down oysters and beer, and the diners in the back are just as delighted with their *pulpo a gallega* (octopus with paprika) and *arroz con bogavantes* (lobster paella).

## Tapas

### El Almendro 13
*C/Almendro 13 (91 365 42 52, almendro13. com). Metro La Latina.* **Open** *1-4pm, 7.30pm-midnight Mon-Thur; 1-4pm, 8pm-12.30am Fri, Sat; 1-5pm, 8pm-12.30am Sun.* **Map** *p62 G16* ❶

A sleepy, traditional bar during the week, it hots up at weekends, and drinkers often drift on to the pavements. A peculiar speciality is the *rosca*, a sort of oversized, filled bagel. These are invariably accompanied by a glass of the house *manzanilla*.

### ♥ Juanalaloca
*Plaza Puerta de Moros 4 (91 364 05 25). Metro La Latina.* **Open** *8pm-midnight Mon; 1-5pm, 8pm-midnight Tue-Thur; 1-5pm, 8pm-1am Fri; 1pm-1am Sat; 1pm-midnight Sun.* **Map** *p62 F17* ❸

Where the hip go to *tapear*, this Uruguayan-run tapas bar attracts a stylish mix of Argentinians, Uruguayans, locals and tourists. It's kind of pricey, but offers undeniably creative cooking – such as wild mushroom and truffle croquettes and tuna carpaccio with almond oil and rice. Its tortilla is also renowned.

### Taberna Matritum
*C/Cava Alta 17 (91 365 82 37, www. tabernamatritum.es). Metro La Latina.* **Open** *1.30-4pm Tue; 1.30-4pm, 8pm-midnight Wed-Sun.* **Map** *p62 G16* ❺

Its name is Latin for 'Madrid', but Matritum has a great selection of tapas and wine from other regions of Spain, principally Catalonia. Try the *gambas all cremat* (prawns with burnt garlic) or fabulous canapés such as Cabrales cheese with apple compôte. The wine list, too, is dominated by Catalan labels, with many notably good bottles from the Penedès.

### El Tempranillo

*C/Cava Baja 38 (91 364 15 32). Metro La Latina.* **Open** *8pm-midnight Mon; 1-4pm, 8pm-midnight Tue-Sun. Closed 3wks Aug.* **Map** *p62 G16* ⑥

Never less than rowdy, decorated in bullring ochre and bare brick, with flamenco on the sound system, El Tempranillo offers an impressive range of labels from nearly every wine-producing region in Spain. The tapas are addictive too: try the wild mushrooms in scrambled egg or the sweetbreads.

### Txirimiri

*C/Humilladero 6 (91 364 11 96, www.txirimiri. es). Metro La Latina.* **Open** *noon-midnight daily.* **Map** *p62 F17* ⑧

The popular Txirimiri specialises in Basque *pintxos*, and despite its aspirational-sounding tag line of 'haute cuisine in miniature', it's a

---

**In the know
Sunday best**

In Madrid, Sunday feels like Friday and preparing for Monday isn't given much thought; *madrileños* like to squeeze the most out of their weekends, hence the Sunday post-Rastro drinking tradition in La Latina. On sunny days, the area's squares brim with hedonism. On rainy days, the best bars burst with drinking, talking *madrileños*. The essence of the tradition is vermouth, and the whole ritual, tapas and all, is sometimes known as *'haciendo el vermut'* – 'doing vermouth'.

---

laid-back, friendly place, and always rammed on a Sunday. The thirtysomething crowd is drawn by the excellent, well-priced tapas (don't miss the croquettes and ravioli) and sociable atmosphere. There's a restaurant area at the far end. **Other locations** C/General Diez Porlier 91, Salamanca (91 401 43 45); C/Ferraz 38, Moncloa (91 559 33 09); C/ Ibiza 25, Retiro (91 028 27 98).

## Cafés & bars

### Almacén de Vinos (Casa Gerardo)

*C/Calatrava 21 (91 221 96 60). Metro Puerta de Toledo.* **Open** *1-5pm, 8.30pm-midnight Mon-Fri; 1-5pm, 8.30pm-1am Sat, Sun.* **No cards.** **Map** *p62 F17* ①

A lively and unpretentious wine bar, Gerardo is an essential part of the neighbourhood, offering excellent sausage, ham and seafood tapas, as well as a particularly good selection of cheeses.

### El Anciano Rey de los Vinos

*C/Bailén 19 (91 559 53 32, www. elancianoreydelosvinos.es). Metro Ópera.* **Open** *9am-midnight Mon, Wed-Sun.* **Map** *p62 E15* ②

Kept much as it has been for the last century – very simple, but spacious and light inside with a wide counter and mirrored walls – the King of Wines serves good canapés, and is a great place for a drink after visiting the cathedral. Prices are quite high, especially if you sit outdoors.

### Delic

*Costanilla de San Andrés 14, Plaza de la Paja (91 364 54 50, www.delic.es). Metro La Latina.* **Open** *11am-2am Tue-Thur, Sun; 11am-2.30am Fri, Sat.* **Map** *p62 F16* ⑦

A perennial favourite with seemingly everybody, from those looking for a morning coffee on the leafy Plaza de la Paja to those meeting up for a few bolstering cocktails before a big night out. In fact, it gets so busy at certain times that they've employed a bouncer and a one-in/one-out policy. A globetrotting menu includes tabbouleh, Japanese dumplings and filled ciabattas, and the Chilean chocolate cake is utterly irresistible.

### El Ventorillo

*C/Bailén 14 (91 366 35 78). Metro Ópera.* **Open** *11am-1am daily.* **Map** *p62 E16* ⑩

Just down from the Palacio Real, this *terraza* offers the finest sunsets in Madrid, looking out over the Casa del Campo and all the way to the Guadarrama.

REINANDO
ISABEL SEGUNDA
DE BORBON
AÑO DE
1844

Teatro Real *p64*

# Sol & Gran Vía

The Gran Vía was created in 1910 by slicing through the Old City so that traffic could easily reach Cibeles from C/ Princesa. Intended to be a broad modern boulevard, it got grander still when World War I made neutral Madrid a clearing house for international money. With the economy booming, developers and architects set out to embrace modernity as hard as they could to show that if you wanted something impressive, they could provide it. In the following decades, each generation added its own stamp, and the result is certainly eclectic. At the heart of this area is the Puerta del Sol, spiritually and geographically the very centre of Madrid, and a place where *madrileños* gather to celebrate victories and mourn losses.

♥ **Don't miss**

**1 Real Monasterio de las Descalzas Reales** *p85*
A 16th-century convent packed with art.

**2 Museo de la Real Academia de Bellas Artes de San Fernando** *p86*
A world-class art museum in a city with no shortage of them.

**3 Círculo de Bellas Artes** *p87*
Exhibitions, masked balls and a stately café.

**4 Real Monasterio de la Encarnación** *p87*
Storied convent off the beaten trail.

**In the know**
**Getting around**

Sol, at the very centre of this area, is crisscrossed by various metro, rail and bus lines, but within the neighbourhood, walking is just as fast, and most streets are pedestrianised.

# EXPLORING SOL & GRAN VÍA

## Puerta del Sol and around

The **Puerta del Sol** represents the very heart of Madrid, both because it contains *kilómetro cero* (the mark from which distances from the city are measured) and for its time-honoured role as chief meeting place. Famously, through the centuries people have come to Sol to find out what's going on. Until the 1830s, the block between C/Correo and C/Esparteros was occupied by the monastery of San Felipe el Real, the steps and cloister of which were, in Habsburg Madrid, one of the recognised *mentideros* – literally 'pits of lies', or gossip-mills – where people came to pick up on the latest news, anecdotes or scurrilous rumours. In a city with no newspapers – but where who was in or out of favour was of primary importance – *mentideros* were a major social institution, and rare was the day when at least one of the great figures of Spanish literature, such as Cervantes, Lope or Quevedo, did not pass by here. The steps of San Felipe were also overlooked by one of the largest brothels of the era, another attraction for men about town. On a more respectable note, the Café Pombo, home to legendary *tertulias* (*see p89* Tertulias), stood on the corner of C/Carretas. It is still Madrid's most popular meeting point, particularly the spot by the monument with the symbols of Madrid (a bear and a *madroño* or strawberry tree) at the junction with C/Carmen.

Under the Habsburgs, the Puerta del Sol, the main, easternmost gate (*puerta*) of 15th-century Madrid, was surrounded by churches and monasteries. It was rebuilt

Puerta del Sol

---

### ❤ Time to eat & drink

**Breakfast among the blue rinses**
La Mallorquina *p90*

**Hearty *cocido madrileño***
La Bola Taberna *p87*

**Tapas with history**
Casa Labra *p90*

**Dessert of champions**
La Casa de las Torrijas *p90*

### ❤ Time to shop

**Covetable ceramics**
Antigua Casa Talavera *p90*

**Ronaldo jerseys**
Área Real Madrid *p91*

**Butter-soft leather gloves**
Guantes Luque *p91*

**Hand-painted fans**
Casa de Diego *p91*

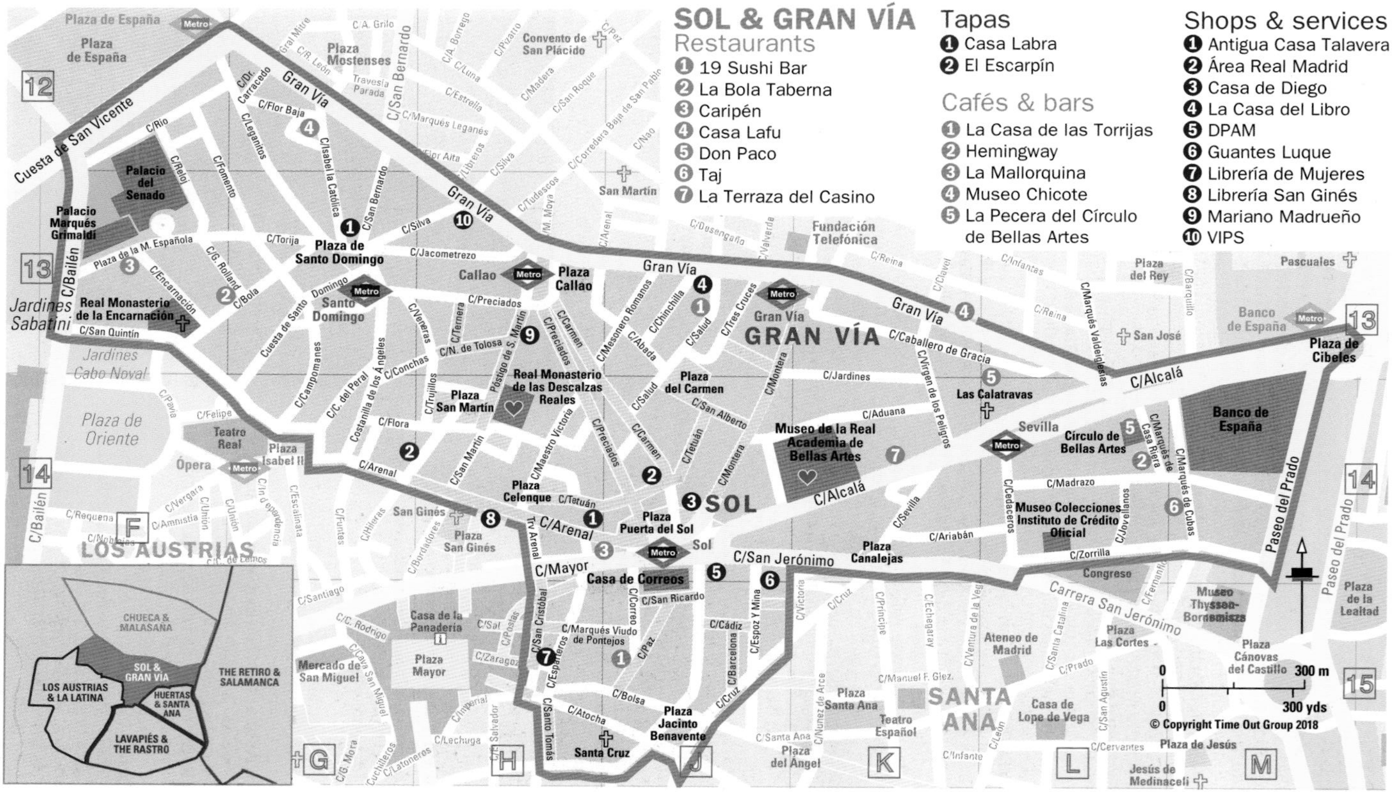

SOL & GRAN VÍA
Restaurants
1 19 Sushi Bar
2 La Bola Taberna
3 Caripén
4 Casa Lafu
5 Don Paco
6 Taj
7 La Terraza del Casino
Tapas
1 Casa Labra
2 El Escarpín
Cafés & bars
1 La Casa de las Torrijas
2 Hemingway
3 La Mallorquina
4 Museo Chicote
5 La Pecera del Círculo de Bellas Artes
Shops & services
1 Antigua Casa Talavera
2 Área Real Madrid
3 Casa de Diego
4 La Casa del Libro
5 DPAM
6 Guantes Luque
7 Librería de Mujeres
8 Librería San Ginés
9 Mariano Madrueño
10 VIPS
GRAN VÍA
SOL
LOS AUSTRIAS
SANTA ANA
Plaza de España
Plaza Mostenses
Palacio del Senado
Palacio Marqués Grimaldi
Plaza de Santo Domingo
Real Monasterio de la Encarnación
Jardines Sabatini
Jardines Cabo Noval
Plaza de Oriente
Teatro Real
Plaza Isabel II
Ópera
Callao
Plaza Callao
Santo Domingo
Real Monasterio de las Descalzas Reales
Plaza San Martín
Plaza del Carmen
Plaza Celenque
Plaza Puerta del Sol
Casa de Correos
Plaza San Ginés
Casa de la Panadería
Plaza Mayor
Mercado de San Miguel
Plaza Jacinto Benavente
Santa Cruz
Fundación Telefónica
Museo de la Real Academia de Bellas Artes
Las Calatravas
Sevilla
Círculo de Bellas Artes
Banco de España
Plaza de Cibeles
Museo Colecciones Instituto de Crédito Oficial
Plaza Canalejas
Congreso
Museo Thyssen-Bornemisza
Plaza Las Cortes
Plaza Cánovas del Castillo
Ateneo de Madrid
Plaza Santa Ana
Teatro Español
Casa de Lope de Vega
Plaza del Ángel
Plaza de Jesús
Jesús de Medinaceli
Plaza de la Lealtad
Plaza del Rey
San José
Pascuales
Convento de San Plácido
San Martín
San Ginés
Paseo del Prado
Carrera San Jerónimo
C/Alcalá
C/Arenal
C/Mayor
C/San Jerónimo
C/Bailén
Cuesta de San Vicente
0 300 m
0 300 yds
© Copyright Time Out Group 2018
CHUECA & MALASAÑA
SOL & GRAN VÍA
THE RETIRO & SALAMANCA
LOS AUSTRIAS & LA LATINA
HUERTAS & SANTA ANA
LAVAPIÉS & THE RASTRO

in its present form in 1854-62. The square's most important building is the **Casa de Correos**, built in 1766 by Jaime Marquet as a post office for Charles III. Today it houses the regional government, the Comunidad de Madrid, but in the Franco era it had much grimmer connotations, as the Interior Ministry and police headquarters. It was altered significantly in 1866, when the large clock tower was added; this is now the building's best-known feature, since it's the clock the whole country sees on New Year's Eve, when revellers crowd into the square to eat their lucky grapes, one for each stroke of midnight. In the 1990s, the tower developed a precarious incline due to rot in its timbers, but it was rebuilt and unveiled once again in 1998. Sol is also where Napoleon's Egyptian cavalry, the Mamelukes, charged down on the *madrileño* crowd on 2 May 1808, as portrayed in one of Goya's most famous paintings.

In 2010, the removal of the iconic Tío Pepe sign from atop the building on the eastern side – now an Apple Store – was an unpopular move, but four years later it was reinstated, this time at no.11, on the north side of the square.

Tucked in the middle of the area between Sol, Arenal, C/Alcalá and Gran Vía is the **Real Monasterio de las Descalzas Reales**, bursting with artworks and a deliciously unexpected oasis amid the traffic and bustle of Sol. At the west side of the area, just above the Plaza de Oriente, is the peaceful and little visited **Real Monasterio de la Encarnación**, also worth a look. Just north of that, occupying the site of another convent, is the old 19th-century **Palacio del Senado** (Senate), now made redundant by its back-to-back counterpart in granite and smoked glass by Santiago Goyarre.

Running almost alongside C/Preciados up to Gran Vía is the pedestrianised and slightly shabby **C/Montera**, lined with cheap, dated shops and the main area for street prostitution in the city centre. At the top, parallel with Gran Vía, is **C/Caballero de Gracia**, with a 19th-century oratory that lays on special Masses for the working girls, many of them Latin American, who operate along the street. While seedy, this area is not generally dangerous, and is heavily policed. Care should be taken when walking around late at night, however, especially if you're on your own.

## Gran Vía

The **Plaza de España**, at the western end of the Gran Vía, is dominated by Franco's bombastic architecture. It is flanked by two classic buildings of the type sponsored by the regime when out to impress: the '50s-modern **Torre Madrid** (1957) and the enormous **Edificio España** of 1948-53. Bought by Mallorcan chain Riu in 2017, the Edificio España is currently being developed into a vast four-star hotel, with around 650 rooms. The three statues standing in the middle – of Cervantes, Don Quixote and Sancho Panza – are by Teodoro Anasagasti and Mateo Inurria, from 1928. The square around them is big, noisy and not a particularly relaxing place to sit, although this is all set to change under mayor Manuela Carmena's grand plans for the area (*see p32* Squaring Up).

Heading down the Gran Vía, the area north and east of Sol was originally the city's financial district, hence the number of grand edifices owned by banks and insurance companies. Its other great avenue

Gran Vía

---

**In the know**
**Pickpockets**

Although Madrid isn't a violent city, petty crime such as pickpocketing and bag-snatching is still rife on the metro and buses, as well as in touristy areas such as the Rastro, Retiro park, Puerta del Sol, Plaza Mayor and around the Gran Vía. To avoid being a victim, don't leave your belongings on the back of café chairs or on the ground; keep your hand on top of your bag in the metro; be wary if someone pulls out a map to ask or offer directions – thieves often work in pairs, and this could be a way to distract you; and beware of fake policemen – if someone asks to see your ID, ask to see theirs first.

# 💜 Real Monasterio de las Descalzas Reales

*Plaza de las Descalzas 3 (information 91 454 88 00). Metro Callao or Sol.* **Open** *10am-2pm, 4-6.30pm Tue-Sat; 10am-3pm Sun.* **Admission** *(by guided tour only) €6; free under-5s. Free to EU citizens Wed & Thur from 4pm.* **Map** *p83 H14.*

The convent of the Descalzas Reales ('Royal Barefoot Nuns') is the most complete 16th-century building in Madrid and still houses a cloistered community. It was originally built as a palace for Alonso Gutiérrez, treasurer of Charles V, but was converted into a convent in 1556-64 by Antonio Sillero and Juan Bautista de Toledo after Philip II's widowed sister Joanna of Austria decided to become a nun. Founded with royal patronage, the Descalzas became the preferred destination of the many widows, younger daughters and other women of the royal family and high aristocracy of Spain who entered religious orders. Hence it also acquired an extraordinary collection of works of art – paintings, sculptures, tapestries and *objets d'art* – given as bequests by the novices' families. Equally lavish is the Baroque decoration of the building itself, belying its sternly austere façade, with a grand painted staircase, frescoed ceilings and 32 chapels.

The largest non-Spanish contingents in its art collection are Italian, with Titian, Bernardino Luini, Angelo Nardi and Sebastiano del Piombo, and Flemish, with Breughel (an *Adoration of the Magi*), Joos Van Cleve and Rubens. The Descalzas is also an exceptional showcase of Spanish Baroque religious art, with works by Gaspar Becerra, Zurbarán, Claudio Coello and even a tiny painting attributed to Goya.

In addition, as you walk around you can catch glimpses of the nuns' courtyard vegetable garden, which has remained virtually unchanged since the convent was built and is closed to the public.

The monastery was seen by very few until the 1980s, when it was restored and partially opened as a museum. It can be visited only with official tours, which leave every 20 minutes and last around 50 minutes. Frustratingly, the guides rarely speak English, there is no printed information about the convent and the paintings are not labelled. Note also that only a limited number of tickets are sold every day, so it's worth arriving early or booking tickets online in advance. It is still an enjoyable place to visit, though, for the sheer sumptuousness of its artworks and fittings.

# ❤ Museo de la Real Academia de Bellas Artes de San Fernando

*C/Alcalá 13 (91 524 08 64, www. realacademiabellasartessanfernando. com). Metro Sevilla or Sol.* **Open** *10am-3pm Tue-Sun. Closed Aug.* **Admission** *€8; €4 reductions; free under-18s, over-65s. Free to all Wed. Calcografía Nacional free.* **No cards.** **Map p83 K14.**

This under-visited museum is in fact one of Madrid's most important and oldest permanent artistic institutions (it was founded in 1794). The eclectic collection is partly made up of works of varying quality donated by aspiring members in order to gain admission to the academy. The museum's greatest possessions, though, are its 13 works by Goya, an important figure in the early years of the Academia. They include two major self-portraits; a portrait of his friend, the playwright Moratín; a portrait of Charles IV's hated minister Godoy; and the *Burial of the Sardine*, a carnival scene that foreshadows his later, darker works. Another of the academy's most prized possessions is the Italian mannerist

Giuseppe Arcimboldo's *Spring*, a playful, surrealistic portrait of a man made up entirely of flowers. It was one of a series on the four seasons painted for Ferdinand I of Austria in 1563: *Summer and Winter* are still in Vienna, but the whereabouts of *Autumn* is unknown. There are also important portraits by Velázquez and Rubens, and several paintings by Zurbarán. Among the later works, the best known are some Picasso engravings and a Juan Gris; the most surprising are the colourful fantasies of Múñoz Degrain and the De Chirico-esque work of Julio Romero de Torres. Look out, too, for Leandro Bassano's superb *La Riva degli Schiavoni*.

The academy also has a valuable collection of plans and drawings, including those of Prado architect Juan de Villanueva, and rare books. In the same building is the Museo de Calcografía Nacional, a similarly priceless collection and archive of engraving and fine printing, which has many of the original plates for the great etching series of Goya.

is **C/Alcalá**, which follows the centuries-old main route into Madrid from the east. In the 18th century, when it was lined by aristocratic palaces, it was described as the grandest street in Europe, and will only improve in mid 2018, when it is to close to all but residential traffic. It is still pretty impressive today, with a wonderful variety of 19th- to early 20th-century buildings, from the dignified 1882 **Banesto** building (corner of C/Sevilla) to the cautiously modernist **Círculo de Bellas Artes**. There are also fine older constructions along the street, such as the austere neoclassical Finance Ministry, built as the **Aduana**, or customs administration, by Francesco Sabatini between 1761 and 1769, and, alongside it, the **Real Academia de Bellas Artes de San Fernando**. At the point where Alcalá and Gran Vía meet stands Pedro de Ribera's exuberantly baroque church of **San José** (1730-42), with a plaque inside to commemorate the fact that Simón Bolívar was married here in 1802.

## Sights & museums

### ❤ Círculo de Bellas Artes
*C/Alcalá 42 & C/Marqués de Casa Riera 2 (91 360 54 00, www.circulobellasartes.com). Metro Banco de España.* **Open** *Café 8am-1am Mon-Thur; 9am-3am Fri, Sat; 9am-midnight Sun. Exhibitions 11am-2pm, 5-9pm Tue-Sun. Roof terrace 9am-2am Mon-Thur; 9am-3am Fri; 10am-3am Sat; 11am-2am Sun.* **Admission** *exhibitions €4 (€5 including access to roof terrace); €3 reductions.* **Map** *p83 L14.*

The Círculo de Bellas Artes occupies a superb building, designed by Antonio Palacios and completed in 1926. It is a key player in every aspect of the Madrid arts scene: as well as a beautifully airy main floor café, with a gracious pavement terrace, the Círculo offers a plethora of classes, exhibitions, lectures and concerts in its theatre and concert hall, as well as an annual masked ball for carnival.

### ❤ Real Monasterio de la Encarnación
*Plaza de la Encarnación 1 (91 547 05 10, information 91 454 88 00, www.patrimonionacional.es/real-sitio). Metro Ópera or Santo Domingo.* **Open** *10am-2pm, 4-6.30pm Tue-Sat; 10am-3pm Sun.* **Admission** *(incl guided tour) €6; free under-5s. Free to EU citizens Wed, Thur from 4pm.* **Map** *p83 F13.*

Before the Alcázar burned down, this understated convent was its treasury, connected by a concealed passageway. In 1611, it was inaugurated as a monastery by Philip III and his wife Margaret of Austria,

and rebuilt to a design by Gómez de Mora. However, much of the original building, including the church, was damaged by fire in 1734 and rebuilt in a classical-Baroque style in the 1760s by Ventura Rodríguez. It still contains a community of around 20 nuns, but most of the building is open to the public. Although not as lavishly endowed as the Descalzas Reales, it contains a great many pieces of 17th-century religious art, the most impressive of which is Jusepe Ribera's shimmering *chiaroscuro* portrait of John the Baptist. The Encarnación's most famous and memorable room, however, is the *reliquiario* (relics room). In its glass casements are displayed some 1,500 saintly remains, bone fragments and former possessions of saints and martyrs, in extravagantly bejewelled copper, bronze, glass, gold and silver reliquaries. Its prize possession is what purports to be the solidified blood of San Pantaleón, kept inside a glass orb. The blood reportedly liquefies each year from midnight on the eve of his feast day, 27 July (*see p65* Saints and Sinners). Note that visits are by guided tour only, so that visitors do not bother the nuns.

## Restaurants

### 19 Sushi Bar €€
*C/Salud 19 (91 524 05 71, www.19sushibar.com). Metro Gran Vía.* **Open** *1.30-4pm, 8-11.30pm daily. Closed 2 wks Aug.* **Map** *p83 J13* ❶ *Japanese*

Going strong since 2005, 19 Sushi Bar is a favourite among aficionados of Japanese cuisine. The Kobe beef sashimi, tuna fillet with wasabi and the king prawn tempura roll are just three of the star dishes. The decor is typically cool and minimalist, but at least there's nothing on display to distract you from the food.

### ❤ La Bola Taberna €€
*C/Bola 5 (91 547 69 30, www.labola.es). Metro Ópera or Santo Domingo.* **Open** *1-4pm, 8.30-11pm Mon-Sat; 1-4pm Sun. Closed Aug.* **Map** *p83 G13* ❷ *Spanish*

Holding court on a quiet backstreet, this dignified, classic Madrid restaurant is considered by many to be the home of *cocido*, the huge and hearty stew beloved of *madrileños* and a test for the biggest of appetites. La Bola Taberna is still run by the same family that founded it in the 19th century, and the *cocido* (which is only served at lunchtime) is still cooked traditionally in earthenware pots on a wood fire. Unfortunately, this hugely impressive pedigree has led to a certain complacency among some of the waiting staff.

Casa Labra

### Caripén €€

*Plaza de la Marina Española 4 (91 541 11 77).*
*Metro Santo Domingo.* **Open** *9pm-2am Mon-*
*Sat. Closed Aug.* **Map** *p83 F13* ❸ *French*

At first glance, this French bistro seems
a wee bit run down, but nonetheless it's
all class – in a campy, Broadway kind of
way. Behind the dangling blue Christmas
tree lights are tables occupied by singing,
dancing, canoodling patrons having a very
good time, oblivious to the excellent skate in
black butter or crêpe with salmon and caviar.
The merry atmosphere owes a lot to the staff,
particularly Juanjo, who floats through the
restaurant spreading his abundant charm.

### Casa Lafu €€

*C/Flor Baja 1 (91 548 70 96, www.casalafu.*
*com). Metro Santo Domingo.* **Open** *noon-*
*midnight Mon-Thur; noon-12.30am Fri-Sun.*
**Map** *p83 G12* ❹ *Chinese*

Superb *huo guo* (Chinese hot pot) restaurant,
with queues out of the door. The dim sum are
also excellent, as are the dumplings and wok
dishes (you can specify how spicy you'd like
them), but don't expect too much by way of
charm from the waiting staff.

### Don Paco €€

*C/Caballero de Gracia 36 (91 531 44 80).*
*Metro Gran Vía.* **Open** *1.30-4pm, 8-11pm*
*Mon-Fri; 1.30-4pm Sat. Closed Aug.* **Map**
*p83 L13* ❺ *Spanish*

Established in 1972 by Don Paco, a former
Jerez bullfighter – who sadly died in 2017 at
the age of 92 – and his brother, this restaurant
is clearly the realm of an Andalucían
matador. With photos of famous visitors (the
former king and his parents were regulars)

and Andalucían memorabilia covering the
walls, it oozes southern style. *Tinto de verano*
('summer wine' cut with lemonade) on tap,
ample sherry options... who needs Seville?
Don't miss the *tortillitas de camarones*
(shrimp fritters).

### Taj €€

*C/Marqués de Cubas 6 (91 531 50 59, www.*
*restaurantetaj.com). Metro Banco de España.*
**Open** *1-4 pm, 8.30-11.30 pm daily.* **Map**
*p83 M14* ❻ *Indian*

Everything about Taj promises serious curry
– from the jingly-jangly muzak to the fanned
linen napkins and plastic flowers. The menu
includes all the usuals, but the *degustación*
of samosa, pakora, tandoori chicken, lamb
curry, pilau and naan is a good bet. Try to get
the curries *picante* (hot), though the waiters
may decide that that can't be what you really
mean and give you *medio* anyway. Desserts
are a bit limited and the decor is slightly naff,
which is curiously reassuring. There's a set
lunch for €12.95, available Monday to Friday.

### La Terraza del Casino €€€€

*C/Alcalá 15 (91 532 12 75, www.*
*casinodemadrid.es). Metro Sevilla.* **Open**
*1.30-3.30pm, 9-11.30pm Mon-Sat. Closed*
*Aug.* **Map** *p83 K14* ❼ *Modern European*

The sumptuous environs of this gentlemen's
club provide the setting for a restaurant
inspired by gourmet god Ferran Adrià. Paco
Roncero, a former disciple, is at the helm in
the kitchen, and has put his own stamp on
the cooking, winning Michelin stars along the
way. The menu changes seasonally, but might
include such delights as lobster sashimi and
crunchy black algae.

# Tertulias

*The favoured forum of the literati*

The intellectual life of Spain once revolved around the ephemeral institution known as the *tertulia*. Originating in the humanist salons of 16th-century Seville, the *tertulia* is a gathering of people united by a common interest, which can range from mathematics to gastronomy, but has traditionally been literature. And Spain being a country where people tend to go out rather than meet in each other's houses, these gatherings have invariably been held in bars and cafés.

The rise of the *tertulia* in Madrid, as depicted in many paintings of the time, coincided with the city's emergence in the early 19th century as the centre of a café life rivalling that of Paris and Vienna. Café life has always flourished at times of great political repression, the café being a place whose proverbial smoky gloom has provided a suitably furtive retreat for dissidents. During the grey, autocratic rule of Spain's Ferdinand VII, the *tertulia* became an expression of political and cultural freedom.

*Tertulias* took place in many of the cafés that, by the 1830s, had almost entirely encircled the Puerta del Sol. But the most influential of these gatherings was the one associated with a tiny, rat-infested basement café next to the neo-classical Teatro Español (the present bland reconstruction bears little resemblance to the original establishment). The place was officially called the Café del Príncipe, but everyone came to know it as the 'Parnasillo' or 'Little Parnassus', on account of its attracting all the fashionable writers of the day. Among these were the much revered satirical essayist Mariano José de Larra and the writer Ramón de Mesonero Romanos, who famously wrote that in 'this miserable little room' they succeeded in shaking the very foundations of Spanish life and culture.

With the evolution towards the end of the 19th century of Madrid's idiosyncratically late eating and drinking hours, *tertulias* proliferated as never before, reaching their apogee in the 1920s under the guidance of a writer sometimes referred to as the 'second of the Ramóns', Ramón Gómez de la Serna. Every Saturday night, from around 10pm until dawn, a *tertulia*, presided over by Gómez de la Serna, was held in what was soon dubbed the 'Sacred Crypt of the Pombo', a now-vanished café off the Puerta del Sol. The solemnity of these celebrated meetings was captured in a sombre painting, *La tertulia del Café Pombo*, by José Gutiérrez Solana. La Serna is seen standing in the centre. These gatherings were also slightly ridiculed by filmmaker Luis Buñuel, who described how, 'We used to arrive, greet each other and order a drink – usually coffee, and a lot of water – until a meandering conversation began about the latest literary publications or political upheavals.'

Most liberal and avant-garde associates of the Pombo went into exile after the Civil War, thus radically diminishing the cultural life of the capital. Subsequently, many of the cafés in the centre of Madrid were succeeded by the HQs of large banks, and many more suffered the humiliation of being transformed into Formica-lined, American-style cafeterias.

▶ La tertulia del Café Pombo *is on display at the Reina Sofía (see p112).*

## Tapas

### ♥ Casa Labra
*C/Tetuán 12 (91 531 00 81, www.casalabra.es). Metro Sol. **Open** 11am-3.30pm, 6-11pm daily. **Map** p83 H14* ❶

Famously the birthplace of the Spanish Socialist Party back in 1879, this legendary bar, with its brown 1950s paintwork and luggage racks, is worth a visit for its history alone. Speciality of the house is the cod *croquetas* served up by dour white-jacketed waiters.

### El Escarpín
*C/Hileras 17 (91 559 99 57, sidreriaelescarpin.com). Metro Ópera or Sol. **Open** 9am-12.30am Mon-Thur; 9am-2am Fri; 10am-2am Sat; 10am-12.30am Sun. **Map** p83 G14* ❷

So vast that you'll always find a seat, this Asturian cider bar has the look – bare bricks and long wooden tables – to go with the regional tapas. Natural cider (*sidra*) should be followed by *lacón* (gammon), *fabada asturiana* (bean and pork stew) or chorizo.

## Cafés & bars

### ♥ La Casa de las Torrijas
*C/Paz 4 (91 025 29 02). Metro Sol. **Open** 11am-5pm Mon, Sun, 11am-11.30pm Tue-Sat. Closed Aug. **No cards**. **Map** p83 J15* ❶

Formerly known as the As de los Vinos, this is a charmingly unkempt bar, tiled and mirrored, with table-tops constructed from old enamel adverts. Since 1907, it has served little more than *torrijas* – bread soaked in wine and spices, coated in sugar and deep-fried – and house wine. If that doesn't appeal, there are a handful of other, simple tapas, along with a basic set lunch.

### Hemingway
*C/Marqués de Casa Riera, Sol (91 200 05 70, www.nh-hotels.com/hotel/nh-collection-madrid-suecia/restaurants). Metro Banco de España. **Open** 8pm-2am daily. **Map** p83 L14* ❷

The *dernier cri* in bar culture is the speakeasy, but none does it better than Hemingway, entered from the street down some stairs and through the toilets. The art deco doors open on to a subterranean film set – a long old-school cocktail bar with a romantic nook of leopard-skin sofas. The DJs who play most nights make this a place that will only really appeal to a youngish crowd, however.

### ♥ La Mallorquina
*Puerta del Sol 8 (91 521 12 01, www.pasteleriamallorquina.es). Metro Sol. **Open** 8.15am-9.15pm daily. Closed 1wk Aug. **Map** p83 J14* ❸

While the atmospheric bakery downstairs supplies box after ribbon-tied box of flaky pastries, croissants and *napolitanas* to what seems like half of Madrid, the upstairs *salón* crackles with the animated chat of *madrileña* blue-rinses and savvier tourists. Windows overlooking the Puerta del Sol make this an unbeatable central spot for breakfast. The coffee is cheap and very good.

### Museo Chicote
*Gran Vía 12 (91 532 67 37, grupomercado delareina.com/es/museo-chicote). Metro Gran Vía. **Open** 7pm-3am Mon-Thur, Sun; 7pm-3.30am Fri, Sat. Closed Aug. **Map** p83 K13* ❹

Its art deco interior is starting to look a bit shabby around the edges, but Chicote is still the doyen of Madrid cocktail bars. This was famously where Hemingway and other international press hacks would spend their days sheltering from the artillery shells flying down the Gran Vía during the Civil War. Grace Kelly and Ava Gardner, along with just about every Spanish writer, actor or artist of the last 60 years, have passed through too. There are various resident DJs, playing electro-soul, funk, hip hop and anything with a groove.

### La Pecera del Círculo de Bellas Artes
*C/Alcalá 42 (91 531 33 02, www.lapeceradelcirculo.com). Metro Banco de España. **Open** 8am-1am Mon-Thur; 9am-3am Fri, Sat; 9am-midnight Sun. **Map** p83 L14* ❺

A quintessential point of reference in the city's café society, the Bellas Artes is utterly elegant. Take a seat amid the columns and female nudes and frown over *El País* with coffee and a croissant to fit right in. A recent addition is the glamorous rooftop terrace bar, where you can pose for a selfie with a cocktail in front of Madrid landmarks like the Metrópolis building.

## Shops & services

### ♥ Antigua Casa Talavera
*C/Isabel la Católica 2 (91 547 34 17, www.antiguacasatalavera.com). Metro Santo Domingo. **Open** 10am-1.30pm, 5-8pm Mon-Fri; 10am-1.30pm Sat. **Map** p83 G13* ❶
*Gifts & souvenirs*

This long-standing family business specialises in traditional blue-and-white Spanish ceramics. Every available space is crammed with hand-painted designs, all sourced from small Spanish producers. The charming owner speaks good English.

### ♥ Área Real Madrid

*C/Carmen 3 (91 521 79 50). Metro Sol.* **Open** *10am-9pm Mon-Sat; 11am-8pm Sun.* **Map** *p83 J14* ❷ *Gifts & souvenirs*

A true emporium for the Real Madrid-inclined. On sale are, naturally, replica shirts and all manner of other stuff bearing the club's logo, from ashtrays to mouse mats, bath towels to undies.

### ♥ Casa de Diego

*Puerta del Sol 12 (91 522 66 43, www. casadediego.info). Metro Sol.* **Open** *9.30am-8pm Mon-Sat.* **Map** *p83 J14* ❸ *Gifts & souvenirs*

This much-loved shop specialises in hand-painted fans, umbrellas and classy walking sticks. **Other locations** C/Mesoneros Romanos 4 (91 531 02 23).

### La Casa del Libro

*Gran Vía 29 (902 026 402, www.casadellibro. com). Metro Gran Vía.* **Open** *9.30am-9.30pm Mon-Sat; 11am-9pm Sun.* **Map** *p83 J13* ❹ *Books & music*

La Casa del Libro covers just about every subject imaginable in Spanish, but also has good sections of literature, reference and teaching material in English and other languages.

### DPAM

*Plaza Puerta del Sol 6 (91 523 16 14, www. dpam.es). Metro Sol.* **Open** *10am-9pm Mon-Sat.* **Map** *p83 J14* ❺ *Fashion*

DPAM (Du Pareil au Même) is a French chain specialising in original, colourful clothes

for kids up to age 12. Its clothes for babies and toddlers are especially funky and make great presents.

### ♥ Guantes Luque

*C/Espoz y Mina 3 (91 522 32 87). Metro Sol.* **Open** *10am-1.30pm, 5-8pm Mon-Fri; 10.30am-1.30pm Sat. Closed Aug.* **Map** *p83 J14* ❻ *Fashion*

This old-fashioned glove shop in Santa Ana was established in 1886. Luque sells gloves in all sizes, colours and materials, covering all types of wool, silk and leather. If you can't find them here you won't find them anywhere. Prices range from €20 to €300.

### Librería de Mujeres

*C/San Cristóbal 17 (91 521 70 43). Metro Sol.* **Open** *Sept-June 10am-2pm, 5-8pm Mon-Fri; 10.30am-2pm Sat. July 10am-2pm, 5-8pm Mon-Fri. Closed Aug.* **Map** *p83 H15* ❼ *Books & music*

Madrid's best women's bookshop goes by the motto *'Los libros no muerden, tampoco el feminismo'* – 'Books don't bite, neither does feminism'.

### Librería San Ginés

*Pasadizo de San Ginés 2 (91 366 46 86). Metro Ópera or Sol.* **Open** *10am-8pm daily.* **Map** *p83 H14* ❽ *Books & music*

This Old Curiosity Shop-style place, in an atmospheric passageway, sells all kinds of books from scruffy English paperbacks to antique first editions.

### Mariano Madrueño

*C/Postigo de San Martín 3 (91 521 19 55, www. marianomadrueno.es). Metro Callao.* **Open** *10am-2pm, 5.30-8.30pm Mon-Sat. Closed 2wks Aug.* **Map** *p83 H13* ❾ *Food & drink*

This classic old *bodega*, dating back to 1895, has a charming interior, complete with wrought-iron columns and carved wooden shelves. As for the booze on sale, the selection is enormous, with wines and spirits, plus the *bodega's* own (lethal) coffee and orange liqueurs. **Other locations** C/Calatrava 19, La Latina (91 521 19 55).

### VIPS

*Gran Vía 43 (91 275 20 93, www.vips.es). Metro Callao or Santo Domingo.* **Open** *9am-2am Mon-Thur, Sun; 9am-3am Fri, Sat.* **Map** *p83 H13* ❿ *Supermarket*

Vip's has branches all over town and stocks basic groceries, along with Spanish- and English-language press. There are unglamorous but occasionally useful cafés for a late-night burger or pizza.

# Huertas & Santa Ana

Spain has more bars and restaurants per capita than any other country in the world, and you can get the impression that most of Madrid's are crowded into the wedge-shaped swathe of streets between C/Alcalá and C/Atocha. Oddly enough, this clearly defined area has an identity problem, for the authorities can never agree on a name; however, if anyone suggests a pub crawl down Huertas, or a jar in Santa Ana, it will always bring you – and several thousand others on any weekend – to the right place.

## ❤ Don't miss

**1 Museo Thyssen-Bornemisza** *p96*
A thrilling collection of world-class art, spanning centuries.

**2 Barrio de las Letras** *p102*
Walk in the steps of Spain's men of letters.

**3 Plaza Santa Ana** *p98*
Favoured meeting place of the literati for many years.

**4 Palacio del Congreso de los Diputados** *p100*
The grandiose home of Parliament.

## In the know
## Getting around

Packing a big punch in a small area (around ten minutes' walk between its furthest reaches), Huertas' bars and restaurants are best accessed on foot, but Anton Martín is a convenient metro station (L1).

UIADOS AL ENEMIGO EN LA GUERRA DE AF

EN 1860.

Palacio del Congreso de los Diputados

# EXPLORING HUERTAS & SANTA ANA

This was once the haunt of Madrid's Golden Age literary set, which explains the district's rather fussy alternative name of **Barrio de las Letras** ('The District of Letters'; *see p102*). Here were the theatres that provided them with a living, along with whorehouses and low dives for entertainment. It is still the city's most distinctive theatre district. Close by, but not too close, lived the nobles who might toss a couple of ducats their way if they buttered them up with a sonnet. Otherwise there were feuds, libellous exchanges and duels to fall back on. A recent tidying up of the area has brought about pedestrianisation of much of Huertas's streets, and literary quotes inlaid in bronze underfoot.

Lope de Vega's charming old house, the **Casa-Museo Lope de Vega**, with its tiny garden, is on the street named after his enemy, Miguel Cervantes, the author of *Don Quixote*. Cervantes lived around the corner on C/León, but was buried in the enclosed convent of the **Trinitarias Descalzas** (*see below* Cervantes' dying wish) on C/Lope de Vega, which seems deliberately confusing. Coming upon the massively plain, slab-like brick walls of the Trinitarias amid the Huertas bars is a great surprise, and gives a vivid impression of what old Madrid must have looked like before the great clear-out of religious houses in the 1830s, of which this is a rare survivor.

A reverential nod is in order to the wonderful **Ateneo** library on C/Prado, the literary and philosophical club that became a cultural institution and has been a major centre of discussion and thought at many times in its history, most notably in the years leading up to the Republic of 1931. In the old days, Ateneo members could also find any number of cafés nearby with a suitably literary atmosphere.

The **Carrera de San Jerónimo** borders the north of the district. Once part of the Ceremonial Route of the Habsburg and Bourbon monarchs, today it is one of the centres of official Madrid. On one side is the **Congreso de los Diputados**, Spain's parliament building, while opposite is the **Westin Palace** hotel, where politicians go to mingle and relax. At the bottom of this stretch, where it meets the Paseo del Prado at the last corner of the neighbourhood, is the world-famous **Museo Thyssen-Bornemisza** (*see p96*), containing one of the world's most important private collections of 20th-century (and other) art. Head up the hill in the other direction and you'll reach **Lhardy**, the classic Franco-Spanish

---

## ♥ Time to eat & drink

**Toast and tortilla**
Pizzeria Cervantes *p100*

**Oxtail stew and a fine Rioja**
Casa Alberto *p101*

**A sherry sharpener**
La Venencia *p105*

**Creative tapas for every budget**
TriCiclo *p101*

### In the know
### Cervantes' dying wish

Had it not been for the nuns at the Convento de Trinitarias Descalzas, the world might have been deprived of one of its all-time greatest works, *Don Quixote*. Its author, Miguel de Cervantes, was shot and injured serving in the navy, and – shortly afterwards – kidnapped by Algerian pirates. After their son had been held in slavery for five years, his parents appealed to the nuns for help. The sisters raised the ransom money and had him released, and it was Cervantes' last request that he be buried in the convent alongside those who had saved his life.

---

## ♥ Time well spent

### Hammam Al Andalus

*C/Atocha 14 (91 429 90 20, madrid. hammamalandalus.com). Metro Sol or Tirso de Molina.* **Open** *10am-2am (last entry midnight) daily.* **Admission** *Baths €33. Baths & massage €47- €195.* **Map** *p95 J15.*

A series of pools spans out beneath arched ceilings, half-lit by flickering lamps. One shallow pool of warm water abuts another of hot water, with a deeper pool of cold water nearby for a chilly plunge. The company behind the hammam, El Grupo Al Andalus, focuses on historic authenticity. Masons from Andalucía were hired to lay the stone floors, which replicate the streets of Granada's Albaicín (Moorish quarter), and the mosaic walls at the entrance are designed in the red, blue and green tiles found in the Alhambra.

Enthusiasts claim that the hammam provides relief for almost any ailment, from the common cold to arthritis and hangovers. The heat improves circulation, eliminates toxins and keeps the skin clean and supple. Most people feel suitably energised and refreshed after a visit, though for even deeper relaxation you can always book a 15-minute massage. Book in advance.

# HUERTAS & SANTA ANA

## Restaurants
1. Ana La Santa
2. Artemisa
3. Come Prima
4. Laverónica
5. Lhardy
6. Pizzeria Cervantes
7. Tandem
8. TriCiclo

## Tapas
1. Alhambra
2. Casa Alberto
3. La Casa del Abuelo
4. Estado Puro
5. La Fábrica
6. Los Gatos
7. La Platería
8. Taberna La Dolores
9. Vinoteca Barbechera

## Cafés & bars
1. Casa Pueblo
2. Cervecería Alemana
3. Cervecería Santa Ana
4. Dos Gardenias
5. Naturbier
6. Salmón Guru
7. La Venencia

## Shops & services
1. González
2. Librería Desnivel
3. Madrid al Cubo
4. Museo del Jamón
5. Piedra de Luna
6. La Violeta

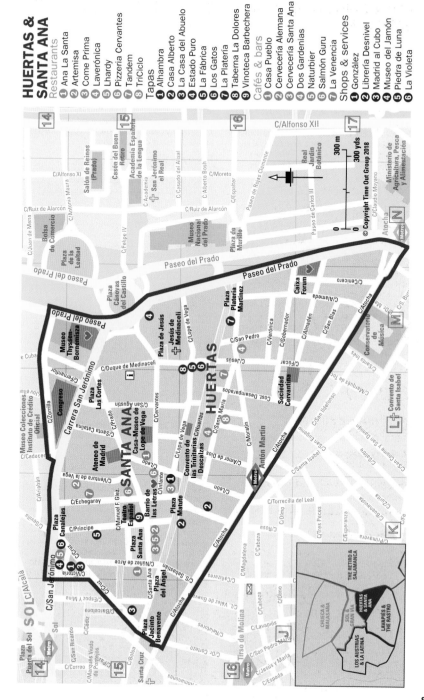

© Copyright Time Out Group 2018

# ♥ Museo Thyssen-Bornemisza

*Palacio de Villahermosa, Paseo del Prado 8 (91 791 13 70, www.museothyssen.org). Metro Banco de España.* **Open** *Permanent collection noon-4pm Mon; 10am-7pm Tue-Sun. Temporary exhibitions 10am-7pm Tue-Fri, Sun; 10am-9pm Sat.* **Admission** *€12; €8 reductions; free under-12s. Free to all Mon. Paseo del Arte ticket €29.60. Temporary exhibitions varies.* **Map** *p95 M15.*

The private collection of the late Baron Hans-Heinrich Thyssen-Bornemisza is widely considered to be the most important in the world. Consisting of some 800 paintings, it came to Madrid on loan, but in 1993 a purchase agreement was signed with the Spanish state. The baron's decision to sell was doubtlessly influenced both by his wife, Carmen 'Tita' Cervera, and by the offer to house the collection in the Palacio de Villahermosa, an early 19th-century edifice superbly converted by architect Rafael Moneo at fantastic cost. Thanks to this revamp, involving terracotta-pink walls, marble floors and skylights, it is possible to view the works with near-perfect illumination. In 2004, the museum unveiled its new wing, containing some 250 works from Carmen Cervera's own collection.

The collection was started by the baron's father in the 1920s but was dispersed among his heirs when he died. The baron bought back the paintings from his relatives and then expanded the collection, buying up first old masters and then contemporary works during the 1960s. The baron's home in Switzerland only had space for 300 works, leading him to look for a larger home for the collection, most of which may now be seen in Madrid, though some paintings are in the MNAC museum in Barcelona.

**The collection**

Works of art are displayed in chronological order. Beginning on the second floor, you'll find 13th-century paintings, notably by the early Italians, such as Duccio di Buoninsegna. You finish the tour on the ground floor, where Roy Lichtenstein's *Woman in Bath* is on show. Along the way, you'll have seen examples of all the major schools. The collection partly complements the Prado and Reina Sofía's collections, with large holdings of 17th-century Dutch painting, plus works of Impressionism, German expressionism, Russian constructivism, geometric abstraction and pop art.

The Thyssen's detractors say the collection is a ragbag of every kind of style. However, one of its great attractions is that, while it is extraordinarily broad in scope, it is recognisably a personal collection that reflects a distinct taste, as seen in the room dedicated to early portraits, with works by Antonello da Messina and Hans Memling. Equally quirky is the section on early North American painting, including the *Presumed Portrait of George Washington's Cook* by

**Hotel Room (Edward Hopper, 1931)**

Gilbert Stuart and works by American artists who are rarely seen in Europe, among them Thomas Cole, Frederick Remington and Winslow Homer.

The Thyssen also has its share of real masterpieces. Among the old masters, the works of Duccio, van Eyck and Petrus Christus stand out. The museum's most famous painting, however, is the great Florentine master Domenico Ghirlandaio's idealised *Portrait of Giovanna Tornabuoni* (1488) in the Portrait Room. Two rooms further on is Vittore Carpaccio's allegorical *Young Knight in a Landscape* (1510), another gem. Among the masters of the Flemish School represented is van Eyck, with his Annunciation diptych. The Thyssen is also strong in the German Renaissance, with works by Cranach the Elder and Dürer.

From the later 16th century and Baroque there are superb paintings, such as Titian's *Saint Jerome in the Wilderness*. There are also representative works by El Greco, Rubens and Tintoretto, and Bernini's *Saint Sebastian*.

The German expressionists are well represented too, with powerful works by Emil Nolde, Ernst Ludwig Kirchner, Otto Dix, Max Beckmann and Blue Rider group artists Franz Marc and Kandinsky. Also present, on the ground floor, are some more familiar modern masters – Braque, Mondrian, Klee, Max Ernst and Picasso (in the shape of his 1911 *Man with a Clarinet*),

among others. The last few rooms focus on the USA, with works by Georgia O'Keeffe and Edward Hopper, among others.

### The Carmen Thyssen-Bornemisza collection

This extension incorporates two adjoining buildings: nos.19 (the Palacio de Goyeneche) and 21 of the C/Marqués de Cubas. The space exhibits some 250 works of the 300 belonging to the private collection of 'Tita' Cervera, which she has ceded to the Spanish state for an indefinite period. In addition, there is a huge area for temporary shows, and the library, restoration workshops and cafeteria have all been enlarged.

Access is from Room 18 on the second floor, which leads straight into rooms with early Italian and Flemish works by the likes of Jan Breughel and van Dyck. Moving on, you will enter a gallery that contains landscapes by Canaletto, Constable, Guardi and van Gogh. In the next room is 18th-century French and Italian painting, and beyond a selection of 19th-century paintings from North America, some of it quite kitsch, and a final room of impressionism, which is continued downstairs. Two rooms are then given over to Gauguin and other post-impressionists. From then on, you move into German expressionists, Fauvists and the early 20th-century avant-garde. The collection also contains four sculptures by Rodin.

Palacio del Congreso de los Diputados *p100*

restaurant founded in 1839. North of San Jerónimo, behind the Congreso, is the grand 1856 **Teatro de la Zarzuela** (*see p234*), the city's most charterfully distinguished music theatre.

To the south of the Carrera de San Jerónimo, several streets run back towards Huertas proper. On C/Echegaray is the former site of Los Gabrieles, until a few years ago a much-loved bar sheathed in perhaps the world's most photographed wall-to-wall tiles, but which has now been converted into luxury flats. However, all is not lost, as another beautifully tiled bar, **Viva Madrid**, lies just around the corner on C/Manuel Fernández y González 7 (91 520 35 96), while the nearby **Villa Rosa** on C/Núñez de Arce also has an impressive tiled exterior.

Last, but in no way least, there is the core of the district, **Plaza Santa Ana**. Like Plaza de Oriente, this popular square was bequeathed to Madrid by poor Joseph Bonaparte, who tore down yet another convent to do so. Somebody should thank him: lined by some of the city's most popular bars and pavement terraces, Santa Ana has long been one of Madrid's favourite places for hanging out for an entire afternoon. On the eastern side of the *plaza* is the distinguished **Teatro Español** (*see p239*), on a site that has been a theatre continuously since 1583 when the Corral del Príncipe opened its doors to the *mosqueteros*, a heckling mob whose reactions were so violent, they sometimes forced terrified playwrights to change plots mid-play.

## Sights & museums

### Casa-Museo Lope de Vega
*C/Cervantes 11 (91 429 92 16). Metro Antón Martín. **Open** (by appt only) 10am-6pm Tue-Sun. Closed Aug. **Admission** free. **Map** p95 L15.*

Spain's most prolific playwright and poet, Félix Lope de Vega Carpio (1562-1635), spent the last 25 years of his life in this simple, tranquil three-storey house. Oddly enough, the street in which it stands is now named after his arch rival Cervantes (who, confusingly, is buried in a convent on the nearby C/Lope de Vega). The house and charming garden – remarkable survivors from the Golden Age – are the most interesting things to see. The furniture and ornaments are approximations to Lope de Vega's household inventory, rather than the originals. However, even the garden contains the same fruit trees and plants he detailed in his journals. Visits are by guided tour only – call ahead to book.

### Museo Colecciones Instituto de Crédito Oficial (ICO)
*C/Zorrilla 3 (91 420 12 42, www.fundacionico. es). Metro Banco de España. **Open** 11am-8pm Tue-Sat; 10am-2pm Sun. **Admission** free. **Map** p95 L14.*

# Paseo del Arte

*The art triumvirate of the Prado, the Thyssen and the Reina Sofía*

In the **Prado** (see *p144*), the **Thyssen** (see *p96*) and the **Reina Sofía** (see *p112*), Madrid has three art palaces that are quite simply world-class. You'll find them dotted along Paseo del Prado, in what has increasingly, and slightly facetiously, come to be known as the 'Golden Triangle'. This formidable trio of museums has made Madrid the world's capital of art for many people in the know, and with extensive revamps of all three museums over the past decade (reckoned to have cost some €150 million in total), this label is only set to stick more firmly.

The city council initiative known as the **Paseo del Arte** ('art stroll') takes advantage of the proximity of the three art collections, promoting the fact that they are barely ten minutes' walk from one another. The idea echoes Berlin's Museum Island and London's Museum District. The axis that unites the big three – as well as avant-garde newcomer the **CaixaForum** (see *p273*) – is the Paseo del Prado.

Of course, it would be far too tiring to approach the Paseo del Arte as a one-day itinerary – a visit to just one of the three museums is likely to take up several hours, and plenty of energy. The idea is more to familiarise visitors with the area – which is becoming more and more pedestrian-friendly – so that the museums can be understood within a historical, geographical and cultural context, and for visits to then be undertaken at one's leisure.

### Tickets

A joint ticket, the **Paseo del Arte**, gives entry to the Prado, the Reina Sofía and the Thyssen-Bornemisza for €29.60. It is available from the ticket desks at all three museums; after visiting one you can visit the other two at any time in the same calendar year. Each museum also has its own 'friends' tickets, giving unlimited entry for a year, which are more expensive and more widely publicised. A better deal is the €36 annual museum ticket (Tarjeta Anual de Museos Estatales), available from any state-run museum, which gives unlimited entry to all the main museums (except the Thyssen).

The Dream (Franz Marc, 1912)

This small museum is run by the ICO, a state bank. Its collection has three main parts: the most important of them is Picasso's *Suite Vollard* series, a milestone in 20th-century prints, dating from 1927 to 1937. There is also a fine selection of modern Spanish sculpture and international painting from the 1980s.

### ♥ Palacio del Congreso de los Diputados (Las Cortes)

*Carrera de San Jerónimo (91 390 65 25, www. congreso.es). Metro Banco de España or Sevilla.* **Open** *Guided tours noon Mon; (by appt) noon Fri, 10.30am-12.30pm Sat. Closed Aug.* **Admission** *free.* **Map** *p95 L14.*

Spain's parliament, the Cortes, was built in 1843-50 by Narciso Pascual y Colomer on the site of a recently demolished monastery, which has led to no end of problems, as the plot is too cramped to accommodate the legislators' ancillary offices. A classical portico gives it a suitably dignified air, but the building is best distinguished by the handsome 1860 bronze lions that guard its entrance. Guided tours can be booked in advance for Fridays and Saturdays, and are available on Mondays without advance reservation; tours may be suspended, depending on parliamentary activity.

## Restaurants

### Ana La Santa €€

*Plaza Santa Ana 14 (91 701 60 13, www. encompaniadelobos.com). Metro Sol.* **Open** *noon-1am Mon-Thur, Sun; noon-2am Fri, Sat.* **Map** *p95 K15* ① *Global*

Bright, comfortable Ana La Santa functions as breakfast room and a kind of extended lobby for the ME Reina Victoria hotel, which dominates the building, but comes into its own in the evenings, when its lounge area and plant-filled gallery brim with groups of friends. Dishes range from tuna sashimi with chipotle and avocado mayonnaise to paella, and there are tapas sharing plates.

### Artemisa €€

*C/Ventura de la Vega 4 (91 429 50 92, www. restaurantevegetarianosolhuertas.com). Metro Sevilla.* **Open** *1.30-4pm, 8.30–11.30pm Mon-Thur, Sun; 1.30-4pm, 9pm-midnight Fri, Sat.* **Map** *p95 K15* ② *Vegetarian*

With the nondescript decor so typical of Madrid's vegetarian restaurants, Artemisa might seem no different from the rest. But the salads are bigger and more creative, and the soy burgers have more flavour. Plus, the menu is entirely vegetarian or vegan, and everything on it is gluten-free. **Other locations** C/Tres Cruces 4, Sol & Gran Vía (91 521 87 21).

### Come Prima €€

*C/Echegaray 27 (91 420 30 42). Metro Antón Martín.* **Open** *9pm-midnight Mon; 1.30-4pm, 9pm-midnight Tue-Sat. Closed 3wks Aug.* **Map** *p95 K15* ③ *Italian*

The toothsome risottos and own-made pastas here are a godsend for Italian gastronomes. Don't miss the risotto with mushrooms, parmesan and white-truffle oil, or the perfectly executed pasta with lobster. Since it opened a few years ago, Come Prima has brought in a classy crew of Spaniards, who pack the place out every night, even on a Monday. With white curtains and tablecloths, green wood-panelled walls and Italian opera posters, you could almost be in the Tuscan countryside.

### Laverónica €€

*C/Moratín 38 (91 429 78 27, restaurantelaveronica.com). Metro Antón Martín.* **Open** *1-4.30pm, 8.30pm-12.30am Mon-Sat; 1-4.30pm Sun.* **Set lunch** *€15 Mon-Fri.* **Map** *p95 M16* ④ *European*

Recently revamped, the white-on-white decor at Laverónica is brightened with multicoloured pouffes and lamps by local designers, which give it the feel of a Parisian gallery. Its Gallic charm attracts a variety, from business types to hipsters, and it's a fine choice for a *menú del día*. Pesto pasta, a giant fillet steak, and sweetbreads or pork cheeks in wine are some of the options.

### Lhardy €€€€

*Carrera de San Jerónimo 8 (91 521 33 85, www.lhardy.com). Metro Sol.* **Open** *1-3.30pm, 8.30-11pm Mon-Sat; 1-3.30pm Sun. Closed Aug.* **Map** *p95 K14* ⑤ *Spanish/French*

This landmark restaurant, which opened in 1839, is credited with having introduced French haute cuisine into the culinary wilderness of Madrid. Founder Emile Lhardy is said to have been enticed to the city by none other than *Carmen* author Prosper Mérimée, who told him there were no decent restaurants in the Spanish capital. These days, it's rated as much for its belle époque decor as for the food. The menu is as Frenchified as ever, although there's also a very refined *cocido*, good game and *callos* (tripe), in addition to an excellent, if pricey, wine list.

### ♥ Pizzeria Cervantes €€

*C/León 8 (91 420 12 98, pizzeriacervantes. com). Metro Antón Martin.* **Open** *8.30am-1.30pm daily. Closed 2wks July.* **Map** *p95 L15* ⑥ *Italian*

Despite the name, this place exceeds the definition of pizzeria, with a long list of salads, crêpes, risottos and meaty fare such as roast beef and steak. Neighbourhood regulars are fans of the cheap breakfast deal and love to linger over *café con leche* with a croissant and the papers.

### Tandem €€
*C/Santa María 39 (91 138 62 98, www. eltriciclo.es/tandem). Metro Antón Martín.* **Open** *10am-4pm Mon-Sat, 11am-3.30pm Sun.* **Map** *p95 L16* **7** *Global*

Casual little sister of TriCiclo (*see below*), Tandem is all shared scrubbed pine tables and yelled orders, but the food is almost as good. Globally influenced dishes are available as *raciones* and half-*raciones* and range from excellent mackerel tartare (not on the menu, just ask) and pork steamed buns to a typically Madrid squid sandwich. Various brunch deals are also on offer.

### ❤ TriCiclo €€
*C/Santa María 28 (91 024 47 98, www. eltriciclo.es). Metro Antón Martín.* **Open** *1.30-4pm, 8.30pm-midnight Mon-Sat.* **Map** *p95 L16* **8** *Global*

Perhaps the most exciting of Huertas' recent raft of openings, TriCiclo offers its dishes in three different sizes, so it's possible to try several without breaking the bank. Peppery steak tartare with a crispy quail's egg is superb, as is the marinated sardine with fennel granita and almond milk – finish with divine fried brioche with ice-cream and fruits of the forest. There's also a seven-course tasting *menú* for €50. Book ahead.

## Tapas
### Alhambra
*C/Victoria 9 (91 521 07 08). Metro Sol.* **Open** *11am-1.30am Mon-Wed, Sun; 11am-2am Thur; 11am-2.30am Fri, Sat.* **Map** *p95 K15* **1**

Named after Granada's magical palace and done up in suitably Andaluz-Moorish style, this is a pretty and peaceful spot during the day, serving basic tapas along with oxtail stew and gazpacho, and a simple set lunch. It's a different place at night, though; awash with Spanish pop, techno and hormones.

### ❤ Casa Alberto
*C/Huertas 18 (91 429 93 56, www.casaalberto. es). Metro Antón Martín.* **Open** *noon-12.30am Tue-Sat; noon-4pm Sun. Closed Aug & 2wks Xmas.* **Map** *p95 K16* **2**

One of the city's most evocative *tabernas*, hung with oil paintings and presided over by a septuagenarian. It still has its old zinc bar complete with running water trough to keep the wine cool and a draught beer head with five founts. Try lambs' trotters,

garlicky prawns, *morcilla* (black pudding) with goat's cheese, or oxtail stew as tapas, or more substantial dishes in the restaurant at the back.

### La Casa del Abuelo
*C/Victoria 12 (91 000 01 33). Metro Sol.* **Open** *noon-midnight Mon-Thur, Sun; noon-1am Fri, Sat.* **Map** *p95 K15* **3**

For over a century, the Casa del Abuelo has stuck to one very simple, and winning, formula – prawns and small *chatos* of slightly sweet red wine served in bright, old-school surroundings. The surprisingly drinkable red is for sale by the bottle (€5.50) and when it's over you can even buy the T-shirt. **Other locations** C/Goya 57, Salamanca (91 000 01 33); C/Núñez de Arce 5, Santa Ana (91 000 01 33).

### Estado Puro
*Plaza Cánovas del Castillo 4 (91 779 30 36, tapasenestadopuro.com). Metro Antón Martín.* **Open** *noon-1am daily.* **Map** *p95 K15* **4**

Chef Paco Roncero oversees the kitchen at this NH Hotel initiative, which turns out classic tapas with a modern twist, from fancy takes on *patatas bravas* to deconstructed tortilla. The cool, black interior evokes an upmarket diner while riffing on the trad Spanish theme, with a wave of white mantilla combs arranged artfully overhead and a thousand flamenco dolls in an eruption of kitsch behind the glass of the counter.

Casa Alberto

# 💜 Barrio de las Letras

This 30-minute walk takes you on a tour of the cafés, theatres and churches around Plaza Santa Ana that were the centre of Spain's literary life during the 16th- and 17th-century Golden Age.

▶ *Begin at the junction of C/Atocha with Costanilla de los Desamparados.*

C/Atocha 87 was once home to the printing press where the first edition of *Don Quixote* was published. It is now the **Sociedad Cervantina**, a cultural centre with a theatre and printing press. See the bronze bas-relief of a scene from the book and, above, the head of Cervantes.

▶ *Walk up Desamparados and turn right down C/Moratín.*

At the **Plazuela de San Juan** is a plaque celebrating poet and playwright Leandro Moratín, born here in 1760.

▶ *Turn left up C/Jesús and left again on C/ Lope de Vega.*

The church ahead of the junction, on the right, is the **Iglesia de Jesús de Medinaceli**, famously a 17th-century centre of rumour and gossip, especially when attended by the great actresses of the time. Up on C/Lope de Vega, on the left, is the **Convento de las Trinitarias**, where Cervantes is buried. On 22 April, the anniversary of his death, a mass is held for him and the other great Spanish writers.

▶ *Turn right up C/Quevedo.*

On the right-hand corner is a plaque marking the house where 17th-century rivals Francisco de Quevedo and Luis de Góngora lived. Quevedo, a satirist, made mincemeat of the hapless and terminally ill poet Góngora in an exchange of verse. He also triumphed posthumously, when the council renamed the street after him, failing to mention Góngora on the plaque. At the end of the street, on C/Cervantes 11, is the **Casa-Museo Lope de Vega** (*see p98*), where Lope de Vega

lived and died. No.2 on this street was built on the site of Cervantes' old house.

▶ *Turn left, and right down C/León to C/Prado.*

At no.21 is the **Ateneo** library, with an impressive marble staircase, walls lined with portraits of Spain's greatest figures and delightfully antiquated rooms. Back up C/Prado, you arrive at the **Plaza Santa Ana**, home to the **Teatro Español** and bars such as the **Cervecería Alemana** (*see p104*), where writers such as the playwright Ramón del Valle-Inclán and, later, Ernest Hemingway were regulars. The theatre itself sits on the site of one of the great open-air *corral* theatres of the Golden Age.

▶ *Facing the theatre, turn left up C/Príncipe.*

This street was home to many of the literary haunts of the day, but the only one that remains is **Las Cuevas de Sésamo** at no.7 (*see p219*), worth a visit for the quotes painted on the walls and the printed history the staff will give anyone who's interested.

▶ *At Plaza Canalejas turn left down C/Cruz.*

C/Victoria on the left has a plaque marking the site of the writers' and politicians' meeting point and subject of Benito Pérez Galdos' eponymous novel, **La Fontana de Oro**. Further up C/Cruz is a mural depicting a reflection of the street, and asking, 'Where has the theatre gone? Or is the street the

theatre?' The theatre in question is the **Corral de la Cruz**, another open-air theatre that stood on the site.

▶ *Turn left down C/Álvarez Gato, through the square and down C/San Sebastián.*

What is now a florist in the yard on the corner with C/Huertas used to be the graveyard for the adjacent **Iglesia de San Sebastián**; the ancient olive tree remains a symbol for all the literary luminaries buried there. Opposite is a plaque showing the site of the **Fonda de San Sebastián** – favoured hangout of the 18th-century writers.

Sociedad Cervantina

Plaza Santa Ana

### La Fábrica

*C/Jesús 2 (91 369 06 71). Metro Antón Martin or Sevilla. **Open** 10am-1am daily. **Map** p95 M16* ⑤

There are long, long lists of the canapés on offer, but most are on display. Try the *matrimonio* (preserved and fresh anchovies – the perfect combination) or the *divorcio* (anchovies and mussels – no kind of match), or the *orgia* (all three). Ahem.

### Los Gatos

*C/Jesús 2 (91 429 30 67). Metro Antón Martin or Sevilla. **Open** 11am-1am Mon-Thur, Sun; 11am-2am Fri, Sat. **Map** p95 M16* ⑥

With their reputation for staying out all night, *madrileños* are popularly known as *'los gatos'* (the cats) and there's nowhere better than here to begin a night prowling the tiles. The bar is hung with all manner of paraphernalia from gramophones to choirboy mannequins – here you can get a selection of tasty canapés and a good frothy beer.

### La Platería

*C/Moratín 49 (91 429 17 22). Metro Antón Martín. **Open** 7.30am-2am Mon-Fri; 9am-3am Sat, Sun. **Map** p95 M16* ⑦

Everything from the smoked salmon and red peppers to *caldo gallego*, grilled asparagus or baked potatoes with eggs and garlic, is available in half portions, so this is a perfect place for a quick snack 'twixt two of the big three museums. The bar is rather cramped, but there are tables outside.

### Taberna La Dolores

*Plaza de Jesús 4 (91 429 22 43). Metro Antón Martín. **Open** 11am-1am Mon-Thur, Sun; 11am-2am Fri, Sat. **Map** p95 M16* ⑧

A Madrid classic, with wonderful tiling outside and rows of dusty beer steins inside, La Dolores has been serving ice-cold frothy beer since the 1920s. There's a short list of tapas, which are good if a bit expensive. Specialities are smoked fish, anchovies and *mojama* (wind-dried tuna).

### Vinoteca Barbechera

*C/Príncipe 27 (91 420 04 78, www.vinoteca-barbechera.com). Metro Antón Martín or Sevilla. **Open** 10am-1am Mon-Thur, Sun; noon-2am Fri, Sat. **Map** p95 K15* ⑨

It looks a lot grander than it is, which is not to say that the tapas aren't good, just that the bill is a pleasant surprise in these rather lofty surroundings. *Pinchos* include smoked salmon with cream cheese, Cabrales cheese with quince jelly and goose liver with apple.

## Cafés & bars

### Casa Pueblo

*C/León 3 (91 420 20 38). Metro Antón Martín. **Open** 6pm-2am Mon-Thur; 3pm-3am Fri-Sun. Closed Aug. **Map** p95 L15* ①

A handsome, old-fashioned jazz bar hung with antique clocks and black-and-white photos, it is popular with a slightly older crowd that knows its whisky. Occasional live music includes jazz and tango (on a Wednesday).

### Cervecería Alemana

*Plaza Santa Ana 6 (91 429 70 33, www.cerveceriaalemana.com). Metro Sol. **Open** 11am-midnight Mon-Thur, Sun; 11am-2am Fri, Sat. **Map** p95 K15* ②

Famous for being Ernest Hemingway's daily haunt (his table was the one in the near right-hand corner). The decor is fin de siècle German *bierkeller*, with dusty old paintings and dark wood. The tapas can be uninspired and the waiters are unfailingly gruff, but for many this will be an essential stop.

### Cervecería Santa Ana

*Plaza Santa Ana 10 (91 429 36 35, www.cerveceriasantaana.es). Metro Antón Martín or Sol. **Open** 11am-1.30am Mon-Thur, Sun; 11am-2.30am Fri, Sat. **Map** p95 K15* ③

Another on this strip of beer houses (the most exotic brew on offer here is Guinness), this one was never frequented by Hemingway and is consequently cheaper. Two entrances lead into two different spaces – one with seating and one without – and there are tables outside. Good for a light lunch, with decent salads and a range of *pulgas* (small rolls).

### Dos Gardenias

*C/Santa María 13 (mobile 627 003 571). Metro Antón Martín. **Open** May-Oct 9.30am-2.30am Tue-Sun. Nov-Apr 9.30am-2.30am Tue-Sat; 9.30am-7pm Sun. **Map** p95 L16* ④

There's no sign on the door – just look out for this mellow little space painted in warm yellow, orange and blue, and the emanating chilled-out vibes, soft flamenco and Brazilian jazz. Kick back on a velvet sofa with the house speciality: a mojito made with brown sugar and Angostura bitters.

### Naturbier

*Plaza Santa Ana 9 (91 429 39 18, www.naturbier.com). Metro Antón Martín or Sol. **Open** mid Mar-Oct 10am-1am Mon-Thur, Sun; 10am-2.30am Fri, Sat. Nov-mid Mar 10am-1am Mon-Thur, Sun; noon-1.30am Fri, Sat. **Map** p95 K15* ⑤

The least exciting-looking of all the beer cellars lining this side of the Plaza Santa Ana,

Cervecería Alemana

Naturbier's big draw is its own-made organic beer – in fact, it's one of only a handful of places in Madrid to brew its own. The tapas are also worth checking out despite the pricing, which is somewhat creative.

### Salmón Guru
*C/Echegaray 21 (91 000 61 85, www. salmonguru.es). Metro Antón Martín. Open 5pm-2am Tue-Sun. Map p95 K15* ⑥

The latest venture of mixologist supreme Diego Cabrera is a crazily eclectic affair, mixing tones of gentlemen's drinking club with colonial garden party and tossing in some Manhattan neon and zebra-skinned barstools for good measure. The list of cocktails includes 25 classics, and a list of house specials – try the Tónico Sprenger, with gin, lemon juice, cardamom, cinnamon, cucumber and ginger beer.

### ♥ La Venencia
*C/Echegaray 7 (91 429 73 13). Metro Sevilla or Sol. Open 3.30-10.30pm daily. No cards. Map p95 K15* ⑦

Totally unreconstructed, La Venencia is gloriously shabby, with old, peeling sherry posters, barrels behind the bar and walls burnished gold by decades of tobacco smoke. It serves only sherry (locals will order a crisp, dry *fino* or *manzanilla*, leaving the sweet stuff to the occasional tourist), along with manchego cheese, *cecina* (air-dried beef) and chorizo by way of tapas. Orders are still chalked up on the bar, and an enamel sign asks customers not to spit on the floor.

## Shops & services
### González
*C/León 12 (91 429 56 18). Metro Antón Martín. Open Sept-June 9am-midnight Mon-Thur; 9.30am-1am Fri, Sat; 11am-6pm Sun. July, Aug 6pm-midnight Mon-Sat. Map p95 K15* ① *Food & drink*

Once a local grocer's, González is now a smart delicatessen with a fine range of cheeses, charcuterie, preserves, fruit and nuts, olive oils and plenty more besides. The back room houses a pleasant, well-stocked wine bar.

### Librería Desnivel
*Plaza Matute 6, Santa Ana (91 369 42 90, www.libreriadesnivel.com). Metro Antón Martín. Open 10am-2pm, 4.30-8.30pm Mon-Sat. Map p95 K16* ② *Books & music*

This excellent travel and adventure bookshop sells a wide range of maps and books covering Spain and other countries. Desnivel's own publications include walking and climbing guides, and the shop also has information on organised walks, hikes and so on.

### Madrid al Cubo
*C/Cruz 35 (mobile 627 45 20 53). Metro Tirso de Molina. Open 10.30am-2pm, 6-9pm Mon-Fri; 11am-3pm, 6-10.30pm Sat. Map p95 J15* ③ *Gifts & souvenirs*

Tourist shop Madrid al Cubo sells a decent range of cool alternative souvenirs, including graphics-based prints, T-shirts and mugs, coffee-table books, tote bags and original postcards.

### Museo del Jamón
*Carrera de San Jerónimo 6 (91 521 03 46, www.museodeljamon.com). Metro Sol. Open 9am-12.30am Mon-Thur; 9am-1am Fri, Sat; 10am-12.30am Sun. Map p95 K14* ④ *Food & drink*

Dotted around town, the various branches of the 'Ham Museum' are a sight to behold, with dozens of hams dangling from the ceiling. Sample their wares at the bar or in their restaurants. **Other locations** throughout the city.

### Piedra de Luna
*C/Príncipe 14 (91 521 63 73). Metro Sevilla. Open 10am-9.30pm Mon-Wed; 10am-10pm Thur, 10am-10.30pm Fri, Sat; 4.30-9.30pm Sun. Map p95 K15* ⑤ *Gifts & souvenirs*

A selection of good-quality craftwork from around the world. Tuareg kilims, Moroccan ceramics, Indian silver jewellery and painted wooden furniture all feature on the shelves.

### La Violeta
*Plaza Canalejas 6 (91 522 55 22, www. lavioletaonline.es). Metro Sol. Open 10am-8pm Mon-Sat. Closed Aug. Map p83 K14* ⑥ *Gifts*

The violet is an emblem of the city, and La Violeta has been doling them out in candied form since 1915, counting Alfonso XIII among its most enthusiastic clients (it is said he used to buy violets for both his wife and his lover here). Little heart-shaped tins of violet-perfumed sweets make perfect gifts, as does violet tea or honey.

# Lavapiés & the Rastro

Once the Jewish quarter, long the main working-class area and still home to a large gypsy community, Lavapiés is also the most racially mixed *barrio* in the city, though the tendrils of gentrification are spreading this way. South of Sol and the Plaza Mayor, this is the area traditionally considered the home of Madrid's *castizos*. *Castizos* are something like London's East End cockneys: rough-diamond chirpy types straight out of a Spanish *My Fair Lady*. Many of them materialise around here in best bib and tucker – cloth caps for the men; long, frilly dresses for the ladies – for the city's summer festivals. These districts have always been the kind of place where newcomers to the city could find a niche.

Historically they were known as the *barrios bajos*, in the double sense of low-lying and full of low life – the closer to the river, the shabbier the surroundings. In imperial Madrid, most of the food brought to the city came in through the Puerta de Toledo, and many of the tasks that the upper classes wanted neither to see nor smell, such as slaughtering and tanning, were concentrated here. Consequently, these districts became home to Madrid's first native working class. In the 18th century, the *majos* and *majas* from these streets were admired by the intelligentsia for their caustic wit (for Goya's portraits of them, see p250 The Majas), sowing the seed for the *castizo* tradition.

♥ **Don't miss**

**1 Museo Nacional Centro de Arte Reina Sofía** *p112*
Spain's temple to 20th-century art.

**2 The Rastro** *p108*
Rambling flea market that forms an essential part of a Madrid weekend.

**3 Iglesia-Catedral de San Isidro** *p114*
Impressively large 17th-century church dedicated to the city's patron saint.

**4 La Casa Encendida** *p110*
Cutting-edge cultural programming and an unbeatable rooftop café.

**In the know
Getting around**

The area is small enough to stroll on foot, but there are various metro stations, including La Latina (L5), Embajadores and Lavapiés (L3), and Tirso de Molina (L1).

Castizos

# EXPLORING LAVAPIÉS & THE RASTRO

The northernmost point of Lavapiés is just south of the Plaza Mayor, where, at the corner of C/Toledo, stand the twin baroque towers of **San Isidro**, perhaps Madrid's most important historic church. Head south of San Isidro down c/Estudios and its continuation, C/Ribera de Curtidores, to reach the **Rastro** flea market.

If, on the other hand, instead of trying to make your way down the **Rastro**, you head from Plaza Cascorro slightly eastwards down **C/Embajadores**, you will enter Lavapiés proper. 'Ambassadors Street' was so named because all Madrid's foreign embassies were moved here during a 17th-century outbreak of the plague. Just by the corner of C/Oso, amid the urban disorder, is the Baroque church of **San Cayetano**, built by a variety of architects, including Ribera and Churriguera, between 1678 and 1761. Despite the many hands involved in its construction, its façade is one of the most finely worked in Madrid. Opposite, a plaque signals the house of the great 18th-century architect Pedro de Ribera.

Because of the rapid changes in the area, Lavapiés has sometimes been portrayed, in local conversations and the press, as an urban crisis zone to be avoided. This is one of the areas with a high incidence of petty crime, commonly associated with gangs of North African boys living on the streets, who have especially bad relations with the local Chinese shopkeepers. However, these images have a tendency to get out of proportion: there are places in Lavapiés it's probably best to steer clear of (the small square halfway down C/Mesón de Paredes, by C/Cabestreros, is the most obvious example), but it would be a shame if this led anyone to avoid the whole neighbourhood, for this web of sloping, winding streets remains one of the most characterful parts of Old Madrid.

**Plaza Tirso de Molina**, with its statue of the Golden Age dramatist whose name it bears, is the main crossroads between these *barrios bajos* and the city centre proper. It was cleaned up a few years ago and is home to a permanent, fragrant flower market, among other sights. At its eastern end is the **Teatro Nuevo Apolo**, part art deco and part neo-Mudéjar. On the south side of the *plaza* is the present headquarters of the CNT anarchist workers' union, a reflection of Lavapiés' long-term association with left-wing politics.

From here C/Mesón de Paredes, which is one of the two main arteries of historic Lavapiés (the other is C/Embajadores), winds off down the hill. The street is named after the long-gone inn of Señor Paredes, inventor of the *emparedado* (a type of sandwich). For refreshment today, there is the historic **La Taberna de Antonio Sánchez** at no.13 (*see p115*). Along Mesón de Paredes there are still some of Madrid's most historic *tabernas*, but they stand next to shops selling tropical fruit, as well as Moroccan teahouses, halal butchers, African

---

### ❤ Time to eat & drink

**An elegant breakfast**
Café Barbieri *p116*

**Lunch with soul**
Los Chuchis *p116*

**Sundowner with a view**
Casa de Granada *p115*

**Old-school tapas**
La Taberna de Antonio
Sánchez *p115*

### ❤ Time well spent

#### La Corrala

C/Mesón de Paredes with C/Sombrerete. Metro Lavapiés. *Map p109 J18.*
The city's best surviving example of an 1880s courtyard tenement, predictably garnished with freshly washed sheets and underwear billowing from the balconies. After the demolition of Madrid's monasteries in the mid 19th century, many streets in these districts were rebuilt with these distinctive, open-balconied tenements. *Corralas* always faced an inner patio, multiplying noise and lack of privacy, factors of urban life that have luckily rarely bothered Spaniards.

#### In the know
#### Squat movement

Squatting first arose in Madrid and other Spanish cities during the rural exodus of the 1960s and '70s, and was later revived as the *okupa* movement during La Movida Madrileña in the '80s, when thousands of squats were legalised.

In the past decade, the movement has been reignited once again, in a highly politicised form and partly in response to house price inflation. In various squatted buildings around Malasaña and, in particular, Lavapiés, grassroots organisations now offer activities such as yoga and film screenings.

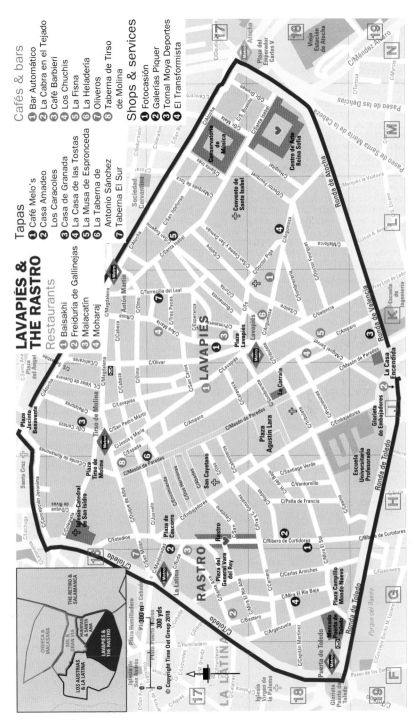

# LAVAPIÉS & THE RASTRO

## Restaurants
1. Baisakhi
2. Freiduría de Gallinejas
3. Malacatín
4. Moharaj

## Tapas
1. Café Melo's
2. Casa Amadeo Los Caracoles
3. Casa de Granada
4. La Casa de las Tostas
5. La Musa de Espronceda
6. La Taberna de Antonio Sánchez
7. Taberna El Sur

## Cafés & bars
1. Bar Automático
2. La Cabra en el Tejado
3. Café Barbieri
4. Los Chuchis
5. La Fisna
6. La Heladería
7. Oliveros
8. Taberna de Tirso de Molina

## Shops & services
1. Fotocasión
2. Galerías Piquer
3. Tornal Moya Deportes
4. El Transformista

© Copyright Time Out Group 2018

fabric stores and any number of Chinese-owned wholesale stores offering discount jewellery and T-shirts.

At the bottom of Mesón de Paredes, is C/Sombrerete. 'Little Hat Street' was named after the hat worn by Portuguese monk Miguel dos Santos when he was paraded through the streets before being hanged in the 16th century. He had been accused of acting as accomplice to chef Gabriel de Espinosa, who claimed to be the missing heir to the Portuguese throne. After the hanging, the hat was left on a muck heap in this street. Where the street becomes the **Plaza Agustín Lara** are the ruins of the 18th-century church/school, **Escuelas Pías de San Fernando**, destroyed in the Civil War. Facing the ruins across from C/Mesón de Paredes is **La Corrala**, a late 19th-century courtyard tenement, *see p108*. The *corrala* has become a characteristic of Madrid life; this one, restored in the 1980s, is used in summer as a setting for a season of *zarzuela*

### In the know
### Local hero

The statue of a dishevelled soldier – so different from Madrid's grand equestrian statues elsewhere – that sits in the Plaza Cascorro is a tribute to Eloy Gonzalo, who grew up in a local orphanage and offered to sacrifice his life in the Cuban War of Independence. Heading over enemy lines clutching a petrol can and a rope, so that his comrades might drag his body back, he set fire to a crucial Cuban stronghold and was able to escape, though he died of disease the following year.

comic operas (*see p234* Zarzuelas). A later *corrala*, not easily visible from the street, is at C/Embajadores 60. At the bottom of this area is a dynamic cultural centre, **La Casa Encendida**.

The **Plaza de Lavapiés** is believed to have been the centre of Madrid's medieval Jewish community, expelled, like all others in her dominions, by the pious Queen Isabella in 1492. Today, the recently renovated square has several good cafés and restaurants, as well as the Teatro Valle-Inclán. The narrow, very steep streets between the *plaza* and C/Atocha are more tranquil than those around Mesón de Paredes, and, with boxes of geraniums on virtually every balcony, often strikingly pretty. Despite all the changes in the area, these closely packed streets of old apartments, shops and workshops still convey the essence of a distinctive urban way of life. At the top of the area by C/Atocha is the Filmoteca Española film theatre, in the Cine Doré building (*see p211*).

Running away from the south-east corner of the Plaza de Lavapiés is **C/Argumosa**, known as the 'Costa Argumosa', with shops, restaurants and outdoor terrace bars that make a popular summer alternative to the more expensive and hectic places further into town. Argumosa leads towards Atocha and the **Museo Nacional Centro de Arte Reina Sofía** (*see p112*). Its opening in 1992 led to the appearance nearby of attractive one-off shops and galleries, while the Jean Nouvel extension, completed in 2005 and consisting of three buildings around a central *plaza*, is a symbol of modern Madrid. Close by, filling up a big stretch of C/Santa Isabel, is the 17th-century **Convento de Santa Isabel**, sponsored, like the Encarnación, by Margaret of Austria, wife of Philip III, and one of the largest religious houses to escape the liberals' axe in the 1830s.

## Sights & museums

### ♥ La Casa Encendida

*Ronda de Valencia 2 (90 243 03 22, www.lacasaencendida.es). Metro Embajadores.* **Open** *10am-9.45pm Tue-Sun.* **Admission** *free. Cinema €3. Theatre €5.* **Map** *p109 N19.*

This exciting multidisciplinary centre in a large neo-Mudéjar building was conceived as a space for cultural interchange. Spread over four floors, it offers exhibitions principally by emerging artists working in all genres, but also features cutting-edge performance art and music (including short seasons of video artists) and activities for kids. It's worth a visit for the rooftop café alone, a chilled-out space with a spectacular view across the city and beyond.

# 💙 The Rastro

*C/Ribera de Curtidores, between Plaza de Cascorro & Ronda de Toledo (no phone, www.elrastro.org). Metro La Latina. **Open** 9am-approx 2pm Sun. **Map** p109 H17.*

The city's most famous flea market dates back nearly five centuries. There are various theories on the origin of its name, which used to mean 'slaughterhouse', and might refer to the abattoir that once sat here (*'curtidores'*, from the name of the market's main drag, means 'tanners' and refers to the workshops that once lined this street). Another meaning of *rastro* is 'trace' or 'vestige', so it may refer to the cast-offs sold here, or perhaps the stolen goods that inevitably ended up here (and still do).

Stalls start setting up from around 8am, with the hardcore bargain-hunters arriving soon afterwards, though trading officially begins at 9am. In truth, there are few real deals to be had these days, but in among the piles of tat are Moroccan stalls selling lovely leather bags (though be sure to haggle hard), and antiques stalls and shops that are worth a trawl. The tributaries that run off the main street mostly specialise: some in art, some in clothes, toys or plants. There is undeniably an awful lot of junk – broken electronic equipment and knock-off toiletries – but it's still a quintessential stop on the tourist map, especially as a pre-La Latina tapas bars jaunt. Do keep an eye on your bag, though.

LAVAPIÉS & THE RASTRO

# 💙 Museo Nacional Centro de Arte Reina Sofía

*Edificio Sabatini* C/Santa Isabel 52.
*Edificio Nouvel* Plaza del Emperador
Carlos V s/n
**Both** 91 791 13 30, www.museoreinasofia.
es. Metro Atocha. **Open** 10am-9pm Mon,
Wed-Sat; 10am-7pm Sun. **Admission** €10 (€8
online); free students, under-18s, over-65s.
Free to all 7-9pm Mon, Wed-Sat; 1.30-7pm
Sun. Paseo del Arte ticket €29.60. **Map**
p109 M18.

Occupying an immense, slab-sided building,
the Reina Sofía boasts an impressive façade
with glass-and-steel lift shafts, designed by
British architect Ian Ritchie. And since 2005,
the museum has had just as impressive
a rear, in the form of three buildings
arranged around a courtyard and covered
by a triangular, zinc-and-aluminium roof,
the work of French architect Jean Nouvel.
This ambitious extension added almost
30,000 square metres to the already
vast space in the patio to the south-west
of the main edifice.

The Reina Sofía's great jewel is still
unquestionably *Guernica*, Picasso's
impassioned denunciation of war and
fascism, a painting that commemorates the
destruction in 1937 of the Basque town of
Guernica by German bombers that flew in
support of Francoist forces in the Spanish
Civil War. Certain art historians have seen

it more in formal terms, as a reflection
on the history of Western painting using
elements from the work of the old masters.
Picasso refused to allow the painting to
be exhibited in Spain under the Franco
regime, and it was only in 1981 that it was
finally brought to Spain from the Museum
of Modern Art in New York. *Guernica* has
been in the Reina Sofía since the museum's
official inauguration in 1992, when it was
transferred from the Casón del Buen Retiro
amid great controversy. The artist had
intended the painting to be housed in the
Prado – of which the Casón is at least an
annexe – and his family bitterly opposed the
change of location. There is no question that
the acquisition of *Guernica* hugely boosted
the prestige of the Reina Sofía. Since the
museum's revamp in 2010, the painting
is displayed under improved lighting
and viewing conditions.

The rest of the Reina Sofía's permanent
collection, which came mainly from the old
Museo Español de Arte Contemporáneo in
Moncloa, has been criticised, with many
questioning its claim to be an international
centre for contemporary art. At best, it is
pointed out, it is a reasonable collection of
Spanish modern art, with thin coverage of
non-Spanish artists. It certainly contains
works by practically all the major Spanish
artists of the 20th century – Picasso, Dalí,

Edificio Nouvel

Miró, Julio González, Tàpies, Alfonso Ponce de León and Antonio Saura are all present – but even here there are few major works.

In response, an active acquisitions policy adopted in the 1990s has sought to fill some gaps and to add works by major foreign artists.

With the appointment of new director Manuel Borja-Villel in 2008 came a total reorganisation – completed in 2010 – of the collection. It is no longer organised along linear historial or grand thematic lines, but in a way that interweaves common influences, themes and ideas; so works by Luis Buñuel are now displayed alongside works by Picasso, Goya and Solana, and even African art. In 2016, it had a record number of visitors, beating the Prado to become the most visited museum in Spain.

### The collection

The permanent collection, comprising more than 1,000 works, is spread over the first, second and fourth floors of the Sabatini building, while temporary shows are weaved throughout. The ground floor also features Espacio Uno, a space for more cutting-edge work.

The second floor is still the most important, housing Collection 1: The Irruption of the 20th Century: Utopias and Conflicts. This includes *Guernica* and the 1930s in Room 206, with works by Joan Miró, Robert Capa, and, of course, Picasso. Other themes and artists explored on this floor include Modernity, Progress and Decadentism, with works by Picasso and José Gutiérrez Solana; The New Culture in Spain; Dalí, Surrealism and Revolution; and Cubism's Break with Space, with more works by Picasso, as well as Georges Braque and Sonia Delaunay.

Collection 2: Is the War Over? Art in a Divided World, is on the fourth floor. This section explores themes such as European art after World War II, and 'The New Blood', with works by Kandinsky, Paul Klee and Miró.

Collection 3: From Revolt to Postmodernity is in the Nouvel building and includes works by Jean Luc Godard and Sol LeWitt.

**In the know**
**Rethinking Guernica**

A new website, www.guernica. museoreinasofia.es, gives unparalleled insight into the history and creation of Picasso's masterpiece, with access to thousands of related documents and interactive features that allow the user to see the finest of details.

Guernica (Pablo Picasso, 1937)

### ❤ Iglesia-Catedral de San Isidro
**(La Colegiata)**

*C/Toledo 37 (91 369 20 37). Metro La Latina or Tirso de Molina.* **Open** *Closed Aug. 7.30am-1pm, 6-9pm daily.* **Map** *p109 H16.*

Still popularly known as La Colegiata, this massive church, built between 1622 and 1633, once formed part of an important Jesuit college attended by many of the Golden Age playwrights. The high-Baroque design by Pedro Sánchez was inspired by the quintessential church of the Jesuits, the Gesù in Rome; the façade was completed by Francisco Bautista in 1664.

In 1768, after Charles III expelled the Jesuits from Spain, the church was separated from the college, dedicated to San Isidro and altered by Ventura Rodríguez to house the remains of the saint and his wife, which had been brought here from the Capilla de San Isidro (*see p75*).

La Colegiata was the city's provisional cathedral for nearly a century, between 1885 and 1993, when the Catedral de la Almudena (*see p64*) was finally finished and inaugurated.

### Puerta de Toledo
*Glorieta de la Puerta de Toledo. Metro Puerta de Toledo.* **Map** *p109 F18.*

Slightly swallowed up by traffic at the meeting point of the Old City and the roads in from the south-west, this neoclassical gate was one of the monuments commissioned by Napoleon's brother Joseph in his brief span as King of Spain.

## Restaurants

### Baisakhi €
*C/Lavapiés 42 (91 506 09 31, www. baisakhimadrid.es). Metro Lavapiés.* **Open** *1-5pm Mon-Thur, 1pm-midnight Fri, Sat.* **Map** *p109 J17* ❶ *Indian*

For good-value Indian food (set lunch is €9.50), Baisakhi is probably the best bet along what has become Madrid's answer to

Iglesia-Catedral de San Isidro

London's Brick Lane. The waiters all speak English, and the dishes on the menu include all the old faves. If you like a bit of poke in your curry, then be sure to ask for a spicier version of your chosen dish, as Spaniards don't generally like their food hot. The terrace is preferable to the slightly shabby interior.

### Freiduría de Gallinejas €

*C/Embajadores 84 (91 517 59 33, www. gallinejasembajadores84.com). Metro Embajadores.* **Open** *11am-11pm Mon-Sat; noon-10pm Sun. Closed 3wks Aug.* **No cards.** **Map** *p109 J19* ❷ *Spanish*

Still going strong after a century, this is the best place in the city for deep-fried lamb's intestines and other tasty titbits. Not for weak stomachs, this offal institution offers superbly prepared testicles, glands and stomach linings, all accompanied by strong red wine. Worth checking out just for the lively scene and a taste of old Madrid's innard circle.

### Malacatín €€

*C/Ruda 5 (91365 52 41, www.malacatin.com). Metro La Latina.* **Open** *11am-5.30pm Mon-Wed, Sat; 11am-5.30pm, 8.15-11pm Thur, Fri. Closed 5wks July-Aug.* **Map** *p109 G17* ❸ *Spanish*

Let us be clear – this is not a place for those who tag their Instagram photos with #cleanliving. This is good, old-fashioned, nose-to-tail eating for unapologetic carnivores, who come for the most traditional local dining experience – the *cocido*, a hearty, meaty chickpea stew – eaten under the dusty bullfighting posters and memorabilia of old Madrid.

### Moharaj €€

*C/Ave María 26 (91 527 17 87, www.moharaj. com). Metro Lavapiés.* **Open** *1-5pm, 8pm-midnight daily.* **Map** *p109 K17* ❹ *Indian*

It may not look fancy, but among curry-lovers Moharaj is widely believed to serve the best Indian food in Madrid. The secret is that most dishes are made from scratch when ordered, avoiding that greasy gloop so prevalent in some establishments. If there are four of you, order the tasty Moharaj platter to start, which has samosas, bhajis and more, then maybe prawns rezala, lamb jalfrezi, beef madras and matar paneer.

## Tapas

### Café Melo's

*C/Ave María 44 (91 527 50 54). Metro Lavapiés.* **Open** *8pm-1am Tue-Thur; 8pm-1.30am Fri, Sat. Closed Aug.* **No cards.** **Map** *p109 K17* ❶

It's got all the aesthetic charm of a kebab shop, but this bright little bar is something of a classic. It's famous for its *zapatillas* – huge, open sandwiches (the word, like ciabatta, means 'slipper') with a variety of toppings. A big favourite for late-night munchies with the bohemian element of the *barrio*.

### Casa Amadeo Los Caracoles

*Plaza de Cascorro 18 (91 365 94 39). Metro La Latina.* **Open** *11am-4pm, 7-11pm daily.* **No cards.** **Map** *p109 G17* ❷

Again, this is no looker, but it's a popular post-Rastro stop. Its specialities include the eponymous snails in spicy sauce, knuckle of ham, and *zarajo*, the lamb's intestines wrapped round sticks, without which your Madrid trip would not be complete.

### ♥ Casa de Granada

*C/Doctor Cortezo 17 (91 420 08 25). Metro Tirso de Molina.* **Open** *noon-midnight Mon-Thur, Sun; noon-1am Fri, Sat.* **Map** *p109 J16* ❸

A very ordinary bar serving very ordinary food, but with an extraordinary view. To get in, ring the buzzer on the street level, and then ride the lift all the way up to the sixth floor – in summer you'll have to fight tooth and nail for a seat on the terrace.

### La Casa de las Tostas

*C/Argumosa 29 (91 527 08 42). Metro Lavapiés.* **Open** *noon-4.30pm, 7pm-midnight Mon-Thur; noon-midnight Fri-Sun.* **Map** *p109 L18* ❹

Welcome to the House of Toast. Toast with scrambled eggs, prawns and wild mushrooms; toast with salmon in white vermouth; toast with gammon and melted cheese; toast with anchovies and Roquefort; toast with cod pâté. And most importantly, toast with wine, many available by the glass.

### La Musa de Espronceda

*C/Santa Isabel 17 (91 539 12 84). Metro Antón Martín.* **Open** *12.30-4pm, 7pm-midnight Tue-Sat; noon-4pm Sun.* **Map** *p109 L17* ❺

La Musa is known for its *pinchos* – don't miss the butternut squash, goat's cheese and caramelised onion, or the brie wrapped in bacon. The tortilla is also excellent, while the mojitos are well made and priced. Blackboards, literary posters and globe lights around a central bar lend the place an arty vibe.

### ♥ La Taberna de Antonio Sánchez

*C/Mesón de Paredes 13 (91 539 78 26). Metro Tirso de Molina.* **Open** *noon-4pm, 8pm-midnight Mon-Sat; noon-4.30pm Sun.* **Map** *p109 J17* ❻

Little changes at this historic bar, from the zinc bar to the bull's head hanging on the wall. Its various owners have all been involved in bullfighting, and *tertulías* of critics, *toreros* and *aficionados* are still held here. It's local and friendly, with superior tapas. Try the fried shrimp *tortillitas* and the tomato salad, followed, perhaps, by the house speciality, *torrijas* – custardy fried bread.

### Taberna El Sur
*C/Torrecilla del Leal 12 (91 527 83 40). Metro Antón Martín.* **Open** *noon-1.30am Tue-Thur, Sun; noon-2am Fri, Sat (open evenings only Aug).* **Map** *p109 K17* ❼

Taberna El Sur is named after Victor Erice's seminal film, decorated with cinematic posters and popular with long-haired soulful types returning from the nearby Filmoteca (*see p211*). Juan, the friendly owner, offers an interesting selection of *raciones*: try *ropa vieja* (shredded beef, Cuban style) with fried potatoes or 'Arabian' lentils.

## Cafés & bars

### Bar Automático
*C/Argumosa 17 (91 530 99 21). Metro Lavapiés.* **Open** *6pm-1.30am Mon-Fri; noon-2am Sat; noon-1am Sun. Closed 2wks Aug.* **No cards. Map** *p109 K18* ❶

A scruffy post-Rastro classic, Automático has been around for over 20 years, and sees all sorts within its turquoise walls, hung with black-and-white photos of the jazz greats. There is a gentle soundtrack to match – jazz, blues and swing – and some decent tapas, from cod brandade to *salmorejo* (a kind of thick gazpacho).

### La Cabra en el Tejado
*C/Santa Ana 29 (91 033 33 59). Metro La Latina.* **Open** *1pm-2am Mon-Thur; 1pm-2am Fri, Sat; 11am-2am Sun.* **Map** *p109 G17* ❷

A clear fave among creative types, the 'Goat on the Rooftop' is a little hidden away, but worth seeking out for its selection of good, cheap and unusual tapas – including quiches, crêpes, *tostas*, salads, and sweet options such as brownies. They also do a great-value lunch *menú* (€10, Monday to Friday). The space is nicely decorated, with a huge mural on one wall and a retro feel.

### ♥ Café Barbieri
*C/Ave María 45 (91 527 36 58). Metro Lavapiés.* **Open** *daily 8am-1am. Closed 2wks Aug.* **Map** *p109 K17* ❸

An airy and peaceful space, this has recently had a facelift, but still features high ceilings, marble-topped tables and plush red-velvet banquettes. A favourite haunt of journos and wannabe travel writers, Barbieri has plenty of newspapers and magazines, but its ordinary coffee comes at a premium.

### ♥ Los Chuchis
*C/Amparo 82 (91 127 66 06). Metro Lavapiés.* **Open** *noon-midnight Tue-Thur; noon-12.30am Fri, Sat; noon-6pm Sun. Closed 2wks Aug.* **Map** *p109 K18* ❹

A warm and welcoming little café, with perky teal paintwork and chequerboard floor, just off the main Rastro drag. The British influence in the team behind it is evident everywhere, from the collection of teapots to the bowler hat on a rack, the Penguin Classics and the complete works of British chefdom – Jamie, Delia, Nigella et al – that influences the kitchen.

### La Fisna
*C/Amparo 91 (91 539 56 15, www.lafisna.com). Metro Lavapiés.* **Open** *7pm-midnight Mon-Fri; 1-5pm, 8pm-1am Sat.* **Map** *p109 K18* ❺

A superb little wine boutique, in a cosy bare-bricked space, with a truly impressive range of wines, spanning many countries and vintages. In the evenings it functions as a bar, where you might occasionally catch a *cata* (wine-tasting). There is a short list of tapas and *conservas* – tinned shellfish, highly prized in Spain.

### La Heladería
*C/Argumosa 7 (91 528 80 09). Metro Lavapiés.* **Open** *10am-11pm daily. Closed Nov-mid Feb.* **No cards. Map** *p109 K18* ❻

Peruvian owner Yoli is unfailingly charming, and happy to let you try her excellent ice-creams before you buy – blackberry (*mora*) and lemon come recommended. Try the *blanco y negro*, a delicious café-frappé with ice-cream, or one of her milkshakes.

### Oliveros
*C/San Millán 4 (91 354 62 52). Metro La Latina.* **Open** *1.30pm-midnight Tue-Sun. Closed Aug.* **Map** *p109 G16* ❼

Oliveros is the genuine article, and although it was closed for years, it has been miraculously preserved in its original mid 19th-century bare-bricked state, complete with tiles and zinc bar. However, it might be worth ringing before going there, as opening hours can be somewhat erratic.

### Taberna de Tirso de Molina
*Plaza de Tirso de Molina 9 (91 429 17 56). Metro Tirso de Molina.* **Open** *8am-2am daily.* **Map** *p109 H16* ❽

Los Chuchis

It has a good stab at looking traditional with tiles, nautically uniformed waiters and exposed brickwork, but this *taberna* is, in fact, relatively new. There are plenty of tables where you can eat a decent breakfast on the way to the Rastro, or a very generous set lunch for €11.50. Tapas are available all day, along with heftier dishes such as the towering *parrillada de marisco* (seafood platter).

## Shops & services

### Fotocasión
*C/Ribera de Curtidores 22 (91 467 64 91, www. fotocasion.es). Metro Puerta de Toledo. Open 10am-2pm, 4.30-8.30pm Mon-Fri; 10am-2pm Sat, Sun. Map p109 H18* ❶ *Photography*

A treasure trove for photographers and camera collectors. Owner José Luis Mur has great offers on spare parts and new and second-hand cameras.

### Galerías Piquer
*C/Ribera de Curtidores 29 (mobile 605 166 447). Metro Puerta de Toledo. Open 10.30am-2pm, 5-8pm Mon-Fri; 10.30am-2pm Sat, Sun. Map p109 H18* ❷ *Antiques*

The antique shops in this Rastro arcade – said to be the oldest antiquarian business in Spain – stock pieces for punters who don't want to have to brush the dust off their purchases. Opening times may vary.

### Tornal Moya Deportes
*Ronda de Valencia 8 (91 527 54 40, www. tornalmoya.com). Metro Embajadores. Open 10am-2pm, 5-9pm Mon-Sat. Map p109 K19* ❸ *Fashion*

This big, well-laid-out shop stocks the lot: top-name sportswear, trainers, walking boots, swimwear, tennis rackets, replica football shirts and bags.

### El Transformista
*C/Mirá el Río Baja 18 (91 539 88 33, www. eltransformista.com). Metro Puerta de Toledo. Open 11am-2pm daily. Map p109 G18* ❹ *Antiques*

Original '50s and '60s furniture and collectibles are up for grabs at this shop. Almodóvar is rumoured to source items for his movies here.

---

**In the know**
**Antiques and arcades**

If you want antiques, head to the **Rastro** (see p108). On the main drag, C/Ribera de Curtidores, are several arcades where you'll find everything from old junk to authentic antiques. The adjoining streets, such as C/Mira el Río Alta and C/Carnero, are more downmarket and can yield real bargains.

# Chueca & Malasaña

Madrid has undergone rapid change in the last few years but nowhere more than around Malasaña and, particularly, Chueca. These two neighbourhoods, roughly divided by the C/ Fuencarral, have always been lively, but many of the area's old *tabernas* and family-run *casas de comida* have been replaced with industrial-themed gin bars, faux vintage cupcake shops and the like. There's still plenty keeping it real, however, particularly in Malasaña, which has retained some of its grungy, studenty feel, and you'll be picking your way through puddles of beer on a Sunday morning. Chueca, gay capital of Madrid (and probably Spain), has spruced up of late, and you can now find boutique hotels and gluten-free bakeries among its leather bars.

## ❤ Don't miss

**1 Museo de Historia** *p123*
A compact and well-organised museum that makes a great intro to Madrid.

**2 Museo del Romanticismo** *p124*
Lavishly furnished 19th-century house with a pretty tea garden.

**3 Centro Cultural de Conde Duque** *p130*
Vast cultural centre with permanent and temporary exhibitions on every topic.

**4 Fundación Telefónica** *p132*
Small but important collection of Spanish art.

In the know
**Getting around**

The area is bisected by C/ Fuencarral, along which various buses run and where you'll also find the Tribunal metro station (L1 and L10); Malasaña is also served by Noviciado (L2) and Chueca station is useful for L5.

AL PUEBLO
DEL
DOS DE MAYO
DE
1808

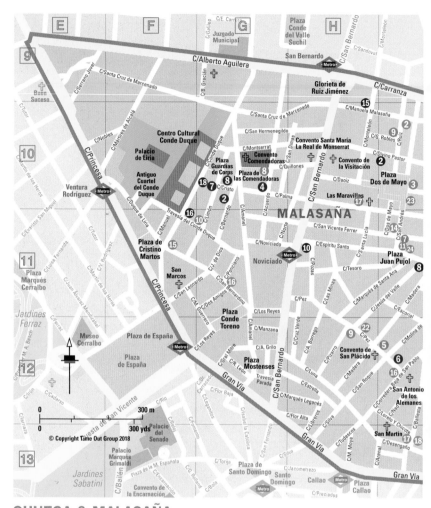

# CHUECA & MALASAÑA

## Restaurants
1. El 26 de Libertad
2. Albur
3. El Bierzo
4. Cannibal
5. La Carmencita
6. Casa Salvador
7. Celicioso
8. Gastromaquia
9. Gumbo
10. Home
11. Meat
12. Media Ración
13. La Mordida
14. Ojalá
15. Ribeira do Miño
16. Siam
17. Taberna Agrado
18. La Tasquita de Enfrente
19. Thai Orchid
20. Tienda de Vinos (El Comunista)
21. Zara

## Tapas
1. El Bocaíto
2. La Casta
3. Conache
4. El Maño
5. Mercado de San Antón
6. Pez Gordo
7. La Taberna de Corps
8. La Tabernilla del Gato Amadeus
9. El Tigre

## Cafés & bars
1. Ángel Sierra
2. La Ardosa
3. Bar El 2D
4. Bar Cock
5. Bar El Palentino
6. Café Comercial
7. Café Manuela
8. Café El Moderno
9. Café de Ruiz

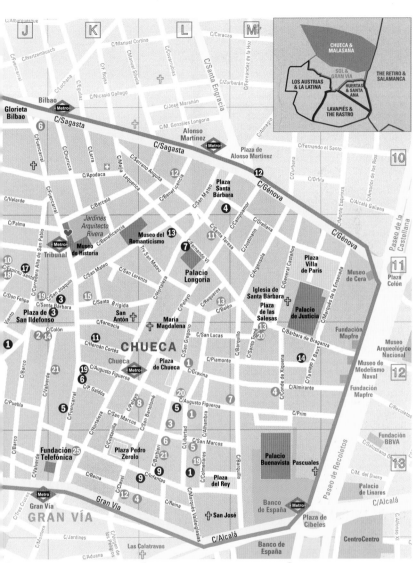

CHUECA & MALASAÑA

⑩ Café Rustika
⑪ Casa Camacho
⑫ Del Diego
⑬ Finnegan's
⑭ La Huida
⑮ El Jardín Secreto
⑯ Levadura Madre
⑰ Lola Loba
⑱ Lolina Vintage Café
⑲ Naif
⑳ Olivera
㉑ La Paca
㉒ Passenger

㉓ Pepe Botella
㉔ El Rincón
㉕ Stop Madrid

## Shops & services
❶ La Antigua
❷ Antigua Casa Crespo
❸ Bunkha
❹ Cacao Sampaka
❺ Custo Barcelona
❻ Desigual
❼ La Duquesita
❽ Happy Day

❾ Isolée
❿ J&J Books & Coffee
⓫ Panta Rhei
⓬ Pasajes
⓭ Patrimonio Comunal Olivarero
⓮ Piamonte
⓯ Popland
⓰ Radio City
⓱ Snapo
⓲ Sportivo
⓳ Vialis

# CHUECA

The neighbourhood of Chueca, bounded by Gran Vía, C/Fuencarral and the Paseo de Recoletos, has been through several transformations. In the 18th century, C/Hortaleza was the site of the Recogida, a refuge for 'public sinners', where women could be confined for soliciting on the street or merely on the say-so of a male family member. Release was only possible through marriage or a lifetime tour of duty in a convent. In the 19th century, Chueca became a more respectable, affluent district, but by the 1970s and early '80s it had turned into a shabby area. Since then, though, it has undergone a spectacular revival, due, above all, to it becoming the gay centre of Madrid.

The epicentre of the scene is **Plaza de Chueca**; its terraces are packed with crowds on hot summer nights, and the only limitation on the scene is whether the *plaza* can actually hold any more people. On the back of the gay scene, many more restaurants, trendy shops, cafés and clubs have opened up, and **C/Fuencarral**, the borderline between Chueca and Malasaña, is now the heart of Madrid's club-fashion scene. Many gay venues have acquired a fashionable crossover status among the hip non-gay crowd (to the extent that some gays now find some Chueca clubs too 'diluted'). Whatever, Chueca has established itself as a booming free zone for socialising of all kinds, gay and heterosexual.

The north side of the district, above C/Fernando VI, is not really Chueca proper and is often known as **Alonso Martínez**, after the metro station. It's not so much part of 'gay Chueca' either, although it, too, has many new restaurants and bars. Instead, it's one of the foremost preserves of Madrid's teen scene. Streets such as C/Fernando VI or C/Campomor and Plaza Santa Bárbara are lined with bars and clubs catering to a young crowd, and on weekend nights the roads are packed, too, with noisy (but safe) crowds of

### In the know
### Palatial awareness

Bienvenidos a Palacio (Welcome to the Palace) is a new initiative from the Madrid tourist board that opens up 23 spectacular buildings to the public on certain days of the year. There are guided tours, and occasionally concerts and other events. Palaces include the Palacio Longoria, owned by the **Sociedad General de Autores y Editores** (see p124); the Palacio del Marqués de Salamanca, now the **Fundación BBVA** (see p153); and many others.

### ❤ Time to eat & drink

**All-American brunch**
Meat *p126*

**Platters of shellfish**
Ribeira do Miño *p126*

**Afternoon tea**
El Jardín Secreto *p135*

**Eastern promise**
Thai Orchid *p127*

### ❤ Time to shop

**Beribboned chocolates**
Cacao Sampaka *p129*

**Pre-loved holiday reads**
J&J Books & Coffee *p137*

**Quirky accessories**
La Antigua *p137*

**Rainbow-coloured espadrilles**
Antigua Casa Crespo *p137*

# ❤ Museo de Historia

*C/Fuencarral 78 (91 701 18 63, www. munimadrid.es/museodehistoria). Metro Tribunal.* **Open** *Sept-July 9.30am-8pm Tue-Fri; 10am-2pm Sat, Sun. Aug 10am-7pm Tue-Sun.* **Admission** *free.* **Map** *p120 K11.*

Previously known as the Museo Municipal, the Museo de Historia has been given a complete makeover and is now one of the most interesting of the city-run museums. Located in an old hospice, it has an exuberantly ornate entrance by Pedro de Ribera, one of the finest examples of Baroque architecture in Madrid, and worth seeing in itself. The collection picks up from where the **Museo de San Isidro** (*see p75*) leaves off – telling the story of the history of Madrid from around the reign of Philip II, in the 16th-century.

Apart from one space filled with antique maps and a scale model of Madrid from 1830, the exhibits are arranged in chronological order and include paintings, sculpture, guns, fans, ceramics and a host of other fascinating objects, such as a beautifully decorated 17th-century litter used to transport the sick to hospital. Perhaps most interesting, however, are the photographs of old Madrid on the top floor, since so many of its squares and landmarks are instantly recognisable today.

Children with a grasp of Spanish (or possibly without), will enjoy the free guided tours tailored to six- to 12-year-olds at noon on Sundays.

CHUECA & MALASAÑA

kids. Just west of here is the city's history museum, the **Museo de Historia** (*see p123*), and the **Museo del Romanticismo**. To the north is C/Glorieta de Bilbao, site of one of Madrid's most traditional (though recently overhauled) cafés, the **Café Comercial** (*see p135*). Towards Recoletos, Chueca also becomes more commercial and more upmarket by day. C/Barquillo is full of hi-fi shops, while C/Almirante and its cross-street C/Conde de Xiquena are important fashion shopping zones. Off Almirante, in C/Tamayo y Baus, is one of Madrid's most important theatres, the **Teatro María Guerrero** (*see p239*).

This area is also part of official Madrid, with the giant **Palacio de Justicia** on C/Bárbara de Braganza. It was formerly part of the complex of the **Convento de las Salesas**, of which the lavishly appointed Baroque church, built in the 18th century, also remains. Built in 1750-58 under the patronage of Queen Bárbara, wife of Fernando VI, it has housed law courts since 1870. Its refined classical Baroque contrasts nicely with the art nouveau of the **Palacio Longoria**, a few streets away. To the south of Chueca, towards C/Alcalá, there is an isolated relic of Philip II's Madrid, the **Plaza del Rey**, and venerable 1580s **Casa de las Siete Chimeneas**, originally designed by Juan de Herrera, architect of El Escorial.

## Sights & museums

### ♥ Museo del Romanticismo
*C/San Mateo 13 (91 448 10 45, museoromanticismo.mcu.es). Metro Tribunal.* **Open** *May-Oct 9.30am-8.30pm Tue-Sat; 10am-3pm Sun. Nov-Apr 9.30am-6.30pm Tue-Sat; 10am-3pm Sun.* **Admission** *€3; €1.50 reductions. Free to all from 2pm Sat.* **No cards.** **Map** *p120 K11.*

The Museo del Romanticismo is essentially a reconstruction of a typical aristocratic house of the Spanish Romantic period (early to mid 19th century); a charming collection of furniture, paintings, ornaments, early pianos and other pieces that evoke the time. As well as these objets d'art, there are paintings from the likes of Francisco Goya and Vicente López Portaña, thousands of prints and lithographs and a substantial number of antique photographs. There's also a tearoom with a pretty garden (you don't need a museum ticket to enter).

### Sociedad General de Autores y Editores (Palacio Longoria)
*C/Fernando VI 4. Metro Alonso Martínez.* **Map** *p120 L11.*

Given the extraordinary output of Catalan Modernista architects such as Gaudí in Barcelona in the early 20th century, it is

Museo del Romanticismo

remarkable – to non-Spaniards at least – that there is not a single example of their work in Madrid. The only thing at all like it is this building in Chueca, designed by José Grasés Riera in 1902 as a residence for banker Javier González Longoria. The voluptuous façade looks as if it was moulded by an expert in giant cake decoration. It was once thought that Catalan architecture influenced Grasés, but Héctor Guimard and French art nouveau seem to have been a more direct inspiration. The building is now owned by the Spanish Writers' and Artists' Association (SGAE), and is not open to the public, except as part of the Bienvenido al Palacio programme (*see p122*, Palatial Awareness).

## Restaurants

### El 26 de Libertad €€

*C/Libertad 26 (91 521 82 23, www.el26madrid. com). Metro Chueca.* **Open** *8.30am-4pm Mon, Sun; 8.30am-1.30am Tue-Thur; 8.30pm-2.30am Fri, Sat.* **Map** *p120 L12* ❶
*Spanish*

Under new ownership, El 26 has thrown some nods to the Italian and Argentinian elements of its team with *burrata* salad, for example, or skirt steak with chimichurri, but you'll still find profoundly Spanish dishes from home-made *croquetas* and *patatas bravas* to paella and fried eggs with *jamón*. No need to break the bank, either – there's a great deal that includes paella for two and a bottle wine for €28, and the *menú del día* is €10.90.

### El Bierzo €€

*C/Barbieri 16 (91 531 91 10, www. restauranteelbierzodebarbieri.com). Metro Chueca.* **Open** *1-4 pm, 9-11.30pm Mon-Sat. Closed Aug.* **Map** *p120 L12* ❸ *Spanish*

El Bierzo is one of the best of Madrid's long-established *casas de comida* – honest, dependable neighbourhood joints where you can get a good *menú del día* at the reasonable price of €12. It buzzes, particularly during lunch, with a loyal crowd feasting on simple dishes: roast chicken, seven types of tortilla and excellent *setas al ajillo* (wild mushrooms fried in garlic). It's worth coming here just for a chat with the friendly owner, Miguel.

### Cannibal €€

*C/Almirante 12 (91 026 87 94, cannibalrawbar.es). Metro Chueca.* **Open** *1-5pm, 8pm-1am Mon-Thur, Sun; 1pm-3am Fri, Sat.* **Map** *p120 M12* ❹ *Global*

Cannibal is a temple to all things raw (though not exclusively – you will find paella with Peking duck and prawns, for example). Expect oysters, steak tartare, ceviche, carpaccio and the like, along with an

impressive wine list. It makes for a handsome nightspot, too, with a sexy, bare-brick, vaulted bar downstairs where DJs spin deep house on Friday and Saturday nights.

### La Carmencita €€

*C/Libertad 16 (91 531 09 11, www. tabernalacarmencita.es/en). Metro Chueca.* **Open** *1pm-1am daily.* **Map** *p120 L13* ❺
*Spanish*

Originally opened in 1854, Carmencita has an illustrious past, and was once a favourite of Pablo Neruda and Federico García Lorca (who lived upstairs). It lay empty for many years but its glorious wall tiles and bronze luggage racks have been sensitively restored, as have some of the original recipes. The emphasis is on slow food, happy cows and chickens, and local produce – try the chicken *en pepitoria* or the oxtail stew.

### Casa Salvador €€

*C/Barbieri 12 (91 521 45 24, www. casasalvadormadrid.com). Metro Chueca.* **Open** *1.30-4pm, 9-11.30pm Mon-Sat. Closed Aug.* **Map** *p120 L13* ❻ *Spanish*

Every inch of this old classic is crammed with bullfighting memorabilia. You'll find good traditional fare – lentil soup, *revueltos* (concoctions with scrambled egg, often with seafood or asparagus), hake, *solomillo* (sirloin steak) with French fries – but the real treat is the atmosphere.

### Celicioso €

*C/Barquillo 19 (91 532 28 99, www.celicioso. com). Metro Chueca.* **Open** *9am-10pm daily.* **Map** *p120 M12* ❼ *Gluten-free bakery*

Opened in 2016 to meet the rising demand for gluten-free products (which here include cupcakes in a kaleidoscope of colours), and every clean-living food trend from spiralised courgette pasta to *matcha* pancakes, Celicioso has now won over the locals and become a favourite brunch stop. **Other locations** C/Hortaleza 3 (91 531 88 87).

### Gastromaquia €€€€

*C/Pelayo 8 (91 522 64 13, www.gastromaquia. com). Metro Chueca.* **Open** *8.30am-midnight Mon-Thur; 1.30-4pm, 8.30am-midnight Fri, Sat; 1.30-4pm Sun.* **Map** *p120 K12* ❽
*Global*

Run by Catalans Hugo Escolies and Ramon Figuls, Gastronomaquia is minimalist in style, with a red, white and black colour scheme and bare-brick walls artistically lined with old soda siphons. The Spanish-fusion food is expertly executed and presented: guacamole and plantain chips, and grilled octopus with potato foam are examples of some of its most celebrated dishes. This is also a popular spot for tapas, and gets rave reviews – it's best to book at weekends.

### ♥ Meat €€
*C/Santa Teresa 4 (91 029 60 41, www. meatmadrid.com). Metro Alonso Martínez.* **Open** *1pm-midnight Mon-Wed, Sun; 1pm-2am Thur; 1pm-2.30am Fri, Sat.* **Map** *p120 L11* ⑪ *American*

Come for the brunch – pancakes with maple syrup; egg and bacon sandwich; avocado toast – and stay for the burgers, made with local beef and available in three sizes, and the triple-cooked fries. The decor is very on point, with its bare bricks, open kitchen, scrubbed pine tables and retro American feel, but there's a lot of heart and soul here.

### Media Ración €€
*C/Beneficiencia 15 (91 447 51 11, www. mediaracion.es). Metro Alonso Martínez.* **Open** *1.30-4pm, 8.30-11pm Tue-Thur; 1.30-4pm, 8.30-11.30pm Fri, Sat.* **Map** *p120 L10* ⑫ *Spanish*

Recent years have seen many new openings in Chueca, but this is one of the best. A cosy, pale-wood dining room is the setting for some supremely tasty dishes like skate *escabeche* and a sublime crunchy pig's trotter with smoked eel. The mixed vegetables served with a velouté is a great accompaniment, and even the bread is superb – but don't eat too much of it because you'll want to leave space for the chocolate ganache with salt and olive oil.

### La Mordida €€
*C/Belén 13 (91 308 20 89, www.lamordida. com). Metro Chueca.* **Open** *1.30-4pm, 8pm-midnight Mon-Thur; 1.30pm-1am Fri, Sat; 1.30pm-midnight Sun.* **Map** *p120 L11* ⑬ *Mexican*

Joaquín Sabina, the gravelly voiced Madrid musician and legend, does restaurants, too, but who'd have expected it to be Mexican food? And such good authentic Mexican food. Usually full to bursting with high-spirited tequila drinkers, this is the place to embrace *mole*, the Mexican chocolate sauce that often scares the uninitiated away. **Other locations** throughout the city.

### ♥ Ribeira do Miño €€
*C/Santa Brígida 1 (91 521 98 54, www. marisqueriaribeiradomino.com). Metro Tribunal.* **Open** *1-4pm, 8pm-midnight Tue-Sun. Closed Aug.* **No cards.** **Map** *p120 K11* ⑮ *Seafood*

Galician in origin, this one's for seafood lovers. Heaped platters of prawns, crab, goose-necked barnacles, lobster and other sea creatures make it the ideal place to roll up your sleeves and get cracking shells. Other typical *gallego* dishes that add a little heat to the fun are pancakes doused in *orujo* (a fiery spirit very similar to grappa) and set aflame, and the *queimada* – a bowl of *orujo* set on fire and then cooled with black coffee. Reservations are recommended, particularly at weekends.

Meat

### ♥ Thai Orchid €€

*C/Colmenares 5 (91 531 85 37, www. thaiorchid.es). Metro Banco de España.* **Open** *1-4.30pm Mon; 1-4.30pm, 8pm-midnight Tue-Thur; 1-4.30pm, 8pm-1am Fri, Sat; 1.30-5pm Sun. Closed 1wk Aug.* **Map** *p120 L13* ⑲ *Thai*

A tiny, simple little Thai restaurant that doesn't look much from outside but is a bit of a gem. The fixed *menú*, available day (€12.50) and night (€14.50), is amazing value, with three properly spicy and generously portioned courses and a drink. As a bonus, the Orchid eschews trickling fountains and garlanded Buddhas for some monochrome Thai prints and a gentle piano soundtrack.

### Tienda de Vinos (El Comunista) €

*C/Augusto Figueroa 35 (91 521 70 12). Metro Chueca.* **Open** *noon-4pm, 8pm-midnight Mon-Sat. Closed mid Aug-mid Sept.* **No cards.** **Map** *p120 L12* ⑳ *Spanish*

This restaurant's popular name comes from its role as a leftie meeting point years ago under Franco (but Tienda de Vinos is all you'll see above the door). It's one of the city's real classics and a visit is essential, but no one makes any grand claims about its unchanging and unchallenging menu. To start, there are soups: gazpacho, lentil or own-made broth, followed by liver and onions, lamb cutlets, kidneys in sherry and plenty of fish. Service is known for being deadpan, but if you're lucky, you'll get one of the two charming great-grandsons of the original owner.

### Zara €€

*C/Barbieri 8 (91 532 20 74, www. restaurantezara.com). Metro Chueca or Gran Vía.* **Open** *1-4pm, 8.30pm-12.15am Tue-Sat. Closed Aug.* **Map** *p120 L13* ㉑ *Cuban*

It's easy to walk right past these wooden doors and miss the little Havana with red-chequered tablecloths that lies within. Inés, the owner, left her home city over 30 years ago, but brought the best Cuban recipes with her – try dishes such as *ropa vieja* (literally, 'old clothes', but actually shredded beef), black beans and rice with pork, and minced beef with fried bananas. Daiquiris are the drink of the house.

## Tapas

### El Bocaíto

*C/Libertad 4-6 (91 532 12 19, www.bocaito. com). Metro Chueca.* **Open** *12.30-4pm, 8pm-midnight Mon-Sat; 12.30pm-4pm Sun. Closed Aug.* **Map** *p120 L13* ❶

El Bocaíto is film-set traditional, from the bullfight posters and Andalucían ceramics

to the old-school tapas and unsmiling, white-jacketed waiters. If you're famous, though, they'll grin for the camera, just as they did with Pedro, Hugh and, goddammit, Mark Knopfler.

### Mercado de San Antón

*C/Augusto Figueroa 24 (91 330 07 30, www. mercadosananton.com). Metro Chueca.* **Open** *Shops 10am-10pm Mon-Sat. Bars/restaurants 10am-midnight Mon-Thur; 10am-1.30am Fri, Sat.* **Map** *p120 L12* ❺

Part gastro market, part tapas village, the covered Mercado de San Antón opened in 2011 and has been rammed with appreciative customers ever since. Stalls selling immaculate produce are on the ground floor; tapas bars specialising in all manner of things, from topped blinis to sushi, are on the next floor; and at the top is a bar-restaurant with a great view over the rooftops.

### El Tigre

*C/Infantas 30 (91 532 00 72). Metro Banco de España or Chueca.* **Open** *11am-1.30am Mon-Thur, Sun; noon-1.30am Fri, Sat.* **Map** *p120 L13* ❾

If you can actually get through the door, order a beer or cider and marvel at the hefty tapas that come with it – patatas bravas, *jamón serrano*, tortilla... It's all free, and each plate varies with each round. The bar itself is noisy, fun and always rammed. **Other locations** C/Infantas 23, Chueca (91 532 02 59); C/ Hortaleza 23, Chueca (91 523 13 28).

## Cafés & bars

### Ángel Sierra

*C/Gravina 11 (91 531 01 26). Metro Chueca.* **Open** *11am-2.30am Mon-Thur, Sun; 11am-3am Fri, Sat.* **Map** *p120 L12* ❶

This battered old bar with its tiled walls, zinc bar top, overflowing sink and glasses stacked on wooden slats has become the Chueca meeting place par excellence, thanks to its position overlooking the main square. A newer room to the back of the bar, however, has a faux pub look enhanced with amplified MOR radio and a rule that only doubles and pints are served after midnight.

### Bar Cock

*C/Reina 16 (91 532 28 26, www.barcock.com). Metro Gran Vía.* **Open** *4pm-3am daily.* **Map** *p120 L13* ❹

A former brothel, Bar Cock is pricey and very stagey, furnished in what Spaniards think to be the style of an English pub (red velvet curtains, embossed leather armchairs and a fake half-timbered effect). It continues to attract those who like to think of themselves as being in the know, and it can get extremely crowded as a result.

### Del Diego

*C/Reina 12 (91 523 31 06, www.deldiego.com). Metro Gran Vía. **Open** 7pm-3am Mon-Thu, Sun; 7pm-3.30am Fri, Sat. Closed 3wks Aug. **Map** p120 K13* ⑫

Not to all tastes, with an unchanging, late 1980s, steel-and-blond-wood *Wall Street* vibe, Del Diego is nevertheless deservedly renowned for its consummately smooth barmen and superb cocktails. Pull up a stool and try a zingy mint julep del Diego to kickstart a night's wheeling and dealing.

### Finnegan's

*Plaza de las Salesas 9 (91 310 05 21). Metro Alonso Martínez. **Open** 8am-2am daily. **Map** p120 M12* ⑬

One for rugby fans, Finnegan's has its own team, the Madrid Lions, and a talent for sniffing out every conceivable match to show on its large screens. In lean sporting times, the void is filled with pub quizzes and DJs (mostly rock) at weekends. Pints of Beamish, Newkie Brown and John Smith's complement burgers and other pub grub.

### Olivera

*C/Santo Tomé 8 (mobile 697 198 543). Metro Chueca. **Open** 7pm-2am Mon-Thur, Sun; 7pm-2.30am Fri, Sat. **Map** p120 M12* ⑳

A relaxed lounge bar, presided over by a portrait of the owner's mother, Yugoslav film star Olivera Markovic. The musical mood is nu jazz and funk, and the mismatched armchairs and sofas make it easy to end up staying all night.

### Stop Madrid

*C/Hortaleza 11 (91 521 88 87, www. stopmadrid.es). Metro Chueca or Gran Vía. **Open** noon-1am Mon-Wed; noon-2am Thur; noon-2.30am Fri, Sat; noon-12.30am Sun. **Map** p120 K13* ㉕

When it opened in 1929, this was the first ham and charcuterie shop in Madrid. It's undergone a few changes since then, but many of the original fittings have been retained, and great pride is taken in sourcing the best ingredients for tapas. Of the 50-strong wine list, all are available by the glass. **Other locations** C/León 10, Huertas, 91 429 56 95; C/Hortaleza 11, 91 521 88 87; C/Atocha 73, Huertas, 91 504 78 43.

Plaza de Chueca

## Shops & services

### ♥ Cacao Sampaka

*C/Orellana 4 (91 319 58 40, www. cacaosampaka.com). Metro Alonso Martínez.* **Open** *10am-9.30pm Mon-Sat.* **Map** *p120 L10* ❹ *Food & drink*

Handmade choccies are arrayed in dazzling displays and for sale singly or in themed boxes, such as 'Spices of the Americas' or 'Flowers and herbs'. There are also chocolate jams, chocolate sauces and chocolate ice-creams.

### Custo Barcelona

*C/Fuencarral 29 (91 360 46 36, www.custo-barcelona.com). Metro Gran Vía or Chueca.* **Open** *10am-9pm Mon-Sat; 11.30am-8.30pm Sun.* **Map** *p120 K12* ❺ *Fashion*

This Catalan designer is famous for his funky patterned T-shirts, but has expanded the range to include creative and flattering dresses, skirts and coats. Custo was all the rage a few years back, but a host of copycat stores have led to the closure of all but this one. **Other locations** throughout the city.

### Desigual

*C/Fuencarral 36-38 (91 521 49 07, www. desigual.com). Metro Tribunal or Gran Vía.* **Open** *10am-9pm Mon-Sat.* **Map** *p120 K12* ❻ *Fashion*

Desigual has become a real hit with the club kids, and it's easy to see why: pumping house music, gorgeous shop assistants, and affordable, quality club and streetwear for men, women and children.

### La Duquesita

*C/Fernando VI 2 (91 308 02 31). Metro Alonso Martínez.* **Open** *8.30am-8.30pm daily. Closed Aug.* **Map** *p120 L11* ❼ *Food & drink*

This traditional *pastelería*, dating from 1914, has featured in lots of period-piece movies. Gorgeous chocolates and cakes are offered, along with *turrón* in the run-up to Christmas.

### Isolée

*C/Infantas 19 (91 522 81 38, www.isolee.com). Metro Banco de España.* **Open** *11am-9pm Mon-Sat.* **Map** *p120 L13* ❾

The tendrils of cool emanating from Chueca are creeping ever further afield, as evinced by Isolée, a concept store that sells CDs, Natura Bissé toiletries, clothes and designer kitchenware. There is also an array of tinned and bottled gourmet goods, whether you're after top-of-the-range olive oil dressing or organic paella rice.

### Panta Rhei

*C/Hernán Cortés 7 (91 319 89 02, www. panta-rhei.es). Metro Chueca.* **Open** *10.30am-8.30pm Mon-Fri; 11am-8.30pm Sat.* **Map** *p120 K12* ⓫ *Books & music*

This friendly Chueca bookshop sells an excellent range of illustrated and photography books. Plenty of them are in English and many have a humorous bent. The shop's stylish cotton totes make nice, cheap souvenirs, too.

### Pasajes

*C/Génova 3 (91 310 12 45, www.pasajeslibros. com). Metro Alonso Martínez.* **Open** *10am-8.30pm Mon-Sat.* **Map** *p120 M10* ⓬ *Books & music*

This linguists' treasure trove sells a great range of fiction and non-fiction, language-learning materials, maps, audio books and videos. Most things are in English, French, German and Spanish.

### Patrimonio Comunal Olivarero

*C/Mejía Lequerica 1 (91 308 05 05, www. patrimonioolivarero.com). Metro Alonso Martínez.* **Open** *10am-2pm, 5-8pm Mon-Fri; 10am-2pm Sat. Closed Aug.* **Map** *p120 L11* ⓭ *Food & drink*

Olive oil from every region of Spain that produces the stuff is on sale at Patrimonio Comunal Olivarero. Quantities go from two-litre bottles to five-litre cans, and some make lovely gifts.

### Piamonte

*C/Marqués de Monasterio 5 (91 702 55 61, www.piamontemadrid.com). Metro Chueca.* **Open** *11am-2.30pm, 5-8.30pm Mon-Sat.* **Map** *p120 M12* ⓮ *Fashion*

Desirable bags in all shapes, sizes and fabrics, from denim to super-soft leather.

### In the know
**Boutique browsing**

The best spots for browsing independent boutiques are Conde Duque, around Plaza Guardias de Corps; the Alonso Martínez part of Chueca, between C/Argensola, C/Génova, Plaza Santa Bárbara and C/Fernando VI; and the trendy triangle now known as triBall (meaning 'triangle of Ballesta', after one of the area's best streets), formed by C/Corredera Baja de San Pablo, C/Valverde and C/Desengaño.

**CHUECA & MALASAÑA**

# MALASAÑA & CONDE DUQUE

By day, the neighbourhood of Malasaña, between C/Fuencarral and San Bernardo, still has a laid-back neighbourhood feel, with grannies watering their geraniums on wrought-iron balconies and idiosyncratic corner shops. By night, though, this has long been an epicentre of Madrid's bar culture. Although less showy than Chueca, this is the city's hipster *barrio*, albeit with a grungy edge. Malasaña is still associated with chilled-out cafés, rock bars and cheap, studenty socialising – although the tentacles of Old City gentrification are taking hold, with scores of new boutiques, cafés and bars opening up in the area in the past few years, especially on C/Espíritu Santo.

On 2 May 1808 this area was the centre of resistance to the French. The name of the district comes from a 17-year-old seamstress heroine, Manuela Malasaña, who was shot by the invaders for carrying concealed weapons (her scissors) or ammunition to the Spanish troops – there are various versions of her exploits. The name of the main square, **Plaza Dos de Mayo**, also recalls that day. Where the square is today was then the Monteleón artillery barracks, from where the artillery captains Daoíz and Velarde galvanised the resistance of the people. The last remaining part of the barracks, a gate, stands in the square with a monument to the two men.

The area gained a tough reputation in the 1980s, when syringes and broken bottles used to litter the *plaza* and side streets in the mornings, but urban renovation schemes have been very successful, and the neighbourhood feels a lot safer to walk around at night. It is now one of the centres of the San Isidro festivals in May (*see p201*), hosting nightly concerts, fairs and outdoor parties.

The streets between Fuencarral and San Bernardo brim with great cafés, bars and restaurants. There are also indications – such as the broad-arched doorways for carriages – that the 19th-century well-to-do once lived here. One of the most rewarding streets is **C/San Vicente Ferrer**, with jewellery shops and a delightful 1920s tile display advertising the long-defunct pharmacy Laboratorios Juanse. Other old ceramic signs on the **C/San Andrés** feature a little boy signalling that his chamber pot is full and a dramatic, reclining vamp. C/La Palma and C/Divino Pastor, with craft and jewellery shops, are equally worth a stroll.

The atmosphere gets more lively as you approach the streets that lead down to the Gran Vía, such as **Corredera Baja de San Pablo**. This is an area of cheap restaurants, wholesale produce dealers in white aprons, shops selling nothing but light bulbs and working-class people who have known each other all their lives. Recent additions are club-style fashion shops, especially towards or on C/Fuencarral. This area contains the triangle (bordered by streets Corredera Baja de San Pablo, Desengaño and Valverde) recently named as **TriBall** by the city council and canny business folk who are looking to create a creative quarter that alludes to New York City's Tribeca. At the corner of the Corredera Baja and C/Ballesta there is an unusual brick church, built by Philip III for his Portuguese subjects in Madrid. Later it was set aside for German Catholic émigrés, and is still known as **San Antonio de los Alemanes**. It is rarely open to visitors. Just a block away along C/Pez, often unnoticed amid the shops, bars and theatres that surround it, is the slab-walled convent of **San Plácido**, another of Madrid's surviving religious houses. Down where C/Fuencarral meets Gran Vía is the **Fundación Telefónica** exhibition space. The area west of C/San Bernardo is most commonly known as Conde Duque after its finest monument, the **Centro Cultural Conde Duque**.

## Sights & museums

### ♥ Centro Cultural Conde Duque

*C/Conde Duque 11 (91 480 04 01, www.condeduquemadrid.es). Metro Noviciado or Ventura Rodríguez. **Open** 10am-2pm, 5.30-8pm Tue-Sat; 10.30am-2pm Sun. **Admission** varies. **Map** p120 F10.*

Housed in a former barracks, built in the 18th century for Philip V's guard by Pedro de Ribera, the magnificently restored Conde Duque is a multipurpose cultural centre. Around a dozen shows, both artistic and historical, are held annually in the two

Centro Cultural Conde Duque

# Poetry of the Absurd

*Surrealist La Serna, the anarchic author*

Few writers have been as central to the life and culture of Madrid as Ramón Gómez de la Serna, one of the most original and influential Spanish authors of the 20th century. Born in 1891 in the old Habsburg heart of Madrid, he trained initially as a lawyer, but never practised. When only 19, he stood on the balcony of his home at C/Puebla 11 and claimed to have had the inspiration for the near untranslatable literary form for which he would best be remembered: *greguerías*.

'Humour + metaphor = *greguerías*' was how Ramón himself defined these brief poetic statements in which words, ideas and objects are brought together in almost stream-of-consciousness fashion ('It is only in botanical gardens that trees carry visiting cards'). These 'attempts to define the indefinable, to capture the fugitive', as La Serna explained them on another occasion, had a major influence on the Spanish surrealist movement, and on avant-garde literature generally, in Europe and Latin America.

La Serna's love of the absurd and the ephemeral, and his ability to uncover the poetical and the extraordinary in the outwardly unremarkable, made him the ideal commentator on Madrid, a city he described as 'the most difficult capital in the world to understand'. He wrote more than 100 books, a great many of which are dedicated to his native city, beginning in 1914 with his first mature work, *El Rastro*. This lengthy work is on the legendary flea market, a place whose diversity of objects echoes his prose style, with an occasionally indigestible medley of aphorisms and random observations.

Exiled to Buenos Aires at the start of the Spanish Civil War, La Serna lived there until his death in 1963, his writings profoundly impacting Argentine author Jorge Luís Borges. Although the memory of Madrid never left him, he returned only once and was bitterly disappointed.

Later his corpse was brought over to Madrid's Sacramental de San Justo, and in 2015 his office was reassembled as part of the **Museo de Arte Contemporáneo** (*see p132*) in the Centro Cultural Conde Duque. It displays his fantastical anarchy, mesmerising with such details as convex mirrors, a stuffed leopard, flying swans on the walls and revolving mirror balls worthy of a suburban disco.

Monument to Ramón Gómez de la Serna, Parque de Las Vistillas

exhibition spaces and the two vast patios. Open-air concerts in summer bring in a range of performers. Also housed here are the city's newspaper and video libraries, as well as the Museo de Arte Contemporáneo, which opened in 2001, and slightly hidden next to it the **Palacio de Liria**.

### ♥ Fundación Telefónica

*C/Gran Vía 28, entrance at C/Valverde 2 (91 580 87 00, www.espacio.fundaciontelefonica. com). Metro Gran Vía. **Open** 10am-8pm Tue-Sun. **Admission** free. Map p120 K13.*

Run by Telefónica, the national telephone company, this foundation functions on several levels. The Museo de las Telecomunicaciones is a permanent exhibition illustrating the history of telecommunications. Another large space is used to display selections from Telefónica's permanent collection of Spanish art, including various works by Eduardo Chillida, Luis Fernández, Miró, Picasso and Tàpies, and it also has a permanent show based around post-Civil War Spanish artists of the so-called Madrid and Paris schools, the latter in exile. Temporary exhibitions feature both the arts and technology.

### Museo de Arte Contemporáneo

*C/Conde Duque 9 & 11 (91 588 58 61). Metro Noviciado. **Open** Sept-June 10am-2pm, 5.30-8.30pm Tue-Sat; 10.30am-2.30pm Sun. July, Aug 10am-2pm, 6-8.30pm Tue-Sat; 10.30am-2pm Sun. **Admission** free. Map p120 F10.*

The council's contemporary art collection covers painting and graphic work, along with sculpture, photography and drawing. Highlights include work by Eduardo Arroyo, Ouka Lele, Eduardo Úrculo, Jorge Oteiza and Eva Lootz.

### Palacio de Liria

*C/Princesa 20 (91 548 15 50, www. fundacioncasadealba.com). Metro Ventura Rodríguez. **Open** Guided tours 10am, 11am, noon Fri. Booking essential. Closed July-Oct. **Admission** free. Map p120 F10.*

This sober, neoclassical palace, completed in 1783 and refurbished in the 1910s by Edwin Lutyens, is still the private property of Spain's premier aristocrat, the Duchess of Alba. The extraordinary collection includes work by Rembrandt, Palma Vecchio, Titian and Rubens, and one of the most important Goyas in private hands: his portrait of an earlier Duchess of Alba in red and white. The Friday guided tours must be booked in advance by phone, email (visitas@fundacioncasadealba. com) or through the website. The waiting list is several months long.

## Restaurants

### Albur €€

*C/Manuela Malasaña 15 (91 594 27 33, www. restaurantealbur.com). Metro Bilbao. **Open** noon-5pm, 7.30pm-midnight Mon-Thur; 12.30-5pm, 7.30pm-1.30am Fri; 1pm-1.30am Sat; 1pm-midnight Sun. **Map** p120 J10* ❷
*Spanish*

The speciality is *revueltos* (scrambled egg) with prawns, wild mushrooms and so on, but there's also a range of paella dishes, good ham, chorizo and black pudding, and a variety of decent wines to accompany them. Generally a quiet place, with soothing buttercup-yellow walls, it gets quite lively later on in the evening with a young Malasaña crowd.

### Gumbo €€

*C/Pez 15 (91 532 63 61, www.gumbo.es). Metro Noviciado. **Open** 2-4pm, 9pm-midnight Tue-Sat; 2-4pm Sun. Closed 2wks Aug. **Map** p120 H12* ❾ *North American*

Bona fide N'Awlins chef Matthew Scott has some good Creole spices simmering in his gumbo pot. In a simple locale tastefully decorated (with a poster of *Gone with the Wind*), you can sample scrumptious New Orleans classics: fried green tomatoes, seafood gumbo, black steak. For festive group dinners, ask Matthew to bring out a parade of tapas-like dishes to share. And only a fool would make any attempt to resist the desserts.

### Home €€

*C/Espíritu Santo 12 (91 522 97 28, www. homeburgerbar.com). Metro Tribunal. **Open** 1.30-4pm, 9pm-midnight Tue-Sat; 1-4pm, 8.30pm-midnight Sun. **Map** p120 J11* ❿
*Burger bar*

If you associate burger bars with junk food, then Home's aim is to make you think again. It's the brainchild of a French Canadian restaurateur, who has created a carefully thought-out menu using 100% organic produce. The attention to detail is fantastic, from the diner-style decor complete with cheesy table lamps to the menus, which come printed on American supermarket paper bags. There are quite a few vegetarian dishes, and even vegans can enjoy a marinated tofu club sandwich. **Other locations** Paseo de la Castellana 210, Salamanca (91 219 56 58); C/ Silva 25, Sol & Gran Vía (91 115 12 79).

### Ojalá €€

*C/San Andrés 1 (91 523 27 47, www. grupolamusa.com/restaurante-ojala). Metro Noviciado or Tribunal. **Open** 10am-1am Mon-Wed; 10am-1.30am Thur; 10am-2am Fri;*

A 2014 makeover gave Ojalá a hipster vibe, with dozens of plants hanging from the ceiling amid strings of fairy lights. The food is a cosmopolitan hotchpotch of designer salads, sandwiches, burgers, tacos and wraps. Waiters are friendly, the food is well presented and the seating comfortable. Below the main dining room is a bar (open at 6pm) that resembles a beach cove with an industrial twist: sand coats the floor and harsh craggy bricks are framed by steel pipes on the walls, on to which old black-and-white movies are occasionally projected.

### Siam €€

*C/San Bernardino 6 (91 559 83 15). Metro Noviciado or Plaza de España.* **Open** *noon-4pm, 8pm-midnight daily.* **Map** *p120 G11* ⑯ *Thai*

Siam was originally set up by a Texan, who poured his heart and the experience of years spent in Thailand into this restaurant, and the investment paid off. Authenticity is key (please don't ask for bread). The new owner imports vegetables and spices that he can't get hold of in the city. Try the spicy Thai green curry, or just ask for a recommendation. Set lunch €12. There is also a fabulous range of cocktails and special teas.

### Taberna Agrado €€

*C/Ballesta 1 (91 521 63 46, www. tabernaagrado.com). Metro Gran Vía or Callao.* **Open** *1-4pm, 9-11pm Mon-Sat.* **Map** *p120 J13* ⑰ *Global*

Named after a character in Pedro Almodóvar's film *All About My Mother*, Agrado opened in 2010 and immediately caused a bit of a stir. It's located on an unpromising street just off Gran Vía, but the area is undergoing a bit of a renaissance. The speciality is the melt-in-the-mouth beef and Iberian pork hamburger. There's also octopus carpaccio and an upmarket Spanish take on fish and chips.

### La Tasquita de Enfrente €€€

*C/Ballesta 6 (91 532 54 49). Metro Gran Vía or Callao.* **Open** *1.30-3.30pm, 8.30-11.30pm Mon-Sat. Closed Aug.* **Map** *p120 J13* ⑱ *Spanish*

One of Madrid's best restaurants, La Tasquita de Enfrente is run by Juanjo López Bedmar, a former executive who chucked it all in to devote himself to cooking. There are only half a dozen tables, so you need to book well ahead. The menu changes according to what is best at any given time, but don't miss the *pochas* (white beans) with clams, if they're available. Also fabulous are the squid

**Fundacion Telefonica**

gnocchi, and the slow-cooked acorn-fed Iberian pork cheeks. But the best idea is to go for the special menu of the day.

## Tapas

### La Casta

*C/Bernardo López García 1 (655 097 026). Metro Noviciado.* **Open** *1-4pm, 7pm-1am daily.* **No cards.** **Map** *p120 G10* ②

A cool and relaxing tapas bar with gently revolving ceiling fans and terracotta floors. Tapas include smoked cod, trout and salmon, or there are wooden *tablas* spread with cheese or ham. More unusually for Madrid, there is Leffe and Guinness on tap. It's on the corner with C/Cristo, which is pedestrianised, and there are some tables outside, but be prepared to be assailed by a mixed bag of buskers.

### Conache

*C/Santa Bárbara 11 (91 522 95 00, www. restauranteconache.com). Metro Tribunal. **Open** 9.30am-2.30am daily. **Map** p120 K11* ❸

The Conache look is an eclectic one, with bits of Indian art and Eastern wall-hangings contrasting with a certain stark approach to furnishings. The food, however, is absolutely where it's at. Try stir-fried vegetables with prawns, little rolls of venison and apple, or spinach and brie with figs, and be sure to finish with the cheese mousse with fruits of the forest.

### El Maño

*C/Palma 64 (91 521 50 57). Metro Noviciado. **Open** 7.30pm-12.30am Mon-Thur; 12.30-4.30pm, 7.30pm-1.30am Fri, Sat; 12.30-4.30pm Sun. **Map** p120 G10* ❹

A relaxed place, with French windows opening on to the street in summer, marble-topped tables and bar, faded yellow paintwork and art deco touches. A good selection of wine is chalked up on the walls, some of it poured from ancient barrels, and there are tortillas served with *pisto*, ragu or squid, brochettes of chicken and lamb and a small selection of canapés.

### Pez Gordo

*C/Pez 6 (91 522 32 08, www.elpezgordo.es). Metro Noviciado. **Open** 7.30pm-2am daily. **Map** p120 J12* ❻

Popular with audiences and actors from the nearby Teatro Alfil, the Fat Fish (the Spanish equivalent to 'Big Cheese') buzzes at night and is fabulously mellow earlier in the evening. The main attraction (aside from the photos of the owner's hideous bulldog) comes in the shape of the creative tapas. Try fried plantain with guacamole, goose confit with red fruit compôte, or the *patatas* Pez Gordo, with alioli, anchovies and hot peppers.

---

**In the know**
**Eating on the run**

It's a phenomenon often noted by visitors that Madrid lacks the sandwich bars found on every corner of most European capitals. The Spanish have always been appalled by the idea of lunch as refuelling, let alone – horror of horrors – eating at one's desk. No, lunch here is a leisurely affair. However, if time is short or if you're eating alone and don't fancy a drawn-out affair, then head to Chueca's C/San Marcos for café/takeaway hotspot **Diurno** (no.37) or grab a quesadilla at **La Chelinda** (no.8). Another street to note is Malasaña's C/Espíritu Santo, which among other places, has the popular **Home** (see p132) for gourmet beef in a bun.

### La Taberna de Corps

*Plaza Guardia de Corps 1 (mobile 690 177 301). Metro Ventura Rodriguez. **Open** 1-6pm Tue-Thur; 1pm-midnight Fri-Sun. **No cards**. **Map** p120 G10* ❼

The *surtido* (mixed plate) of canapés and excellent selection of wines aside, the main attraction in this tiny bar is the location – on a quiet leafy plaza. Grab a Rioja or a draught *vermut* and settle down with the papers.

### La Tabernilla del Gato Amadeus

*C/Cristo 2 (91 541 41 12). Metro Noviciado. **Open** 1pm-1am daily. **Map** p120 G10* ❽

Named after a late, great, Persian cat, this is a tiny, welcoming bar, whose *croquetas* are the stuff of legend. The other favourite is the *patatas con mojo picón* (baked new potatoes with a spicy sauce). Although there's not much seating inside the premises (the sister bar nearby is bigger), in summer there are tables outside. **Other location** C/Limón 32, Malasaña & Conde Duque (91 542 54 23).

---

## Cafés & bars

### La Ardosa

*C/Colón 13 (91 521 49 79, www.laardosa.com). Metro Tribunal. **Open** 8am-2am Mon-Thur; 8am-2.30am Fri; 11am-2.30m Sat; noon-2am Sun. **No cards**. **Map** p120 J12* ❷

Having an affair? Then simply duck under the counter to find the most intimate bar room you could wish for. Out front, meanwhile, this is a lovely old tiled *taberna* lined with dusty bottles, old black-and-white lithographs and beer posters. A range of canapés has just been added, and the speciality of the house is its draught beer – Bombardier, Budvar and, especially, Guinness.

### Bar El 2D

*C/Velarde 24 (91 448 64 72). Metro Tribunal. **Open** noon-2am Mon-Thur; 11.30am-2.30am Fri, Sat; 11.30am-2am Sun. **Map** p120 J10* ❸

The emblematic Malasaña hangout, packed at weekends and drowsily mellow in the afternoons, with a tiled bar and engraved mirrors, nicotine-stained walls and lazily circling ceiling fans. To drink, there's vermouth, lager and Beamish on tap, plus plenty of bottled beers and a small selection of wines, served (if you dare) in *porrones*, which are long-spouted drinking jars.

### Bar El Palentino

*C/Pez 12 (91 532 30 58). Metro Callao or Noviciado. **Open** 7am-2am Mon-Sat. **No cards**. **Map** p120 J12* ❺

Something of a Madrid institution, this old-school neighbourhood bar is popular with seemingly everyone – the place is always packed in the evenings. Wooden panelling, fluorescent strip ceiling lamps, a much-loved owner and notoriously cheap (but good) drinks attract punters of all ages, creating a buzzing, sociable and quintessentially *madrileño* vibe. Sandwiches help to soak up the *cañas*.

## Café Comercial

*Glorieta de Bilbao 7 (91 521 56 55). Metro Bilbao. **Open** 7.30am-midnight Mon-Thur, Sun; 7.30am-2am Fri, Sat. **Map** p120 J10* ⑥

There was city-wide mourning when this scruffy but classic Madrid bar closed down, but it reopened in 2017 with a brand new look. Some of its original fittings remain – brown leather seats, revolving doors and marbled walls – but it's an altogether glitzier proposition nowadays, and you'll no longer be able to observe old men playing chess as you sip your beer. For one thing, you're more likely to be drinking a vodka martini.

## Café Manuela

*C/San Vicente Ferrer 29 (91 531 70 37). Metro Tribunal. **Open** 4pm-2am Mon-Thur, Sun; 4pm-2.30am Fri, Sat. **Map** p120 J11* ⑦

Stacked to the rafters with board games, Café Manuela has been a hive of activity since the Movida days. Its handsome art nouveau decor and conveniently nicotine-coloured walls are still the backdrop to occasional live music and other performances, but otherwise it's a great place to reacquaint yourself with Cluedo and Mastermind.

## Café El Moderno

*Plaza de las Comendadoras 1 (mobile 693 528 169, www.cafemodernomadrid). Metro Noviciado. **Open** 11am-2am Mon-Thur, Sun; 11am-3am Fri, Sat. **Map** p120 G10* ⑧

El Moderno's art deco look is entirely fake, but none the worse for it, and, along with its large terrace, it attracts a mixture of local characters and curious tourists. The specialities are teas, milkshakes and hot chocolates, with an impressive 30 varieties of each. Fans of *Sex and Lucía* will recognise the building as Lorenzo's apartment block.

## Café de Ruiz

*C/Ruiz 11 (91 446 12 32). Metro Bilbao. **Open** 4pm-2am Mon-Thur; 4pm-2.30am Fri; 3.30pm-2.30am Sat. **Map** p120 J10* ⑨

A quiet favourite with the smarter denizens of the neighbourhood, Café de Ruiz is an elegant place, with comfortable sofas and dramatic flower arrangements. A big draw is its own-made ice-cream and other tempting sweet treats, such as milkshakes and home-made cakes.

## Café Rustika

*C/Limón 11 (91 542 15 67, www.rustikacafe. net). Metro Noviciado. **Open** 7.30pm-12.30am Wed, Thur; 7.30pm-2.30am Fri, Sat; 5.30pm-12.30am Sun. **Map** p120 G11* ⑩

Whimsical interiors, funky lo-fi music and lots of hanging lanterns make this one of the most relaxing cafés in a neighbourhood full of them. A randomly international menu, with dishes from couscous to chop suey to chocolate cake and a wide selection of cocktails.

## Casa Camacho

*C/San Andrés 4 (91 531 35 98). Metro Tribunal. **Open** noon-2am Mon-Fri; noon-2.30am Sat. Closed Aug. **No cards**. **Map** p120 J11* ⑪

A rough diamond, the diminutive Casa Camacho has changed little since it opened in 1928, except for the addition of a fruit machine and a TV – both in constant use. Pre-war dust coats the bottles and plastic flowers on display and the floor is a sea of toothpicks and cigarette ends, but for a slice of real neighbourhood life it can't be beat.

## La Huida

*C/Colón 11 (mobile 600 870 509). Metro Tribunal. **Open** 1pm-2am daily. **No cards**. **Map** p120 J12* ⑭

La Movida meets *Friends* in this cramped but jolly little café, where everybody knows everybody else. This is where the neighbourhood's painfully cool neo-punks come to let their guard down, tucking into leek and mushroom quiche at the scrubbed pine tables. Sundays are especially mellow: the perfect set for The One Where They All Got Tattoos.

## ❤ El Jardín Secreto

*C/Conde Duque 2 (91 541 80 23, www. eljardinsecretomadrid.com). Metro Plaza de España or Ventura Rodríguez. **Open** 6pm-1am Mon-Thur; 6.30pm-2.30am Fri, Sat; 5.30pm-2.30am Sun. **Map** p120 F11* ⑮

Although it also functions as a restaurant, El Jardín Secreto – decked out with mismatched furniture and arty knick-knacks – is most popular as a *merienda* (afternoon tea) spot. The crowds tend to show up when the place opens. Its cakes and desserts – in particular the chocolate orgasm – are much talked about, and there's a large selection of chocolate drinks, teas and coffees on the menu. Open late, it's also popular as a cocktail spot.

## Levadura Madre

*C/Pez 1 (91 058 65 68, www.levaduramadre.
es). Metro Santo Domingo. **Open** 8.30am-9pm
daily. **Map** p120 J12* ⑯

'*Levadura madre*' means 'sourdough' and
this little café is all about bread, brought
out from its ovens in myriad forms. Equally
importantly, it's one of very few places
hereabouts where you can get an early
morning coffee – along with smoothies, fresh
juices, home-made cakes and quiches. If
you're in town for a while, you might enjoy
the breadmaking courses.

## Lola Loba

*C/Palma 38 (mobile 630 839 816). Metro
Noviciado. **Open** 6pm-2.15am Mon-Thur;
5pm-2.15am Fri, Sat. **No cards. Map** p120
H10* ⑰

Lola Loba is named after a *copla* singer
who ran away from her abusive American
millionaire husband and opened this bar.
In 1872 he found her and murdered her, and
it's said her ghost still prowls within the red-
brick walls. What is not known is whether she
approves of the jazz, funk and house, or the
tasty *tostas*, slathered in mozzarella, tomato
and basil, caramelised onion with brie, or
smoked salmon with camembert.

## Lolina Vintage Café

*C/Espíritu Santo 9 (91 523 58 59, www.
lolinacafe.com). Metro Tribunal.
**Open** 10am-midnight Mon-Thur, Sun;
10am-2.30am Fri, Sat. **Map** p120 J11* ⑱

Now a few years old, Lolina was among the
new wave of openings on Calle Espíritu
Santo. The cute, retro space – with its 1970s
wallpaper and vintage floor lamps – is a
popular hangout for arty types and young
expats, drawn by its pan-European vibe,
brunch-style menu and large selection of
teas, coffees and juices. The good-value
breakfasts start from €3; and if you visit
in the evening, be sure to order a mojito or
caipirinha – the house specialities.

## Naif

*C/San Joaquín 16 (91 007 20 71). Metro
Tribunal. **Open** 1pm-12.30am Mon-Wed;
1pm-2am Thur-Sat; 1pm-1am Sun. **Map** p120
J11* ⑲

Naif is very much of its time; a high-ceilinged
post-industrial space with Banksy-inspired
murals, exposed ventilation ducts, recycled
furniture and a bit of attitude behind the bar.
It's sympathetically lit, though, does a great
burger and is one of very few places to serve
BLTs or pastrami with mustard.

## La Paca

*C/Valverde 36 (662 119 067). Metro Alonso
Martínez. **Open** 3pm-1.30am Mon-Thur;
3pm-2.30am Fri; 4pm-2.30am Sat. **Map** p120
K12* ㉑

A peaceful option on a less transited
Malasaña street. Whitewashed brick walls,
a lazy ceiling fan, some comfy chairs and
sofas, antique mirrors and a funky music
selection make this a relaxed place to flick
through the papers with coffee and a slice of
home-made cake.

## Passenger

*C/Pez 16 (91 169 49 76). Metro Noviciado.
**Open** 8pm-3am Mon-Thur; 4pm-3.30am Fri-
Sun. Closed Aug. **Map** p120 H12* ㉒

Party like it's 1939 in this supremely elegant
Orient Express lookalike bar. Long and
narrow, with wood panelling, an art deco
bar, leather banquettes and screens showing
footage of scenery in mocked-up windows
– sure, it's a gimmick, but it's one hell of
a gimmick. Cocktails are the speciality
and there's a long list of tequilas and
organic whiskies.

## Pepe Botella

*C/San Andrés 12 (91 522 43 09, www.
pepebotella.com). Metro Tribunal. **Open**
10am-2am Mon-Thur, Sun; 10am-2.30am Fri,
Sat. **Map** p120 J10* ㉓

The name ('Joe Bottle') was the nickname
of Joseph Bonaparte, who slashed taxes on
alcohol when he was put on the Spanish
throne during the French occupation of
Spain. A cineaste's delight, the colourful
Pepe Botella is frequented by the likes of
director Alejandro Amenábar and actor
Eduardo Noriega. For all that, it's wonderfully
unpretentious, and attracts an intelligent
bunch of mainly thirty- and fortysomethings,
engaged in lively debate.

## El Rincón

*C/Espíritu Santo 26 (91 522 19 86). Metro
Tribunal. **Open** 9am-2am daily. **Map** p120
J11* ㉔

Popular with both locals and expats, laid-back
El Rincón has a new-wave Malasaña feel, with
chequered floors, powder blue walls, black-
and-white photos on the walls, mismatched
wooden tables and a boho vibe (a sign outside
reads 'Don't smoke joints on the terrace').
For a bite to eat, try the delicious *tortilla de
patatas* (€3.90) or the excellent sandwiches
and cakes. There's also good coffee and a
range of teas.

## Shops & services

### ♥ La Antigua

*C/Corredera Baja de San Pablo 45 (91 142 54 99, www.laantiguadepez.blogspot.com.es). Metro Tribunal.* **Open** *11am-9pm Mon-Sat.* **Map** *p120 J12* ❶ *Fashion*

Run by three designers, this kooky little boutique sums up all that is good about Malasaña, with a playful selection of clothes, jewellery and accessories. You might also pick up a *Royal Tenenbaums* tote, a *Fantastic Mr Fox* enamel mug or a pair of socks in a seahorse pattern.

### ♥ Antigua Casa Crespo

*C/Divino Pastor 29 (91 521 56 54, www.alpargateriacrespo.com). Metro Bilbao.* **Open** *10am-1.30pm, 5-8.15pm Mon-Sat. Closed last 2wks Aug.* **No cards.** **Map** *p120 J10* ❷ *Fashion*

This perfectly preserved, old-fashioned, family-run store, founded in 1863, is dedicated to espadrilles of all sizes and colours.

### Bunkha

*C/Santa Bárbara 6 (91 522 09 50, www.bunkha.com). Metro Tribunal or Gran Vía.* **Open** *11am-3pm, 5-9pm Mon-Sat.* **Map** *p120 K11* ❸ *Fashion*

The stylish boutique stocks a host of upmarket yet hip labels, such as Swedish brand Uniforms for the Dedicated, Spanish brand Broken Porcelain and Italian label Camo. Menswear is in the front space, while womenswear is in the mezzanine area.

### Happy Day

*C/Espíritu Santo 11 (91 522 91 33, www.happydaybakery.es). Metro Tribunal.* **Open** *11am-10pm Mon-Thur, Sun; 11am-midnight Fri, Sat.* **Map** *p120 J11* ❽ *Food & drink*

The cupcake phenomenon is now huge in Madrid, and Happy Day was one of the pioneers. The 1950s-style *pastelería* is kitted out in pastel shades, and has a café table if you want to indulge your sweet tooth in-store. **Other locations** In the El Corte Inglés stores at C/Preciados 3, C/Goya 76, C/Raimundo Fernández Villaverde 79.

### ♥ J&J Books & Coffee

*C/Espíritu Santo 47 (91 521 85 76, www.jandjbooksandcoffee.com). Metro Noviciado.* **Open** *4-11.30pm Mon-Thur; 4pm-1.30am Fri; noon-11.30pm Sat; noon-6pm Sun.* **Map** *p120 H11* ❿ *Books & music*

J&J is at once a relaxing little café (at ground-floor level) and a well-stocked second-hand bookshop (in the basement). Activities include language exchanges (Wednesdays, Thursdays and Saturdays from 8pm) and quizzes (Fridays from 11pm).

### Popland

*C/Manuela Malasaña 24 (91 591 21 20, www.popland.es). Metro Bilbao.* **Open** *11am-9pm Mon-Sat.* **Map** *p120 H10* ⓯ *Gifts & souvenirs*

For times when only a Jesus action figure will do, Popland saves the day. The shop is packed with all things pop culture and plastic, but also film posters, shower curtains and T-shirts. There's also a good range of greetings cards – quite a rarity in Madrid.

### Radio City

*C/Conde Duque 14 (91 547 77 67,). Metro Noviciado, Plaza de España or Ventura Rodríguez.* **Open** *11am-2pm, 6-9pm Mon-Sat.* **Map** *p120 F11* ⓰ *Books & music*

One of the city's best record shops, with a host of independent labels covering everything from indie folk to rare soul and R&B via Latin beats, on vinyl and CD. A selection of vintage LPs is also stocked.

### Snapo

*C/Espíritu Santo 5 (91 532 12 23, www.snaposhoponline.com). Metro Noviciado or Tribunal.* **Open** *11am-2pm, 5-8.30pm Mon-Sat.* **Map** *p120 J11* ⓱ *Fashion*

Snapo stocks streetwear with attitude. Designs are funny and cheeky. The collection is mainly T-shirts, plus some shoes, bags, caps and womenswear.

### Sportivo

*C/Conde Duque 20 (91 542 56 61, www.sportivostore.com). Metro San Bernardo.* **Open** *10am-9pm Mon-Sat.* **Map** *p120 G10* ⓲ *Fashion*

With a great range of menswear labels, including Barena, Libertine Libertine, YMC and Sunspel, Sportivo is an unmissable stop. The staff are extremely helpful.

### Vialis

*C/Fuencarral 40 (91 199 74 84, www.vialis.es). Metro Chueca.* **Open** *10.30am-8.30pm Mon-Sat.* **Map** *p120 K12* ⓳ *Fashion*

Madrid's only branch of the stylish Spanish footwear store is located on Malasaña's main shopping drag. Expect chunky but hip shoes and boots, and a small selection of high-quality leather bags.

# The Retiro & Salamanca

Most visitors encounter the area around the verdant Retiro park within the first few days, when they visit Madrid's star attraction of their trip, the Museo del Prado. The world-famous art museum is often referred to in relation to the 'Paseo del Arte' it forms with the nearby Thyssen-Bornemisza and the Reina Sofía. This 'art stroll' nowadays also includes the postmodern CaixaForum arts centre. To the east of the museum district is the Retiro. North of here is the *barrio* of Salamanca, an area known for its designer shopping, expensive restaurants and futuristic architecture (along the Paseo de la Castellana).

## ❤ Don't miss

**1 Museo Nacional del Prado** *p144*
Centuries of oil paintings from Spain's greatest artists.

**2 The Retiro** *p143*
Manicured gardens, a picture-perfect boating lake and the world's only statue of Lucifer.

**3 CaixaForum Madrid** *p273*
Groundbreaking building showing exhibitions to match.

**4 Museo Lázaro Galdiano** *p157*
Dazzling and quirky collection, off the beaten track.

## In the know
## Getting around

Many buses run up and down the *paseos* – Prado, Recoletos and Castellana – but the area is also well served by the metro. Banco de España station (L2) is useful for the Prado and Retiro, and Colón (L4) is a good hopping-off point for Salamanca, but there are many more.

Ángel Caído *p143*

# THE RETIRO & AROUND

## Paseo del Prado

The most attractive section of Madrid's north–south avenue, and the one that most new arrivals in Madrid first become familiar with, is the oldest: the **Paseo del Prado**, from Atocha up to Plaza de Cibeles. Once an open space between the city wall and the Retiro (*prado* means 'meadow'), it was given its present form between 1775 and 1782, from a design chiefly by José de Hermosilla; it was the most important of Charles III's attempts to give his shabby capital the kind of urbane dignity he had seen in Paris and Italy. The king intended it to be a grand avenue lined with centres of learning and science. It was originally called the Salón del Prado (*see p142* Stop the Car!), and the form of the main section, from Cibeles to Plaza Cánovas del Castillo, was modelled on Piazza Navona in Rome, with three fountains by Ventura Rodríguez: **Cibeles** at the most northerly point, **Neptune** to the south and a smaller figure of **Apollo** in the middle. The southern stretch of the Paseo, tapering down to Atocha, has another statue, the *Four Seasons*, in front of the Museo del Prado. In the 19th century, the Paseo del Prado was the great promenade of Madrid. Virtually the entire population, rich and poor, took a turn along it each evening, to see and be seen, pick up on the latest city gossip, make assignations and show off new clothes.

Despite the traffic, the tree-lined boulevard still has many attractions on and around it, most notably Madrid's 'big three' art museums: the **Museo Thyssen-**

Cuesta de Moyano

---

### 💚 Time to eat & drink

**Aperitivos and tapas**
José Luis *p160*

**A literary breakfast**
Café Gijón *p160*

**Mexican with a view**
Salón Cascabel *p160*

**Spanish delicacies**
La Castela *p152*

### 💚 Time to shop

**Classy gift-shop souvenirs**
Museo del Prado *p144*

**Fine wines**
Lavinia *p163*

**Gourmet treats**
Mantequerías Bravo *p163*

**Splashy, colourful clothing**
Agatha Ruiz de la Prada *p161*

### 💚 Time well spent

**Museo de Modelismo Naval**
*C/Bárbara de Braganza 14, Salamanca (91 581 46 09, www.museomodelismonaval. com). Metro Colón or Banco de España.* **Open** *2-8pm Mon; 10am-8pm Tue-Sat; 11am-7pm Sun.* **Admission** *free.* **Map** *p141 N12.*
A delightful little free museum for naval enthusiasts, opened in 2014 by the Fundación Mapfre (*see p158*). It comprises just one room filled with beautifully painted and constructed models of well-known ships of every era, from the *Cutty Sark* and *HMS Endeavour* to the *Titanic*.

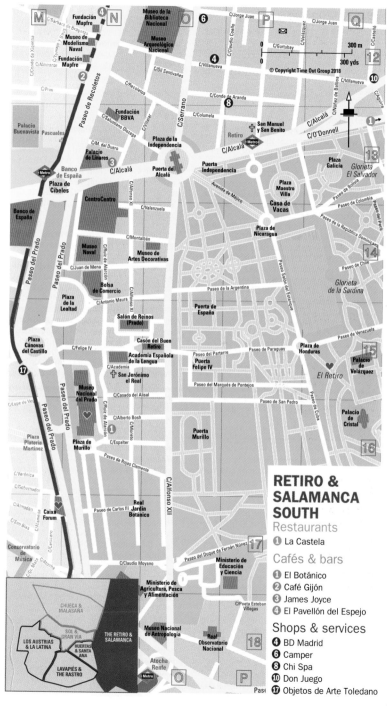

## RETIRO & SALAMANCA SOUTH

### Restaurants
**1** La Castela

### Cafés & bars
**1** El Botánico
**2** Café Gijón
**3** James Joyce
**4** El Pavellón del Espejo

### Shops & services
**4** BD Madrid
**6** Camper
**8** Chi Spa
**10** Don Juego
**17** Objetos de Arte Toledano

Bornemisza (*see p96*), near the statue of Neptune, at the border with Santa Ana; Charles III's **Museo Nacional del Prado** (*see p144*), with its new wing on Calle Ruiz de Alarcón; and, at the very bottom, in the south-east corner of Lavapiés, the **Museo Nacional Centro de Arte Reina Sofía** (*see p112*). Together with the cutting-edge **CaixaForum** (*see p273*), these spaces form the Paseo del Arte (*see p99*).

To the left of the Paseo, looking north, streets lead off into Huertas and the Old City, while to the right is the tranquil district of the Retiro. The knot of elegant streets in between the Paseo and the Retiro make up Madrid's most concentrated museum district, with, as well as the Museo del Prado, the **Museo Naval**, the **Bolsa de Comercio de Madrid** and the **Museo Nacional de Artes Decorativas**.

Heading south from here, other highlights include the **Real Jardín Botánico**, on the Paseo del Prado itself; the rows of second-hand bookstalls on the pedestrianised **Cuesta de Moyano**, which runs along the southern side of the botanical garden; the magnificently grandiose 1880s **Ministerio de Agricultura**, right on Glorieta de Atocha and designed by Ricardo Velázquez, the same architect who created the delicate exhibition halls inside the Retiro itself; and the landmark 19th-century **Atocha** station. A few blocks east from here along the (traffic-filled) Paseo Reina Cristina, a turn right down C/Julián Gayarre leads to the

**Real Fábrica de Tapices**. On Julián Gayarre there is also the much rebuilt **Basílica de Atocha** and the odd, often deserted, **Panteón de Hombres Ilustres** containing the elaborate tombs of Spanish politicians of the 19th century (*see p150* The Quick and the Dead).

## Plaza de Cibeles

Midway between the Puerta del Sol and the Retiro, this four-way intersection and its statue signifies Madrid to Spaniards as much as the Eiffel Tower or the Empire State Building identify their particular cities. It is surrounded by some of the capital's most prominent buildings: the **Palacio de Cibeles** (formerly the Palacio de Comunicaciones, the main post office, which has been turned into a stunning information centre and exhibition space, **CentroCentro**), the **Banco de España**, the **Palacio Buenavista** (now the Army headquarters) and the Palacio de Linares, which houses the **Casa de América**. The Ventura Rodríguez statue in the middle is of Cybele, Roman goddess of fertility and symbol of natural abundance, on a chariot drawn by lions. The goddess and the fountain around her have traditionally been the gathering point for victorious Real Madrid fans (Atlético supporters head for the fountain of Neptune, by the Thyssen museum) and the place where wins by the Spanish national team have been celebrated.

# Stop the Car!

*Giving the paseos back to the people*

Thanks to Charles III's efforts in the 18th century, the Paseo del Prado was to become the social heart of the city. Charles's idea was for this to become a centre of learning, with the main research institutions for arts and sciences, all open to the public, based here. He had it adorned with statues and fountains, and the area became known as El Salón del Prado. Early photos show women strolling with parasols while men in black bowlers hold ardent discussions. The 19th-century writer Richard Ford effused: 'The Prado, a truly Spanish thing and scene, is unique; and as there is nothing like it in Europe, and oh, wonder! no English on it, fascinates all who passes the Pyrenees.'

Oh, wonder! In time, however, thanks to the invention of the combustion engine, the Paseo del Prado was to become less of a promenade and more of a motorway, with cars speeding through red lights and tour buses blocking the view of the fountains. A succession of recent mayors has tried to address the

situation, but the most successful looks to be Manuela Carmena.

Carmena's plan to close the centre of Madrid to all traffic but residents and public transport is not specific to the area, but should make a considerable difference when it comes into force in mid 2018. It should create a broader expanse of walkable promenade that will link the Plaza de Colón and the big three museums to Atocha train station, with minimal interference from passing traffic. The stretch from Colón along Paseo Recoletos to Cibeles has already been remodelled, along with isolated spots around the Retiro, such as the now pedestrianised bookstall-lined Cuesta de Moyano.

Further remodelling is planned and should mean that strollers will, at some point in the future, be able to amble in a leisurely fashion between Madrid's best art museums, and that the fountain-filled Prado 'salon' will be returned to its 19th-century self as Madrid's best place to see and be seen.

# 💙 The Retiro

When Philip II ruled Madrid, this whole area was just open country, apart from the church of **San Jerónimo** (*see p152*) and a few other royal properties. In the 1630s, it was made into gardens – unprecedented in size for the era, at nearly 122 hectares (300 acres) – that became part of the **Palacio del Buen Retiro**, built by the Conde Duque de Olivares for Philip IV to impress the world. Gardeners were brought in from across Europe to create the park and its lake, and to ensure that it would feature shade and flowers throughout a Madrid summer. Charles III first opened sections of the park to the public in 1767, but it was only after the fall of Isabel II in 1868 that the gardens became entirely free to the public. After it became a park, the Retiro acquired most of its many statues, most notably the giant 1902 monument to King Alfonso XII presiding over the lake.

Since it was made open to all, the Retiro has found a very special place in the hearts and habits of the people of Madrid. On a Sunday morning stroll, especially before lunch, you will see multigenerational families watching puppet shows, dog-owners and their hounds, children playing on climbing frames, vendors hawking everything from *barquillos* (traditional wafers) to etchings, palm and tarot readers, buskers from around the world, couples on the lake in hired boats, kids playing football, elderly men involved in leisurely games of *petanca* (boules), cyclists, runners, and a good many bench-sitters who want nothing

more than to read the paper. During the week it's much emptier, and it's easier to take a look at some of the 15,000 trees, the rose garden and the park's fine exhibition spaces: the **Palacio de Cristal**, the **Palacio de Velázquez** and the **Casa de Vacas**. Built in the 19th century, they were extensively renovated during the 1980s.

At the southern end of the park is the **Real Observatorio Nacional**, a fine neoclassical building. However, the greatest curiosity of the park is Madrid's monument to Lucifer, in the moment of his fall from heaven. Known as the **Ángel Caído** (Fallen Angel), this bizarrely unique statue on the avenue south of the Palacio de Cristal is thought to be the only monument to the Devil in the world.

After the death of Philip IV in 1665, little use was made of the Retiro, although the palace gained a new lease of life when the Alcázar burned down in 1734, as it became the primary royal residence in Madrid until the Palacio Real was completed in 1764. However, in 1808 Napoleon's troops made it a barracks, and when the British army arrived in 1812 to fight over Madrid, much of the palace was destroyed.

On the north side of the park, forming a bridge between it and Salamanca, is the grand **Puerta de Alcalá**, still imposing despite being surrounded by the hectic traffic of the Plaza de la Independencia. The districts around and south of the Retiro are in some ways similar to Salamanca, but less emphatically affluent and more mixed.

THE RETIRO & SALAMANCA

# ❤ Museo Nacional del Prado

*C/Ruiz de Alarcón 23, off Paseo del Prado (91 330 28 00, 91 330 29 00, www. museodelprado.es). Metro Atocha or Banco de España.* **Open** *10am-8pm Mon-Sat; 10am-7pm Sun.* **Admission** *€15; €7.50 reductions; free under-18s, students aged 18-25. Free to all 6-8pm Tue-Sat, 5-7pm Sun. Paseo del Arte ticket €29.60.* **Map** *p141 N16.*

Housed in a vast neoclassical building begun by Juan de Villanueva for King Charles III in 1785, the Prado is Madrid's best-known attraction. Charles originally wanted to establish a museum of natural sciences, but by the time it opened in 1819, the plan had changed: the Prado was to be a public art museum – one of the world's first – displaying the royal art collection.

The main phases of the Prado's ambitious expansion programme have now come to fruition, making the collection more comprehensive than ever before. In 2007, the new extension opened, on the site of the San Jerónimo cloisters behind the main building. The highly controversial cube-shaped edifice designed by Rafael Moneo houses the museum's temporary galleries, as well as a huge foyer containing the café-restaurant, information points, and a book and gift shop.

Director Miguel Zugaza's 'second expansion' involved a massive internal reorganisation in order to increase the number of works displayed by 50 per cent (to around 1,500). In 2009, 12 new rooms opened (arranged chronologically) on the ground floor, containing a total of 176 pieces from the museum's 19th-century collection (many moved from El Casón del Buen Retiro).

In 2010, a further seven new rooms opened, containing newly restored works. Dedicated to medieval and Renaissance Spanish art, they complete the ground floor collections of the Villanueva building, and significantly expand the museum's displays of 12th- to 16th-century Spanish painting. The next major extension is the Salón de Reinos, which previously held the military museum and was once a wing of the Buen Retiro palace (fittingly, it was where most of the royal collection of paintings was held). It was purchased by the museum in order to create more exhibition space and stitch the various buildings of the Museo del Prado together. Norman Foster is behind the new design and building work will begin in 2018.

### The collection

The Prado embraces art from the 12th to the 20th centuries, and contains the world's largest collection of Spanish works. Its core is still the royal holdings, however, so it reflects royal tastes and political alliances from the 15th to the 17th centuries: court painters Diego de Velázquez and Francisco de Goya are well represented. Political ties with France, Italy and the southern, Catholic Netherlands also assure the presence of works by Titian, Rubens and Hieronymous Bosch.

But Spanish monarchs had begun collecting long before this time. By the 1500s, Queen Isabella already had a substantial collection of works by Flemish artists. During the reigns of Emperor Charles V (1519-56) and Philip II (1556-98), Italian and Flemish works continued to dominate. Titian was a favourite of both kings, and the eclectic Philip II also purchased several

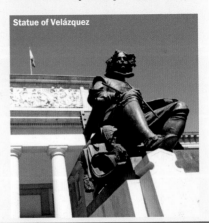

Statue of Velázquez

---

### ❤ Don't miss

**1 Goya's *The Third of May***
A devastating depiction of the horrors of war.

**2 Bosch's *Garden of Earthly Delights***
Apocalyptic, hallucinatory and exquisitely detailed.

**3 Velázquez's *Las Meninas***
Often described as the 'greatest painting in the world'.

works by Bosch, among them the triptych *Garden of Earthly Delights* (*see p146* Visions of Hell), which he had hanging on his bedroom wall in El Escorial.

Philip IV (1621-65), a major patron of Rubens, is seen as the greatest Habsburg art collector. He was contemptuous of Spanish painters until he saw the work of the young Velázquez, who served him as court painter for nearly 40 years (1623-60). Velázquez also supervised the acquisition of other works, adding some 2,000 paintings by Renaissance and 17th-century masters.

Spain's first Bourbon King, Philip V (1700-46), brought with him one of the museum's most extraordinary possessions, displayed in the basement: the Tesoro del Delfín ('Treasures of the Grand Dauphin') – mostly 16th- and 17th-century Italian objets d'art. The last monarch to add significantly to the royal collection was Charles IV (1788-1808), the employer of Goya, who was possibly the least respectful court painter who ever lived, as shown by his portraits of Charles IV's family.

### Highlights and basic floor plans

It's impossible to do the Prado justice in a single visit, and we don't suggest you try. When you arrive, pick up a floor plan (or download one from the website, where you'll also find suggested thematic routes) to help you track down the don't-misses.

The ground floor contains Flemish works from the 17th century and Italian paintings from the 15th to the 18th centuries, such as Breughel the Elder's *Triumph of Death* and Bosch's *Garden of Earthly Delights* (Room 56A), as well as Spanish art from the 16th to the 19th centuries, including some of Goya's major works, and in particular his masterpiece *The Third of May* (Rooms 64-65; *see also p252* The Third of May). There's also a room dedicated to Joaquín Sorolla (Room 60A). The ground-floor central gallery displays many works from the sculpture collection.

The highlight of the first floor is undoubtedly the Velázquez rooms, in the Central Gallery. Here you'll find the Prado's most famous work, *Las Meninas* (Room 12), which is often described as the finest painting in the world because of its complex interplay of perspectives and realities. Elsewhere on this floor are Italian paintings from the 15th to 18th centuries and Spanish art from the 16th to the 19th centuries, including several works by El Greco and Goyas from the period 1780 to 1800 (there are more rooms dedicated to Goya on the second floor).

Las Meninas (Diego Velázquez, 1656)

# Visions of Hell

*The Prado is home to two of the world's finest Last Judgement paintings*

In Room 56A of the Prado are two of the greatest paintings ever done of the Last Judgement: Pieter Breughel the Elder's *The Triumph of Death,* painted in 1562; and *The Garden of Earthly Delights*, the triptych by Hieronymus Bosch (El Bosco to the Spanish), thought to have been completed around 1501. The latter is one of the greatest canvases of all time. And *The Triumph of Death* is no lightweight effort either; even if Breughel had not also been Flemish and an unabashed admirer of Bosch's painting, it would still be a good choice to display near *Earthly Delights*. It is smaller, a single canvas, but imagined in hallucinatory detail that is every bit a counterweight to the Bosch. In it, hundreds of skeletons herd the living into a huge coffin. The humans are terrified, helpless, shoved, pushed and prodded along by the skeletons. There is a huge bony horse and astride it is a skeletal general in death's army, huge scythe in one hand, reaping as he tramples through the waves of fearful human beings. A dog feeds on a dead woman's body. The horizon is high on the painting; the whole shocking scene in the foreground fades into dark spectral colours punctuated by pockets of leaping flames.

On the facing wall is Bosch's triptych, two metres high, the centre panel twice the width of the wings, which fold in over it. Painted on the back of the wings, forming another scene when they are covering the centre panel, is the third day of creation as described in Genesis. The main triptych depicts our peopled world in its implacable fullness and flesh, its joys and sufferings, all in amazingly modern detail.

The left panel shows the Garden of Eden in its innocence, but even here all is not peace and light, as beasts swallow other beasts, hinting at the savage brute world on which ours is built. In the centre panel is the antediluvian world of the senses – the world as we know it, a variety of human pleasure as modern as television or Hollywood's latest scandal. Sensual romps we have no trouble recognising as our own – the pleasures of the flesh in trysts, threesomes, group gropes, everyone indulging. Beside it, in the last panel, is hell itself, Judgement Day, when the former revellers are tied and tortured by ghouls and animals: miserable, dominated, impaled, ensnared and enslaved, their cities burning in the implacable darkness of the last days.

The *Garden of Earthly Delights* is full of the most modern of physical forms, from a round earth to airships. The power of its images is undimmed across the centuries, and they still resonate to this day.

Garden of Earthly Delights (detail)

The Triumph of Death (Pieter Bruegel the Elder, c1562)

Garden of Earthly Delights (Hieronymous Bosch, 1501)

## Sights & museums

### Banco de España

*Plaza de Cibeles. Metro Banco de España.*
**Map** *p141 M14.*

This grandiose pile on the corner of Calle Alcalá was designed in 1882 by Eduardo Adaro and Severiano Saínz de la Lastra to house the Bank of Spain. The eclectic style was strongly influenced by French Second Empire designs, with a few Viennese touches. The decorative arched window and elaborate clock above the main entrance are best appreciated from a distance.

### Bolsa de Comercio de Madrid

*Plaza de la Lealtad 1 (91 589 10 20, www. bolsamadrid.es). Metro Banco de España.*
**Open** *(guided tour only) Individuals noon Thur. Groups 10am Mon-Fri. Closed July.*
**Admission** *free.* **Map** *p141 N14.*

In the same *plaza* as the Hotel Ritz, Madrid's stock exchange is a landmark as well as a business centre. Enrique María Repullés won the competition to design it in 1884, with a neoclassical style chosen to reflect that of the nearby Prado. The building has two distinct areas: one is the trading area; the other, open to the public, houses an exhibition on the market's history. Guided tours last 60 minutes; phone or email visitas@grupobme.es to arrange a visit (although waiting lists can be long).

### Casa de América

*Palacio de Linares, Plaza de Cibeles 2 (91 595 48 00, www.casamerica.es). Metro Banco de España.* **Open** *11am-7.30pm Mon-Fri; 11am-3pm Sat. Guided tours 11am, noon, 1pm Sat, Sun. Closed Aug.* **Admission** *free. Guided tour €8; €5 reductions; free under-8s.*
**Map** *p141 N13.*

Housed in the 1872 Palacio de Linares, the Casa de América showcases Latin American art, both by established figures and emerging talents. It also has the important role of promoting cultural contacts between Spain and South America. As well as this, there are film seasons, music, theatre and talks given by leading writers, film directors, playwrights and political figures. There are also print and video libraries, a good bookshop and a terrace with arts events in summer.

### Centro Cultural Casa de Vacas

*Parque del Retiro (91 409 58 19). Metro Retiro.*
**Open** *10am-9pm daily. Times may vary.*
**Admission** *free.* **Map** *p141 P14.*

This exhibition space in the Retiro, close to the boating lake, is run by the local council and offers shows ranging from children's books to wildlife photography.

### CentroCentro

*Plaza de Cibeles 1 (91 480 00 08, www. centrocentro.org). Metro Banco de España.* **Open** *10am-8pm Tue-Sun. Mirador 10.30am-1.30pm, 4-7pm Tue-Sun.* **Admission** *free. Mirador €2; 50¢ under-12s. Free to all 1st Wed of mth.* **Map** *p141 N14.*

Estación de Atocha

This extraordinary construction, which dwarfs the Plaza de Cibeles and is regularly compared to a sandcastle or a wedding cake, was until recently the world's most spectacular post office. It was designed in 1904 by Antonio Palacios and Joaquín Otamendi and completed in 1918, and is the best example of the extravagant style favoured by Madrid's elite at its most expansive. The design was influenced by Viennese art nouveau, but it also features many traditional Spanish touches, with a grand entrance (complete with an oversized revolving door), a Hollywood film-set staircase, soaring ceilings, stunning columns and grand marble floors. In 2011, the building was transformed into a five-storey exhibition space, with a cultural information centre in the main entrance hall. There's a colourful and comfortable reading area, with sofas, beanbags, newspapers and iPads, and a café, while upstairs are various exhibition halls and the *mirador* – a lookout point with a panoramic view of the city.

### Estación de Atocha
*Glorieta del Emperador Carlos V. Metro Atocha.* **Map** *p141 O18.*

Madrid's classic wrought-iron and glass main rail station was completed in 1892, to a design by Alberto del Palacio. It remained much the same, gathering a coating of soot, until the 1980s, when Rafael Moneo – he of the Museo Thyssen and Prado extension – gave it a complete renovation in preparation for Spain's golden year of 1992. Entirely new sections were added for the AVE high-speed train to Andalucia and Barcelona, and for the *cercanías* local rail network; an indoor tropical garden was installed in an imaginative blend of old and new. To the front of the station you can visit the monument to the victims of the horrific terrorist bombings of March 2004, a large glass cylinder inside which thousands of messages to the victims are written and displayed on a type of 'membrane', although in recent years the monument has fallen into disrepair.

### Museo Nacional de Antropología
*C/Alfonso XII 68 (91 539 59 95, mnantropologia.mcu.es). Metro Atocha.* **Open** *9.30am-8pm Tue-Sat; 10am-3pm Sun.* **Admission** *€3; €1.50 reductions; free under-18s, over-65s.* **Map** *p141 O18.*

This three-storey building between the Retiro and Atocha station houses several levels, each devoted to a specific region or country. The first level has an extensive collection from the Philippines (a former Spanish colony), dominated by a six-metre dugout canoe. Among the bizarre highlights are a 19th-century Philippine helmet made from a blowfish, shrunken human heads from Peru, and the skeleton of Don Agustín Luengo y Capilla, an Extremaduran who stood 2.25m (7ft 4in) tall. Even more enticing is a shrivelled tobacco leaf-skinned mummy, said to have once been in Charles III's royal library. Both are in the annexe to the first level.

# The Quick and the Dead

*In search of some of Spain's more famous departed*

Spanish philosopher Miguel de Unamuno famously wrote that the dead in Spain were never allowed to rest. The truth of this observation will become apparent to anyone who wonders what has happened to the tombs of famous Spaniards who have died in Madrid. Remarkably, the remains of none of the city's outstanding Golden Age figures – including Cervantes, Lope de Vega and Calderón de la Barca – have survived, though there was a brief moment of excitement in 1999 following the discovery of bones wrongly believed to be those of Velázquez and his wife.

Even those Spaniards wealthy enough in the past to have paid for *sepultura perpetua* (others still have their bodies automatically removed from their tombs after ten years) have not been guaranteed a tranquil posthumous life. The expansion and destruction of churches has led to constant transfers of corpses, during the course of which a high proportion have been mislaid or misidentified.

In view of this unfortunate situation, a decision was finally taken in 1869 to create what Spain so obviously lacked – a national pantheon for its heroes. The domed late 18th-century **Basílica de San Francisco** (*see p74*) was set aside for this purpose, and the remains of Calderón and other famous Spaniards were taken to the church in a triumphant procession involving cannon fire and horse squadrons. But barely had the corpses had time to recover from their journey than the parishes from where they had come began to reclaim them. In the case of Calderón, the body would be moved several more times before disappearing entirely.

The fiasco of San Francisco did not put an end to the idea of a Spanish pantheon. In the 1890s, next to the then ruined 16th-century Basilica and Monastery of Atocha, the **Panteón de Hombres Ilustres** was built. However, this too proved a failure, and most of the illustrious corpses for whom it was intended were taken away, leaving just the remains of largely forgotten politicians. Today, it's one of Madrid's least visited sites, but worth a look for its inappropriately Italianate architecture, and its splendidly elaborate tombs by Benlliure and other fashionable Spanish sculptors of the period.

While the Panteón de Hombres Ilustres is centrally located, visitors with a love of cemeteries will find themselves travelling to some of the city's poorest outlying districts. The largest of the city's cemeteries is that of the **Almudena**, out to the east (metro García Noblejas), the terrifying scale of which, not to

mention the dusty, grim surroundings, gives it a compellingly morbid appeal. Across the road is the comparatively intimate **Civic Cemetery**. Tidied up in the early 1990s following the burial here of the Communist leader Dolores Ibarruri ('La Pasionaria'), this contains the tombs of hundreds of opponents to Franco and the Catholic Church. At the end of the Civil War, numerous Republican prisoners were shot here and thrown into a mass grave.

But the most absorbing of Madrid's cemeteries is the **Sacramental de San Justo**, attached to the cemetery of the Hermitage of San Isidro (bus 17) out west. In a state of poignant neglect, this overgrown, cypress-shaded wasteland is the resting place of some of the more distinguished writers of 19th- and 20th-century Spain, from the romantic Madrid poet Mariano José de Larra to prolific writer and man-about-town Ramón Gómez de la Serna. Luis Buñuel was greatly drawn to this cemetery; his memory of coming across the hair of a woman protruding from a cracked grave here was used by him in his film *The Phantom of Liberty*.

Almudena Cemetery

## Museo Nacional de Artes Decorativas

*C/Montalbán 12 (91 532 64 99, www.mecd. gob.es/mnartesdecorativas). Metro Banco de España.* **Open** *Sept-June 9.30am-3pm Tue, Wed, Fri, Sat; 9.30am-3pm, 5-8pm Thur; 10am-3pm Sun. July, Aug 9.30am-3pm Tue-Sat; 10am-3pm Sun.* **Admission** *€3; €1.50 reductions; free under-18s, over-65s. Free to all Thur pm, Sat 2-3pm & all day Sun.* **Map** *p141 O14.*

The Decorative Arts Museum houses more than 15,000 objets d'art, furniture and tapestries from all over Spain, plus many from China. One of the most prized rooms is the fifth-floor tiled kitchen, painstakingly transferred from an 18th-century Valencian palace, whose 1,604 painted tiles depict a domestic scene, with a huddle of servants making hot chocolate. Also of great interest is the second floor, where the Spanish Baroque pieces are concentrated, among them ceramics from Talavera and Teruel, textiles, gold and silver work and jewellery cases from the Tesoro del Delfín (Treasure of the Grand Dauphin), the rest of which is in the Prado. Elsewhere are 19th-century doll's houses, antique fans, an ornate 16th-century four-poster bedstead and a Sèvres porcelain jug given to Queen Isabel II by Napoleon III.

## Museo Naval

*Paseo del Prado 5 (91 523 87 89, www.armada. mde.es/museonaval). Metro Banco de España.* **Open** *Sept-July 10am-7pm Tue-Sun. Aug 10am-3pm Tue-Sun.* **Admission** *free.* **Map** *p141 N14.*

Madrid's naval museum contains examples of the booty accumulated by Columbus and other mariners during Spain's period of maritime expansion, and an array of navigational instruments, muskets, guns and naval war paintings. Glass display cases enclose primitive weapons, some of which, like the swords lined with sharks' teeth from the Gilbert Islands, promise greater damage than their Western counterparts. The most impressive room is dominated by a huge mural map that traces the routes taken by Spain's intrepid explorers; in front of it are two equally impressive 17th-century giant globes. This same room also holds the museum's most valuable possession: the first known map of the Americas by a European – a parchment paper drawing by royal cartographer Juan de la Cosa, believed to have been made for Ferdinand and Isabella in 1500. Also worth a look is the room occupied by items salvaged between 1991 and 1993 from the *Nao San Diego*, which sank in the China Seas in 1600. You'll need to show a passport or other form of ID to gain entry.

## Palacio de Cristal

*Parque del Retiro (91 774 10 00). Metro Retiro.* **Open** *Nov-Mar 10am-6pm daily. Apr-Sept 10am-10pm daily. Oct 10am-7pm daily.* **Admission** *free.* **Map** *p141 Q16.*

This 1880s glass and wrought-iron construction, which is an outpost of the Reina Sofía, is a lovely, luminous space for viewing art. Shows here often involve large-scale installations, sculpture or pieces specially conceived for the space.

## Palacio de Velázquez

*Parque del Retiro (91 573 62 45). Metro Retiro.* **Open** *Nov-Mar 10am-6pm daily. Apr-Sept 10am-10pm daily. Oct 10am-7pm daily.* **Admission** *free.* **Map** *p141 Q15.*

Built by Ricardo Velázquez for a mining exhibition in 1883, this pretty brick and tile building amid the trees of the Retiro is topped by large iron and glass vaults. Another Reina Sofía annexe, its galleries are wonderfully airy and host very good temporary shows. Contemporary dance has also featured.

## Puerta de Alcalá

*Plaza de la Independencia. Metro Retiro.* **Map** *p141 O13.*

A short distance along C/Alcalá from Cibeles, in the middle of another traffic junction, stands one of the most impressive monuments built for King Charles III, a massive neoclassical gate designed by his favourite Italian architect, Francesco Sabatini, to provide a grand entrance to the city. It was built between 1769 and 1778, using granite and stone from Colmenar. Possible to miss in daytime traffic, it is hugely impressive at night.

Palacio de Velázquez

### Real Fábrica de Tapices
*C/Fuenterrabía 2 (91 434 05 50, www.
realfabricadetapices.com). Metro Menéndez
Pelayo.* **Open** *Guided tours only 10am-2pm
Mon-Fri (last tour 1pm; tour in English noon).
Closed Aug.* **Admission** *€5. No cards.* **Map** *Pull-out Q19.*

Goya created some of his freshest images as
designs for Madrid's royal tapestry factory,
founded in 1721. Originally it was in Chueca,
but has been here since 1889. The hand-
working skills and techniques used haven't
changed, and are evident from the intricate,
painstaking work carried out in its two
sections – the carpet room and the tapestry
room. Goya designs are a mainstay of the
work that's done here today (the factory also
maintains carpets for royal palaces and the
Ritz, as well as private clients).

### Real Jardín Botánico
*Plaza de Murillo 2 (91 420 30 17, www.rjb.csic.
es). Metro Atocha.* **Open** *Nov-Feb 10am-6pm
daily. Mar, Oct 10am-7pm daily. Apr, Sept
10am-8pm daily. May-Aug 10am-9pm daily.*
**Admission** *€4; reductons 50¢-€2; free
under-10s. No cards.* **Map** *p141 N17.*

Madrid's luscious botanical gardens were
created for Charles III by Juan de Villanueva
and the botanist Gómez Ortega in 1781. They
sit alongside the Paseo del Prado, just south
of the Prado museum, but inside this deep-
green glade, with over 30,000 plants from
around the world, it's easy to feel that city life
has been put on hold. A sign at the entrance
asks that you treat the gardens as if they were
a museum, but don't feel bad about getting
comfortable with a book for a while. The
building in the middle of the gardens is used
as a gallery space.

### Real Observatorio Nacional
*C/Alfonso XII 3 (91 527 01 07, www.ign.es/rom/
visitas/index.html). Metro Atocha.* **Open**
*Guided tours (by appt only) Oct-May 4.30pm
Fri; noon, 4.30pm Sat; noon Sun. June-Sept
5.30pm Fri; noon Sat (also 5.30pm in June);
noon Sun.* **Admission** *€5; €3 reductions; free
under-3s.* **Map** *p141 O18.*

One of Charles III's scientific institutions, the
Observatorio was completed after his death in
1790. Beautifully proportioned, it is Madrid's
finest neoclassical building, designed by
Juan de Villanueva. It still contains a working
telescope, which can only be seen by prior
request. One room is also open to the public,
as part of a guided tour.

### San Jerónimo el Real
*C/Moreto 4 (91 420 30 78). Metro Banco de
España.* **Open** *Sept-June 10am-1pm, 5-8pm
Mon-Sat; 9.30am-2.30pm, 5.30-8.30pm*
*Sun. July, Aug 10am-1pm, 6-8.30pm daily.*
**Map** *p141 N15.*

Founded in 1464 and rebuilt for Queen
Isabella in 1503, this church near the Retiro
was particularly favoured by the Spanish
monarchs, and used for state ceremonies.
Most of the original building was destroyed
during the Napoleonic Wars, and the present
church is largely a reconstruction that was
undertaken between 1848 and 1883. The
cloisters at the side of the church have been
taken over for use as galleries by the Prado.

## Restaurants

### ♥ La Castela €€
*C/Doctor Castelo 22 (91 574 00 15, www.
restaurantelacastela.com). Metro Ibiza.*
**Open** *noon-4.30pm, 9pm-midnight Mon-Sat;
noon-4.30pm Sun. Closed Aug.* **Map** *p141
Q13* ❶ *Spanish*

The neighbourhood just east of the Retiro
has recently become something of a gastro
hunting ground, but La Castela was ahead of
the curve, and has been around for decades.
Smart but thoroughly authentic, with a zinc
bar, pillars and marble tables, it serves top-
notch tapas at a noisy bar area, or you can sit
in a quieter dining room for dishes such as
sirloin with sweet sherry and foie, or bream
baked in salt.

## Cafés & bars

### El Botánico
*C/Ruiz de Alarcón 27 (91 420 23 42). Metro
Banco de España.* **Open** *8am-2am daily.*
**Map** *p141 N16* ❶

Confusingly, this quiet bar-restaurant
actually sits on C/Espalter, overlooking the
botanical gardens. Tucked away from the
tourist drag, it's very quiet considering its
proximity to the Prado, and has a peaceful,
shaded terrace. It's a good spot for breakfast,
and there are tapas later in the day.

## Shops & services
The shop at **Museo del Prado** (*see p144*) is a
great source of gifts and souvenirs.

### Objetos de Arte Toledano
*Paseo del Prado 10 (91 429 50 00, www.
armasmedievales.com). Metro Banco de
España.* **Open** *10am-8.30pm Mon-Sat.* **Map**
*p141 M15* ❶ *Gifts & souvenirs*

Located across from the Prado, this souvenir
shop par excellence sells traditional
*españoladas* such as fans, and flamenco and
bullfighting dolls. A great place to find that
gift for your kitsch-loving friends.

# SALAMANCA & AROUND

## Paseo de Recoletos and Paseo de la Castellana

While other cities have rivers cutting through them as navigational points of reference, Madrid has two great avenues: the Gran Vía and its continuation, C/Alcalá, running east–west, and the **Paseo del Prado** – which becomes the **Paseo de Recoletos** and the **Paseo de la Castellana** as it runs north.

The stretch north of Cibeles, Paseo de Recoletos, was mostly added in the 1830s and '40s. The curiously grand marble palace a little further north on the right, which is now the **Fundación BBVA** (a cultural foundation), was built in the 1840s to be the residence of the Marqués de Salamanca, 19th-century Madrid's huckster-in-chief (*see p156*). It famously had the first flushing toilets in Madrid, an amenity the marquis later offered to residents in his new housing developments.

At the north end of Recoletos, on the right, stands the huge building that houses the **Biblioteca Nacional** and, behind it, the **Museo Arqueológico Nacional**. The most ambitious project of the reign of Isabel II, the building was commissioned in 1865, but only completed in 1892. It overlooks the **Plaza de Colón**, which has a statue of Columbus in the central roundabout. The square houses the **Fernán Gómez** theatre and arts centre.

In 1860, when he designed Madrid's 'extension', Carlos María de Castro took the significant decision, since the Paseo del Prado and Paseo de Recoletos were already there, to continue along the same route with the main avenue of the new district. Thus the Castellana was born. Until the Republic of 1931 demolished Madrid's old racetrack, the avenue reached only as far as C/Joaquín Costa. Today it snakes away freely northwards, through thickets of office blocks (*see p154* Changing the Skyline). It also contains, near the junction with C/Juan Bravo (location of the **Museo Arte Público de Madrid**), Madrid's 'beach' of upmarket terrace bars, at the height of fashion in the mid 1990s and still thronged with *pijos* (akin to London's Sloanes; *see p156* Salamanca's pijos). To the east is the Salamanca district, the heart of affluent Madrid and the city's most upscale shopping area.

## Salamanca

In the mid 19th century, as it became evident that Spanish cities needed to expand beyond their old walls, attempts were made to ensure that this happened in an orderly way. Madrid and Barcelona had plans approved for *ensanches* ('extensions'). Carlos María de Castro's 1860 plan for Madrid envisaged the expansion of the city north and east in a regular grid pattern, with restrictions on building height and public open spaces at regular intervals within each block to ensure a healthy, harmonious landscape. The problem, though, was that for a good while few members of Madrid's middle classes seemed to have the money or motivation to invest in such a scheme, and

Paseo de Recoletos

# Changing the Skyline

*The buildings that jostle for attention along the Paseo de la Castellana*

▶ *Sights along the upper Castellana are listed here from bottom to top, south to north. The metro system partly avoids the avenue, but the 27 bus runs up and down the whole stretch, covering the Paseo del Prado, Recoletos and the Castellana.*

In the 1970s and '80s, banks and insurance companies vied with each other to commission trendy architects to create corporate showcases along the upper Castellana; see the **Bankinter** building at No.29 and **Bankunión** at No.46. Beyond the latter, the **Museo de Ciencias Naturales** is set back from the road on a grassy hill; further still, on the left, is the Kafka-esque grey bulk of the enormous **Nuevos Ministerios** government complex. Begun in 1932, it contains many government ministries, and is one of the largest projects bequeathed by the Spanish Republic to Madrid. It was designed by a team led by Secundino Zuazo, chief architect of the Gran Madrid plan, in a monolithic '30s rationalist style; then, after the victory of General Franco, the same architect added to the still-unfinished building some curving, traditionalist details more to the taste of the new regime. Inside it has a park-like garden, open to the public.

Beyond that, a huge branch of the Corte Inglés signals your arrival at the **AZCA** complex. The Asociación Zona Comercial A, known to some as 'Little Manhattan', is a glitzy skyscraper development first projected during the Franco regime's industrial heyday in the '60s, which gained extra vigour in

Torre Picasso

democratic Spain's 1980s boom to become a symbol of Madrid yuppiedom. At its centre is the **Plaza Picasso**, a small park, and amid the office blocks is a chic shopping mall, restaurants and other facilities to make it a self-contained 'workers' city'. At its north end is the **Torre Picasso**, designed by Japanese architect Minoru Yamasaki (also responsible for New York's World Trade Center) in 1988 and, at 157 metres (515 feet), one of Madrid's tallest buildings. Beyond it is the circular **Torre Europa**.

A little further up again, opposite each other, is the Real Madrid stadium, **Estadio Bernabéu** (*see p169*), and the **Palacio de Congresos** conference centre. By this time, the view up the Paseo de la Castellana is dominated by the two leaning towers officially known as the **Puerta de Europa** at Plaza Castilla. These remarkable smoked-glass blocks, leaning in at 15 degrees off the perpendicular, are perhaps the greatest monument to Spain's 1980s boom. They were begun with finance from the Kuwait Investment Office (the towers are often called the **Torres KIO**) and left unfinished for years after a financial scandal in 1992. With their rather phallic fountain in the middle, they have joined the landmarks of modern Madrid.

Puerta de Europa

# SALAMANCA NORTH

## Restaurants

2 Salón Cascabel
3 Tepic

## Tapas

1 Estay
2 Hevia
3 José Luis

## Shops & services

1 ABC Serrano
2 Adolfo Domínguez
3 Agatha Ruiz de la Prada
5 La Boulette
7 Centro de Anticuarios Lagasca
9 Don Deporte
11 El Jardín de Serrano
12 Joaquín Berao
13 Lavinia
14 Loewe
15 Mantequerías Bravo
16 Mercado de la Paz
18 ¡Oh, qué Luna!
19 Purificación García

© Copyright Time Out Group 2018

they preferred to stay within the cramped, noisy Old City. That Madrid's *ensanche* got off the ground at all was due to a banker, politician and speculator notorious for his dubious business practices, the Marqués de Salamanca.

The marquis had previously built his own vast residence on Paseo de Recoletos, now the **Fundación BBVA** (*see p153*). He spent one of the several fortunes he made and lost in his lifetime building a first line of rectangular blocks along C/Serrano, from C/Goya up to Ramón de la Cruz. However, his ambitions overstretched his resources, the apartments proved expensive for local buyers, and he went terminally bankrupt in 1867. Nevertheless, it is to the rogue Marqués, not the old Castilian university town, that Madrid's smartest *barrio* owes its name.

It was only after the Restoration of 1874 that Madrid's wealthier citizens really began to appreciate the benefits of wider streets and residences with more class than the musty old neighbourhoods could supply. Once the idea caught on, the exodus proceeded apace, and the core of Salamanca was built up by 1900. The wealthiest families of all built individual palaces along the lower stretch of the Paseo de la Castellana, in a wild variety of styles: French imperial, Italian Renaissance, neo-Mudéjar. The block on C/Juan Bravo between Calles Lagasca and Velázquez contains a magnificent example: the neo-Baroque palace of the **Marqueses de Amboage**, now the Italian Embassy. From the C/Velázquez side it's possible to see the extraordinarily lush gardens. Other mansions are scattered around the district, tucked in between apartment blocks. Those who couldn't quite afford their own mansion moved into giant apartments in the streets behind. The area has been the centre of conservative, affluent Madrid ever since.

Salamanca is a busy area, with streets that often boom with traffic, and so the best time to explore it is Saturday morning, when the shops are open but traffic has slackened. Streets such as calles Jorge Juan, Ortega y Gasset, Goya and Juan Bravo yield top designers, art galleries and dealers in wine, silver or superior leather goods. Salamanca also has its own social scene, based around C/Juan Bravo, with shiny, smart bars and discos. Towards the east end of C/Goya there is a slightly more affordable shopping area; on the very eastern flank of Salamanca is Madrid's bullring, **Las Ventas**; and south of here is the numismatic **Museo Casa de la Moneda**.

Art buffs are advised to head for the marble tower with sculpture garden at C/Castelló 77, base for the **Fundación Juan March**'s first-rate collection of modern art, which also hosts great contemporary art shows and free classical concerts. For private art galleries, C/Claudio Coello, parallel to C/Serrano, is the city's most elegant centre. At the north end of Serrano is the eclectic **Museo Lázaro Galdiano**.

The blocks of Serrano, Claudio Coello and Lagasca below C/Ortega y Gasset are the oldest part of Salamanca, the first section built up by the Marqués in the 1860s. Streets here are narrower, traffic less intense and shops closer together. There are charming buildings with intriguing details – such as the glass-galleried block on the corner of Claudio Coello and C/Ayala. The block between Claudio Coello and Lagasca on C/Ayala also contains the **Mercado de la Paz**, Salamanca's excellent market.

## Sights & museums

### Fundación Juan March
*C/Castelló 77 (91 435 42 40, www.march. es). Metro Núñez de Balboa. **Open** Mid Sept-June 11am-8pm Mon-Sat; 10am-2pm Sun. Guided tours in English (by appointment only) 11am-1pm Wed. **Admission** free. **Map** p155 Q9.*

This cultural foundation, set up by the wealthy financier Juan March in 1955, is one of the most important in Europe. Each year, a couple of major exhibitions are held here, and a decent selection of the foundation's 1,300 works of contemporary Spanish art is also on permanent display.

### Fundación Mapfre – Sala Bárbara de Braganza
*C/Bárbara de Braganza 13 (91 581 46 09, www.fundacionmapfre.org/fundacion/en/exhibitions/barbara-braganza-hall). Metro Colón or Banco de España. **Open** 2pm-8pm Mon; 10am-8pm Tue-Sat; 11am-7pm Sun. Closed June-Sept. **Admission** €3; €2 reductions; €5 combined admission with the Sala Recoletos; free under-16s. Free to all 2-8pm Mon. **Map** p141 N12.*

# ❤ Museo Lázaro Galdiano

*C/Serrano 122 (91 561 60 84, www.flg.es). Metro Gregorio Marañón.* **Open** *10am-4.30pm Tue-Sat; 10am-3pm Sun.* **Admission** *€6; €3 reductions; free under-12s. Free to all 3.30-4.30pm Tue-Sat, 2-3pm Sun.* **Map** *p155 P6.*

This unjustifiably little-known museum holds the extraordinarily eclectic collection of 15,000 paintings and objets d'art, covering 24 centuries, that was accumulated over 70 years by the financier and bibliophile José Lázaro Galdiano (1862-1947). Its holdings include paintings by Goya and Bosch, an important collection of work from the Dutch and English schools, with paintings by Jan Breughel and Constable, and some wonderful Renaissance ornamental metalwork, as well as suits of armour, weaponry, jewellery and illuminated manuscripts.

The four-storey mansion and its gardens are a sight in themselves. Be sure to take the creaky antique lift – with its original red velvet banquette – up to the first floor, where you can see the carefully restored ceiling frescoes and some of the original furniture in what were once the dining and billiard rooms.

Within the museum, temporary exhibitions – in various mediums and across a wide range of subjects –are included in the ticket price, and in the grounds is a further exhibition space, free to enter. It's worth exploring the website for more detail on some of the paintings, most notably an interactive look at the secrets hidden within Hieronymus Bosch's *St John the Baptist in Meditation.*

This striking space hosts four photography exhibitions every year, showing works by celebrated artists such as Cartier-Bresson and Paul Strand, as well as contemporary photographers such as Fazak Sheikh and Lynne Cohen.

## Fundación Mapfre – Sala Recoletos

*Paseo de Recoletos 23 (91 581 61 00, www. fundacionmapfre.org/fundacion/en/ exhibitions/recoletos-hall). Metro Colón or Banco de España. **Open** 2pm-8pm Mon; 10am-8pm Tue-Sat; 11am-7pm Sun. **Admission** €3; €2 reductions; €5 combined admission with the Sala Bárbara de Braganza; free under-16s. **Map** p141 N12.*

Set in the Palacio de la Duquesa de Medina de las Torres, the Mapfre shows some of the city's most interesting exhibitions – in various media. Until 2021, however, its greatest attraction is the 'Espacio Miró', a stunning collection of over 60 paintings ceded by the artist's family, which also includes wire sculptures by Miró's great friend Alexander Calder.

## Museo Arqueológico Nacional

*C/Serrano 13 (91 577 79 12, man.mcu.es). Metro Serrano. **Open** 9.30am-8pm Tue-Sat; 9.30am-3pm Sun. **Admission** €3. Free after 2pm Sat & all day Sun. **Map** p141 O12.*

One of Madrid's oldest museums, dating back to 1867, the Museo Arqueológico Nacional shares the same building as the Biblioteca Nacional and Museo del Libro. It traces the evolution of human cultures, from prehistoric times up to the 15th century, and the collection of artefacts includes finds from the Iberian, Celtic, Greek, Egyptian, Punic, Roman, Paleochristian, Visigothic and Muslim cultures. Remarkably, the great majority of pieces came from excavations carried out within Spain, illustrating the extraordinary continuity and diversity of human settlement in the Iberian peninsula. Begin in the basement, which holds palaeontological material such as skulls, tombs and a mammoth's tusks, still attached to its skull. Some of the most interesting relics are from the area around Madrid itself, such as the many 4,000-year-old neolithic bell-shaped pottery bowls. The first floor holds the museum's most famous possession, the *Dama de Elche*, the stone bust of an Iberian priestess, believed to date from 500BC. In the garden, steps lead underground to a reproduction of the renowned Altamira prehistoric cave paintings in Cantabria.

## Museo Arte Público de Madrid

*Paseo de la Castellana 41. Metro Rubén Darío. **Admission** free. **Map** p155 P8.*

An unconventional museum, this 1970s outdoor space at the junction of the Castellana with C/Juan Bravo was the brainchild of engineers José Antonio Fernández Ordoñez and Julio Martínez Calzón. Designing a bridge across the avenue, they thought the space underneath would be a good art venue, and sculptor Eusebio Sempere convinced fellow artists to donate their work. All the major names in late 20th-century Spanish sculpture are represented – including Pablo Serrano, Miró and Chillida – and much of their work is spectacular, especially the dynamic stainless-steel *Món per a infants* ('A world for children') by Andreu Alfaro and the cascade by Sempere that forms the museum's centrepiece.

## Museo Casa de la Moneda

*C/Dr Esquerdo 36 (91 566 65 44, www. museocasadelamoneda.es). Metro O'Donnell. **Open** 10am-5.30pm Tue-Fri; 10am-2pm Sat, Sun. **Admission** free.*

This museum, dedicated to coins and currency, has a huge collection, dating from the 18th century, among the most important in the world. The history of coins is represented in chronological order, and complemented by various displays of seals, bank notes, engravings, rare books and medals, plus around 10,000 sketches and drawings from Spain, Italy and Flanders, dating from the 16th to the 18th centuries.

## Museo de Cera (Wax Museum)

*Paseo de Recoletos 41 (91 319 26 49, www. museoceramadrid.com). Metro Colón. **Open** 10am-2.30pm, 4.30-8.30pm Mon-Fri; 10am-8.30pm Sat, Sun. **Admission** €12-€19. No cards. **Map** p155 N11.*

Madame Tussauds it isn't (there's no queueing for starters), yet this waxwork museum still has a certain tacky charm. The usual collection of rogues, celebrities and politicians includes the Beatles, Clark Gable and Melania Trump – but doesn't include Donald. Sad.

## Museo de la Biblioteca Nacional

*Biblioteca Nacional, Paseo de Recoletos 20 (91 580 77 59, www.bne.es). Metro Colón. **Open** 10am-9pm Tue-Sat; 10am-2pm Sun. **Admission** free. **Map** p141 O12.*

With over three million volumes, Spain's national library has been called the 'Prado of paper'. Among the wealth of printed matter is every work published in Spain since 1716, Greek papyri, Arab, Hebrew and Greek manuscripts, Nebrija's first Spanish grammar, bibles, and drawings by Goya, Velázquez, Rembrandt and many others. Given the precious and fragile nature of the texts, access was limited to scholars, but in 1996 the administration opened this museum to allow the public a glimpse of the library's riches. The displays are conceived as interactive, steering visitors through bibliographical history via multimedia applications including laser shows, videos and holographs.

## Plaza de Toros de Las Ventas

*C/Alcalá 237 (91 356 22 00, museum 91 725 18 57, www.las-ventas.com). Metro Ventas.* **Open** *Museum 10am-6pm daily (until 4pm on fight days).* **Admission** *Museum free.*

More than 22,000 spectators can catch a bullfight in this, Spain's largest arena, completed in 1929. Like most early 20th-century bullrings, it is in neo-Mudéjar style, with often playful use of ceramic tiling. Around it there is ample open space to accommodate the crowds and food vendors, so it's easy to get a good look at the exterior. It's not necessary to go to a *corrida* to see the ring from within. When the bulls are back on the ranch, concerts are often held here, and alongside the ring there is the small Museo Taurino. The museum holds portraits of famous matadors, as well as *trajes de luces* (suits of lights), including the pink-and-gold outfit worn by the legendary Manolete on the afternoon of his death in the ring in 1947. Among the 18th-century paintings

is a portrait of *torero* Joaquín Rodriguez Costillares.

## Teatro Fernán Gómez Centro Cultural de la Villa

*Plaza de Colón 4 (91 436 25 40, www. teatrofernangomez.es). Metro Colón.* **Open** *Exhibitions 10am-9pm Tue-Sun.* **Admission** *Exhibitions free.* **Map** *p155 O11.*

Previously called the Centro Cultural de la Villa, the city council's only purpose-built cultural centre has been renamed after the late Spanish actor and director Fernán Gómez, who died in 2007. On offer is a mixed bag of theatre, puppets, opera and *zarzuelas* in the summer, as well as art exhibitions, usually featuring important Hispanic artists.

## WiZink Center (Palacio de Deportes de la Comunidad de Madrid)

*Avda Felipe II s/n (91 444 99 49, www. wizinkcenter.es). Metro Goya.*

This state-of-the-art 16,000-capacity sports venue was inaugurated in early 2005 and occupies the site where its predecessor stood until it was destroyed by fire four years previously. It is a multipurpose arena that can host a wide range of indoor sports thanks to a system of retractable stands. It's

Plaza de Toros de Las Ventas

THE RETIRO & SALAMANCA

the home arena of one of the less successful of Madrid's basketball clubs, Estudiantes, which nevertheless has passionate supporters. Among them, the most vociferous are a group known as 'La Demencia', who make for a great atmosphere home or away. You can order tickets (€10-€60) at www.clubestudiantes.com or through the WiZink website. Hoop stars Real Madrid Baloncesto also play here, have a trophy record to match that of the football team, and, under the guidance of head coach Pablo Lasal, have been on top form in recent years. Expect goals galore and exuberant professional cheerleaders. As well as sports, you can catch spectacles at WiZink such as *Disney on Ice* or any number of big-name concerts; Lady Gaga, Rihanna and J-Lo have all performed here.

### In the know
### Basketball

Basketball is Spain's second most popular sport, and Madrid has two of the country's top teams: **Estudiantes** (see *above*) is the city's best-supported club, while **Real Madrid** (see *p168*), affiliated to the football club of the same name, is traditionally the more successful. Both teams regularly qualify for the all-important league play-offs that run in May to eventually decide the national champions.

## Restaurants

### ♥ Salón Cascabel €€
*C/Serrano 52 (in El Corte Inglés), (91 432 54 90, www.saloncascabel.com). Metro Serrano. **Open** 1.15pm-midnight Mon-Wed, Sun; 1.15pm-2am Fri, Sat. **Map** p155 P10* ❷
*Mexican*

A groundbreaking haute Mexican restaurant/tapas bar, sitting in a former ironmonger's on the top floor of El Corte Inglés (the view is spectacular). The vibe is glam disco food-truck, but the food is impeccable, from the humble guacamole to the Flintstones-style femur out of which you scoop creamy roast bone marrow, the house speciality. Ingredients are mostly grown and smoked on their own land – pick up a jar of the fab chipotle sauce when you leave..

### Tepic €€
*Ayalá 14 (91 522 08 50, www.tepic.es). Metro Serrano. **Open** 1pm-1.15am Mon-Thur; 1pm-2.15am Fri, Sat; 1pm-5pm Sun. **Map** p155 O10* ❸ *Mexican*

The name comes from the capital of Nayarit state in Mexico, and a huge photo of a typical Mexican city takes up one wall of

this chic restaurant. There is no doubt about what you're going to eat here: quesadillas, guacamole, tacos, enchiladas, enmoladas... all of a much higher standard than at most Mexican joints in Madrid, plus the margaritas are so good, there's no way you're going to have just one.

## Tapas
### Estay
*C/Hermosilla 46 (91 578 04 70, www.estayrestaurante.com). Metro Velázquez. **Open** 8am-12.30am Mon-Thur; 1-4.30pm, 8pm-1.30am Fri, Sat. **Map** p155 Q11* ❶

The bright, air-conditioned interior, usually filled with baying young mothers heavily laden with shopping bags, does not immediately suggest gastronomic promise. Stick with the place, however, and you'll enjoy scrumptious and sophisticated tapas and cheap wines by the glass.

### Hevia
*C/Serrano 118 (91 562 30 75, www.heviamadrid.com). Metro Gregorio Marañón. **Open** 10am-midnight Mon-Sat. Closed 1wk Aug. **Map** p155 P7* ❷

A quiet, well-heeled crowd frequents this smart bar. Tapas are correspondingly sophisticated – foie gras, caviar, crab and duck liver pâté – and pricey. In summer, the tables outside can prove irresistible.

### ♥ José Luis
*C/Serrano 89 (91 563 09 58, www.joseluis.es). Metro Núñez de Balboa. **Open** 9am-1am Mon-Sat; noon-1am Sun. **Map** p155 P7* ❸

Despite its relatively anodyne interior, this is probably one of Madrid's most famous tapas bars and namechecked in a song by the Catalan folk singer Serrat. The food here is little changed since the 1950s and of a high standard. If your appetite is up to it, try the superb *brascada* (sirloin with ham and onions). **Other locations** throughout the city.

## Cafés & bars
### ♥ Café Gijón
*Paseo de Recoletos 21 (91 521 54 25, www.cafegijon.com). Metro Banco de España or Colón. **Open** 7.30am-1.30am daily. **Map** p141 N12* ❷

Still charming after all these years, this is Madrid's definitive literary café, open since 1888. It still holds poetry *tertulias* on Monday nights, and publishes a magazine filled with doodles and thoughts from visiting writers. A pianist tinkles the ivories to a packed terrace in summer.

### James Joyce

C/Alcalá 59 (91 575 49 01, www.jamesjoycemadrid.com). Metro Banco de España. **Open** noon-2am Mon-Thur; noon-2.30am Fri; 11am-2.30am Sat; 11am-2am Sun. **Map** p141 N13 ❸

This is the Madrid outpost of what is now a global chain of Oirish theme pubs. With both Guinness and Murphy's on tap, pub grub, chatty staff and plenty of rugby and Premier League matches showing on two big screens and three TVs, it's all much as you'd expect. Of more interest, perhaps, is the fact that the pub sits on the site of the historic Café Lion, a haunt of post-Civil War literati.

### El Pavellón del Espejo

Paseo de Recoletos 31 (91 308 23 47,). Metro Colón. **Open** 8am-midnight daily. **Map** p141 N12 ❹

Not nearly as historic as the neighbouring Gijón, although it may look it: when it opened in 1978, 'The Mirror' set out to be the art nouveau bar Madrid never had, with positively Parisian 1900s decor. Its terrace bar out on the Paseo de Recoletos occupies a splendid glass pavilion reminiscent of a giant Tiffany lamp. Fashionable and comfortable, it's a good spot for breakfast, but the tapas can be mediocre.

## Shops & services

### ABC Serrano

C/Serrano 61 & Paseo de la Castellana 34 (91 577 50 31, www.abcserrano.com). Metro Rubén Darío. **Open** 10am-9pm Mon-Sat. **Map** p155 P8 ❶ Shopping centre

Occupying the building that once housed the ABC newspaper, this upmarket and perfectly located shopping mall has eight floors. Four of them are dedicated to designer and high street fashion, as well as sportswear, jewellery, crafts and electronics. There are three restaurants on the upper floors, a café on the ground floor and a lively summer terraza on the fourth, plus a gym at the top.

### Adolfo Domínguez

C/Serrano 96 (91 576 70 53, www.adolfodominguez.es). Metro Rubén Dario. **Open** 10am-8.30pm Mon-Sat. **Map** p155 P8 ❷ Fashion

Simple, classic pieces from the well-known Galician designer. The suits are well cut and long-lasting, while the accessories and shoes are also some of the brand's strong points. **Other locations** throughout the city.

### ♥ Agatha Ruiz de la Prada

C/Serrano 27 (91 319 05 01, www.agatharuizdelaprada.com). Metro Serrano. **Open** Sept-July 10am-8.30pm Mon-Sat. Aug 10am-2pm, 5-8pm Mon-Fri, 10am-2pm Sat. **Map** p155 P10 ❸ Fashion

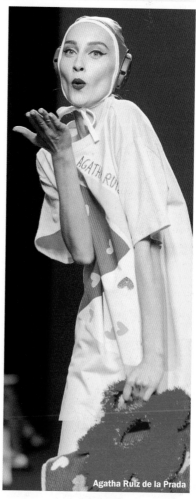

Agatha Ruiz de la Prada

Loud, colourful patterns characterise this designer's work, with many pieces emblazoned with her trademark hearts and flowers. The childrenswear range is hugely popular, as are the homewares.

### BD Madrid
*C/Villanueva 5 (91 435 06 27, www.bdmadrid. com). Metro Serrano. **Open** 9.30am-1.30pm, 4.30-8pm Mon-Fri; 10am-2pm Sat. Closed Aug. **Map** p141 O12* ❹ *Homeware*

BD carries a stunning selection of contemporary furniture designs from Spanish and international names, many with a retro feel. The company is now producing its own pieces, including a kitchen range. There are hefty price tags, but it's worth a visit if only to peruse.

### La Boulette
*Stands 63-68, Mercado de La Paz, C/Ayala 28 (91 431 77 25, www.laboulette.com). Metro Serrano. **Open** 9am-8pm Mon-Fri; 9am-2.30pm Sat. **Map** p155 P10* ❺ *Food & drink*

La Boulette probably has the largest selection of cheeses in Madrid and possibly the country, with over 400 varieties, both Spanish and imported, on sale. The range of goods in the charcuterie section is similarly impressive.

### Camper
*C/Serrano 24 (91 578 25 60, www.camper. com). Metro Serrano. **Open** 10am-9pm Mon-Sat; noon-8pm Sun. **Map** p141 O12* ❻ *Fashion*

Branches of the Mallorcan family firm continue to spring up all over the city (and

Lavinia

all over the world). At this one, two large plinths display the entire men's and women's collection – brightly coloured, fun shoes and sandals. **Other locations** throughout the city.

### Centro de Anticuarios Lagasca
*C/Lagasca 36 (91 577 37 52). Metro Serrano. **Open** 11am-2pm, 5-8.30pm Mon-Fri; 11am-2pm Sat. Closed Aug. **Map** p155 P11* ❼ *Antiques*

An upmarket antiques arcade selling furniture, art and ornaments of every stripe.

### Chi Spa
*C/Conde de Aranda 14 (91 578 13 40, thechispa.com). Metro Retiro. **Open** 10am-9pm Mon-Fri; 10am-6pm Sat, Sun. **Map** p141 P12* ❽ *Spa*

A sleek, sophisticated space that has separate areas for men and women offering specialised body and relaxation treatments, massages with essential oils and spices, hydrotherapy and aromatherapy.

### Don Deporte
*C/Goya 50 (91 575 88 68). Metro Goya. **Open** 10.15am-2pm, 5-8.30pm Mon-Sat. Closed Aug. **Map** p155 R11* ❾ *Fashion*

Selling shirts and other memorabilia from over 500 clubs worldwide, Don Deporte can usually kit out fans of even the most obscure teams.

### Don Juego
*C/Alcalá 113 (91 435 37 24, www.donjuego. es). Metro Príncipe de Vergara. **Open** 10am-2.30pm, 5-9pm Mon-Sat; 11am-3pm Sun. **Map** p141 Q12* ❿ *Gifts & souvenirs*

This shop specialises in board games for both kids and adults; as well as mah-jong, solitaire, Chinese chequers and chess, it stocks Go.

### El Jardín de Serrano
*C/Goya 6-8 (91 577 00 12, www. jardindeserrano.es). Metro Serrano. **Open** 9.30am-9.30pm Mon-Sat. **Map** p155 P11* ⓫ *Shopping centre*

This Salamanca mall may be small but it's a retail gem, with designer boutiques, expensive shoe shops and a classy café.

### Joaquín Berao
*C/Lagasca 44 (91 577 28 28, www. joaquinberao.com). Metro Serrano. **Open** Sept-July 10am-8.30pm Mon-Sat. Aug 10am-2pm, 5-8.30pm Mon-Fri; 10am-2.30pm Sat. **Map** p155 P11* ⓬ *Fashion*

Chunky, twisted and contorted, but also fluidly elegant, Joaquín Berao's solid silver bracelets, necklaces, earrings and chokers are increasingly the choice of those in the know.

Mantequerías Bravo

### ♥ Lavinia

*C/José Ortega y Gasset 16 (91 426 06 04, www. lavinia.es). Metro Nuñez de Balboa.* **Open** *10am-9pm Mon-Sat.* **Map** *p155 P9* ⑬ *Food & drink*

No oenophile should miss visiting Lavinia, which claims to be Europe's largest wine shop. In stark contrast to many of Madrid's dusty old *bodegas*, it's bright, airy and spacious, and staff are knowledgeable and helpful.

### Loewe

*C/Serrano 34 (91 577 60 56, www.loewe.com). Metro Serrano.* **Open** *10am-8.30pm Mon-Sat; 11am-8pm Sun.* **Map** *p155 O11* ⑭ *Fashion*

This is the flagship store for the world-famous, elite Spanish leather goods company, selling bags, shoes, cases and an expanding range of clothes for men and women. **Other locations** throughout the city.

### ♥ Mantequerías Bravo

*C/Ayala 24 (91 575 80 72). Metro Serrano.* **Open** *9.30am-2.30pm, 5.30-8.30pm Mon-Fri; 9.30am-2.30pm Sat. Closed Aug.* **Map** *p155 P10* ⑮ *Food & drink*

A marvellous selection of foodstuffs is on sale in this Salamanca shop, including meats and cheeses, wines and spirits, and coffees and teas. Homesick Brits will be pleased with imports such as English mustard and cream crackers.

### Mercado de la Paz

*C/Ayala 28 (91 435 07 43, www. mercadodelapaz.es). Metro Serrano.* **Map** *p155 P10* ⑯ *Market*

A high-end market, with a dazzling range of products. Don't miss gourmet cheese stall La Boulette (*see p162*).

### ¡Oh, qué Luna!

*C/Ayala 32 (91 431 37 25, www.ohqueluna. com). Metro Serrano.* **Open** *10am-8.30pm Mon-Fri; 11am-2pm, 5-8.30pm Sat.* **Map** *p155 P10* ⑱ *Fashion*

Glam, sexy lingerie, negligées and dressing gowns. It also does a line in bedlinen and swimwear.

### Purificación García

*C/Serrano 28 (91 435 80 13, www. purificaciongarcia.es). Metro Serrano.* **Open** *10am-8.30pm Mon-Sat.* **Map** *p155 O11* ⑲ *Fashion*

Purificación García is where the capital's older but elegant woman heads when she wants something smart for the office. Well cut and using natural materials, the clothes are very well priced for the quality of the fabrics. **Other locations** throughout the city.

> **In the know**
> **Salamanca shopping**
>
> Salamanca is a shopper's paradise, with several specialities. If you're all about labels, then this is the place to be, in particular C/Serrano, where on the same block you will find Loewe, Yves Saint Laurent and La Perla, as well as smaller designer boutiques throughout the area. On and around C/Claudio Coello are lots of upmarket, specialist antique dealers. A great place for cheap second-hand books, from rare editions to remainders, is the line of kiosks on Cuesta de Moyano, (also known as C/Claudio Moyano), by the Jardín Botánico.

# Beyond the Centre

Building restrictions over the centuries have kept even Madrid's more far-flung attractions within reasonably easy reach of the city centre. Many visitors never stray out of the old city and the triangle defined by the big three art museums. That's all very well – and if this is your first visit it's certainly a reasonable decision – but go further afield and you can take in the Madrid skyline by cable car, visit an authentic Egyptian temple or inspect General Franco's old home. The more distant areas are a welcome green escape from Madrid's centre, with the woods and hills around El Pardo serving as a refuge for wildlife and humans seeking respite from the summer heat. But this is Madrid, so there's some magnificent art to see as well, from frescoes adorning Goya's tomb to Europe's finest collection of pre-Columbian American art. And away from the attractions are the quiet pleasures of suburbs such as Vallecas, secure in their own identity.

## ❤ Don't miss

**1 Casa de Campo** *p167*
Madrid's green lung is a rambling space with acres of parkland.

**2 Parque El Capricho** *p170*
A delightful 18th-century garden that's worth the metro ride.

**3 Matadero Madrid** *p178*
The spectacular reinvention of a former slaughterhouse.

**4 Museo del Ferrocarril** *p181*
Quirky, old-time train museum.

Faro de Moncloa *p169*

# NORTH & WEST

## Argüelles and Moncloa

West of Conde Duque lie the districts known as Argüelles and Moncloa. **Argüelles**, properly speaking, is the grid of streets between Plaza de España, C/Princesa, Plaza de Moncloa and Paseo del Pintor Rosales. The Paseo is known for its *terrazas* – open-air bars that are ideal for taking the air on summer evenings. The Paseo sits above the **Parque del Oeste**. Designed by Cecilio Rodríguez in the 1900s, it's one of Madrid's most attractive spaces. The park was completely relaid after forming part of the front line in the Civil War. **La Rosaleda**, the rose garden, is beautiful in spring. The **Montaña del Príncipe Pío**, at its southern end, is one of the city's highest points, with great views of the Palacio Real and the incongruous **Templo de Debod**, an Egyptian temple that was presented to Spain in 1968. This was the site of the Montaña barracks, the Nationalists' main stronghold at the start of the Civil War, before it was demolished and the hill incorporated into the park. Below the Teleférico stop a path leads to the **Ermita de San Antonio de la Florida** with its Goya frescoes, and beyond that, the river. The fountain below the Teleférico used to preside over the roundabout at Príncipe Pío station, but was moved to the park in 1994. In its place by the station there is now the **Puerta de San Vicente** – an entirely new, quite convincing reconstruction of the 18th-century gate that once stood on this side of the city. On Sundays Madrid's Andean community takes over the Parque del Oeste, organising volleyball tournaments and picnics; after dark, the area around the fountain becomes a prostitution zone.

In the southern corner of the district, just off Plaza de España, is the **Museo Cerralbo**. In the opposite, northern corner, unmissable at the end of C/Princesa, stands one of the biggest, most significant creations of the Franco regime, the **Ministerio del Aire** or Air Ministry, built in the 1950s, in kitsch Castilian Baroque style and popularly known as the 'Monasterio del Aire', because of its resemblance to El Escorial.

Alongside the Ministry is Plaza de Moncloa, Moncloa metro station and the departure points for many bus services to towns north and west of Madrid. There is also Franco's fake Roman triumphal arch, built to commemorate victory in the Civil War. To the north of the *plaza*, in the **Moncloa** district, lies the sprawling campus of the Universidad Complutense, the **Ciudad Universitaria**. Within the university, specific attractions are the **Museo de América** and the **Faro de Moncloa** observation tower and, beyond that, the **Museo del Traje**.

## Chamberí

Directly north of Malasaña is the *barrio* of Chamberí, one of the first working-class districts outside the walls to be built up in the second half of the 19th century. Consequently, and generally justifiably, it has become one of the few areas outside the old city considered to have genuine *castizo* character (*see p106*). A pleasant place to while away an evening in this area is the circular **Plaza de Olavide**, ringed with pavement cafés. Just to the east of here is the charming **Museo Sorolla**. On the north side of Chamberí is Madrid's main water supply, the Canal de Isabel II. On C/Santa Engracia, a neo-Mudéjar water tower has been converted into a unique photography gallery, the **Sala del Canal de Isabel II**.

## Tetuán and Chamartín

North of Chamberí is **Tetuán**, a modern working area centred on C/Bravo Murillo, and, to the east, **Chamartín**, which contains the major business area of modern Madrid. The main point of interest for visitors is the local market, the **Mercado de Maravillas**, at C/Bravo Murillo 122, just north of Cuatro Caminos – it's one of the largest markets in the city. On Sunday mornings, too, a 'Rastro' gets going on C/Marqués de Viana. Also well worth a visit is the **Museo Tiflológico** just north of here. A museum designed especially for blind and partially sighted visitors, it by no means excludes others; in fact, its hands-on approach is particularly suitable for those with children in their group.

Across the Castellana, north-east of Nuevos Ministerios, is **El Viso**, an anomaly in high-rise Madrid. It was developed in the 1920s as a model community on garden-city lines, on the fringes of the city at that time, and some of its individual houses are museum-worthy examples of art deco. Unsurprisingly, the district has

### In the know
### Strawberry train

In May, June and October, the 1920s Tren de la Fresa departs from the Príncipe Pío station (Argüelles, 91 232 03, 20, www.renfe.com, map C12) for a relaxing steam train ride to Aranjuez (see p191). Departures are 9.50am on Saturday and Sunday only, and ticket prices start at €23 return (€9 reductions).

# ♥ Casa de Campo

Once a royal hunting estate, the verdant, sprawling parkland of the **Casa de Campo**, to the west of the city in Moncloa, was only opened to the public under the Republic in 1931. Five years later, it became a key site for Franco's forces in the Civil War battle for Madrid, its high ground being used to shell the city centre and the university. Remains of trenches still exist.

Today, the Casa is home to the **Parque de Atracciones** funfair (*see p173*) and the **Zoo** (*see p175*), as well as swimming pools (*see below* Splashing out), tennis courts, and a large boating lake. The cafés that ring the lake are good for an outdoor lunch, and cyclists should note that most of the park's roads are closed to cars on Sunday mornings.

Once you stray away from the criss-crossing roads, much of the park is surprisingly wild, and it's possible to have a real country walk through its woods and gullies. A favourite way to visit is via the **Teleférico de Madrid** cable car from the **Parque del Oeste**, which runs over the trees almost to the middle of the Casa, where there are viewpoints, an (undistinguished) bar-restaurant and picnic spots.

Couples seeking seclusion favour the Casa de Campo, both by day and by night, and the area by the Teleférico has been a gay cruising spot, although police have been cracking down on this. Prostitution used to be a major problem, but in recent years the park has mostly been closed to traffic, which has vastly improved the situation.

**In the know**
**Splashing out**

Within the Casa de Campo is a leafy complex of swimming pools (Avda del Ángel, 91 463 00 50) set in green meadows (expect queues on midsummer weekends). Topless bathing is tolerated and there's an informal gay area. It's open June to September, 11am-8.30pm daily.

BEYOND THE CENTRE

retained its desirable (and expensive) status. At the southern tip of this area is the incongruously political cultural centre, the **Residencia de Estudiantes**. Further east again is **La Prosperidad**, also once a model housing development, although most of its early buildings have been replaced by modern blocks. Within it is the **Auditorio Nacional de Música** (*see p234*).

## Northern suburbs

The northern and western *extrarradio* offers a radical contrast to the south. The thing to do for those with the necessary cash in Madrid has been to adopt the Anglo-Saxon way of life and move out of city flats into house-and-garden districts like **Puerta de Hierro**, north of the Casa de Campo. Named after the 1753 iron gate to the royal hunting reserve of El Pardo, its grand homes are no match for those in **La Moraleja**, off the Burgos road, an enclave for executives, diplomats and Real Madrid players.

The growing districts to the east are not nearly so lush. The area along the A-2 towards the airport is intended to be a major commercial development zone, with the Feria de Madrid trade fair complex and the **Parque Juan Carlos I**, which lies between the airport and the Feria de Madrid centre. Oddly enough, the area already contains, swallowed up in the urban spread, one of Spain's most appealing 18th-century gardens, the **Parque El Capricho de la Alameda de Osuna**. Just south of here is the **Wanda Metropolitano stadium**, the new home of the Atlético football team.

## El Pardo

Around 15 kilometres (10 miles) to the north-west of the city lies a vast expanse of verdant and well-tended parkland. This area contains the main residence of the Spanish royal family, the **Palacio de la Zarzuela**, but the reason most people will venture up here is for the peculiar sensation of nosing around in the house where General Franco lived and worked for the 35 years up to his death in 1975, the **Real Palacio de El Pardo**, situated in the peaceful 18th-century town of El Pardo. Today the place serves mainly to host foreign dignitaries and heads of state, for events such as the wedding of the now King Felipe VI. The hills and woodlands are also worth a visit, being remarkably unspoilt thanks to those long protected years of dictatorial and regal status. They contain an amazingly rich array of wildlife.

# Football Crazy

*Catch a match with one of Madrid's teams, in a stadium or bar*

Madrid has four main clubs: the world-famous **Real Madrid** (known as 'El Madrid'), **Atlético de Madrid** ('El Atleti', and the third most successful Spanish team behind Real Madrid and FC Barcelona), and the modest **Rayo Vallecano** and **Getafe** clubs. Real Madrid have historically been the most successful club in both Spain and Europe, boasting a dazzling collection of silverware. They have won La Liga 33 times and the Champions League a record 17 times.

While El Atleti may not be considered among Europe's elite teams, they overshadowed Real Madrid in 2010 by winning the Europa League (and won the UEFA Super Cup in the same year, and again in 2012). They lost on penalties to Real Madrid in the nail-biting Champions League final in 2016.

Getafe has also had some glory in recent years, reaching the final of the Copa del Rey for the first time in their history in 2007, then repeating the feat the following year. Since promotion in 2004, they have been relegated only once (in 2015–2016) and have also become a mainstay in the Primera Liga.

League matches are played on Saturday or Sunday evenings, from September to May or June; at least one of the teams plays in Madrid every weekend. Cup and European matches are held during the week. Tickets can be very hard to come by, especially for Real Madrid games; if you can't get one at the ticket office, you might have to resort to buying a *'reventa'* ('resale') from one of the touts outside the ground. For shirts and various bits of fan-junk, head to the Adidas shops in the stadium or at C/Carmen 3, or shop online.

Good coverage of Spanish football can be found weekly in Sid Lowe's column at www.guardian.co.uk/football.

Real Madrid fans

# Sights & museums

## Ermita de San Antonio de la Florida

*Glorieta de San Antonio de la Florida 5, Moncloa (91 542 07 22). Metro Príncipe Pío. **Open** 9.30am-8pm Tue-Sun. **Guided Tours** 1pm Sat, in Spanish and English, free. **Admission** free. **Map** pull-out B11.*

This plain neoclassical chapel was completed by Felipe Fontana for Charles IV in 1798. North of Príncipe Pío station on the Paseo de la Florida, it is famous as the burial place of Goya, and for the unique frescoes of the miracles of St Anthony, incorporating scenes of Madrid life, which Goya painted here in 1798. In contrast to the staid exterior, the colour and use of light in his images are stunning. Featuring a rare mix of elements, including his unique, simultaneously ethereal and sensual 'angels', they are among his best and most complex works. On the other side of the road into the park is a near-identical second chapel, built in the 1920s to allow the original building to be left as a museum.

## Estadio Santiago Bernabéu

*Paseo de la Castellana 144, Chamartín (91 398 43 00, www.realmadrid.com). Metro Santiago Bernabéu. **Open** (guided tours) 10am-7pm Mon-Sat; 10.30am-6.30pm Sun; tours stop 5hrs before kick-off on match days. **Tickets** Stadium tours €25; €13-18 reductions. Match tickets €40-€325.*

After a few years blighted by infighting and power struggles, the Whites are thriving under the leadership of coach Zinedine Zidane. They won four major titles for the first time in their 115-year history during the 2016-2017 season, making it their best ever year. Tickets can be purchased online or at the stadium's ticket offices, but getting hold of one can be extremely difficult as 90% of tickets are taken up by club members. For more information on stadium tours, visit the Real Madrid website. *See also p168* Football Crazy.

## Estadio Wanda Metropolitano

*Av de Luis Aragones 67, northern suburbs (902 26 04 03, www.clubatleticodemadrid. com). Metro Estadio Metropolitano. **Open** Ticket office 10am till kick-off on match days. **Tickets** €30-€180.*

Atlético Madrid, or 'El Atleti', won the UEFA Europa League in 2010 and 2012, and La Liga in 2014, and only just lost out to arch-rivals Real Madrid in the finals of the Champions League in 2016 and 2017. The loyal '*rojiblanco*' faithful always created a vibrant atmosphere in the Calderón stadium, which was their home until 2017. Their new 68,000-seater home is the Estadio Wanda Metropolitano, nicknamed 'La Peineta' and inaugurated

Estadio Santiago Bernabéu

in late 2017 with a match between Atlético Madrid and Málaga CF, attended by King Felipe VI. Tickets can be bought via the website, through entradas.com, or at the stadium ticket office.

## Faro de Moncloa

*Avda de los Reyes Católicos, Moncloa (91 550 12 51, www.esmadrid.com/faro-de-moncloa). Metro Moncloa. **Open** 9.30am-8pm Tue-Sun. **Admission** €3; €1.50 reductions; free under-6s.*

This former radio and communications tower, 92m (302ft) tall, provides one of the best views of the whole of the city and the *sierras* in the distance. Diagrams along the floor point out highlights of the city. The best bit, though, is the ride up in the glass lift.

## Museo de América

*Avda de los Reyes Católicos 6, Moncloa (91 543 94 37, www.mecd.gob.es/museodeamerica). Metro Moncloa. **Open** 9.30am-3pm Tue, Wed, Fri, Sat; 9.30am-7pm Thur; 10am-3pm Sun. **Admission** €3; €1.50 reductions; free under-18s, free to all Sun.*

This museum comprises the finest collection of pre-Columbian American art and artefacts in Europe, a combination of articles brought back at the time of the Conquest and during the centuries of Spanish rule over Central and South America, plus later acquisitions generally donated by Latin American governments. The collection includes some near-matchless treasures: there is the *Madrid Codex*, one of only four surviving Mayan illustrated glyph manuscripts in the world; the *Tudela Codex* and illustrated manuscripts from central Mexico, which depict the Spanish Conquest; superb carvings from the Mayan city of Palenque, sent back to Charles III by the first-ever modern survey expedition to a pre-Hispanic American ruin in 1787; and the Gold of the Quimbayas, a series of exquisite gold figures from the Quimbaya culture of Colombia, which were presented to Spain by the Colombian government. All the main pre-Columbian cultures are represented – further highlights include Aztec obsidian

# 💜 Parque El Capricho de la Alameda de Osuna

*Paseo de la Alameda de Osuna 25, northern suburbs (91 588 01 14). Metro El Capricho.* **Open** *Oct-Mar 9am-6.30pm Sat, Sun. Apr-Sept 9am-9pm Sat, Sun.* **Admission** *free.*

Head out to the suburbs to explore this impossibly romantic garden. Just to the north of the A-2 motorway, now surrounded by Madrid's eastern sprawl, the Parque El Capricho de la Alameda de Osuna is a jewel of a fantasy garden, a remarkably preserved monument to 18th-century taste. Within its 14 hectares (2.5 acres) is an artificial river that meanders between lakes, woods, rose gardens, mock temples and a whole range of cool, surprising corners. The gardens were begun in the 1780s for the Duke and Duchess of Osuna, the most cultivated couple among the Spanish aristocracy, who were enthusiastic promoters of the ideas and enquiring spirit of the Enlightenment and great patrons of the artists, writers and musicians of their day. The Capricho was their country estate and, under the direction of the Duchess, became a special combination of salon and pleasure garden. In the 1790s, an invitation to spend a day there was the hottest ticket in Madrid, for both the aristocracy and the intelligentsia.

The Capricho has been called 'the essence of a feminine garden', and its design closely reflected the duchess's personal taste. Her main architect was Jean-Baptiste Mulot, a French gardener who had previously worked for Marie Antoinette, although much of the Capricho is in the English style, with simulated natural landscapes between smaller formal gardens. An Italian theatre designer, Angelo Maria Borghini, was brought in to construct many of the Capricho's fanciful buildings. Wandering visitors were to be surprised and delighted by a succession of different ambiences and experiences: from secluded alcoves to broad vistas; from tranquil boat rides on the lakes out to tiny artificial islands to sampling the simple life at the Casa de la Vieja, a mock peasants' cottage. Also waiting to be discovered were replica Greek and Egyptian temples, a ballroom, an open-air theatre and even an ornate beehive in the shape of a classical temple.

Within the Capricho, the Osunas' aristocratic friends, men and women, could mingle with artists and intellectuals and talk freely, whether of gossip or great ideas, in an atmosphere that was very different from the paralysing etiquette of the royal court. New poems were read, and operas and music performed: Haydn was a favourite composer. This liberal informality encouraged by the duchess – already deeply suspect for her 'French' ideas – soon led to unstoppable rumours that far more illicit activities were going on among the Capricho's intimate arbours than just chat.

The Duke and Duchess of Osuna were also among the first important patrons

of Goya, and their support played a major part in winning him acceptance among high society. Among the several paintings that Goya produced for the Osunas' house at El Capricho were two oddities, the *Aquelarre* (Witches' Sabbath) and *Escena de Brujas* (Witchcraft Scene) – both now in the Museo Lázaro Galdiano (*see p157*) – precursors of his later macabre, sensual paintings. These artworks perhaps indicate a more decadent taste in the duke and duchess alongside their more celebrated Enlightenment rationalism.

The Capricho is also famous as the place where Goya, then aged 40, met the 23-year-old Duchess of Alba in 1786, and where his obsession with her began. Scandalous and impulsive, known for breaking whichever social conventions suited her, dressing as a Madrid *maja* or street girl and having a string of male escorts from aristocrats to bullfighters, the Duchess of Alba was nevertheless a good friend of the high-minded Duchess of Osuna, and a frequent visitor to El Capricho.

The gardens were badly knocked about by Napoleon's troops – who also shot the head gardener, the French émigré Pierre Prévost – but were later reclaimed by the Duchess of Osuna, who lived on there until her death, aged 82, in 1834. El Capricho then suffered decades of decay and occasional destruction – during the Civil War – before it became the property of the city of Madrid in the 1970s.

masks from Mexico, Inca stone sculptures and funeral offerings from Peru, and finely modelled, comical and sometimes highly sexual figurines from the Chibcha culture of Colombia. There are also exhibits from the Spanish colonial period, such as the *Entry of the Viceroy Morcillo into Potosí* (1716) by the early Bolivian painter Melchor Pérez Holguín; a series of paintings showing in obsessive detail the range of racial mixes possible in colonial Mexico; and a collection of gold and other objects from the galleons *Atocha* and *Margarita*, sunk off Florida in the 18th century and only recovered in 1988.

The collection is arranged not by countries and cultures but thematically, so that rooms are dedicated to topics such as 'the family', 'communication' and so on, with artefacts from every period and country alongside each other. Without some knowledge of the many pre-Columbian cultures, this can be confusing and uninformative. Frustrating, then, but it's still a superb, intriguing collection, and temporary shows are usually interesting.

### Museo Cerralbo

*C/Ventura Rodríguez 17, Argüelles (91 547 36 46, museocerralbo.mcu.es). Metro Plaza de España. **Open** 9.30am-3pm Tue, Wed, Fri, Sat; 9.30am-3pm, 5-8pm Thur; 10am-3pm Sun. **Admission** €3; €1.50 reductions; free under-18s, over-65s. Free to all Thur pm, Sat from 2pm, all day Sun. **Map** pull-out E12.*

Laid out in a sumptuous 19th-century mansion is the remarkable collection of artworks and artefacts assembled by Enrique de Aguilera y Gamboa, the 17th Marqués de Cerralbo. A politician, traveller and a man of letters, who collected pieces everywhere he went, he bequeathed his collection to the state with the stipulation that it should be displayed exactly how he had arranged it himself. Thus the contents are laid out in a crowded manner, with paintings in three levels up the walls, and few items labelled. Among the many paintings, though, there is El Greco's *The Ecstasy of St Francis of Assisi* – the real highlight – and works by Zurbarán, Alonso Cano and other Spanish masters. The upstairs area contains an astonishing collection of European and Japanese armour, weapons, watches, pipes, leather-bound books, clocks and other curiosities. The mansion itself is of interest; it gives a good idea of how the aristocracy lived in the Restoration period.

## Museo Sorolla

*Paseo del General Martínez Campos 37, Chamberí (91 310 15 84, museosorolla.mcu. es). Metro Gregorio Marañón or Iglesia. **Open** 9.30am-8pm Tue-Sat; 10am-3pm Sun. **Admission** €3; €1.50 reductions; free under-18s & over-65s. Free to all 2-8pm Sat, all day Sun.*

Often regarded as a neo-Impressionist, Valencia-born Joaquín Sorolla was really an exponent of 'luminism', the celebration of light. He was renowned for his iridescent, sun-drenched paintings, including portraits and family scenes at the beach and in gardens. Sorolla's leisured themes and greetings card-style aesthetic (and indeed his paintings are often used as such) are easy to dismiss, but most find his luminous world at least a little seductive. This delightful little museum, housed in the mansion built for the artist in 1910 to spend his latter years, holds 250 works. The works are exhibited on the main floor, in his former studio areas and his living space on the first floor. The salon, dining room and breakfast room are furnished in their original state with the artist's eclectic decorative influence in evidence. The garden, Moorish-inspired but with an Italianate pergola, is a delightful, peaceful oasis of calm, seemingly miles away from the roaring traffic outside.

## Museo Tiflológico

*C/La Coruña 18, Tetuán (91 589 42 19, museo. once.es). Metro Estrecho. **Open** 10am-2pm, 5-8pm Tue-Fri; 10am-2pm Sat. Closed Aug. **Admission** free.*

Owned and run by ONCE, the organisation for blind and partially sighted people, this special museum presents exhibitions of work by visually impaired artists (the name comes from the Greek *tiflos*, sightless). Work here is intended to be touched, and is generally sculptural, three-dimensional, rich in texture and highly tactile. As well as staging temporary shows, the museum holds a large permanent collection of instruments devised over the years to help the blind and a series of scale models of monuments from Spain and around the world.

## Museo del Traje (Museum of Clothing)

*Avda Juan de Herrera 2, Moncloa (91 550 47 00, museodeltraje.mcu.es). Metro Moncloa. **Open** 9.30am-7pm Tue-Sat; 10am-3pm Sun. **Admission** €3; free under-18s, over-65s. Free to all 2.30-7pm Sat, all day Sun.*

This museum is a must for those interested in any aspect of clothing. The collections comprise around 21,000 garments covering six centuries of Spanish fashion, although there are some much older items, among

Museo del Traje

them fragments of Coptic cloth and Hispano-Muslim pieces. The permanent exhibition shows up to 600 items at any one time, rotating garments frequently both to protect them and to allow returning visitors to appreciate the breadth and diversity of the collection. It is arranged chronologically, in 14 spaces, among which are two outstanding monographic rooms, one covering regional costume, the other containing pieces by Mariano Fortuny y Madrazo, son of the painter, whose creations were worn by the likes of Isadora Duncan. Other rooms cover costume from the Enlightenment to the *castizos* (Madrid's working classes), early 19th-century French influences, Romanticism, belle époque, the avant-garde, post-Civil War fashion and the modern era. A room is dedicated to the great couturier Balenciaga and another to Spanish haute couture. Visitors can learn about how clothes are made in 'didactic areas' and a further exhibition space shows temporary displays. Facilities include reading rooms, a bookshop, a café and a restaurant.

## Palacio de Hielo

*C/Silvano 77, northern suburbs (ice rink 91 716 01 59, www.sporthielo.com, www. palaciodehielo.com). Metro Canillas.* **Open** *Ice rink Sept-May 8.45-10.30pm Wed, Thur; 5.30-10.30pm Fri; 12.30-3pm, 5.30-10.30pm Sat, Sun. Closed June-mid Sept. Bowling alley 3-11pm Mon-Thur; 11am-2am Fri, Sat; 11am-11pm Sun.* **Admission** *Ice rink €7-€12.50. Bowling alley €6-€8.50.*

The Ice Palace is a huge leisure complex dominated by an 1,800sq m (20,000 sq foot) ice rink. With a curling and skating school, 24-lane bowling alley and 15-screen cinema, it's a good option for a rainy day. The site, out towards Barajas Airport, is also home to a shopping centre (10am-10pm daily), numerous cafés and restaurants, and a nursery for kids aged three to 11.

## Parque de Atracciones

*Casa de Campo, Moncloa (902 345 009, 91 526 80 30, www.parquedeatracciones.es). Metro Batán.* **Open** *times vary (see website for details).* **Admission** *€31.90 over 120cm; €24.90 90cm-120cm; €16 over-65s.*

A funfair with something for everyone. The wildest rides are El Abismo (the Abyss), which is a 49m (160ft) high-roller that follows a route of scary drops at 100km/h (60 mph), and the Star Flyer, the park's symbol and tallest attraction at 80m (260ft) high. Other features include indoor paintball and a 4D cinema. There are long queues for some rides. For more on Casa de Campo, *see p167*.

## Parque del Canal de Isabel II

*Entrance on Avda de las Islas Filipinas, Chamberí (91 533 17 91). Metro Canal or Rios Rosas.* **Open** *8am-10pm daily.*

This lovely outdoor sports complex and park – located between Avenida de las Islas Filipinas, Calle de Santander and the Paseo de San Francisco de Sales – consists of a 1.5km (one mile) running track and pedestrian pathway, a golf course, two football pitches and eight *pádel* courts, as well as a gym, tennis courts and outdoor pools. It is beautifully landscaped with lavender, rose bushes, cypress trees, water fountains, benches and shaded areas, and there's a great vibe on summer evenings, when the park buzzes with runners, old folk on their evening strolls, families and more serious sporty types. Officially called the Centro de Ocio y Deportes Tercer Depósito del Canal de Isabel II, it's referred to by locals as simply Parque del Canal or, increasingly, Parque Green Canal.

## Parque Juan Carlos I

*Avda de Logroño & Avda de los Andes, northern suburbs. Metro Campo de las Naciones.*

This huge park, one of Madrid's newest green (and brown) spaces, lies between the airport and the Feria de Madrid trade fair centre. It is slowly becoming one of the city's more attractive spaces, but it has taken a while for the trees to grow to provide shade. The park's current draws include a series of different gardens within a circle of olive trees, an artificial river and other water features.

## Real Palacio de El Pardo

*C/Manuel Alonso, El Pardo (91 376 15 00, www.patrimonionacional.es). Bus 601 from Moncloa.* **Open** *Apr-Sept 10am-8pm daily. Oct-Mar 10am-6pm daily.* **Admission** *€9; €4 reductions; free under-5s. Free to EU citizens 5-8pm (3-6pm Apr-Sept) Wed, Thur pm.*

In 1405, Henry III constructed a hunting lodge here, but the first monarch to take a really serious interest in El Pardo's excellent deer and game hunting estate was Charles I of Spain (Charles V of the Holy Roman Empire), who built a sizeable palace here. His successor, Philip II, added many important works of art but most of these were lost in a fire in 1604, and after various architectural changes the building was finally reconstructed on Charles III's orders by 18th-century architect Francesco Sabatini; superb murals by Bayeu and Maella were added at this time. The current furnishings, paintings and tapestries were added during the 19th and 20th centuries.

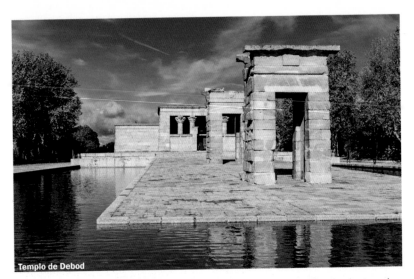
Templo de Debod

In addition to its main role today as a diplomatic rendezvous, the palace is partially open to the public and there are tours of its ornate and gaudy interior with ornamental frescoes, gilt mouldings and some fine tapestries, many of which were woven in the Real Fábrica de Tapices to Goya designs. There's an ornate theatre, built for Charles IV's Italian wife María Luisa of Parma, where censorious film fan Franco used to view films with his cronies before deciding on their suitability for the great unwashed but, in truth, the only rooms of real fascination are the Generalísimo's bedroom, dressing room and '70s bathroom – decorated to his own specifications.

Outside, you can wander in the palace's attractive gardens or picnic in at least part of the magnificent surrounding parkland known as Monte de Pardo – even though much of this is still closed to the public. Other nearby highlights include the Convento de los Capuchinos del Pardo (Ctra del Cristo, 91 376 08 00, open 8am-1pm, 4.30-8pm daily), famed for Gregorio Fernández's wooden Baroque sculpture of Christ; the Quinta del Pardo, a small 18th-century summer house; and the single-storey Casita del Príncipe, built in 1785 by Juan de Villanueva and noted for its lavish lounges, though both have been closed to the public for some years.

### La Residencia de Estudiantes

*C/Pinar 21-23, Chamartín (91 563 64 11, www.residencia.csic.es). Metro Gregorio Marañón.* **Open** *(during exhibitions, phone to check) 11am-8pm Mon-Sat; 11am-3pm Sun.* **Admission** *free.*

From its foundation in 1910 until the war in 1936, the Residencia de Estudiantes was the most vibrant cultural centre in Madrid, and a powerful innovative force in the whole country. Although it was a students' residence – García Lorca, Buñuel and Dalí all stayed here in the early days – 'La Resi' also organised visits to Madrid by leading artists and scientists of the day and was active in the propagation of avant-garde ideas from outside Spain. The Civil War and subsequent regime severely stifled intellectual freedom and the Residencia languished until the late 1980s, when it was resurrected as a private foundation sponsored by Spain's official scientific research council. It hosts talks by international figures, conferences and exhibitions, recitals, films and concerts.

### Sala del Canal de Isabel II

*C/Santa Engracia 125, Chamberí (91 545 10 00, www.madrid.org). Metro Ríos Rosas.* **Open** *11am-2pm, 5-8.30pm Tue-Sat; 11am-2pm Sun.* **Admission** *free.*

This water tower, built in elaborate neo-Mudéjar style between 1907 and 1911, is considered to be a gem of Madrid's industrial architecture. It is now home to a

### In the know
### Plaza de Olavide

Chamberí's Plaza de Olavide is something of a neighbourhood hub, and makes a great place to enjoy tapas alfresco. On summer evenings, the place buzzes with relaxed conversation. Try **Arco Iris** (no.2), renowned for its excellent *tortilla de patata*.

stylish exhibition space that specialises in photography, ranging in quality from good to world-class. Two kilometres north of here, just off the Plaza de Castilla, is the Fundación Canal (www.fundacioncanal.com), another arts and education centre run by the Canal de Isabel II.

### Teleférico de Madrid

*Paseo del Pintor Rosales, Argüelles (91 541 11 18, www.teleferico.com). Metro Argüelles.* **Open** *May-Aug noon-1.45pm, 3-9pm Mon-Fri; noon-9.30pm Sat, Sun. Opening times for rest of year change on a weekly and monthly basis (see website).* **Tickets** *€5.90/€4.20 (return/single); €5.20 price of a single return with reduction; free under-3s.* **Map** *pull-out C10.*

An extraordinary 2.5km (1.5-mile) trip over the Casa de Campo and Parque del Oeste in a cable car. The views of the Palacio Real, Río Manzanares, city skyline and park are breathtaking. There are even interesting close-ups of the park's seedier goings-on. In the winter, the cable cars rarely operate on weekdays.

### Templo de Debod

*Paseo de Pintor Rosales s/n, Argüelles (91 366 74 15, templodedebod.memoriademadrid.es). Metro Plaza de España or Ventura Rodríguez.* **Open** *10am-8pm Sun.* **Admission** *free.* **Map** *pull-out D11.*

This Egyptian structure, which sits on the outskirts of the Parque del Oeste, dates back 2,200 years and is dedicated to the gods Amun and Isis. It was sent, block by block, by the Egyptian government in 1968 in thanks for Spain's help in preserving monuments threatened by the Aswan Dam.

### Zoo Aquarium Madrid

*Casa de Campo (91 512 37 70, www. zoomadrid.com). Metro Batán.* **Open** *times vary (check the website or call for details).* **Admission** *€23.30; €18.90 reductions; free under-3s. Discounts for tickets purchased through website.*

This attractively landscaped zoo is located slap bang in the heart of the Casa de Campo (*see p167*). The animals look as happy as can be expected of beasts held in captivity, although the big cats could really do with a bit more leg-room. At the Tierra de Gorilas ('Land of Gorillas'), a sheet of reassuringly thick glass separates you from the massive, glowering silverbacks prowling about. Children will enjoy walking through the shark tank and dolphinarium. There's also a petting zoo and a train ride.

## Restaurants

### Asador Donostiarra €€€

*C/Infanta Mercedes 79, Tetuán (91 579 08 71, www.asadordonostiarra.com). Metro Tetuán.* **Open** *1.30-4pm, 8.30pm-midnight Mon-Sat; 1.30-4pm Sun.* Steakhouse

If you love meat and you love Real Madrid, you may want to splurge on a night out at the once-preferred *asador* (steakhouse) of David Beckham and the rest of the team, located near the Bernabéu stadium. The celeb crowd is as legendary as the *solomillo*, and they often give away signed photos and other goodies from the team. Dissenting voices say that all the press has had an adverse effect, and the run-of-the-mill salad, steak and potato offerings are not commensurate with the hefty prices; others still claim it's the best *asador* in Madrid.

### Bar Tomate €€

*C/Fernando El Santo 26, Chamberí (91 702 38 70, www.grupotragaluz.com). Metro Colón.* **Open** *8am-2am daily.* **Map** *pull-out N10.* Mediterranean

Open all day, this establishment is great for breakfast, a snack, lunch or dinner. Part of the wildly successful Tragaluz group, which has several restaurants in Barcelona, Bar Tomate specialises in light and tasty Mediterranean cuisine, such as gorgonzola croquettes, anchovies and red piquillo peppers on toast, rice cooked in squid ink with clams, and carpaccios. There are good deals available at breakfast time, with a selection of little rolls and pastries, and later on you can have cocktails.

### Casa Mingo €

*Paseo de la Florida 34, Casa de Campo (91 547 79 18, www.casamingo.es). Metro Príncipe Pío.* **Open** *11am-midnight daily.* **No cards.** **Map** *pull-out B11.* Spanish

A vast and noisy Asturian cider house, open since 1888. This is a great opportunity to rub elbows with *madrileños* really enjoying themselves at one of the long wooden tables. The restaurant specialises in roast chicken and cider, and also serves classic *madrileño cocido* on weekday lunchtimes. Turn up before the city gets hungry (around 1.30pm) if you want a terrace seat, or take out a chicken and a bottle of cider and head for the River Manzanares for a picnic. At other times, expect to queue.

### El Club Allard €€€€

*C/Ferraz 2, Argüelles (91 559 09 39, www. elcluballard.com). Metro Plaza de España.* **Open** *1.30-5pm, 9-11.30pm Mon-Fri; 9-11.30pm Sat.* **Map** *pull-out E12.* Modern European

Club Allard began as a private members club, opening its doors to the public a few years later and earning a second Michelin star in 2011 and again under a new chef in 2014. Things are often not what they seem: fruit and vegetables are reconstructed, mimicked in form and in flavour, to a level that would confound Mother Nature herself, and eating here is an intellectual challenge as much as it is a culinary delight. There is no à la carte, only tasting menus (€115 and €145).

### DiverXO €€€€
*NH Eurobuilding, C/Padre Damián 23, Chamartín (91 570 07 66, www.diverxo.com). Metro Cuzco.* **Open** *2pm-1am Tue-Sat. Closed 3wks Aug. Modern Spanish/Asian*

A gastronomic temple in the heart of an unprepossessing business neighbourhood, DiverXO offers some of the most exciting food in the country at the hands of wunderkind chef David Muñoz. The restaurant's aesthetic is bizarre and playful, with flying pigs erupting from the walls and giant ice-cream sculptures. A little like the food, in fact, which might include dishes such as yoghurt, strawberry and coffee kimchi with cuttlefish or tortilla 'dim sum'. These days the restaurant has three Michelin stars, and you'll need to book a few weeks in advance.

### La Favorita €€€
*C/Covarrubias 25, Chamberí (91 448 38 10, www.lafavoritarestaurante.com). Metro Alonso Martínez or Bilbao.* **Open** *9pm-midnight Mon-Sat.* **Map** *pull-out L9. Spanish*

Opera fanatic Javier Otero converted this charming 1920s mansion into a restaurant and filled it with singing waiters – conservatoire students or artists just starting out on their careers. It's a surprisingly fun way to dine. And the food, made using fresh ingredients from Navarra, also hits a high note. Reservations are essential.

### Fismuler €€€
*C/Sagasta 29, Chamberí (91 827 75 81, www.fismuler.es). Metro Alonso Martínez.* **Open** *1.30-4pm, 8.30-11.30pm Mon-Thur; 1.30-4pm, 8.30pm-12.30am Fri, Sat.* **Map** *pull-out L10. Spanish*

Nino Redruello is of good Madrid restaurant stock, and draws on old family recipes, adding his own distinctive stamp and drawing praise from the likes of Anthony Bourdain. Fismuler is his latest venture, a sociable, welcoming place with long wooden shared tables. Dishes change daily depending on what looks good in the market, but don't miss the sea anemone tortilla, if it's on offer.

### Sacha €€€
*C/Juan de Hurtado de Mendoza 11, Chamartín (91 345 59 52). Metro Cuzco.* **Open** *1.30-4pm, 8.30pm-midnight Mon-Sat. Spanish/French*

Larger-than-life chef Sacha Hormachea is such a Madrid institution that local foodie types refer to '*sachismo*' – the concept of flavour and enjoyment of simple food made with great produce but without the frills and furbelows employed by most of Madrid's top restaurants. His parents set the place up in 1972 and he has remained faithful to their philosophy ever since: signature dishes include crab lasagne with sea urchin, battered hake and sole meunière.

### Santceloni €€€€
*Hotel Hesperia Madrid, Paseo de la Castellana 57, Chamberí (91 210 88 40, www.restaurantesantceloni. com). Metro Gregorio Marañón.* **Open** *2-4pm, 9-11pm Mon-Fri; 9-11pm Sat. Closed Aug.* **Map** *pull-out N6. Spanish*

Named after the village where the late famed Barcelona restaurateur Santi Santamaria was born, and run by his former protégé Óscar Velasco, Santceloni won its first Michelin star in less than a year (it now has two). The menu changes frequently to make the most of the best seasonal ingredients, but might include crab in sherry with creamed onion and celery, or one of Santamaria's trademark dishes: ravioli with sliced raw prawn with a filling of ceps. The tasting menu will set you back a pretty penny, but it's a chance to relish the talents of one of Spain's celebrity chefs.

### Sudestada €€
*C/Ponzano 85, Chamberí (91 533 41 54, www.sudestada.eu). Metro Ríos Rosas or Cuatro Caminos.* **Open** *1-4pm, 9pm-midnight Mon-Sat. Asian*

Run by young Argentines with a passion for Asian food, Sudestada is the Madrid branch of a Buenos Aires favourite. It can get very booked up, and given the authentic spiciness of its curries – from all over south-east Asia – this gives the lie to the idea that Spanish diners prefer their food bland. Less *picante* options include Vietnamese rolls and dim sum from Singapore. Reserve ahead, especially at weekends.

## Tapas
### Bodegas la Ardosa
*C/Santa Engracia 70, Chamberí (91 446 58 94). Metro Iglesia.* **Open** *11am-3pm, 7-11pm Mon, Tue, Thur-Sun. Closed mid July-mid Aug.* **No cards.**

A tiny bar with a lovely old tiled exterior (confusingly marked no.58) and walls lined with bottles. There are especially good *patatas bravas* and fried pigs' ears, as well as sardines and beer. Not to be confused with the Malasaña bar of the same name (no relation).

## Shops & services

### Bodegas Santa Cecilia
*C/Blasco de Garay 74, Chamberí (91 445 52 83, www.santacecilia.es). Metro Islas Filipinas.* **Open** *10am-9pm Mon-Sat. Food & drink*

This *bodega*, occupying two almost-adjacent *locales*, stocks a vast array of wines, beers and spirits – over 4,000 in total. Wines are mainly Spanish, while beers and spirits come from all over. The gourmet shop, no.72, hosts frequent tasting sessions. **Other locations** C/Bravo Murillo 50, Cuatro Caminos (91 442 35 32) & C/Núñez de Balboa 103, Salamanca (91 562 95 13).

### Booksellers
*C/Fernández de la Hoz 40, Chamberí (91 442 79 59, www.booksellers.es). Metro Iglesia.* **Open** *Sept-July 9.30am-2pm, 5-8pm Mon-Fri; 10am-2pm Sat. Aug 9.30am-2pm, 5-8pm Mon-Fri. Books & music*

Madrid's best English-language bookshop sells a wide selection of literature, videos and DVDs, as well as materials for TEFLers. The branch below also has a children's book section. **Other locations** C/Santa Engracia 115, Chamberí (91 702 79 44).

### La Cava de Magallanes
*C/Magallanes 16, Chamberí (91 446 28 17, www.estancomagallanes.com). Metro Quevedo.* **Open** *8.30am-8.30pm Mon-Fri; 9am-2pm Sat.* **Map** *pull-out H8. Gifts & souvenirs*

A temple to tobacco, La Cava de Magallanes stocks over 350 different types of cigar, all maintained at optimum temperature in a special humidified room. The knowledgeable owner speaks a little English. There is a good range of accessories, too.

### Centro Comercial Príncipe Pío
*Paseo de la Florida s/n, Argüelles (91 758 00 40, www.principepio.es). Metro Príncipe Pío.* **Open** *10am-10pm Mon-Sat; 11am-10pm Sun.* **Map** *pull-out C13. Shopping centre*

A welcome addition to one of the city's main transport hubs. Built into the shell of the old train station, the mall manages to pack in a deceptively large number of shops and eateries, ranging from the Body Shop and H&M to a VIPS restaurant and the obligatory Starbucks.

### Mercado de Chamartín
*C/Bolivia 9, Chamartín (91 457 53 50, mercadodechamartin.com). Metro Colombia. Market*

In an upmarket neighbourhood with many affluent foreign residents, and produce to match.

### Mercado de Chamberí
*C/Alonso Cano, 10, Chamberí (91 446 95 74, www.mercadodechamberi.es). Metro Iglesia. Market*

Big, with lots of variety. The fruit and veg stalls in the middle are among the best in town.

### NaturaSí
*C/Doctor Fleming 1, Chamartín (91 458 32 54, www.naturasi.eu). Metro Santiago Bernabéu.* **Open** *10am-9pm Mon-Sat. Food & drink*

This 'natural' supermarket sells a huge range of ecological and natural foodstuffs, among them fresh fruit and veg, cheese and herbal products. **Other locations** C/Guzmán El Bueno 28, Moncloa (91 544 5663).

### Ocho y Medio
*C/Martín de los Heros 11, Argüelles (91 559 06 28). Metro Plaza de España.* **Open** *10am-11.30pm Mon-Thur; 10am-12.30am Fri; noon-12.30am Sat.* **Map** *pull-out E11. Books & music*

This superb cinema bookshop and café is a treat for film buffs, with plenty of works in English and other languages, plus DVDs and film paraphernalia.

### Sana Sana
*C/Zurbano 51, Chamberí (91 310 54 24, www.sanasaludsana.es). Metro Rubén Dario.* **Open** *11am-9pm Mon-Fri; 11am-3pm Sat.* **Map** *pull-out M7. Spa*

An instant massage chain that offers a ten-minute workover for the harassed exec using specially designed chairs. It also offers shiatsu, sports and anti-stress massage, and beauty treatments. No booking is necessary for the short massage.

### La Tienda Verde
*C/Maudes 23, Chamberí (91 534 38 10, www.tiendaverde.es). Metro Cuatro Caminos.* **Open** *10am-2pm, 5-8pm Mon-Fri; 10am-2pm Sat. Books & music*

Madrid's original and best shop for travel books and maps, the 'Green Shop' has a complete range of tourist and nature guides, along with maps and specialised mountaineering books.

## SOUTH OF THE CENTRE

The *barrios* of southern **Embajadores** – namely **Delicias**, **Arganzuela** and **Legazpi** – occupy a triangular chunk of land just south of the old city, bordered by the Manzanares river, the M-30 motorway and the rail lines from the nearby Atocha station. Low rents attract a fair number of resident foreigners. Conventional attractions are few – there is the **Museo del Ferrocarril** and the **Parque Tierno Galván**, and the **Planetario de Madrid** – but the area contains the Estación Sur bus station, and two symbols of Madrid, Atlético Madrid's Wanda Metropolitano stadium and, alongside it, the Mahou brewery. It's also now home to the spectacular cultural centre **Matadero Madrid** (*see p178*), in the city's old abattoir (hence the name). Beyond that is the river and the **Puente de Toledo**, which was built by Pedro de Ribera for Philip V in 1718-32.

Just south of the river is the **Parque de San Isidro**, containing a charming 18th-century hermitage dedicated to the city's patron saint. The hermitage is the traditional focus of the Romería (Procession) de San Isidro (*see p201*). The park still fills with life and crowds during the San Isidro *fiestas* every May. At other times it's very tranquil.

### Vallecas

Vallecas, beyond the M-30 in the south-east of the city, was already an industrial suburb in the 1930s and remains an area of Madrid with a firm sense of its own identity. The area has its own football team, **Rayo Vallecano**, forever struggling to keep up with its money-laden neighbours. Car stickers proclaim 'Independence for Vallecas' (spelled 'Vallekas' by hipper natives, who have their own punky sense of cool). It also has a pleasant tree-lined main drag, more than enough to mark it out from the other areas around it. There are problem districts not far away, such as **Entrevías**, which is home to some of Madrid's largest gypsy communities.

---

**In the know**
**Madrid Río**

The Manzanares river has been given a makeover thanks to the Madrid Río project, which took the M-30 ring road underground and created a eight-kilometre park along the riverbank in its wake. Pick up a leaflet from the tourist office or check out www.esmadrid.com to see where the main points of interest are. These include sports areas, picnic zones and fountains designed for children to cool off in on hot summer days.

---

**Top 20**

# 💜 Matadero Madrid

*Plaza de Legazpi 8 (91 517 73 09, www. matadero madrid.org). Metro Legazpi.* **Open** *Site 9am-10pm Mon-Fri; 11am-10pm Sat, Sun. Cineteca 5-10pm Mon. Exhibitions 4-9pm Tue-Fri; 11am-9pm Sat, Sun.* **Admission** *free; Cineteca €3.50.*

In a recession-defying measure, Madrid's city council launched one of its most dynamic cultural projects ever in the shape of the **Matadero**, an innovative and multidisciplinary arts centre, which has become a key socio-cultural symbol for the city.

The vast, ambitious space consists of ten impressive neo-Mudéjar buildings strung along the bank of the Manzanares. These once formed the city's slaughterhouse (*matadero*), and the painted tiles at the entrance to each announce *'deguello de ganado'* (throat cutting of cattle); *'deguello de cerdos'* (throat cutting of pigs), and so on, which can create a slightly melancholy air, though the architecture itself is far too ornate to be gloomy.

Each building is dedicated to a different discipline, with the exception of the offices and the Cantina, an excellent café-restaurant in the former boilerhouse.

The Nave de la Música contains rehearsal rooms, a recording studio and a performance space, while the Nave del Español is all about theatre, with auditoria and exhibition spaces. The foyer comprises a café with a small stage for theatre groups to showcase work, but the loveliest space is the *plaza*. Mobile platforms carry, variously, speaker stacks or small trees to provide shade for daytime performances.

Other buildings include the Casa del Lector (Reader's House), which has a children's library, literature exhibitions and a Kindle-lending service; the Cineteca, which focuses mainly on documentaries (€3.50); and the Central de Diseño, which holds design-related workshops, conferences and exhibitions. There are reading rooms with newspapers and Wi-Fi and even a seed bank.

Unusually, the Matadero has been created with Madrid's citizens in mind, rather than its visitors, but there's plenty here to see and be inspired by, all just a short ride south of Atocha station.

**BEYOND THE CENTRE**

# 🖤 Museo del Ferrocarril de Madrid

*Paseo de las Delicias 61, Delicias (91 506 83 33,www.museodelferrocarril.org). Metro Delicias.* **Open** *Oct-Mar 9.30am-3pm Mon-Thur; 10am-8pm Fri-Sun (until 6pm every second Fri); June-Sept 10am-3pm daily.* **Admission** *€6 Mon-Thur, €2.50 Fri from 2pm, Sat, Sun; €4-1.50 reductions; free under-4s. No cards.*

Housed in the elegant but disused Delicias station, with ironwork by Gustave Eiffel, Madrid's railway museum has an evocative collection of models, old locomotives, railway equipment and memorabilia. There is also a room dedicated to clocks, including the one that marked time when Spain's first-ever train chugged from Barcelona to Mataró in 1948, and displays of antique stationmasters' caps, old tickets, Bakelite telephones, punching machines and the like.

The real attraction, however, for both kids and adults, are the trains themselves, including the sleek 1954 American electric locomotive, 'Marilyn', named after Monroe. You can climb aboard a steam engine, have a drink in an elegant 1928 restaurant car and watch surprisingly absorbing (even – or especially – for children) film footage of Spanish railways. Another hit with the kids is the section of model railways, including engines puffing actual smoke running through miniature landscapes. Real fans won't want to miss the second-hand market for all things railway-related, which takes place here on the first Sunday of every month.

## Sights & museums

### Caja Mágica
*C/Camino de Perales, Parque Lineal de Manzanares, San Fermín (91 722 04 00, www.madrid-open.com/caja-magica). Metro San Fermín-Orcasur.*

Madrid's main venue for top-level tennis, La Caja Mágica ('Magic Box', also known as the Manzanares Park Tennis Center), is the host venue for the Madrid Open, the most prestigious event in the Spanish tennis calendar. Its retractable roofs are its most celebrated feature. It is used for various other events, including music festivals.

### Faunia
*Avda de las Comunidades 28, Vallecas (91 154 74 82, www.faunia.es). Metro Valdebernardo.* **Open** *times vary, check website or call for details.* **Admission** *€26.45; €19.95 reductions; free under-3s. Discounts for tickets purchased through website.*

Part zoo, part theme park, Faunia recreates the world's different ecosystems in a series of domes. Best of the bunch is the Amazon jungle house, which echoes with the screech of exotic birds; an intense tropical storm is simulated every half hour. In summer, Penguin World – an impressive reconstruction of a polar zone, where you can see the little fellas zipping about – is wildly popular. Faunia is not a cheap day out, and queues can be long.

### Planetario de Madrid
*Avenida del Planetario 16, Parque Tierno Galván, Legazpi (91 467 34 61, www.planetmad.es). Metro Arganzuela-Planetario.* **Open** *5-7.45pm Tue-Fri; 11am-1.45pm, 5-8pm Sat, Sun.* **Admission** *€3.60; €1.65 2-14s, over-65s.*

The Planetarium has three exhibition spaces, with shows on the solar system (though the narration is only in Spanish and may test your kids' interest in the heavens if they don't speak it) and an observation tower.

## Restaurants

### Bodegas Rosell €€
*C/General Lacy 14 (91 467 84 58, www.bodegasrosell.es). Metro Atocha.* **Open** *noon-4pm, 7pm-midnight Tue-Sat; noon-4pm Sun.*
*Spanish*

A great pit-stop if you're coming in or out of Atocha station, or even for the Reina Sofía museum, Bodegas Rosell is a fabulous old tavern that has been around since 1920. It serves *raciones* of shellfish and cheese alongside more substantial dishes such as lamb cutlets or duck magret.

# Day Trips

It's a tough call. Spend the entire long weekend in Madrid in order to fit in all three of the mandatory museums? Or take advantage of one of the city's extraordinary day trips? Three words: change your ticket. Because you'll want to do both. In summer, the cool mountain air of the sierras beckons, along with excellent hiking. In winter, what better than to hole up in a traditional *mesón* in the stately cities of Toledo or Segovia, with red wine, a log fire and some suckling pig? Year round, the palaces, monasteries and gardens at Aranjuez, La Granja, Riofrío and El Escorial make for a compelling visit.

The areas to the north and west of Madrid have the most spectacular landscapes, following the three main sierra ranges. The less dramatic country to the south and east – where dry tableland, tufty hillocks and fertile river basins gently intermingle – is full of fascinating towns.

❤ **Don't miss**

**1 Segovia** *p186*
Suckling pig and a fairy-tale castle.

**2 Toledo** *p193*
UNESCO site and crucible of cultures, learning and religion.

**3 Aranjuez** *p191*
Concerto-inspiring palace and gardens.

**4 Chinchón** *p191*
One of Spain's prettiest *plazas mayores*.

**5 El Escorial** *p184*
Philip II's vast and forbidding monastery.

**In the know**
**Getting around**

A large number of buses depart from Estación Sur de Autobuses (C/Méndez Álvaro, 91 468 42 00, www.estacionautobusesmadrid.com), but there are also five major interchange terminals within the city: Plaza de Castilla, Moncloa, Avenida de America, Príncipe Pío and the Plaza Elíptica. The system of local trains (*cercanías*) runs to Alcalá de Henares, Aranjuez, El Escorial, Cercedilla and many more destinations. The ageing but efficient single-gauge extension line, the scenic C-9, wends its way up from Cercedilla through mountain pinewoods to Cotos, which adjoins ski slopes and a glacial lake. Services to other destinations leave from mainline stations Chamartín and Atocha, though many trains also stop between them at Nuevos Ministerios and Recoletos stations. For RENFE trains, *see p282*.

San Lorenzo de El Escorial

# EL ESCORIAL & AROUND

The grand, austere monastery of **San Lorenzo de El Escorial** never fails to divide opinion, but is undoubtedly one of the most significant buildings in the history of Spain. Many people see it as the outward manifestation of its founding monarch's mind – Philip II was at once fanatically religious and wildly ambitious, and so his legacy in stone is both spartan and vast. The gloomy building is also symbolic architecturally, and it was the grey slate and spiky turrets of El Escorial that inspired decades of the 'Herreran' style (also known as Castilian Baroque). Construction was completed in record time between 1563 and 1574, initially by Juan Bautista de Toledo – who died shortly after work started – and subsequently by Juan de Herrera. Everything here is on a grand scale: the main façade is 200 metres (700 feet) long, the overhead cupola measures 92 metres (302 feet), and there are 15 cloisters, 16 kilometres (10 miles) of corridors, 86 stairways, 88 fountains, 1,200 doors and 2,675 windows.

Two other small palaces lie in the spacious gardens and parklands surrounding the monastery, and can be visited with a guided tour: the **Casita del Infante** and the **Casita del Príncipe** (Prince's House), with paintings by Lucas Jordan and a charming garden. The park is open year-round (10am-6pm Tue-Sun).

Outside the monastery, El Escorial is really two separate towns. Down below, next to the train station, is **El Escorial de Abajo**, and at the top of the hill, alongside the monastery, is the grander **San Lorenzo**. Look out here for Charles III's 18th-century **Real Coliseo** theatre and the parish church of **San Bartolomé**. A couple of kilometres out on the road towards the Casita de Arriba is the **Silla de Felipe**, 'Philip's Seat', from where he used to watch progress on the building.

Built between 1940 and 1959 by Civil War prisoners of the defeated Republican army, Franco's giant mausoleum, the **Valle de los Caídos**, or 'Valley of the Fallen' (the fallen on Franco's side, at least), stands in a forested valley a few miles from El Escorial. It was the Generalísimo's grand project, and its stark, grandiose, authoritarian style is worthy of the likes of Mussolini or Ceaucescu. It is easily spotted from up to 50 kilometres (31 miles) away, thanks to the huge 150-metre (500-foot) high cross (said to weigh over 180,000 tons), which is placed 150 metres (492 feet) above the main esplanade.

---

## Sights & museums

### Real Monasterio de San Lorenzo de El Escorial

*91 890 59 03/05, www.patrimonionacional.es.* **Open** *Oct-Mar 10am-6pm Tue-Sun. Apr-Sept 10am-8pm Tue-Sun.* **Admission** *Monastery €10; €5 reductions; free under-5s. Casita del Príncipe €5 (including guided tour). Casita del Infante €5 (including guided tour). Free (to EU citizens only) Oct-Mar 3-5pm Wed, Thur; Apr-Sept 5-8pm Wed, Thur.*

Philip conceived the palace as a mausoleum and contemplative retreat, built as a final resting place for his father, Charles I, and to celebrate the 1557 Spanish victory over the French at St Quentin on St Lawrence's (San Lorenzo) day. It's laid out to resemble the grid-iron on which the saint himself was martyred. The jasper, gold and marble Panteón de los Reyes, designed by Gian Battista Crescenzi in the 1620s, contains all but two of the sovereigns who reigned over four centuries (absentees being Philip V, who was buried at La Granja, and Ferdinand VI, whose remains are in Madrid). The Basilica, with its notable *Christ Crucified* in Carrara marble by Benvenuto Cellini, has no fewer than 45 altars.

The main galleries are located on what was the lower floor of Philip's own austere rooms, above the Basilica. There is a small jalousie window overlooking the high altar so he could participate in Mass even if he was ill and confined to his surprisingly small bed. His cherished Hieronymous Bosch triptych was just a tiny part of a huge Habsburg art collection that includes celebrated works by Velázquez, Ribera, Alonso Cano and individual masterpieces like El Greco's *Adoration of the Name of Jesus* and Titian's *Last Supper*, concentrated mainly in the museum, church, chapterhouse and the ornate barrel-vaulted library – whose 50,000 volumes rival the Vatican's holdings.

The most refreshing section of El Escorial is the Palacio de los Borbones, remodelled by Charles IV in a light neoclassical style that contrasts with the general austerity and

---

**In the know**
**Combined ticket for the Reales Sitios**

The Reales Sitios ticket gives entry to all palaces and monasteries in and around Madrid and costs €30 (€19 reductions). It gives admission for a year to the Palacio Real, Real Sitio de San Lorenzo de El Escorial, Palacio Real de Aranjuez, Real Sitio de El Pardo, Real Monasterio de las Descalzas Reales, Real Monasterio de la Encarnación and the Abadía Benedictina de la Santa Cruz del Valle de los Caídos.

gloom. Highlights here are the tapestries designed by Goya and his contemporaries. Guided tours can be arranged on Fridays and Saturdays.

### El Valle de los Caídos

*91 890 56 11, www.patrimonionacional.es.* **Open** *Oct-Mar 10am-6pm Tue-Sun. Apr-Sept 10am-7pm Tue-Sun.* **Admission** *€9; €4 reductions; free (to EU and Latin American citizens only) Oct-Mar 3-5pm Wed, Thur; Apr-Sept 5-8pm Wed, Thur.*

The monument was completed at great financial and human cost and many Republicans perished while quarrying the dense granite rock needed to build it. Ironically, and to the grief of their families, many of the Republican prisoners' bodies probably now lie side by side with those of their oppressors.

Like it or loathe it, the monument's cold, atmospherically lit underground chambers, lined with eerie cowled figures, do exert a certain mesmerising aura. The mausoleum is basically a huge tunnel, driven 260m (867ft) into the granite rock. At its entrance are 16th-century monoliths, 12m (40ft) high, while deep in the interior you can see bright-coloured tapestries of the *Apocalypse of St John*, a cupola decorated with mosaics showing heaven-bound saints and martyrs of Spain, and an altar-bound polychrome wooden sculpture of Christ crucified. The monument contains a subterranean church, an ossuary of six chapels bearing the remains of Civil War dead and the tombs of two men – Franco himself and José Antonio

Patio de los Reyes, El Escorial

Primo de Rivera, the rich young founder of the Falange who died in the early phases of the Civil War, thus conveniently leaving El Caudillo from El Ferrol unchallenged as leader. After a Socialist Party proposal to remove these remains failed to get through parliament, there are moves afoot to exhume the bodies and move them somewhere out of sight, in an attempt to deter the Francoist pilgrims who come here to worship their deceased figurehead.

The views are quite staggering, especially from the base of the cross, reached via a funicular (closed at the time of writing).

## Restaurants

**Fonda Genara** (Plaza San Lorenzo 2, 91 890 16 36, www.restaurantegenara.com, €€€) is a pretty if slightly pricey restaurant with old theatre posters on the walls. **Parrilla Principe** (C/Floridablanca 6, 91 890 16 11, €€€-€€) is a small, peaceful 18th-century palace with a hotel on the upper floors and a blend of Castilian and seafood cuisine available in the restaurant below. **Madrid Sevilla** (C/Benavente 1, 91 890 15 19, madridsevilla.com, €€) has simple but reasonably priced dishes and tapas, while **La Chistera** (Plaza Jacinto Benavente 7, 91 890 37 26, €€) is principally a tapas bar.

Up above the town in the Monte Abantos district, **Horizontal** (Camino Horizontal, 91 890 38 11, www.restaurantehorizontal.com, €€) offers outdoor eating in summer and a seat by the fire in winter.

## Essential information

**Tourist information**
**Oficina de Turismo** *C/Grimaldi 2 (91 890 53 13, www.sanlorenzoturismo.org).* **Open** *10am-2pm, 3-6pm Tue-Sat; 10am-2pm Sun.*

**Getting there**
**Herranz** (91 890 41 22, www.autocaresherranz.com) buses 661 and 664 run from the Moncloa interchange (journey time 55mins) to El Escorial, every 15-30mins 7am-11.30pm Mon-Fri, every 30-60mins 10am-10.15pm Sat, 8.45am-11pm Sun. Last return journey is at 10.30pm Mon-Fri, 9pm Sat, 10pm Sun. Bus 660 runs hourly Mon-Fri from San Lorenzo de El Escorial to Valle de los Caídos. Last return at 8.45pm. Journey time 15mins.
**RENFE** (www.renfe.com) *cercanías* operate from Atocha station. There are 27 trains daily Mon-Fri; hourly trains Sat and Sun. Trains run to El Escorial town, from where it's a 2-km (1.25-mile) walk or bus ride uphill to San Lorenzo and the monastery.

### In the know
### Train trip

The **Philip II Train** (www.trendefelipeii.com) is a vintage sightseeing train that leaves from Príncipe Pío in Madrid in the morning, returning from San Lorenzo de El Escorial in the afternoon. It's €32 (€20 children) for the train and a guided visit to the monastery and town.

# MANZANARES EL REAL & LA PEDRIZA

**La Pedriza** is a rocky crag crisscrossed with paths. Birthplace of the Manzanares river, it is home to the Sierra's biggest colony of griffon vultures, protected in the Parque Regional de la Cuenca Alta del Manzanares. The area fills up on Sundays, but don't be fooled – many experienced climbers still get lost in La Pedriza, and fatalities have been known. The starting point for a hike is the town of **Manzanares el Real**, dominated by the almost cartoonish vision of a perfect 'Spanish' castle, the 15th-century **Castillo de Manzanares el Real** (91 853 00 08), once the stronghold of the Mendozas, one of the most powerful aristocratic clans of medieval Castile. Much of its interior is the product of restoration work, but the castle still retains a fascinating mix of late Gothic and Mudéjar features, especially in the courtyard and the beautiful upper gallery, which has a spectacular view over the valley. Nearby are a couple of lively bars with outdoor terraces.

## Essential information

**Getting there**
**Herederos de J Colmenarejo** (91 845 00 51, www.hjcolmenarejo.com) operates bus 724 from the Plaza de Castilla interchange every 30mins 7am-11.30pm Mon-Fri, 8am-11.30pm Sat and Sun. The last return is at 10.25pm.

# SEGOVIA & AROUND

Segovia combines beautiful architecture with visual warmth in a region more associated with austerity. In contrast with the traditional grey chill of Castile it glows, radiant and mellow. Make the approach by road across vast plains and it appears as if by witchcraft, rising on a burnished hillock like an acropolis or ship in full sail. The scene is dominated by the **Alcázar** fortress, with its sharply angled ramparts, spiky towers and high gables; a fantastical fairy-tale vision.

Close by is the huge, airy and very light Gothic **Cathedral de Segovia** (Plaza Mayor, 921 46 22 05, admission church, museum & cloister €3; church only 9am-1pm Sun free; guided visit of tower €5). The current structure was built to replace a predecessor destroyed in a 1521 revolt. Inside there's a tiny museum that holds an interesting collection of tapestries, paintings and a wonderful 16th-century grandfather clock.

Very different, but just as extraordinary as the Alcázar, is the 728-metre (2,426-foot) Roman **aqueduct**, made of Guadarrama granite in rough-hewn blocks that mesh perfectly without mortar, although it no longer brings water from the Riofrío as it first did over 2,000 years ago. The **Plaza del Azoguejo** below, where markets are now held, was a rendezvous for thieves and vagabonds in Cervantes' day. Steps rise up the wall at the place where the aqueduct merges into the hill, or you can spiral up the streets channelling traffic up and down. A warren of intricate lanes criss-crosses the old town like a demented spider's web, weaving you past squares, gardens, mansions, palaces and museums. The town is never short of tourists but is still resolutely traditional: in the Plaza Mayor the atmosphere of the past blends with real-life bustle and you can still find plenty of bars and cafés filled only with locals.

Of its dozen or so churches and convents, all built between the 12th and 16th centuries, **San Esteban**, noted for its striking bell tower, and **San Millán**, with its Moorish-influenced decor and elaborately carved wooden ceiling, stand out. Among its secular buildings the **Casa de los Picos**, with waffle-iron studs on its façade, can be found in the shopping streets downhill from the cathedral. Also not to be missed is the **Monasterio de Santa María del Parral**, founded by Henry VI and now a national monument. One of the best views is from 13th-century **Iglesia de Vera Cruz** built by the Knights Templars with spoils from the Crusades.

About 11 kilometres (seven miles) southeast from Segovia back towards Madrid on the N-101 is the **Palacio Real de La Granja de San Ildefonso**. This palace, which started life as a hunting lodge, was later converted by the Bourbons.

The charming village of **San Ildefonso** has long been a favourite resort for escaping the oppressive Madrid summer heat; if you have your own transport it offers a relaxing alternative to staying in Segovia. Among its imposing private houses is the **Casa de Infantes**, which was built by Carlos III for his sons Gabriel and Antonio.

The **Palacio de Riofrío** and its beautiful estate were built in the best deer-hunting country near Madrid, south-west of Segovia.

## Sights & museums

### Alcázar de Segovia
*Plaza de la Reina Victoria Eugenia (921 46 07 59). **Open** Oct-Mar 10am-6pm daily. Apr-Sept 10am-8pm daily. **Admission** Castle €5.50. Torre de Juan II €2.50.*

Impregnably poised on the edge of a hair-raising abyss – into which a negligent 14th-century nurse once accidentally dropped an heir to the throne and then flung herself after him to avoid punishment – the Alcázar was originally built as a modest stone fort in the 12th century, and underwent radical changes over time. Most of the world-

DAY TRIPS

Alcázar de Segovia

famous fairy-castle architecture seen today is a brilliant work of restoration carried out after a disastrous fire in 1862. Though owned by the army, the bastion's purpose is now purely commercial and its chambers are open daily for the public to inspect the weapons, armour, tapestries and artworks on display. Climb the 156 steps of the Torre de Juan II for stunning views from the panoramic terrace.

### Palacio de Riofrío

*921 47 00 19, www.patrimonionacional.es.* **Open** *Oct-Mar 10am-6pm Tue-Sun. Apr-Sept 10am-8pm Tue-Sun.* **Admission** *€4; €2 reductions; free (to EU and Latin American citizens only) Oct-Mar 3-5pm Wed, Thur; Apr-Sept 5-8pm Wed, Thur.*

After the death of Philip V, Isabel Farnese could not bear to stay on at La Granja with her stepson Fernando VI, and so had another palace built at Riofrío. She was to survive Fernando as well, however, and Riofrío was never completely finished. Later Alfonso XII came here to mourn the death of his new bride, Mercedes, and the whole palace still has a melancholy air, despite the warm pinks and greens of its exterior.

Later sovereigns also came to this estate to blast away to their hearts' content. With this in mind, half the palace has been turned into a hunting museum – a mandatory and overlong part of the guided tour. Unless row after row of antlers and stuffed animals really rock your boat, it is probably best admired from outside, particularly with a picnic.

### Palacio Real de La Granja de San Ildefonso

*921 47 00 19, www.patrimonionacional.es.* **Open** *Oct-Mar 10am-6pm Tue-Sun. Apr-Sept 10am-7pm Tue-Sun. Fountains Apr-July 5.30pm Wed, Sat, Sun.* **Admission** *Palace €4.50; €5 guided tour; €2.50 reductions; free (to EU and Latin American citizens only) Oct-Mar 3-5pm Wed, Thur; Apr-Sept 5-8pm Wed, Thur. Gardens free. Fountains €4; €2 reductions.*

This palace was built on the site of a former shrine, San Ildefonso, by Philip V, homesick for his youth in Versailles. His wife Isabel Farnese also added some distinctive touches, not least of which are the fountains. The result is perhaps the loveliest of all the Bourbon palaces.

Work on the palace structure was carried out in record time between 1721 and 1723 by Teodoro Ardamans, and on the extensive gardens over a longer period under the main supervision of René Carlier. Amid all the formal hedgerows, lawns and rows of trees you'll find voluptuous statues, limpid pools and the famous fountains, some of which spring to life three times a week in the summer (unless there is a drought, as occurred in 2017) and all of which are turned on for one memorable evening each year, on 25 August. Water comes from an artificial lake called El Mar, which is set in woodland at the end of the estate and backed by the dramatic sheer wall of the Peñalara, the highest peak in the Guadarrama.

The palace itself, which was restored after a devastating fire in 1918, is an opulent maze of elegant salons and chambers that abound in classical frescoes, dazzling cut-glass chandeliers (made in the palace's own glass factory, which still functions today) and priceless *objets d'art*. The tapestry selection, although representing only a part of the Spanish and Flemish royal collection, is among the finest you'll see anywhere. Unfortunately visits are only by guided tours of up to 45 people at a time.

## Restaurants

In Segovia, **Casa Duque** (C/Cervantes 12, 921 46 24 87, www.restauranteduque. es, €€) is a long-standing favourite, with colourfully decorated dining rooms on several floors serving excellent Castilian fare. **Restaurante José María** (C/Cronista Lecea 11, 921 46 11 11, €€€) is a traditionally styled *mesón* serving first-rate *cochinillo* (suckling pig) and probably the best lamb in town. It also has a good tapas bar. **Cuevas de San Esteban** (C/Valdelaguila 15, 921 46 09 82, www.lacuevadesanesteban.com, €€) is another place to avoid the tourist-trap market with reasonably priced Castilian food. For something different, **Narizotas** (Plaza Medina del Campo 1, 921 46 26 79, www.narizotas.net, €€) has a few unusual dishes (such as shiitake mushrooms with ham and garlic), as well as the usual parade of roast meats.

In La Granja de San Ildefonso is the wildly popular **Casa Zaca** (C/Embajadores 6, 921 47 00 87, www.casazaca.com, €€); it offers home-style cuisine, so instead of the standard roast lamb or *cochinillo* there are gutsy casseroles and braised ox tongue. It's essential to reserve ahead. Alternatively, try the tapas at the old-fashioned and friendly **El Hábito** (C/Baños 4 1, 921 47 16 46).

## Essential information

### Tourist information
**Oficina de Turismo** *C/Azoguejo 1 (921 46 67 20, www.turismodesegovia.com).* **Open** *July, Aug 9am-3pm, 4-7pm Mon-Fri; 10am-3pm, 4-6.30pm Sat; 9.30am-3pm, 4-6.30pm Sun. Sept-June 9am-2pm, 5-8pm daily.*

**Getting there**
**La Sepulvedana** (902 11 96 99, www.
lasepulvedana.es) runs around 20 buses
daily from the Príncipe Pío interchange in
Madrid to Segovia (journey time 1hr 15mins).
From Segovia there are frequent connecting
buses to La Granja (journey time 20mins).
There are six **trains** Mon-Fri and four
trains Sat and Sun from Chamartín to
Segovia, but it's a slow journey (1hr 50mins).
Alternatively, you can catch the fast train
connecting Madrid and Valladolid, which
stops at Segovia on the way. There are ten
daily trains and the journey is quicker
(30mins) but more expensive. Segovia trains
stop at Navas de Riofrío-La Losa, about
2.5km from Riofrío.

# ALCALÁ DE HENARES & AROUND

After the horrific terrorist attacks in 2004,
Alcalá de Henares was descended upon by
the world's camera crews and catapulted to
fame for all the wrong reasons. Centuries
before, all eyes were on Alcalá as Spain's
centre of learning and culture, with a superb
university, founded in 1498, and later as
the birthplace of Cervantes. As far back as
Roman times, Complutum, as it was known
then, was a large and important city.

The university moved to Madrid in the
19th century, but there is still a strong sense
of the city's educational history here today.
The streets in the old quarter are lined
with **colegios mayores** – student halls of
residence in the 16th and 17th centuries,
now converted into hotels and restaurants.
One of the most impressive is the **Colegio
de San Ildefonso**, famous for its stunning
Plateresque façade and its three-tiered
patio, which is still the setting for the
solemn opening of university terms and for
the presentation of the Cervantes Prize for
Literature.

The main square, named after the
city's most famous literary son, is a great
spot to relax over a coffee and admire the
buildings that line it, such as the **Casa
Consistorial** (town hall) and the **Capilla
de Oidor**, a 15th-century chapel now used
for exhibitions. If you want to know more
about the creator of *Don Quixote*, head to the
author's birthplace, now the **Museo Casa
Cervantes** (C/Mayor 48, 91 889 96 54, www.
museo-casa-natal-cervantes.org, closed
Mon, admission free). On the city's west side
are the **Catedral Magistral** and the **Museo
de Esculturas al Aire Libre**, an open-air
museum with 50 or so sculptures.

One of the most entertaining ways to
get to Alcalá is via the **Tren de Cervantes**
(which runs weekends in autumn and
spring, leaving Atocha station in Madrid
at 11am, and returning at 7pm). Guides in
Golden Age costume ply passengers with
information about the city, and, on arrival,
give them a tour of the town.

From Alcalá you can take a short
excursion 17 kilometres (9.5 miles) down
the M-204, to **Nuevo Baztán**. A peaceful
little place, it was founded by a banker in
the early 18th century and the entire village
was designed by renowned architect José
de Churriguera, giving it a wonderfully
harmonious feel.

## Restaurants

Alcalá's best-known restaurant is the
**Hostería del Estudiante** (C/Colegios
3, 91 888 03 30, www.parador.es, closed
Aug, €€€), which occupies a stunning
16th-century *colegio* and specialises in
hearty Castilian food – roast lamb and
suckling pig, garlic soup and the Alcalá
dessert speciality, *costrada*, which is
something like a sweet millefeuille. For
good tapas washed down with draught
*vermut*, check out the attractive, tiled bar
**Cerveceria El Hidalgo** (C/El Bedel 3, 91
883 43 48).

In Nuevo Baztán, **Mesón El Conde** (Plaza
la Iglesia 5, 91 873 53 27, €€) is a reasonably
priced, traditional place with balconies over
the square and tables outside in summer.

## Essential information

### Tourist information
**Oficinas de Turismo** *Callejón Santa María
1, Plaza de Cervantes (91 889 26 94, www.
turismoalcala.es). Open 10am-2pm, 4-7pm
daily.
Plaza de los Santos Niños s/n (91 881 06 34).
Open Sept-May 10am-2pm, 4-7pm daily.
June-Aug 10am-8pm daily.*

### Getting there
**Alsa** (91 177 99 51, www.alsa.es) bus 223
leaves the Avda de América interchange
every 10-20mins, 6.15am-midnight Mon-Fri,
every 15-20mins, 6.20am-midnight Sat, Sun.
The journey time is around 40mins.
**By car** it's approximately a 25min drive on
the A-2 (31km/19miles).
**RENFE** *cercanías* C-2 (from Chamartín)
and C-7 (from Atocha) depart from Madrid
station approximately every 10mins (15-
25mins weekends), 5.14am-11.51pm daily.
Journey time 38mins. From the station it's a
10min walk to the centre (go straight down
Paseo de la Estación).

# Spires and Tyres

*Religious recycling*

You may think you're doing your bit for the environment with that weekly trip to the recycling bins, but the average person's attempts at recycling pale into insignificance compared to the efforts of **Justo Gallego**, a pensioner in the small town of **Mejorada del Campo**, to the east of Madrid.

In the early 1960s, Justo took it upon himself to start building a **cathedral** (C/Antoni Gaudí), using stuff other people had thrown away. Neither architect nor engineer, he was a farmer before entering the Convento de Santa María de Huerta, a Trappist monastery in Soria, northern Spain. He stayed there for seven years until he caught TB and the other monks asked him to leave.

He was at something of a loose end after that, until 12 October 1961 – the feast day of Our Lady of the Pillar – when it suddenly came to him that he had been put on this earth to construct a cathedral in his home town. Justo flogged his belongings and started right away, on a patch of land he'd inherited from his parents. Unsurprisingly, the money didn't go very far, and soon he was using whatever

he could scavenge. More than 50 years later, he's still at it. Local firms sometimes donate supplies they no longer need, but otherwise he has recycled the most unlikely of materials, helped along by occasional contributions.

It's a curious sight, but the structure does somehow resemble a cathedral, and mass has even been held there. It is, however, a long way from completion. Now in his seventies, Justo is desperate for more funds and materials to complete his mission while he is still able to do so. Local builders and architects are reluctant to take the project on because it never had planning permission – or, indeed, any kind of official authorisation. In fact, Justo himself readily admits he never drew up any sort of plans and there is no guarantee it won't fall down at any minute.

The structure could be described as neo-Romanesque, and is 40 metres (131 feet) high with 12 towers. It has a large nave, partly covered by a dome with a diameter of almost 12 metres (39 feet). There's also a crypt, along with cloisters, a library and various other as yet unspecified spaces. Columns are made from oil drums, arches constructed from piles of old tyres and towers built with bits of bricks and piping. Bicycle wheels have been transformed into pulleys to get materials up the structure. The main entrance is approached by mosaic steps and spiral staircases link different levels. The structure has become a symbol of the town and attracted global media attention. If and when it will ever be completed, though, only God knows.

▶ *Bus 341 (www.redtransporte.com) departs from Conde de Casal every 15-20 minutes on weekdays and every 50-60 minutes on Saturday and Sunday. If travelling by car, it's 21km (13 miles) from Madrid via the A-3, then M-203.*

Justo Gallego

# CHINCHÓN & AROUND

Out of season Chinchón is a sleepy little town, famous for its *anís* liqueur and pretty, arcaded Plaza Mayor, overlooked by wooden balconies all the way round, and occasionally used for bullfights. This is where you'll find the town hall, tourist office and, most importantly, plenty of balcony restaurants and bars, where the traditional lunch is lamb cooked in a wood-burning oven, washed down with red from the *cuevas* (cellars) and finished off with a glass of the famous local brew.

The neoclassical **Iglesia de la Asunción** overlooking the plaza houses Goya's depiction of the Assumption. Just next door is the **Teatro Lope de Vega**, where the playwright wrote *El Blasón de los Chavos de Villalba* and which now doubles as a cinema. Just outside the town is the 16th-century castle, built on the site of the original 12th-century fortress. Sadly, only the ground floor remains, and it's home to sheep and the local outdoor drinking scene.

Chinchón hosts an open-air folk festival in the plaza at the beginning of June, and during the *fiestas* in August the bulls run the C/Huertos, and there are fireworks, a fairground and bands performing near the castle.

It's worth driving to **Colmenar de Oreja**, five kilometres away on the M-311. A quiet, untouristy place, it has an unspoilt Plaza Mayor, again ringed with wooden galleries, though on a smaller scale than Chinchón's, and a handsome 13th-century church, the **Iglesia de Santa María**. The tower is by Juan de Herrera.

## Restaurants

The balcony restaurants lining the Plaza Mayor all offer similar Chinchón fare – garlic soup and roasted red peppers, roast lamb and suckling pig. **La Casa del Pregonero** (Plaza Mayor 4, 91 894 06 96, www.lacasadelpregonero.com, €€), is slightly different – it uses local ingredients with some interesting twists, and has an attractive patio at the back. **Mesón Cuevas del Vino** (C/Benito Hortelano 13, 91 894 02 06, www.cuevasdelvino.com, €€€) is an atmospheric place, with an ancient oil press and some old carriages.

## Essential information

### Getting there
**La Veloz** (902 55 15 80, www.crtm.es) bus 337 runs from Plaza Conde de Casal (Metro Conde de Casal, line 6). Buses leave every

Plaza Mayor, Chinchón

30-45mins, 7am-11pm Mon-Fri; every 30-60mins, 8am-midnight Sat, and every 90mins, 9am-11pm Sun. The last return is at 9.30pm Mon-Fri; 10pm on Sat and Sun. Journey time is approximately 45mins.

# ARANJUEZ

Aranjuez was the official spring residence of the Spanish monarchy and its hangers-on from the 17th to the 19th century. It was probably originally chosen for its setting and lush countryside – it is an oasis in the arid plains of central Spain, situated in a wide valley formed by the Jarama and Tajo (Tagus) rivers. The royals have long gone, but the **Palacio Real de Aranjuez** (91 891 07 40, www.patrimonionacional.es) is still the principal tourist attraction, along with the town's famous asparagus and strawberries.

Originally built as a hunting lodge for Charles I of Spain (Charles V of the Holy Roman Empire), the palace took its current shape under Philip II in the 1560s, and was extended in the 1770s by Charles III. It's a charming mix of Baroque and classical styles, and typical of the Bourbon palaces, with a sumptuous throne room and a cosy ballroom. It is the gardens, however, that provide the real attraction, particularly the 16th-century-designed **Jardín de la Isla** and **Jardín del Príncipe**. The gardens inspired Rodrigo's famous *Concierto de Aranjuez* (*see p192* Garden Composition) and the music continues today with a summer season of mostly open-air concerts and musical promenades, principally featuring Baroque music. It's in the gardens that you'll find

# Garden Composition

*Aranjuez was the inspiration for Rodrigo's famous Concierto*

Influenced by Aranjuez's vast palace gardens, the *Concierto de Aranjuez*, composed in 1939 by **Joaquín Rodrigo** (1901-99), is probably the best-known piece of Spanish music. Sneered at by classical snobs, it's nonetheless a 20th-century classic, covered by greats such as flamenco guitarist Paco de Lucía and, famously, Miles Davis, who used its 'Adagio' section as the cornerstone of his *Sketches of Spain* album. The *Concierto* has featured in commercials and World Championship-winning skating routines, and even inspired Jack Black to start his 'School of Rock'.

Blinded after a diphtheria attack aged three, Rodrigo wanted the piece to depict the aural and olfactory pleasures he experienced in the Bourbon monarchs' summer retreat: 'the fragrance of magnolias, the singing of birds and the gushing of fountains'. Rodrigo drew on Spain's musical heritage – the formality of 17th- and 18th-century Baroque composers, as well as more passionate folk styles – to conjure up the magical flow of nature, as well as the splendour and darkness of the palace's history.

Unusual for pitting a solo guitar against a full orchestra, the *Concierto* comprises three movements. The first, 'Allegro con spirito', feels like an alfresco jaunt and is built on a series of switching elements – between solos and the orchestra, between the flamenco-tinged strumming of the guitar and the melody. The famous second movement, 'Adagio', is based on an Andalucían lament. Guitar and cor anglais swap the same mournful refrain back and forth, until the whole orchestra deliver an aching climax. The third movement, 'Allegro gentile', reverts back to the jauntiness of the opening movement, with a forthright mix of Baroque-like counterpoint and folk-dance melody.

'After listening to it for a couple of weeks I couldn't get it out of my mind,' said Miles Davis, in early 1959. He and collaborator Gil Evans set about reworking that haunting central 'Adagio' section for their third album together, *Sketches of Spain*. Reportedly, Rodrigo wasn't all that impressed with the end result, but many other listeners were. In his autobiography, Davis recounts the story a woman had told him of a retired matador, now raising *toros* himself, who after hearing *Sketches of Spain* had got out of his chair, put on his old bullfighting gear, gone outside and fought and killed one of his bulls. 'He said that he'd been so moved by the music that he just had to fight the bull,' Davis remembered. 'It was hard for me to believe the story, but she swore that it was true.'

The *Concierto* had its premiere in 1940 in Barcelona and brought Rodrigo worldwide fame. It is Aranjuez, though, that best commemorates the composer, with a statue off C/Infantas and, set into the pavement nearby, an inscription that includes musical notation from the *Concierto*. King Juan Carlos awarded Rodrigo the hereditary title of Marquis of the Gardens of Aranjuez in 1992. Rodrigo died in 1999 and was buried in Aranjuez's cemetery.

the delightfully over-the-top **Real Casa del Labrador** (91 891 03 05, 91 891 07 40, www. patrimonio nacional.es), which was built for Charles IV. This early 19th-century folly – complete with painted ceilings, tapestry-lined walls, and porcelain and marble floors – is said to be one of the most important examples of neoclassicism in Europe.

In the town itself, **Museo del Toro** (Avda Plaza de Toros s/n, 91 892 16 43, open Mon, Sat, Sun, admission €5, €3 reductions) aims to recreate the atmosphere of the bullfight and the traditions and entertainments of the court.

If you're so inclined you can travel to Aranjuez on the **Tren de la Fresa** steam train, with hostesses in period costume (*see p166*).

## Restaurants

**Casa Pablo** (C/Almíbar 42, 91 891 14 51, www.casapablo.net, €€€) serves up superb seafood, along with traditional local grilled meats and stews.

## Essential information

### Tourist information
**Oficina de Turismo** *Antigua Ctra de Andalucía s/n, next to Plaza de San Antonio (91 891 04 27). **Open** 10am-6pm daily.*

### Getting there
**Bus** 423 (www.redtransporte.com) from Estación Sur runs every 15-30mins, 6.30am-11.30pm Mon-Fri; every 30mins-1hr, 7am-11.30pm Sat, Sun. Last return 11pm Mon-Fri, 11.30pm Sat, Sun.
**RENFE** *cercanías* C-3 from Atocha depart every 15-30mins, 5.36am-11.50pm daily (last return 11.29pm). The steam-powered 'Strawberry Train' (Tren de la Fresa) runs on summer weekends and during holidays.

# TOLEDO

Once the imperial capital of Spain (1087-1561) and still the ecclesiastical heart of the country, 'Holy Toledo' represents two millennia of history and so holds incomparable cultural riches. Its impregnable hilltop position, tremendous fortified walls and the natural moat formed by the River Tagus have made this an important strategic stronghold for everyone from the Romans to the Visigoths, Muslims and Christians.

During the Middle Ages, Toledo was known as 'the city of three cultures', at a time when the Jewish, Muslim and Christian population lived in a uniquely heterogeneous society; many religious buildings still bear a strange palimpsest of crucifixes, stars of David and Arabic script. Over time, these religions blurred into one another, creating the Mozárabes (Christians who lived under Muslim rule with a semi-Arabic liturgy), and later the Mudéjars, Muslims who did the reverse after the Christian conquest. This air of tolerance also attracted many world-class scholars, and Toledo became a famous centre of learning with prominent schools of science, mathematics, theology and mysticism.

Now enjoying a golden age of tourism, Toledo is by far the most popular day trip from Madrid, and the cobbled streets are mobbed with tour groups until the buses depart at sundown. The city is absolutely gridlocked for the duration of the Corpus Christi processions, during which the route is marked by white awnings over the streets and the cobblestones are strewn with rosemary, thyme and rose petals. Incense and chanting give the town an eerie medieval air, as do the period costumes and the priceless Flemish tapestries hung on the cathedral walls.

## The Bisagra to the Cathedral

If you come from Madrid by bus, car or train, the main point of entry to the old walled city is the imposing **Puerta de Bisagra**. This was built at the end of the reign of Emperor Carlos V to replace the original 11th-century Moorish gate and bears his imperial crest of the two-headed eagle, the symbol of Toledo. The **Museo de Hospital de Tavera** (C/Duque de Lerma 2, 925 22 04 51, admission €4.50) is housed in the 1541 **Hospital de Tavera**, with a fine chapel and Renaissance courtyards; it has works by Tintoretto, Zurbarán and the city's adopted son, El Greco. Part of it may only be visited by guided tour.

To avoid the steep climb from here to the city, take the free escalator (7am-10pm Mon-Fri, 8am-10pm Sat, Sun). Alternatively, behind the gate, the superb Mudéjar church of **Santiago del Arrabal** stands out, with an impressive brick tower and horseshoe arches. Part of it was once a mosque, but after the Christian reconquest it was rebuilt as a church. The maze of streets on either side as you head up C/Real del Arrabal was (as the name implies) the Arrabal – an area originally outside the Christian city. Off to the right on C/Cristo de la Luz are the gardens and stunning latticed brickwork of the **Mezquita del Cristo de la Luz** (925 25 41 91, admission €2.80). Built in 999, this mosque is the oldest surviving building in Toledo. According to legend, its name came from the fact that as Alfonso VI entered

Sinagoga de Santa María la Blanca

altar, Narciso Tomé's unique 16th-century *Transparente*, a Baroque frenzy of bronze, stucco, coloured marble and painting lit by beams of light via a circular 'sunroof' dripping with alabaster putti.

## Santo Tomé and the synagogues

Just round the corner from the cathedral, the narrow alleys that lead to **Plaza del Salvador** are the most visited parts of Toledo. They are lined with shops selling Toledo's artisan products: Toledan steel has been famous for its strength since Roman times and C/Santo Tomé is packed with shops selling everything from flick-knives to sabres. Equally ubiquitous is *damasquinado* – the Damascus style of decoration brought by the Moors, in which fine threads of gold and silver are hammered into blackened metal – which covers everything from chess sets to knife handles and jewellery. For the sweet-toothed, Toledan marzipan is sold in all shapes and flavours.

The first major building en route is the **Taller del Moro** (C/Taller del Moro s/n, 925 22 71 15, 9.45am-2.15pm, 4-6.15pm Tue-Sat; 10am-2pm Sun; admission €2.80; free Wed afternoon and Sun morning), a Mudéjar workshop that houses exhibitions of Toledo crafts. Behind the Taller, down C/San Juan de Diós, follow the crowds to the Mudéjar church of **Santo Tomé** (Plaza del Conde 4, 925 25 60 98, admission €2.80), which holds only one painting: El Greco's masterpiece, *El Entierro del Conde de Orgaz*.

Round the corner lies the **Casa-Museo de El Greco** (C/Samuel Leví s/n, 925 22 36 65, admission €3), although, despite the fanfare, it has never actually been confirmed that the artist lived here. The house – a reconstructed 16th-century Toledan home – holds an impressive collection of El Greco's later works.

In medieval times this area was Toledo's **judería**, the Jewish quarter, once the world's most important centre of Jewish scholarship. Many of its finest works of Jewish-Mudéjar architecture were restored in 1992 as an act of atonement on the 500th anniversary of the expulsion of Jews from Spain. The most recent beneficiary of the makeover is the **Sinagoga del Tránsito**, a richly decorated multicultural blaze of Hebrew inscriptions, Gothic carvings and Moorish columns. It was built in 1357 and its immense size is a testimony to the huge Jewish population that once lived in Toledo. Today, there is not even the minimum number of adult males (ten) to hold a service. After 1492, the synagogue was used as a church, but it now pulls in crowds with its fascinating museum of Sephardic Jewish culture, the **Museo Sefardí** (C/Samuel

Toledo after the reconquest, his horse knelt at the door of the mosque, where, behind a stone in the archway, stood Christ, illuminated in the light of an oil lamp.

Dominating the skyline is the grim, black-turretted **Alcázar**, an enormous fortress built on the highest point of Toledo, where Roman, Visigothic and Muslim forts stood before. Using the Alcázar as a landmark, head up C/Real de Arrabal and C/Cuesta de Armas to the social nerve centre of the city, **Plaza de Zocodover**. Originally known as the *suk-al-dawad*, or animal market, it became the site for *autos-da-fé* after the reconquest, but is now lined with restaurant and café terraces serving everything from partridge to Big Macs. Nearby, the Renaissance **Hospital de Santa Cruz** (C/Miguel de Cervantes 3, 925 22 10 36, admission free) is linked to the Prado Museum, and contains tapestries, and a superb art collection including works by El Greco and Ribera.

C/Comercio, the old town's main street, leads from the Zocodover to the Plaza Mayor, dominated by the **Palacio Arzobispal** (the Archbishop's Palace) and the jaw-dropping **Cathedral** (C/Cardenal Cisneros 1, Plaza del Ayuntamiento, 925 22 22 41, admission €10, or €12.50 including access to the belltower).

Spain's second-largest cathedral (after Seville) but for many the more beautiful of the two, Toledo's cathedral was completed in 1493 after 250 years of construction. A Christian church is said to have been founded here in the first century AD by Saint Eugene, the first Bishop of Toledo. Mainly Gothic in style with touches of Mudéjar, neoclassical and Baroque, the cathedral has 750 stained-glass windows, 70 cupolas and five naves, and is supported by 88 columns with 22 side chapels. You could easily spend a whole day exploring its dark interiors but some of its most extraordinary features include the sacristy's prestigious art collection (including El Greco's *The Disrobing of Christ*), the lavishly carved central choir and, behind the main

Leví s/n, 925 22 36 65, museosefardi.mcu. es, admission €3, €1.50 reductions) where displays include crystal circumcision instruments and a 2,000-year-old ossuary.

Another surviving medieval synagogue, the **Sinagoga de Santa María la Blanca** (C/Reyes Católicos 4, 925 22 72 57, www. toledomonumental.com/sinagoga, admission €2.80) lies at the opposite end of narrow C/Judería. Its small, plain interior, dominated by horseshoe arches, is extremely beautiful, in spite of the gaudy Baroque altar that was added later.

The main street of the *judería* is now, ironically, called C/Reyes Católicos, and is topped by the very Catholic **Monasterio de San Juan de los Reyes** (C/Reyes Católicos 17, 925 22 38 02, www.sanjuandelosreyes.org, admission €2.80). Built by Ferdinand and Isabella, it was originally intended to be the royal pantheon and has a dramatic Gothic cloister and an exterior garlanded with grim black chains; during the reconquest, these chains were supposedly taken from Christian prisoners and used to hang Jewish dissidents.

Next to the monastery is a long stone balcony with impossibly romantic views over the River Tagus, the San Martín bridge and the typical *cigarrales* (Toledan country homes) on the hill opposite. For another great view, back over the whole city, head out of town over the River Tagus by the San Martín bridge, and turn right along the Carretera de Piedrabuena.

## Restaurants

As Toledo province is the hunting centre of Spain, hearty game dishes dominate. Partridge (*perdiz*) is the most typical dish, and is usually served *a la toledana* – cooked slowly with onion, garlic and bayleaf – or else with *pochas* (succulent white beans) or pickled and eaten cold. Venison and wild boar stews are another speciality, along with roast suckling pig and *cuchifrito* (fricassée of lamb with egg and wine) and *tortilla a la magra* (cured ham omelette).

All these and more are on offer at traditional restaurants such as **La Abadía** (Plaza de San Nicolás 3, 925 25 11 40, www. abadiatoledo.com, €€) where a labyrinth of bars and dining rooms fill a 16th-century palace. **Restaurante Aurelio** (C/Sinagoga 6, 925 22 20 97, www.casa-aurelio.com, €€) is in the heart of the Jewish quarter and filled with ancient farming tools. It has another branch near the Ayuntamiento (City Hall) – check the website for details. After more than a century serving food, **Venta de Aires** (Paseo Circo Romano 35, 925 22 05 45, www.ventadeaires.com, €€) must be doing something right. For a sophisticated twist

on local staples – quail fried with ginger and lemon or pork with berries – **Los Cuatro Tiempos** (C/Sixto Ramón Parro 5, 925 22 37 82, www.restauranteloscuatrotiempos.com, €€) is located in a charming 16th-century National Heritage building. For a real treat, the famous **Adolfo Restaurante** (C/Hombre de Palo 7, 925 22 73 21, www. adolforestaurante.com, €€€) is worth a visit for its fantastic wine list and light cuisine such as tempura courgette flowers with saffron.

## Essential information

### Tourist information
**Oficina Municipal de Turismo** *Plaza del Consistorio (925 25 40 30).* **Open** *10am-6pm Tue-Sun.*
**Oficina de Turismo** *Puerta de Bisagra (925 22 08 43).* **Open** *Oct-June 9am-6pm Mon-Fri; 9am-7pm Sat; 9am-3pm Sun. July-Sept 9am-7pm Mon-Sat; 9am-3pm Sun.*

### Getting there
**Alsa** (902 42 22 42, www.alsa.es, www. redtransporte.com) provides at least four buses an hour to Toledo from the Plaza Elíptica interchange terminal in Madrid. They leave every 15-30min, 6am-11pm Mon-Sat, 8am-10pm Sun. Last return at 11pm. Journey time is around 50mins on the express services, and between 60 and 90mins on standard services.
**RENFE** operates 16 trains daily to Toledo from Atocha station. The first train leaves at 6.50am Mon-Fri, and 9.20am Sat and Sun. The last train leaves at 9.50pm daily; returning, the last train is at 9.30pm daily. The average journey time is 30mins. From Toledo station, take bus L-6 to the Puerta de Bisagra or you'll face a long uphill walk.

Toledo

Experience

# Events

*A plan for all seasons*

Practically all year round – apart from perhaps during the late winter lull (when everybody is worn out and broke from Christmas, New Year and Reyes celebrations) and at the end of summer – anyone coming to the Spanish capital is likely to encounter some sort of arts festival, music festival, *fiesta* or themed film season.

Events and festivals that receive official sponsorship come under the aegis of either the Ayuntamiento (city council) or the Comunidad de Madrid (regional government), and the influence of politics, inevitably, is felt in culture. Other events, such as the annual photographic extravaganza PHotoEspaña, are independent and still more are semi-independent, functioning with a mix of public and private money.

---

**In the know**
**What's on when**

Advanced festival information is scarce as programming tends to be finalised close to the starting date. For details on Ayuntamiento-backed events, call 010 or visit www. esmadrid.com; for Comunidad-backed events, call 012 or go to www.madrid.org (Spanish only). Listings magazines such as *Time Out Madrid*, (www.timeout.es/madrid), *Guía del Ocio* (www.guiadelocio.com/madrid) and *Metrópoli* (a supplement of *El Mundo*, www.elmundo.es/metropoli) are useful.

## Spring

### Festival de Arte Sacro
*Various venues (contact tourist offices & 012, www.madrid.org).* **Date** *Mar-Apr.*

This two-month festival of music, dance, theatre, poetry, movies and conferences focuses on the role of religion in art, music, dance and film through the centuries.

### Semana Santa (Holy Week)
*All over Madrid (contact tourist offices & 010, www.esmadrid.com).* **Date** *wk leading up to Good Friday and Easter weekend (Mar/Apr).*

Easter is usually a good time to be in Madrid, as many *madrileños* get out of town for the long weekend, and the weather is usually good. In Madrid and nearby towns there are many parish processions in which hooded *penitentes* schlep figures of Christ and the Virgin around. The most impressive one is considered to be Jesús Nazareno El Pobre from San Pedro El Viejo and around La Latina. All over town there are organ and choral performances in churches.

### Día de la Mujer/Semana de la Mujer
*Various venues (contact Dirección General de la Mujer, 91 720 62 46).* **Date** *8 Mar & surrounding wk.*

International Women's Day is celebrated with a march through central Madrid (the route changes from year to year). Some of the many other related events taking place over the week include short film seasons and concerts.

Semana Santa

**Top 20**

# ♥ San Isidro

*Plaza Mayor, Los Austrias & all over Madrid
(91 578 78 10 & 010, www.sanisidromadrid.
com).* **Date** *few days around 15 May.*

For a few days around 15 May, you can
see *madrileños* doing what they do best:
taking to the streets and having a rollicking
good knees-up. The *fiestas* celebrate San
Isidro, Madrid's patron saint, a humble
12th-century labourer and well-digger to
whom all manner of miracles are attributed
and whose wife, María de la Cabeza, was
also canonised, making them the only
sainted couple in history.

The action centres on the Plaza Mayor,
where nightly gigs are held, including
*zarzuela* performances and the odd classical
concert. There is more music and dancing in
Las Vistillas park; music, theatre, painting
workshops and more are put on for kids at
parks throughout Madrid. An associated
event is the Feria de la Cacharrería, a
ceramics market, held in the Plaza de las
Comendadoras, close to Conde Duque. Also
on offer is Documenta (*see p202*), a short
season of international documentary films,
and Universimad (universimad.org), a rock
festival at the Pradera de San Isidro.

Throughout the week there are also
numerous religious ceremonies in various
churches. The 15th itself sees a procession
of vintage cars in the Castellana. Possibly
most fun of all is the traditional *romería*
(pilgrimage) in and around the Ermita de
San Isidro, in the park of the same name;
families in traditional castizo garb, looking
like something out of a Goya painting, drink
from wine skins and stuff themselves with
traditional *madrileño* delicacies such as
chorizo, morcilla and other offal dishes.

## Teatralia

*Various venues (contact tourist offices & 012, www.madrid.org/teatralia). **Date** 3wks Mar.*

A regional jamboree of performing arts, including theatre, puppet shows, circus and dance, as well as workshops and other activities aimed at children and young people.

## Dos de Mayo

*District of Malasaña (contact tourist offices & 012, www.somosmalasana.com). Metro Bilbao, Noviciado or Tribunal. **Date** late Apr-early May. **Map** p120 J10.*

Commemorating the fateful day in 1808 when the people of Madrid rose up against Napoleon's occupying troops and paid for their audacity by being massacred, 2 May is now the region's official holiday and kick-starts a nearly continuous series of *fiestas* that go on throughout the rest of the spring and summer. Things get going in the Malasaña neighbourhood – named after the uprising's teenage heroine, Manuela Malasaña – in the Plaza Dos de Mayo, where the Monteleón barracks, a main bastion of resistance, then stood. The neighbourhood association organises homespun activities, from kids' workshops to outdoor gigs and exhibitions.

## Feria del Libro Antiguo y de Ocasión

*Paseo de Recoletos, Salamanca (www.feriadeprimavera.com). Metro Banco de España or Colón. **Date** late Apr-mid May.*

This antiquarian and second-hand book fair, spanning a week either side of the San Isidro weekend, has been held annually for more than 40 years. Here you may stumble across rare treasures, out-of-print editions or recent remainders. Don't expect much in English.

## Fiesta del Trabajo (May Day)

*City centre & Casa de Campo. Metro Batán or Lago. **Date** 1 May.*

The largest May Day march, attracting upwards of 60,000 people, is organised by the communist-led CCOO and the socialist UGT unions, which converge on Sol. Smaller in scale but quite animated is the anarcho-syndicalist CGT's march from Atocha to Plaza Jacinto Benavente. The anarchist purists CNT/AIT, meanwhile, march up C/Bravo Murillo from Cuatro Caminos. Many of the participants then head to the Casa de Campo where the UGT organises a lively party with stalls run by the *casas regionales*, clubs representing Spain's regions.

## Documenta Madrid

*Various venues (91 318 44 76, www.documentamadrid.com). **Date** early-mid May.*

This popular international documentary film festival, which is organised by the Ayuntamiento de Madrid, celebrated its 14th year in 2017. It consists of screenings, workshops and related activities, in high-profile venues such as Matadero Madrid (also the festival's main office; *see p178*), Cine Doré (the Filmoteca; *see p211*) and cultural centres.

## Summer

## Suma Flamenca

*Various venues (012, www.madrid.org/sumaflamenca). **Date** May & June.*

The month-long Suma Flamenca is Madrid's high-profile flamenco festival, a feast of music, dance and intense emotion. Concert venues include Teatros del Canal (Sala Roja; *see p240*) and Pavón Cultural Kamikaze in Embajadores, plus a host of other buildings and theatres.

## La Feria del Libro (Book Fair)

*Parque del Retiro (91 533 88 36, www.ferialibromadrid.com). Metro Atocha or Ibiza. **Date** 2wks end May-June. **Map** p141.*

First celebrated in 1933, the Book Fair is now a major international event. Hundreds of publishers are present and well-known writers show up to sign copies of their works. There are also talks, children's workshops and concerts.

## PHotoEspaña

*Various venues (91 360 13 26, www.phe.es). **Date** May-Aug.*

Every spring/summer since 1998, PHotoEspaña has swept through Madrid's major museums and galleries, redefining the city as an international photography epicentre. In recent years, the retinue of

---

**In the know**
**Fiestas**

*Fiestas* usually celebrate a religious or historical event, though this is really just a pretext for dressing up, getting out and partying, something for which *madrileños* seem to have an innate talent. **Dos de Mayo, San Isidro, San Antonio de la Florida** and **La Paloma** are *fiestas* that people take part in with great gusto, and all are normally accompanied by good weather. Not that freezing temperatures or a few drops of rain are an impediment for the thousands who step out for **Reyes** (Three Kings' Day) and **Carnaval**.

# 💜 Mad Cool

*Caja Mágica, Camino de Perales 23, San Fermín (www.madcoolfestival.es). Metro San Fermín-Orcasor.* **Date** *3 days July.*

Mad Cool crashed on to the scene in 2016, with a line-up that ranged from old-timers such as Neil Young and The Who to hi-energy EDM acts such as Die Antwoord and a whole bunch of bands in between (The Prodigy, it seems, are back). The following year pulled in Foo Fighters, Green Day, Wilco, MIA, Alt-J, the Manics, Savages and a whole lot more. Bands play across five stages: the two main stages are outdoors – one perpendicular to the other, so that audiences don't need to do more than swivel between acts – and three smaller stages are indoors. It's not just about music – there are art exhibitions, theatre, and documentary screenings.

The space itself has a Coachella look to it, with a big wheel, towering art installations and an awful lot of neon, and the crowd, similarly, has a glam-hippie California vibe. The area in front of the two main stages is entirely carpeted in Instagram-friendly Astroturf, and consequently there's always somewhere non-muddy to sit. Rows of food trucks cater to every taste, and the payment system (credit loaded on to bracelets), means that the queues are bearable.

As ever, though, tips for maximum comfort include good shoes, sun cream and something to throw over your shoulders in the evening – Madrid can get very hot during the day, but it cools down a lot at night.

Foo Fighters

Savages

photographic stars has included Anders Petersen, Karlheinz Weinberger, Adam Broomberg and Pierre Molinier. PHotoEspaña also puts on projections at the Real Jardín Botánico (*see p152*). As well as exhibitions, there are workshops, courses, talks and competitions related to photography and the visual arts.

### San Antonio de la Florida
*Ermita de San Antonio de la Florida (see p169, 91 547 07 22). Metro Príncipe Pío.* **Date** *9-13 June.* **Map** *pull-out B11.*

One of the first of the summer's biggest street parties, these celebrations can trace their history back a very long way; 13 June is the feast day of San Antonio, the patron saint of seamstresses. Single women used to place 13 pins in the baptismal font of the hermitage. If one stuck to her finger she would marry within a year. The main party, including events for kids, takes place across the Paseo de la Florida, in the Parque de la Bombilla.

### LGBT Pride
*Around Chueca (www.orgullolgtb.org).* **Date** *1wk late June-early July.*

One week of partying in Chueca, Madrid's gay neighbourhood, and a huge parade on the Saturday that runs from Puerta de Alcalá to Plaza de España. There's also film, theatre, exhibitions and other cultural activities.

LGBT Pride

### Veranos de la Villa
*Various venues (www.veranosdelavilla.com).* **Date** *end June-early Sept.*

The Veranos de la Villa summer festival offers a huge variety of events, many of them free, including opera, classical music concerts, flamenco and fado performances, fireworks and even parkour. A good selection of top names have appeared over the years, and while the big names have been scaled down of late, you can still expect a range of decent acts. In 2017 these included Susana Baca and Bonnie Prince Billy. Elsewhere, *zarzuelas* are programmed in both the Centro Cultural de la Villa and in the Sabatini Gardens beside the Royal Palace. The puppet season for kids takes place in the Retiro, and fringe venues all over town offer plenty of 'alternative' shows. There are also many outdoor film screenings at venues throughout the city, including the Parque de la Bombilla, which hosts Fescinal (*see right*).

### La Casa Encendida
*Ronda de Valencia 2 (902 43 03 22, www. lacasaencendida.es). Metro Lavapiés.* **Date** *early July-late Aug.* **Map** *p109 K19.*

Concerts and low-cost films are hosted outdoors on the rooftop terrace of this cultural centre during its summer cultural programme, the Magnetic Terrace.

### Urban Beach Cinema
*C/Conde Duque 11, Malasaña (91 318 44 50, condeduquemadrid.es). Metro Ventura Rodríguez or Plaza de España.* **Date** *mid July-mid Aug.* **Map** *p120 F10.*

Every summer, the Conde Duque Cultural Centre (*see p130*) organises the Urban Beach Cinema. It features outdoor film screenings, along with hammocks, a sandy fake 'beach', cafés, food trucks and a weekend market stalls selling jewellery, clothes and homeware.

### Cibeles de Cine
*Palacio de Cibeles, Plaza Cibeles 1 (sunsetcinema.es). Metro Banco de España.* **Date** *July-Sept.* **Map** *p141 N14.*

This movie festival screens film classics under the grand glass roof of the Palacio de Cibeles. Also on offer are film-themed events with exhibitions and DJs.

### Fescinal (Cine de Verano)
*Parque de la Bombilla, Avda de Valladolid, La Florida (91 541 37 21,www.fescinal.es). Metro Príncipe Pío.* **Date** *July-Sept.*

This open-air night-time venue in Parque de la Bombilla shows double bills of mainstream films during the Veranos de la Villa festival (*see p204*). As well as the massive screen (with wayward sound), Fescinal also offers a smaller one for kids, plus the opportunity to munch on *bocadillos* washed down with *cerveza*. Some of the films are dubbed – check out the website for details.

### Verbenas de San Cayetano, San Lorenzo & La Paloma
*La Latina & Lavapiés (contact tourist offices & see www.madrid.es). Metro La Latina.* **Date** *6-15 Aug.*

This is Madrid popular culture at its best – the streets and squares of the Lavapiés, Rastro and La Latina neighbourhoods are dolled up with flowers and bunting and the locals don their *castizo* gear for some serious street partying. San Cayetano is first, on 2-8 August, followed by San Lorenzo on the 9-11 and La Paloma on the 12-15. Daytime sees parades and events for kids; by night there are organ grinders, traditional *chotis* dancing, the aroma of grilled chorizo and *churros*, sangría by the bucketful and a lot of good fun.

Verbenas de San Cayetano

## Autumn

### Estampa
*Matadero Madrid (see p178, 91 544 77 27, www.estampa.org). Metro Legazpi.* **Date** *late Sept.*

A firm fixture on the arts calendar, Estampa is a well-attended contemporary art fair that brings together galleries and collectors from around the world to exhibit prints and other artworks.

### Fiesta del Partido Comunista
*Auditorio Municipal Villa de Vallecas, C/ Monte de Montjuich 7, Vallecas (91 300 49 69, www.fiesta.pce.es).* **Date** *late Sept-early Oct.*

Now in the political minority, the Spanish Communist Party still has enough clout to stage this three-day *fiesta*. There are performances by flamenco and rock bands, stalls run by political groups, debates on many political and social issues, and lots of regional cuisine.

### Luna de Octubre
*Various venues (www.esmadrid.com/ agenda/luna-de-octubre).* **Date** *late Oct.*

Formerly known as La Noche en Blanco, La Luna de Octubre was repurposed and renamed in 2017, with a focus on light, including light installations and video mapping on iconic buildings. To have '*una noche en blanco*' means to spend a sleepless night, and this is insomniac heaven. In Madrid, as in other Spanish cities like Seville, Granada and Malaga, as well as Paris, Brussels and Riga, for one night only you can wander from exhibition centre to museum, from fashion show to concert all night long and all for free.

### Festival de Otoño a Primavera
*Various venues (contact tourist offices & 012, www.madrid.org).* **Date** *Oct-June.*

Named, somewhat clunkily, the 'Autumn to Spring Festival', this event offers numerous Shakespeare, contemporary theatre, dance and music spectacles, and remains one of the city's major performing arts events.

## Winter

### Feria de Artesanía
*Plaza de España (www.esmadrid.com). Metro Plaza de España, Sol & Gran Via.* **Date** *early Dec-5 Jan.* **Map** *pull-out F12.*

This large and crowded crafts fair is an ideal place to look for original presents and coincides with Christmas, New Year and Reyes.

### Navidad (Christmas)
*All over Madrid.* **Date** *25 Dec.*

Less hyped than in northern climes, Christmas is traditionally less important than Epiphany (Reyes; *see p206*). Father Christmas, tinsel, flashing lights and baubles are far more evident than a few decades ago, however; all these trappings, plus lots of other

Rain (Anne Teresa De Keersmaeker) performed by Rosas, Festival de Otoño a Primavera 2016 *p205*

cheap festive junk, are sold in the Christmas market in Plaza Mayor from late November to the end of December. The big family blow-out is usually on Nochebuena (Christmas Eve), with shrimps, red cabbage and either roast lamb, sea bream or both. Some families exchange presents on the otherwise fairly quiet Christmas Day, but the big ones are usually saved for 6 January.

### Noche Vieja (New Year's Eve)
*Puerta del Sol, Sol & Gran Vía. Metro Sol.* **Date** *31 Dec.* **Map** *p83 J14.*

New Year's Eve is celebrated with gusto, usually *en familia*, and involves another blow-out meal, litres of cava and the curious tradition of eating 12 grapes as the clock chimes midnight. Ever resourceful, many supermarkets now sell seedless grapes pre-packed in dozens for the occasion. The Puerta del Sol is where thousands throng. Clubs and bars organise parties.

### Reyes (Three Kings)
*All over Madrid.* **Date** *5-6 Jan.*

On the evening of 5 January, Noche de Reyes, thousands of children and their parents line up along C/Alcalá to watch the annual *cabalgata* (parade), which is also televised. Dozens of elaborate floats pass by and the riders hurl sweets to the children. Later, most families have a big dinner, and the following day presents await those who have been good. Those who haven't get a piece of coal.

### Carnaval
*Various venues.* **Date** *wk of Shrove Tuesday (Feb/Mar).*

Carnival is a very good excuse for dressing up and partying, either in the street or in Madrid's many bars and clubs. It opens in the Plaza Mayor, followed by a parade around old Madrid. On Ash Wednesday, the last day, there is a ribald ceremony during which a fish is carted around to the strains of a marching band, before being interred (*see right* Burial of the Sardine).

Puerta de Sol at New Year

# Burial of the Sardine

*A fishy festival*

It doesn't get much weirder. On Ash Wednesday, the last day of Carnival, Madrid mourns the death of a sardine. With Pythonesque absurdity, its scaly little corpse, dressed in Sunday best, is sombrely paraded through the streets of old Madrid by the Alegre Cofradía de la Sardina (Happy Brotherhood of the Sardine). They carry its diminutive coffin from bar to bar, enjoying a tongue-in-cheek display of funereal ceremony along with their *cañas*. The route changes annually, but always winds up at the Fuente de los Pajaritos in the Casa de Campo.

The origins of this wacky pageant are sadly unclear. Some say that it derives from the days when sardines were sold in abundance on the last day before Lent, and that the ripe little fellow came to symbolise the many sacrifices that lay ahead until Easter. The fish may also have phallic implications, and its burial could be a harbinger of sexual abstinence during Lent. Other sources link it to the reign of Carlos III (1759-88), when a shipload of rotten sardines arrived at his court and he ordered that they be buried immediately.

Despite the ritual's uncertain roots, Goya's masterful and macabre painting suggests that the custom was in full swing by the early 1800s (the precise date of the painting is unknown). Goya depicts a frenzied bacchanal of cavorting, masks and partner-swapping, overseen by a gruesome death mask. Despite the title of the painting, no sardines are in sight.

The sardine, its burial and other carnival merriment were suppressed during the dictatorship. La Alegre Cofradía, a small group of high-spirited friends, thought they'd chance it anyway. One Ash Wednesday in the early

▶ *Information 91 365 38 64, www. elentierrodelasardina.es.*

1950s, they marched the fish to the Casa de Campo, singing and dancing en route. The police were summoned by a priest, who felt this spectacle to be sacrilegious. The police found the entourage to contain so many venerable old lawyers, doctors and journalists, however, that they simply joined the throng.

Nowadays, the Cofradía has more than 90 members and a sister organisation, La Peña del Boquerón (Anchovy Club), for the widows of the dead sardine. The march usually begins at 10am, from sardine HQ at C/Rodrigo de Guevara 4 in La Latina (you will know the building by the fish on the door). But be prepared for a mournful moment, as all of the ornately painted miniature coffins from previous years are on display at the Cofradía site, and you will be expected to pay proper respects to the dearly departed fish.

Goya's *Burial of the Sardine* is found at the **Real Academia de Bellas Artes de San Fernando** (*see p86*).

# Film

*Madrileños and movies go together like chocolate and churros*

Spanish film goes from strength to strength, but it's been a mixed few years for Madrid's cinephiles, with several of the city's much-loved movie-houses, such as La Enana Marrón, closing down. However, the opening of Sala Berlanga, in the refurbished California cinema in the district of Argüelles, has been something of a silver lining. The cinema offers Spanish, Iberoamerican and European films in their original (undubbed) versions, and it joins a decent list of arthouse cinemas in the city – including the excellent Cine Doré Filmoteca (the national film theatre) in Lavapiés, showing old films in VO (*versión original*) – as well as a host of multiplexes.

## Spanish cinema

Spain has no film censorship and its movie aficionados have long indulged their considered taste for avant-garde cinema, which, in turn, has inspired the works of home-grown masters such as Pedro Almodóvar and Julio Médem. Once the enfant terrible of Spanish cinema, the deservedly garlanded Almodóvar now makes mature and richly textured films that are both emotionally and stylistically audacious. The metaphysical Médem, whose thrilling documentary on the Basque conflict, *Basque Ball*, made him a controversial figure in Spain, continues to court attention, as he did with his 2010 erotic lesbian drama *Room in Rome*.

Other names to keep an eye out for are the social realists Iciar Bollaín and Fernando León de Aranoa; Catalan director Isabel Coixet; the satirist Álex de la Iglesia; and the precocious maestro that is Alejandro Amenábar, who directed Nicole Kidman in *The Others*. Added to this roster are veterans such as Carlos Saura, who is still going strong.

Due to complex funding and distribution policies, an enormous number of films are made in Spain when compared with how many eventually make it into mainstream cinemas. However, a plethora of film festivals of every persuasion provides a springboard for new filmmakers and the production of short films is booming, with arthouse cinemas programming some of the best before their main features. For more on Spanish film, *see p262* Movida Movies.

## Venues

There is no shortage of multiplexes throughout the city showing Hollywood fodder dubbed into Spanish. However, if you're after a more refined experience, try the commercially viable arthouse cinemas showing Spanish auteurs, documentaries, foreign films in VO (*versión original* – undubbed and with subtitles), and an exhilarating variety of quirky, classic and controversial features. For film seasons and older films, both in Spanish and VO, head for the grand **Filmoteca** (**Cine Doré**).

---

**In the know**
**The price is right**

Monday and Wednesday are often *días del espectador* ('spectator days'), offering special discounts, though every cinema has its own policy on price reductions.

**In the know**
**Film festivals**

There are a number of film festivals in Madrid, particularly in the summer months. *See pp198-206* Events for more information.

Sala Berlanga *p212*

## Tickets and times

Daily newspapers, the weekly *Guia del Ocio* and the www.timeout.es/madrid website have film reviews and full listings. Screenings (*pases*) usually start at around 4pm. The 8pm screening is the most popular, though the late screenings (*sesiones de madrugada*) at midnight and 1am can be surprisingly packed if they're showing cult films or current favourites. Screenings tend to start promptly with few trailers or ads, though a brisk turnover means that credits are curtailed and latecomers are a constant hazard.

Read the newspapers for VO listings, and once there check whether your seating is allocated (*numerada*) before paying. Be warned of the rarity of adequately tiered seating – Spaniards are getting taller but the screens are yet to be put any higher. Internet reservations are available through www.entradas.com, and many cinemas will take advance bookings for busy times and popular films.

## VO cinemas

### Cine Doré (Filmoteca Española)
*C/Santa Isabel 3, Lavapiés (box office 91 369 11 25, information 91 369 21 18, bookshop 91 369 46 73, www.mecd.gob.es/cultura-mecd/ areas-cultura/cine/mc/fe/cine-dore). Metro Antón Martín.* **Open** *Bar-cafés 4-11pm Tue-Sun. Bookshop 5-10pm Tue-Sun.* **Tickets** *€2.50; €2 reductions. 10 films €20; €15 reductions. No cards.* **Map** *p109 K16.*

Known affectionately as 'la filmo' and featured in films by Almodóvar, this chic art nouveau national film theatre was founded more than 50 years ago. The neon-lit foyer/ café is a lively meeting place and the tiny bookshop is always full of browsers. A free, expansive, fold-out monthly programme guide features details of its eclectic seasons of films from the Spanish National Archive and world cinema. The grand auditorium is an especially marvellous place to see silent movies, sometimes accompanied by live music. The outdoor rooftop cinema and bar are open – and unsurprisingly very popular – during the summer months. Note that the box office opens at 4.15pm and stays open until 15 minutes after the start of the last performance of the night. Advance tickets can only be bought for the following day's performance and then only until a third of the capacity has been booked. Note also that you can only buy three tickets per person for each performance.

### Cine Estudio de Bellas Artes
*C/Alcalá 42, Sol & Gran Vía (91 389 25 00, www.circulobellasartes.com). Metro Banco de España.* **Tickets** *€7-€5.50; €4-€5.50 members & reductions. No cards.* **Map** *p83 L14.*

Originally a theatre, this repertory cinema is part of the grand Círculo de Bellas Artes building. The sound system is excellent, and the programme of themed film seasons goes down well with the trendy audience.

## Conde Duque Verdi

*C/Alberto Aguilera 4, Malasaña (91 447 71 84, www.cinescondeduque.es). Metro San Bernardo. **Tickets** €8.90, €10 for VIP seats; €4.95 Mon, Wed. **Map** p120 H9.*

A small selection of recent indie and mainstream films is complemented by 'Cultural Thursdays', when shows include documentaries and live screenings of classical concerts and opera. Note that films are shown in both dubbed and subtitled versions, so it pays to check listings carefully.

## Golem

*C/Martín de los Heros 14, Argüelles (information 91 559 38 36, www.golem.es). Metro Plaza de España. **Tickets** €5 Mon, Wed, Sun; €8.30 Tue, Thur, Fri; €8.90 Sat. **Map** pull-out E11.*

This legendary four-screener, once known as the Alphaville, was the first of Madrid's arthouse cinemas and played a crucial role in the Movida during the 1980s. The screens and sound systems are showing their age and tiering is inadequate, but the basement café is still a fashionable meeting place with a bohemian atmosphere.

## Pequeño Cine Estudio

*C/Magallanes 1, Chamberí (91 447 29 20, www.pcineestudio.es). Metro Quevedo. **Tickets** €8.50; €6.50 Mon & reductions; 6 films €30, 10 films €45. No cards. **Map** pull-out H8.*

It's always worth keeping an eye on this peculiar little VO cinema because its rapid turnover means that rarely viewed classics from Hollywood and world cinema often make it on to the programme.

**In the know**
**Matadero movies**

A building at the slaughterhouse-turned-cultural centre Matadero Madrid (see *p178*) has been turned into **La Cineteca** (www.cinetecamadrid.com), showing mostly documentaries and shorts. Entrance is normally free.

## Renoir Plaza de España XXXI

*C/Martín de los Heros 12, Argüelles (information 91 541 41 00, box office 91 542 27 02, www.cinesrenoir.com). Metro Plaza de España. **Tickets** €6.30 Mon; €8 Tue-Sun. **Map** pull-out F11.*

This is the flagship cinema of the enterprising Renoir chain. Screens are on the small side and the queuing system in the cramped foyer is somewhat haphazard, but good sound systems and a keen crowd of film fans ensure enjoyable viewing. **Other locations** (phone number as above): Renoir Retiro, C/Narváez 42.

## Renoir Princesa

*C/Princesa 3, Moncloa (box office 91 542 27 02, www.cinesrenoir.com). Metro Plaza de España. **Tickets** €6.30 Mon; €8 Tue-Sun. **Map** pull-out F11.*

The Renoir Princesa features an eclectic mix of Spanish, European and independent American cinema.

## Sala Berlanga

*C/Andrés Mellado 53, Argüelles (91 455 08 77, www.salaberlanga.com). Metro Argüelles, Islas Filipinas or Moncloa. **Tickets** €3. No cards.*

Named after Spanish film director Luis García Berlanga, the 250-seat VO-only cinema is one of the city's most technologically advanced. It runs special seasons and festivals, with a strong focus on documentaries, shorts and underground films.

## Verdi

*C/Bravo Murillo 28, Chamberí (information 91 447 39 30, www.cines-verdi.com/madrid). Metro Canal or Quevedo. **Tickets** €4.90 Mon; €8 Tue-Thur; €9 Fri-Sun (€6 early sessions Fri, Sat); €7 reductions. No cards.*

This relative newcomer to the ranks of VO cinemas has five screens showing a lively mix of arthouse, Spanish, independent and mainstream foreign films.

## Yelmo Cines Ideal

*C/Doctor Cortezo 6, Lavapiés (information 91 369 25 18, box office 902 22 09 22, www.yelmocines.es). Metro Tirso de Molina. **Tickets** €7.30-€7.90 Mon, Wed; €9.20 Tue, Thur-Sun.**Map** p109 J15.*

This hugely popular nine-screen multiplex is an efficient if somewhat characterless venue for international mainstream films in *versión original*.

# Essential Madrid Films

*Celluloid city*

### Día de la Bestia (The Day Of The Beast)
*Alex de la Iglesia 1995*

A devilishly funny horror-comedy in which a priest becomes convinced that the Antichrist will be born in Madrid on Christmas Day. Immersing himself in evil, he searches for clues among the city's human detritus and in the lyrics of death metal songs, before kidnapping, with the help of a gonzoid record-shop assistant, a famous TV para-psychologist.

### Abre Los Ojos (Open Your Eyes)
*Alejandro Amenábar 1997*

A dazzling thriller that toys with our perceptions to exquisite effect. Playboy César seems to have it all – until his obsessive ex-girlfriend tries to kill him, leaving him so disfigured that he needs a prosthetic mask. But his problems are just beginning as the film lurches from noir-ish poser to latter-day *Beauty and the Beast*, and eventually to head-spinning sci-fi mode.

### Lovers of the Arctic Circle
*Julio Medem 1999*

A love story that burns like ice. Otto is just eight years old when he falls in love with Ana. The first time she lays eyes on him, she sees her dead father looking back at her. And Otto's father, Alvaro, also falls in love, with Ana's mother Olga. They make a family with a faultline running through its heart. Teasing, allusive and elusive, this is also perhaps Medem's most deeply felt movie.

### El Método (The Method)
*Marcel Piñeyro 2005*

Competing for a post at a Madrid corporation, seven candidates are exposed to the sadistic 'Grönholm Method' that forces them to identify a mole in their midst, eliminate others and plead to stay on. The anti-capitalist argument is hammered home (as the candidates clash, anti-globalisation protestors rip up the city), but the strong cast maintains the intensity and malicious humour.

### Volver
*Pedro Almodóvar 2006*

Penélope Cruz stars as a working-class housewife in this fable of long-suffering drudgery overcome by domestic homicide and the whiff of quotidian magic (and bodily odours). The story is at once hysterical and mundane, founded in abuse, rape, murder and corpse disposal, yet ultimately about none of these so much as the endurance of the characters involved.

### The Bourne Ultimatum
*Paul Greengrass 2007*

Madrid plays itself and also stands in for Turin in this, the third part of the satisfying action franchise. Bourne (Matt Damon) is still on the run, gradually remembering how US security forces reshaped him as a super-assassin while trying to avoid their determined efforts to neutralise him. A UK newspaper exposé makes his position all the more dangerous.

Volver

# Nightlife

*From funk to flamenco, the capital shines brightly after dark*

While the pace of Madrid's nightlife scene may have slowed down somewhat from its early noughties heyday, *madrileños* still party harder – and later – than most. And they do so in spite of interference from the local council, which fails to see the value of the capital's after-dark antics, though that gives the whole scene an underground feel. Many Madrid clubs double up as gig venues too, giving much-needed space to the city's up-and-coming bands. The best way to see flamenco is to bar-hop in the streets that live and breathe it, such as C/Echegaray. Rule of thumb: the more the punters look like the performers, the more chance there is that you've found the right place.

## CLUBS & LIVE MUSIC VENUES

Nightlife here has distinct stages. In the early evening, from 6pm until midnight, teenagers take to the streets. Most of them congregate in parks and squares, and engage in what is known as the *botellón*.

At around 11pm, a more mature crowd starts to spill out of the restaurants and hits the bars. Generally, bars break down into a few distinct categories. *Bares de copas* sell spirit-based drinks with or without a DJ in the corner. Next come the *discobares*, which may require a cover charge and bang out international and Spanish pop, perfect for their alcohol-fuelled clientele. Then there are the funkier pre-club bars, often with a house DJ warming you up for a night on the town. City legislation says that bars must close at around 3am: precisely the moment when the clubs or *discotecas* start to fill up. (*Discoteca* carries no cheesy connotations in Spanish; in fact, be careful what you ask for when talking to locals – *club* in Spanish usually means brothel.)

A lot of nightclubs will let you in free before 1am (though you might find the place a bit lonely). Any later and there'll be a cover charge of €10-€15, but that will normally include one or even two drinks at the bar. The late-night clubs start closing their doors at around 6am, but the night's still not over. Plenty of clubbers spill out into what are commonly referred to as 'old men's bars' for a few early morning beers, before finally staggering home. But those with energy to burn seek out the after-hours bars (*los afters*). There aren't as many as there used to be, but they are out there; you just need to ask around.

Ocho y Medio DJs

### In the know
### Price to party

The ticket you're given on the door of a club is almost always valid for a drink, so don't toss it away. Spain has recently seen a hike in prices across the board and some of the swankier clubs will charge you as much as €15 for a long drink, and €10 for a beer. Remember, though, measures for long drinks are huge, so if you're on a tight budget, stick to the rum and Coke. Before you head out, it's also worth checking club websites for printable flyers or guest lists that'll get you in for a discount.

### ♥ Best for night owls

**Café Central** *p219*
For class jazz acts.

**Casa Patas** *p227*
For foot-stomping flamenco.

**Gymage** *p230*
For rainbow-hued lounging.

**Medias Puri** *p222*
For speakeasy glamour.

**El Sol** *p218*
For scruffy Movida vibes.

**Teatro Kapital** *p221*
For a choice of dancefloors.

Apart from the Palacio de Deportes (**WiZink Center**, *see p159*), concert venues are mostly small, intimate affairs in the centre of the city, with bigger acts usually requiring a trip out to the suburbs. Venues listed don't charge admission unless otherwise stated. These days, smaller bands usually pay to play in venues, with the take on the door going directly to them – along with a cut of the bar take, too, if they're lucky. Few venues accept credit cards on the door, although many will at the bar. To make licensing issues easier, a lot of listed venues stay open as nightclubs after the concerts.

## Los Austrias & La Latina

### Contraclub

*C/Bailén 16 (91 365 55 45, office 91 523 15 11, www.contraclub.es). Metro La Latina.* **Open** *10pm-6am Thur-Sat (11pm-6am non-concert nights).* **Admission** *free; €10 (incl 1 drink) after 1.30am.* **Concerts** *prices vary.* **Map** *p62 E16.*

A dark and rather labyrinthine venue, Contraclub is a favourite with the acting set – local lush Javier Bardem has been known to drop in with Woody Harrelson. The groups appearing here tend to be Spanish acts, and range from singer-songwriters and jazz groups to fusion outfits. DJs take over after the gigs are done.

### Marula

*C/Caños Viejos 3 (91 366 15 96, www.marulacafe.com). Metro La Latina.* **Open** *11pm-6am Tue-Sun.* **Admission** *varies. No cards.* **Map** *p62 F16.*

This small venue serves as bar, club and live music venue. There are gigs on weekday nights (check the website for details), followed by DJ sessions. But the place really hots up at weekends, attracting DJ sessions from local talent such as Antonio Requena, Casbah 73 and Comandante Kwenya. The summertime terrace is a big pull, filling up by midnight and staying that way.

### Shôko Restaurant & Lounge Club

*C/Toledo 86 (91 354 16 80, www.shokomadrid.com). Metro Puerta de Toledo or La Latina.* **Open** *11.30pm-6am Fri, Sat.* **Admission** *varies.* **Map** *p62 F18.*

This popular space houses an oriental restaurant (at the top), and a slick lounge-club with high ceilings and minimalist decor made up of bamboo, water features, Japanese panels and contemporary furniture. Its non-fussy music policy – commercial dance and Latin – attracts a fun-seeking crowd in their twenties and early thirties, who get

dressed up for the occasion and are mostly on the pull.

### Terraza Atenas

*C/Segovia & C/Cuesta de la Vega (91 161 01 37, 91 868 422 24, www.terrazaatenas.com). Metro Ópera or Puerta del Ángel.* **Open** *6pm-3am daily. Closed Nov-Mar.* **Admission** *free. No cards.* **Map** *p62 D15.*

A super-cool *terraza* that's set in its own small park. The plentiful tables in the front bar are filled by midnight and the overflow swells on to the surrounding gentle grass slope. With no neighbours to worry about, the crowd can enjoy the easy sounds of soul, funk and lounge long after other *terrazas* have called it a night. There are live gigs on Thursday nights.

## Sol & Gran Vía

For the much-loved cocktail/DJ bar **Museo Chicote**, *see p90*.

### Café Berlin

*C/Costanilla de los Ángeles 20 (91 559 74 29, berlincafe.es). Metro Callao.* **Open** *10pm-5.30am Tue-Sat; 9pm-3am Sun.* **Admission** *varies.* **Map** *p83 G13.*

A stalwart on the Madrid scene, the legendary Café Berlin was forced to move from its old location in 2016, but its fancy new digs (just around the corner) are bigger and plusher. Gigs usually get going around 10pm, with salsa on Tuesdays and flamenco on Wednesdays. The concerts are followed by club sessions from 1am (Tue-Sun)..

### La Coquette

*C/Hileras 14 (91 530 80 95). Metro Ópera or Sol.* **Open** *Sept-Apr 8pm-3am Tue-Sun. May-Aug 9pm-3am Tue-Sun.* **Admission** *free. No cards.* **Map** *p83 H14.*

This basement bar, which has been going since the 1980s, was Madrid's first venue dedicated exclusively to blues. It's run by a Swiss-Spanish guy called Albert, who has a large collection of old records that won't disappoint, and there are live acts featuring local bluesers from Tuesday to Thursday, plus a great Sunday night jam session

### Costello Club

*C/Caballero de Gracia 10 (91 522 18 15, www.costelloclub.com). Metro Sol or Gran Vía.* **Open** *8pm-2.30am Tue; 8pm-3am Wed, Thur; 8pm-3.30am Fri, Sat.* **Admission** *€5-€10.* **Map** *p83 K13.*

Don't be put off by the seedy street – Costello Club is a centrally located, popular live music venue, with two distinct areas. Head to the comfy ground-floor space to enjoy an expertly mixed gin and tonic before heading downstairs to the cave-like basement to catch a live gig. The schedule takes in everything from pop and rock to indie and folk, and there are also theatre productions, stand-up comedy and even magic shows

## Joy Eslava

*C/Arenal 11 (91 366 37 33, joy-eslava.com). Metro Ópera or Sol.* **Open** *Club nights midnight-6am daily.* **Admission** *€20 (incl 2 drinks).* **Map** *p83 H14.*

Unusual in that it retains some original trappings of its former incarnation as a 19th-century theatre, in every other respect this is an ordinary high-street club, where the vast dancefloor is crammed with a young and dressed-up set, enjoying staple disco house. As a live music venue, Joy Eslava hosts some of the best Spanish names, from flamenco supremo Tomasito and beloved crooner Raphael to Catalan popsters Manel.

## Sala Cocó

*C/Alcalá 20 (913 60 16 11, www.mondodisko. es). Metro Sevilla.* **Open** *12.30am-6am Thur-Sun.* **Admission** *varies.* **Map** *p83 K14.*

Sala Cocó is located on the site of the former Alcalá 20 club, where 81 people lost their lives in a fire in 1983. The site lay empty

### In the know
### Sweet endings

The *madrileño* chocolate and *churros* tradition truly comes into its own in the *madrugada* (pre-dawn hours). Old-school fave **Chocolatería San Ginés** (see p71) is open 24 hours a day, and is a hive of activity once the bars and clubs shut.

for years, but finally reopened in 2010 and soon regained its pre-eminent role in *madrileño* nightlife. Mondo, a Thursday night electronica session, is one of the city's biggest nights out, while DJs spin R&B, funk, house and hip hop on Fridays and Saturdays..

## ♥ El Sol

*C/Jardines 3 (91 532 64 90, www. salaelsol.com). Metro Gran Vía or Sol.* **Open** *10pm-5.30am Tue-Sat.* **Concerts** *vary.* **Admission** *(incl 1 drink) €12.* **Map** *p83 K13.*

To call this Movida remnant 'no-frills' is an understatement – as its faded yellow walls and middle-aged bar staff attest. However, as everyone knows, it's the music and crowd that make a night, and that's where El Sol is a winner. A steady flow of live acts pass through, offering a mix of rock, R&B, punk, soul and hip hop. The DJ serves up an equally eclectic selection. Before long you're lured on to the floor and there you'll stay, getting down with a varied crowd of twenty- and thirtysomethings. The venue is the city's classic climax to a big night out.

# Huertas & Santa Ana

## El Burladero

*C/Echegaray 19 (mobile 620 370 662). Metro Sevilla or Sol.* **Open** *9pm-3.30am daily.* **Admission** *free.* **Map** *p95 K15.*

A cosmopolitan crowd, buzzing to the sound of flamenco and rumba, throngs the Moorish arches amid Andalucian tiles and a rogues' gallery of bullfighters. Upstairs the rumba rumbles but doesn't dominate. Head up here for respite and a chat with the languid barman, but the frenzied guitar and pistol-shot hand-clapping will eventually lure you back.

Joy Eslava

## ♥ Café Central

*Plaza del Ángel 10 (91 369 41 43, www.*
*cafecentralmadrid.com). Metro Antón*
*Martín or Sol.* **Open** *11am-2.30am Mon-*
*Thur, Sun; 11am-3.30am Fri, Sat.* **Concerts**
*9-11pm daily.* **Admission** *Concerts €15-€24.*
**Map** *p95 J15.*

For many years now, this beautiful space, with high ceilings and elegant decor, has been *the* place to get your jazz fix in Madrid. The artists it attracts place it among Europe's best jazz venues. Recent acts include the Jean Toussaint Quartet, Wallace Roney, Rick Margitza Quartet, and Pia Tedesco, who is one to look out for.

### Las Cuevas de Sésamo

*C/Príncipe 7 (91 429 65 24). Metro Sevilla*
*or Sol.* **Open** *6pm-2am Mon-Thur, Sun;*
*6pm-2.30am Fri, Sat.* **Admission** *free. No*
*cards.* **Map** *p95 K15.*

If you want proof that partying Spaniards are among the noisiest, most raucous people on the planet, then Sésamo is the ideal place to put that to the test. You'll be attended to by smartly dressed waiters, who will accommodate you at a table no matter how big your group. A piano player does his best to make himself heard above the cacophony that reigns between 9pm and 1am, as a young crowd that's mostly composed of students enjoys the cheap beers and jug after jug of the famous sangria. A good choice to start the night rather than a final destination.

### La Fontana de Oro

*C/Victoria 1 (91 531 04 20, www.*
*fontanadeoro.com). Metro Sol.* **Open**
*1pm-6am daily.* **Concerts** *at 10pm.* **Prices**
**vary.** **Map** *p95 K15.*

With the kudos of being Madrid's oldest bar, this place used to be a real institution. These days, though, it's an Irish theme pub. It's run of the mill by day, but everything changes when night falls. Then the crowd packs in, fuelling up for the night ahead and losing themselves to a mix of classic beer anthems and a variety of live music.

> **In the know**
> ### Survival tips
>
> Having changed your body clock to suit your schedule in Madrid, there are just a few more things you need to bear in mind before you go out seeking *la marcha*, or a good time. Firstly, don't get too dolled up; with some exceptions, Madrid is not a town where people dress to impress. Creativity is more important than couture. Secondly, be careful with the drinks; measures poured here are such that you may, for once, ask the bartender to put a little less in. And finally, be aware that there's a specific window of time for every venue in Madrid – if you turn up to a club or bar and it's empty, you might just have arrived at the wrong hour.

Café Central

# Essential Madrid Albums

*Sounds of the city*

### De Alaska A Fangoria (Alaska, 2005)
Alaska – a feisty flame-haired darling of the Movida cultural explosion of the late 1970s and '80s (see p264), is Mexican-born but viewed as the quintessential *madrileña*. As a performer, she's still going strong as part of electro pop duo Fangoria, but this album chronicles her various incarnations.

### Songhai (Ketama, 1988)
Leading proponents of the New Flamenco movement, this trio opened up musical horizons when they adopted rhythms from around the world – rumba, reggae, salsa and funk among them – and created a whole new sound. While *Songhai* isn't their most typically Spanish album, it's probably their best.

### Concierto de Aranjuez (Joaquín Rodrigo, 1939)
The best-known piece of Spanish classical music in the world, the *Concierto de Aranjuez* was inspired by the gardens of the royal palace at Aranjuez (see p191), just 40 minutes from Atocha station. Composer Joaquín Rodrigo was a pianist, but wrote the piece for classical guitar and orchestra.

### Descanso Dominical (Mecano, 1988)
Unabashedly poppy trio Mecano have sold over 25 million albums in their time, and had more international success than any other Spanish group. *Descanso Dominical* contains perhaps their two most popular hits – 'Mujer contra mujer' (radical for its time in that it deals with lesbianism), and 'La fuerza del destino'.

### Malas Compañías (Joaquín Sabina, 1980)
After a period of exile in London in the '70s, Sabina moved to Madrid following Franco's death and had his musical breakthrough when he was signed by Sony and produced *Malas Compañías* (Bad Company). This yielded his best-loved hit, 'Pongamos que hablo de Madrid' ('Let's say I'm talking about Madrid').

### Fuerteventura (Russian Red, 2011)
Singer-songwriter Lourdes Hernández, known as Russian Red, is inspired by artists such as Joanna Newsom and Feist, which comes through in her own brand of fey nu folk. She sings in English and, on this Glasgow-produced album, collaborated with Belle & Sebastian, with whom she has also toured.

Teatro Kapital

### The Roof

*Hotel ME Madrid Reina Victoria, Plaza Santa Ana 14 (91 701 60 20, www.es.melia. com). Metro Sol or Antón Martín.* **Open** *Winter 9pm-2am Wed, Thur; 9pm-3am Fri, Sat. Summer 9pm-3am daily.* **Map** *p95 K15.*

If you're looking to impress on a date and feel like splashing some cash then head to the side door of the ME Madrid hotel, which is guarded by a couple of menacing-looking bouncers. If your attire passes muster they'll usher you into an express lift, which will take you up to one of the swishest terraces in town, with amazing views of the city in all its neon glory. Drinks are pricey (a G&T costs €18), but the loungers, bed-like chill-out booths and carefully crafted soundtrack make it worth a visit.

### ♥ Teatro Kapital

*C/Atocha 125 (91 420 29 06, www.grupo-kapital. com). Metro Atocha.* **Open** *midnight-5.30am Thur; midnight-6am Fri, Sat.* **Admission** *€10-€30.* **Map** *p95 M17.*

This giant among Madrid clubs offers splendid views of the main dancefloor from many of the upper balconies. Each of the seven levels has something different to offer: the main dancefloor and bars are at ground level; the first floor has a VIP area; the second has karaoke; the third R&B and hip hop; the fourth a cosy cocktail bar; the fifth is the so-called 'Party Zone'; the sixth is all about mojitos; and at the top is a terrace with a retractable roof and smoking area. Smart casual is the order of the day.

### Torero

*C/Cruz 26 (91 523 11 29, www. discotecatorero.es). Metro Sol.* **Open** *10pm-5am Thur; 10am-6am Fri, Sat.* **Admission** *€12 (incl 1 drink) Thur-Sat; free Mon-Wed, Sun.* **Map** *p95 J15.*

Don't be put off by the forbidding exterior, the only thing not dancing inside Torero is a wall-mounted bull's head that stares down impassively. A mixed crowd of Spaniards and tourists gyrates to Spanish and Latin beats on one floor, and commercial dance and house on the other.

## Lavapiés & the Rastro

If you're interested in some impromptu late-night flamenco, try **Candela** (*see p227*).

### El Juglar

*C/Lavapiés 37 (91 528 43 81, www.salajuglar. com). Metro Lavapiés.* **Open** *7.30pm-3am Wed; 9pm-3am Thur; 9pm-3.30am Fri, Sat.* **Concerts** *usually at 10pm or 10.30pm.* **Admission** *varies.* **Map** *p109 J17.*

Epitomising Lavapiés, El Juglar is a laid-back hangout for those who like the tempo of their evening to be energetic but not too frenetic. The bare red brick and chrome front bar provides a chilled background for the broad-based crowd to enjoy a soundtrack of jazz and soul. After midnight the rhythm speeds up in the back as the resident DJs play a mix of souped-up soul, Latin and funk.

# All That Jazz

*Madrid's jumping joints*

Madrid is a city lacking a long history of jazz culture, but things are changing. Practically every night of the week there's a jazz jam in some corner of the capital, often featuring foreign musicians living in Madrid. But there are also more and more local jazz talents – many of whom have spent time living and playing in other cities around the world.

Founded in 1982, **Café Central** (see *p219*) is the classic venue on the scene, often booking invited artists for a whole week, thus allowing performances to evolve. On Mondays, you could catch the jazz jam session with Groovin Santa at **El Intruso** (see *p223*). If it's the quality of the sound that really matters, then the best blue notes in the city are to be heard at **Bogui Jazz** (see *p223*) and **El Junco** (see *p223*). Stalwart venue **Café Berlin** (see *p217*) has a new home and a new lease of life, while **BarCo** (see *p223*) is a relative newcomer that attracts interesting performers from the School of Creative Music. But the granddaddy of them all is still **Clamores** (see *p225*), which first opened its doors in 1979 and offers jam sessions on Fridays and Saturdays.

El Intruso

### ♥ Medias Puri

*Plaza Tirso de Molino 1 (91 521 69 11, mediaspuri.com). Metro Tirso de Molina.* **Open** *10.30pm-5.30am Thur (Karate Kid Sessions); 11.30pm-6am Fri, Sat.* **Admission** *€18 (incl 1 drink) 1st visit, when you're given a key card; thereafter €15 (incl 1 drink).* **Map** *p109 J16.*

The hottest address in town, Medias Puri plays on all the best speakeasy traditions and was designed by the creators of *The Hole*, a risqué show which combines burlesque and Cirque du Soleil-style showmanship. First of all, the entrance is through what appears to be an old-fashioned haberdashery. Once inside, you'll find three dancefloors, one with spectacular dance and acrobatic shows, and a fabulous cocktail bar decked out like an old apothecary. There's a complicated key system: you're given one on your first visit, and it gets you a discounted admission price on subsequent visits.

## Chueca

For gay clubs in Chueca (and elsewhere), see *p229*.

### Areia

*C/Hortaleza 92 (91 310 03 07, www. areiachillout.com). Metro Chueca.* **Open** *4pm-3am Mon-Fri; 2pm-3am Fri, Sat.* **Admission** *free.* **Map** *p120 L11.*

Areia is a chill-out space that has all the angles covered: by day it's somewhere to get lunch or a snack, in the afternoon it becomes a place to chill, and by the evening the vibe has hotted up enough for a cool crowd that passes through on their nightly tour of the city (there are DJ sessions from Wednesday to Saturday nights). The seductive eastern decor, along with sofas and cushions for lounging, can make it difficult to leave.

## Bogui Jazz

*C/Barquillo 29 (91 521 15 68, bogui.es). Metro Chueca.* **Open** *10pm-1.30am Wed, Thur; 10pm-6am Fri, Sat; 6.30-9.30pm every other Sun.* **Concerts** *10.30pm, 11.30pm.* **Admission** *varies.* **Map** *p120 M12.*

The pet project of an American who has lived in Madrid for almost half a century, Bogui is now a reference point for local and visiting jazz musicians alike. It has an intimate 50-seat concert space and a basement bar with TVs screening the show. Once the live stuff is over, DJs take over: mainly pop upstairs, mainly R&B and hip hop downstairs.

## Búho Real

*C/Regueros 5 (91 308 48 51, www.buhoreal. com). Metro Alonso Martínez or Chueca.* **Open** *from 7pm daily.* **Concerts** *from 8pm.* **Admission** *varies. No cards.* **Map** *p120 L11.*

The lights go down very low in the Búho Real, and the spots come up on a tiny stage. The size limitations here dictate the acts – expect local jazz or acoustic groups, most of them just two- or three-piece bands. The name means the 'Royal Owl', which goes some way towards explaining the large collection of miniature owls on display.

## El Intruso

*C/Augusto Figueroa 3 (91 531 89 96, www. intrusobar.com). Metro Chueca.* **Open** *9pm-5.30am Mon-Thur, Sun; 9pm-6am Fri, Sat.* **Admission** *varies.* **Map** *p120 K12.*

The name means 'the intruder', and that's what you may feel like as you slip into this new venue, which is housed in what looks like an office block and lies behind a large, intimidating wood-panelled door. But you're on safe ground once inside, where you can get comfy at the tables or perch on the diner-style bar stools. The small stage plays host to a variety of local acts, including bigger names such as Gecko Turner, as well as international visitors such as Bob Stroger. Late opening makes it perfect if you're on a midweek bender.

## El Junco

*Plaza Santa Bárbara 10 (91 319 20 81, www. eljunco.com). Metro Alonso Martínez.* **Open** *11pm-5.30am Tue-Thur, Sun; 11pm-6am Fri, Sat.* **Admission** *€6-€10 (incl 1 drink).* **Map** *p120 L11.*

This is the ultimate late-night jazz spot in the city, boasting jam sessions and gigs nearly every night of the week. When there aren't live musicians for your listening pleasure, DJs spin vinyl with just the right amount of off-beats.

## Ocho y Medio

*Sala But, C/Barceló 11 (no phone, www. ochoymedioclub.com). Metro Tribunal.* **Open** *midnight-6am Fri, Sat.* **Admission** *€15 (incl 1 drink).* **Concerts** *€10-€25.* **Map** *p120 K10.*

This popular club night has been running since the late 1990s, and relies on an alcohol-fuelled mass of party energy that's driven by the eclectic mix of indie, electro-clash, electro-pop, new wave and New York rock spun by the resident DJs. Located practically in the basement of Teatro Barceló *(see p223)*, this is the place to head to if the glammed-up crowds jostling to get in via the VIP queue of that club fill you with dread.

## Teatro Barceló

*C/Barceló 11 (91 447 01 28, teatrobarcelo. com). Metro Alonso Martínez.* **Open** *midnight-6am Thur-Sat.* **Admission** *€15 (incl 1 drink).* **Map** *p120 K10.*

This club (formerly Pachá) calls itself the 'best in Madrid', and it does a good job of living up to its own hype with its roster of top national and international DJs and a glamorous crowd. Thursday nights are student nights, while Friday and Saturday nights are for the over-25s (bring ID). There are two dancefloors, with reggaeton in the smaller of the two and house and electro pop in the larger one.

## Ya'sta

*C/Valverde 10 (no phone, www.facebook. com/YastaClub). Metro Gran Vía.* **Open** *8pm-5am Mon; 9pm-5am Tue; midnight-5am Wed; midnight-6am Thur-Sat; 5pm-5am Sun.* **Admission** *€9-15 (incl 1 or 2 drinks). No cards.* **Map** *p120 J13.*

There's perhaps only one place in Madrid where you'll find funk, breaks, reggae, techno, dubstep, salsa, swing, country and boogie all under one roof – and Ya'sta is it. The club itself is industrial-style, with psychedelic projections on the walls and graffiti in the corridors. Depending on the night, the venue attracts anyone from young techno-heads and breakdancers to a more grown-up rock crowd.

## Malasaña & Conde Duque

## BarCo

*C/Barco 34 (91 531 77 54 www.barcobar. com). Metro Tribunal or Gran Vía.* **Open** *10pm-5.30am daily.* **Concerts** *times vary.* **Admission** *Concerts free to €12 (incl 1 drink). Club €8 (incl 1 drink).* **Map** *p120 J12.*

The lines snaking up Calle del Barco will give away the location of this excellent venue, which hosts concerts in the early evening and then DJs till the wee small hours. Everything from funk and soul to rap-metal goes on the turntables, letting the crowd go wild in the near pitch-black ground floor and basement areas. A classic in the 'hood.

## Café la Palma

*C/Palma 62 (91 522 50 31, www.cafelapalma. com). Metro Noviciado. **Open** 5pm-3am Mon-Thur, Sun; 5pm-3.30am Fri, Sat. **Concerts** 10pm; DJs from midnight. **Admission** Concerts €5-€10 (incl 1 drink). DJ sets free. **Map** p120 G10.*

This is a longstanding favourite with the Malasaña crowd and has been going for more than two decades. Choose from an area with tables; a chill-out zone where everyone lazes around on cushions on the floor; or the main room, where you can catch concerts from big local names such as La Bien Querida or Vetusta Morla from Thursday to Saturday.

## Démodé

*C/Ballesta 7 (mobile 680 202 576). Metro Gran Vía. **Open** 11pm-3.30am Thur-Sat. **Admission** free. **Map** p120 J12.*

A juxtaposition of the über-trendy and the super-cheesy, this hugely popular pre-club joint is housed in an old brothel. Faux oil paintings still adorn the walls, but red lighting, sofas and an ample sound system have transformed it into one of the coolest nightspots in town. DJs spin everything from nu disco and tech-house to deep house and disco for an appreciative mixed gay/straight crowd.

## El Fabuloso

*C/Estrella 3 (mobile 651 829 373). Metro Noviciado or Callao. **Open** 8.30pm-3.30am Wed-Sat. **Admission** free. **Map** p120 H12.*

The glamorous Silvia Superstar is behind this neighbourhood favourite, which is tucked away in a corner off one of the seedier squares in the capital. The former frontwoman of the splendidly monikered Killer Barbies rock group, Silvia is often to be found behind the decks, either in the kitsch upstairs lounge or on the heaving basement dancefloor. Along with the other Fabuloso DJs, she plays a heady mix of northern soul, swing, rock 'n' roll and 1960s and '70s classics. A magnet for gorgeous Malasaña hipsters.

## El Perro de la Parte Atrás del Coche

*C/Puebla 15 (mobile 618 783 054). Metro Gran Vía or Callao. **Open** 10pm-3.30am Thur-Sat. **Admission** €10 (incl 1 drink) Fri, Sat; free Tue, Thur & before 1am. Concerts €3-€10. No cards. **Map** p120 J12.*

You're guaranteed a top night at El Perro, a quirky basement club with a vaulted ceiling whose full name translates as 'the nodding dog'. After the early live gigs, resident DJ and owner Jamie Steel mixes up everything from pop and rock to early electro on Friday and Saturday nights, while there are all kinds of weird and wonderful live acts on Thursdays, followed by DJ sessions.

## Siroco

*C/San Dimas 3 (91 532 13 57, www.siroco.es). Metro Noviciado. **Open** 8pm-5am Thur-Sat. **Admission** varies. **Map** p120 G10.*

A wonderfully creative crew run Siroco, something that is abundantly clear from the programme and the visuals of the club itself. Doubling as a live music venue, it starts to hot up after concerts finish at around 2am, when a crowd composed mainly of wannabe b-boys, club kids and beardy young students get down to the soul, funk and rare groove seven-inchers deftly woven together by the resident DJs.

## Tempo

*C/Duque de Osuna 8 (91 547 75 18, www. tempoclub.net). Metro Plaza de España. **Café** 6pm-3am Mon-Thur; 4pm-3.30am Fri, Sat; 4pm-3am Sun. **Club & concerts** 11pm-5.30am Thur-Sat. Closed Aug. **Admission** Café free. Club & concerts varies. **Map** p120 F11.*

A very cosy little venue that doubles as a daytime café and a nighttime venue for live acts and DJs. You can sit and have a bite or an early cocktail in the pleasant upstairs lounge, before heading downstairs to the dancefloor to enjoy the funk, afrobeat and soul tunes from the DJs or local bands.

## Tupperware

*C/Corredera Alta de San Pablo 26 (91 446 42 04, www.facebook.com/tupperwarebar). Metro Tribunal. **Open** 8pm-3am Mon, Tues, Sun; 9pm-3am Wed, Thur; 9pm-3.30am Fri, Sat. **Admission** free. **No cards**. **Map** p120 J11.*

Truly postmodern, this popular bar is outrageously kitsch but with a pop art sensibility that saves it from crossing over too far into tackiness. The fake fur, *Star Wars* pictures, 1970s toys and faux-cool psychedelia hang together surprisingly well, and there's a pleasant anything-goes music policy that brings all kinds of sounds, from rock and indie to funk and soul, to a sociable, slightly older crowd. Something of a neighbourhood nightlife institution.

## The Retiro & Salamanca

### Almonte

*C/Juan Bravo 35, Salamanca (91 563 54 70, www.almontesalarociera.com). Metro Diego de León.* **Open** *9pm-5am Mon-Thur, Sun; 9pm-6am Fri, Sat.* **Admission** *free.* **Map** *p155 R8.*

This 'flamenco disco' attracts a youthful crowd. The beautiful patrons flaunt it freestyle before *sevillanas* prompt a free-for-all. Try to work your way downstairs, where the most attention-grabbing moves can be admired and – go on – attempted.

### Goya Social Club

*C/Goya 43, Salamanca (681 650 040, www. goyasocialclub.com). Metro Serrano.* **Open** *midnight-6am Fri, Sat.* **Admission** *€15 (incl 1 drink), €18 (incl 2 drinks).* **Map** *p155 Q11.*

Not one of Madrid's largest clubs, but possibly the one with the best sound (thanks to the Funktion One sound system). With the likes of Maceo Plex, Alex Metric, Gonçalo and Oliver Heldens having all played here, it's for serious house and techno fans, but get here early-ish or you might not squeeze in. Look out, too, for their special sessions at the Roof bar at the Hotel ME Madrid Reina Victoria (*see p279*).

### Opium

*C/José Abascal 56, Salamanca (91 752 53 22, www.opiummadrid.com). Metro Gregorio Marañón.* **Restaurant and bar** *noon-12.30am daily.* **Club** *midnight-5am Mon-Thurs, Sun; midnight-6am Fri, Sat.* **Admission** *€20 (incl 1 drink).* **Map** *pull-out N6.*

A glitzy restaurant and club (part of the Spain-wide Costa Este group), this has a sumptuous interior with lots of white sofa beds for lounging, and attracts a dressy, uptown crowd. Every night is different: Latin music on Mondays; funk and pop on Tuesday nights; R&B on Wednesdays; pop (usually) on Thursdays; house and electro pop with resident DJs Jesús Llanos and Michael K on Fridays and Saturdays; and finishing up with funk and hip hop on Sunday nights.

### Palacio de Deportes (WiZink Center)

*Avda. Felipe II s/n, Salamanca (91 444 99 49, www.wizinkcenter.es). Metro Goya.* **Open** *times vary.* **Admission** *varies.*

Doubling as a sports stadium, this excellent venue has played host to big-hitters as varied as Muse, Metallica, Justin Bieber and Foals. There's room for 18,000 people between the pitch and the stands. Tickets are not always for a specific area, so check carefully and get there early if you want access to the mosh pit. Look out for the little red lights in the crowd – they're attached to backpacks full of beer for those who don't want to make a bar run.

## Beyond the centre

### Clamores

*C/Alburquerque 14, Chamberí (91 445 79 38, 91 445 54 80, www.salaclamores.com). Metro Bilbao.* **Open** *6pm-2am Mon-Thur, Sun; 6pm-6am Fri, Sat.* **Admission** *varies.* **Map** *pull-out K9.*

This legendary jazz club opened in 1979, and for eight years served as the set for TV show *Jazz Entre Amigos*. It has a hugely varied programme these days, with tango, pop, rock, bossa, samba and folk all on the bill, as well as the jazz that made its name. The live acts sprawl into late-night DJ sessions on Friday and Saturday nights, helped along by the exotic list of cocktails (God Save the Queen, anyone?).

### Fabrik

*Avda de la Industria 82, Ctra Fuenlabrada–Moralejos de Enmedio, south of the centre (mobile 902 930 322, www.grupo-kapital. com/fabrik). Metro Fuenlabrada then bus 496, 497.* **Open** *11.30pm-6am Sat; 3pm-3am occasional Sun.* **Admission** *varies.*

Fabrik is a converted warehouse that's kitted out with a dazzling array of disco surprises: there's a huge outdoor terrace complete with a fake river and two covered dance floors; and, in the main arena, a vertical and horizontal megatron to shoot freezing bursts of nitrogen gas into the crowd. The nighttime sessions attract a young, up-for-it crowd seeking hard techno or electronica, but the monthly all-day Sunday Goa party is the highlight (see www.tripfamily.com for more information). It's a bit of a trek to get here, but buses are usually laid on from the centre.

### Galileo Galilei

*C/Galileo 100, Chamberí (91 534 75 57, www. salagalileogalilei.com). Metro Islas Filipinas or Quevedo.* **Open** *5pm-2am Mon-Wed; 5pm-5.30am Thur-Sun.* **Admission** *varies. No cards.*

Galileo Galilei presents possibly the widest range of artists in Madrid. Whatever kind of music you like, you'll probably find it here. There's Latin jazz, flamenco, salsa, singer-songwriters and myriad types of fusion. There are also occasional comedy nights. It's a former cinema, and as such is very spacious, though the mock-Hellenic decor can be a bit over the top.

## Gotham

*C/Hilarión Eslava 38, Moncloa (no phone, gothamtheclub.es). Metro Moncloa.* **Open** *midnight-6am Fri, Sat.* **Admission** *free before 1am, otherwise varies.*

Right in the middle of Madrid's main university district, this club fills up with students. Expect crowd-pleasing electro pop and house on Friday nights, and a mix of commercial pop and reggaeton on Saturdays.

## Gruta 77

*C/Cuchillo 6, south of the centre (91 471 23 70, www.gruta77.com). Metro Oporto.* **Open** *9pm-4am midweek concert nights; 11pm-6am Fri, Sat.* **Admission** *varies. No cards.*

A mix of local unsigned groups and touring bands from the US, Australia and Japan pass through this 300-seater *sala*, on the corner of Cuchillo and Nicolás Morales. Punk, rock, ska and *mestizaje* tastes are catered for. An excellent sound system makes it worth the trip out to the suburbs.

## Honky Tonk

*C/Covarrubias 24, Chamberí (91 445 61 91, www.clubhonky.com). Metro Bilbao.* **Open** *9.30pm-5am Mon-Thur, Sun; 9.30pm-6am Fri, Sat.* **Concerts** *12.30am. Closed Sun Aug.* **Admission** *free Mon-Thur, Sun; €5 Fri, Sat.* **Map** *pull-out L9.*

Honky Tonk hosts local pop and rock acts nightly, and also offers an open mic night on Mondays, should you fancy stepping up and belting out a few tunes yourself. Get here early, as the large pillars that hold up the building tend to restrict your view if you're not up the front.

## Moby Dick

*Avda del Brasil 5, Tetuán (91 555 76 71, www.mobydickclub.com). Metro Cuzco or Santiago Bernabéu.* **Open** *9pm-3am Wed; 9pm-5am Thur; 9pm-5am Fri, Sat.* **Admission** *€5-€20.*

With music on two different levels, Moby Dick caters for a range of tastes. It's mainly a venue for local tribute bands and touring Spanish bands, but it can still pull a few surprises. Start the evening off with a pint of Guinness in its sister bar, the Irish Rover, next door.

## The Monkey

*Paseo de los Olmos 13 (mobile 653 83 00 79, www.themonkey.es). Metro Puerta de Toledo or Pirámides.* **Open** *10pm-6am Fri, Sat.* **Admission** *€10 (incl 1 drink).* **Map** *pull-out F19.*

The fact that this indie club is a little off the beaten track only adds to its appeal, as the clientele knows exactly what they came here for. Pop, rock, nu jazz and funk all get an outing, while the friendly crowd is lubricated by well-mixed – and very strong – cocktails and long drinks. Get there early to check out a mix of local cabaret acts, stand-up and bands.

## Palacio Vistalegre

*C/Utebo 1, south of the centre (91 563 94 93, palaciovistalegre.com). Metro Oporto or Vista Alegre.* **Open** *times vary.* **Admission** *varies.*

This venue is what the Spanish call *multiusos*, so it serves as a basketball stadium and conference hall, as well as a concert venue. Visiting bands have included All Time Low, Placebo and R5. For smaller gigs, a stage is erected underneath the stands, which sounds odd, but it works well.

## La Riviera

*Paseo Bajo de la Virgen del Puerto s/n (91 365 24 15, www.salariviera.com). Metro Puerto del Ángel.* **Open** *Concerts times vary. Club midnight-6am Fri, Sat.* **Admission** *varies.* **Map** *pull-out C16.*

This club on the banks of the Manzanares river is a major player on the Madrid music scene and ranked by many as the city's best medium-sized venue. It's certainly popular, and comes equipped with an excellent sound system. All sorts of acts have passed through in recent times, among them Lana del Rey, Eels and Mogwai.

## Sala Caracol

*C/Bernardino Obregón 18, south of the centre (91 527 35 94, www.salacaracol.com). Metro Embajadores.* **Open** *times vary.* **Admission** *varies. No cards.* **Map** *pull-out K19.*

The much-cherished Caracol may be a cosy venue, but it has still hosted the likes of Queens of the Stone Age, Placebo and Dr Feelgood since it opened more than 25 years ago. Once known for flamenco and world music, it's now more likely to feature rock and has its own competition for up-and-coming bands.

## Sala Pirandello 1, 2, 3

*C/Martín de los Heros 14, Argüelles (91 547 57 11). Metro Plaza de España.* **Open** *midnight-6am Thur-Sat.* **Admission** *free; €12-15 (incl 1 drink) after 2.30am.* **Map** *pull-out E11.*

Sala Pirandello gives you three clubs, spread out over five floors, for the price of one. Thursday night's Crossbeast is for hip hop, techno and breakbeat. Fridays are a night for younger clubbers at Sala Pirandello, who go wild for electro house, dubstep, drum'n'bass, rock and rap. Hysterical Pop on Saturdays is one of the most popular gay parties in town.

# FLAMENCO

The most authentic flamenco inhabits a closed world and is proud of it; but if you know where to go and are lucky on the night, you might be granted a peek. Where people are most likely to see flamenco, though, is at a *tablao*, of which there are several in Madrid; below is a selection of those with more genuine performances. As well as the show, you can dine or just drink; both are appallingly expensive, but if you stay until closing you may get your money's worth. The fun really starts around midnight, when most tourists go off to bed and the major artists appear; until then you may just get the kitsch jollity of the *cuadro de la casa* (the house musicians and dancers). Flamenco purists are notoriously snobbish about what's on offer in Madrid, but even they are thrilled by the performances at **Casa Patas**, where guitarists are skilled, dancers ooze power and grace, and singers are as they should be – bloody terrifying.

## Festivals

A great way to experience flamenco is as part of the city festivals in honour of **San Isidro** and the summer's **Veranos de la Villa**, while the **Festival Flamenco Madrid** is held in May and June in the Teatro Fernán Gómez Centro de Arte (*see p239*). The biggest flamenco festival, though, is the month-long **Suma Flamenca**. For details of these festivals and others, *see pp198-206*.

## Venues

### Café de Chinitas

C/Torija 7, Sol & Gran Vía (91 559 51 35/91 547 15 02, www.chinitas.com). Metro Santo Domingo. **Open** 7pm-midnight Mon-Sat. **Performances** 8.15pm, 10.30pm Mon-Sat. **Admission** €36, or €67 (incl dinner). **Map** p83 G13.

An indulgent evening's entertainment for those who like to play at being 19th-century

aristocrats – and don't mind paying 21st-century prices. At least this self-styled 'Cathedral of Flamenco' makes an effort, with sumptuous decor that contributes to the experience. The food and floorshow are expensive, yes, but at least it means the owners can afford to pay top euro for flamenco stars, who will send you reeling into the night.

### Candela

C/Olmo 2, Lavapiés (91 467 33 82, flamencocandela.com). Metro Antón Martín. **Open** 10.30pm-6am daily. **Performance** 11pm Fri, Sat. **Admission** Show €15 (includes a drink). Bar free. No cards. **Map** p109 K16.

An ideal place to soak up some atmosphere, though performances are impromptu (except for the regular Thursday slot) and only take place downstairs and after hours. Still, this in-the-know watering hole for professional musicians and amateurs is welcoming to knowledgeable and respectful aficionados.

### Las Carboneras

Plaza del Conde de Miranda 1, Los Austrias (91 542 86 77, www.tablaolascarboneras.com). Metro Sol. **Open** 7.30pm-midnight Mon-Sat. **Performances** 7.30pm, 8.30pm, 10pm, 10.30pm Mon-Thur; 7.30pm, 8.30pm, 10pm, 11pm Fri, Sat. **Admission** (incl 1 drink) €36, (incl dinner) €70.50-€78. **Map** p62 G15.

Packed with tourists, this bar-restaurant still offers an energetic, passionate show, although the set menus comprise typical fare. Highly polished flamenco guarantees an inauthentic but unashamedly fun night out.

### Cardamomo

C/Echegaray 15, Santa Ana (91 429 98 75, www.cardamomo.es). Metro Sevilla. **Open** 6pm-4am daily. **Performance** 6pm, 8pm, 10pm, 11.30pm daily. **Admission** (incl 1 drink) €39, set tapas and dinners €15-€65 (plus admission). **Map** p95 K15.

A firm fixture on the scene, this frenetic flamenco bar plays a mixture of flamenco and rumba tunes, often to thundering effect.

### ❤ Casa Patas

C/Cañizares 10, Lavapiés (91 369 04 96, www.casapatas.com). Metro Antón Martín. **Open** Sept-July 1-4.30pm, 8pm-midnight Mon-Thur; 1-4.30pm, 7.30pm-1am Fri; 7.30pm-1am Sat. Aug 8pm-midnight Mon-Thur; 7.30pm-1am Fri, Sat. **Performances** 10.30pm Mon-Thur; 9pm, midnight Fri, Sat. **Admission** (incl 1 drink) €34. **Map** p109 J16.

This is a plush and somewhat pricey place to savour traditional or *nuevo* flamenco. Recent headliners have included Chaquetón, Remedios Amaya and Niña Pastori. Casa Patas is deservedly proud of its reputation and treats its loyal, knowledgeable and sometimes intimidating audience with respect. The same owners have a bar, Pata Chico, alongside for pre-flamenco drinks.

### Corral de la Morería

*C/Morería 17, Los Austrias (91 365 84 46, www.corraldelamoreria.com). Metro La Latina.* **Open** *8pm-12.30am daily.* **Performances** *9pm, 11pm daily.* **Admission** *(incl 1 drink) €47.* **Map** *p62 E16.*

More serious and exacting than Las Carboneras, this longstanding *tablao* sports seemingly authentic Arab decor and an atmosphere to match. A relaxed mix of tourists, fans (Hemingway, Che Guevara and Picasso all paid a visit) and professionals enjoy a solid, expensive and sometimes exhilarating show.

### Corral de la Pacheca

*C/Juan Ramón Jiménez 26, north of the centre (91 353 01 00, www. corraldelapacheca.com). Metro Cuzco.* **Open** *8.30pm-midnight daily.* **Performance** *10pm daily.* **Admission** *€30 (incl 1 drink); €15 if dining.*

This grand centre of popular and traditional flamenco boasts a history of star performers and even starrier punters. Built on the site of a 17th-century theatre, it began life as a *tablao* but has grown into an imposing venue with a large auditorium and stage.

### Torres Bermejas

*C/Mesonero Romanos 11 (91 532 33 22, www.torres bermejas.com). Metro Callao.* **Open** *8.30pm-1.30am daily.* **Performance** *9.30pm daily.* **Admission** *(incl 1 drink) €37.* **Map** *p83 J13.*

Modelled somewhat kitschly on the Alhambra, this bar plays hosts to authentic gypsy flamenco and a faithful in-crowd, managing to absorb the tour parties without spoiling the mood. The paella and Rioja veal are, like the flamenco, rich and satisfying.

Corral de la Morería

Gymage *p230*

# LGBT Madrid

The throbbing heart of the LGBT scene (*el ambiente*) is the Plaza de Chueca. Tightly packed around what is an otherwise nondescript square in the centre of town, the dazzling array of bars and services are aimed almost exclusively at one of Madrid's most vociferous and dynamic communities. With bars, cafés, hotels, saunas, travel agencies and bookshops, the formerly rundown neighbourhood has emerged as one of the city's liveliest and trendiest areas. But Chueca has become, perhaps, a victim of its own success, because in recent years its hip hangouts have started attracting a non-gay crowd. Now, many want their ghetto back, at least for cruising, and plenty of shag-and-go male-only bars have popped up all over the place. Special events aimed at specific subcultures are a growth industry, too: there are camping weekends for bears in the nearby mountains, an action-packed 'Sleazy Madrid' long weekend every spring, plus lesbian raves with dyke-y darkrooms, body-shaving bashes and sloppy mud parties.

For more information about the scene and helplines, *see p289*.

## Gay cafés & restaurants

As well as the places listed below, **El 26 de Libertad** (*see p125*) is also noticeably popular among the gay community. **Ángel Sierra** (*see p127*), while not a gay bar per se, is smack on the Plaza de Chueca and therefore an ideal place to start the evening.

### Café Acuarela
*C/Gravina 10, Chueca & Malasaña (91 524 99 35). Metro Chueca.* **Open** *2pm-2.30am daily.* **Map** *p120 L12.*

By day a quiet, mixed haven to duck into and catch your breath: curl up with a book and sample one of the teas. After sundown, sip a cocktail, sink into a deep sofa and admire the decor – a mix of kitsch, retro glamour and exuberant baroque.

### Café Figueroa
*C/Augusto Figueroa 17, Chueca & Malasaña (91 521 16 73). Metro Chueca.* **Open** *Oct-May noon-1am Mon-Thur; noon-2.30am Fri, Sat; 4pm-1am Sun. June-Sept 4.30-11.30pm daily.* **No cards**. **Map** *p120 K12.*

Madrid's original gay café is a sedate place. The lace curtains and 19th-century chandeliers have gone in a smart revamp, but it's still a cosy destination for those who want gay in an old Spain way. It's a popular place for a late breakfast.

### D'Mystic
*C/Gravina 5, Chueca & Malasaña (91 308 24 60). Metro Chueca.* **Open** *9.30am-2am Mon-Thur; 10am-2.30am Fri, Sat; 1pm-2am Sun.* **Map** *p120 L12.*

This den of cool is located at a strategic crossroads, and its bigger-than-average cocktails make up for the aloof staff. Watch the real world stroll by outside or gaze at the natural world on the New Age-y videos on the screens inside. Relax, listen to the whale songs and the waterfalls. Then get out and head for Leather Club (*see p231*).

# Pride Without Prejudice

*LGBT Madrid marches on*

Spain's Socialist government of the noughties made history when it became one of the first to legalise gay marriage and to allow transsexuals to choose whichever gender they wished on their identity cards. These were milestone achievements that were celebrated with leather, rubber, bears, tanned toned flesh and non-stop hedonism in the LGBT Pride parade.

Organised by COGAM and FELGBT (*see p289*), the parade has continued to grow since then, despite continued threats to the event by some Chueca residents, who want the week-long June party to be moved to the outskirts of the city. The parade runs from the Puerta de Alcalá to Plaza España, and attracts some two million people. For an entire week, the city is invaded by visitors from all over the world, partying hard by night and sporting an array of ludicrously coloured banana hammocks at the swimming pools by day, with the rooftop terrace of the Room Mate Oscar hotel (*see p281*) a big hotspot. In 2017, Madrid hosted World Pride, a spectacular city-wide event that was attended by three million people.

As well as the parties and the parades, the week boasts some 300 cultural, artistic and sporting events – kicking off with the Carrera en Tacones (a race where contestants run in stilettos) – as well as off-site parties at the end of the week.

Despite such leaps, bounds and high-heeled trotting towards an equal Spain, there is much still to be done, according to Madrid's numerous gay rights associations. Madrid may be one of the most tolerant cities in the world, but this is still a deeply conservative country in many ways and there is still plenty to march for.

### Diurno

*C/San Marcos 37, Chueca & Malasaña (91 522 00 09, www.grupomercadodelareina.com/es/diurno). Metro Chueca.* **Open** *10am-2am Mon-Thur; 10am-2.30am Fri; 11am-2.30am Sat; 11am-2am Sun.* **Map** *p120 L13.*

A minimalist and sexy café spinning all-day chill-out sounds (and occasional techno), this offers great brunches, delicious tapas, and cakes, plus a good value set lunch. A peaceful place to start the day, upbeat and lively at night.

### ♥ Gymage

*C/Luna 2, Chueca & Malasaña (91 532 09 74, www.gymage.es). Metro Gran Vía.* **Open** *7am-1.30am Mon-Thur, Sun; 10am-2.30am Fri, Sat.* **Map** *p120 H12.*

Located on top of the old Luna cinema, Gymage describes itself as an 'urban resort', which is really just a fancy way of saying it's a gym with a restaurant. The (gay-friendly) gym is great, the restaurant decent, but the real draw here is the spectacular rooftop terrace, where Madrid's glitterati like to lounge about on the white-on-white furnishings and sip cocktails.

### Mama Inés

*C/Hortaleza 22, Chueca & Malasaña (91 523 23 33). Metro Gran Vía.* **Open** *10am-2am Mon-Thur, Sun; 10am-3am Fri, Sat.* **No cards.** **Map** *p120 K13.*

Mama Inés successfully combines a decent breakfast (and fantastic cakes) with plenty of eye candy. Chill-out and nu flamenco tunes waft through this modern but surprisingly intimate café during the daytime; then, in the evening, house music takes over and the T-shirts get progressively tighter and tighter.

## Gay clubs & discobares

A *discobar* treads the line between club and regular drinking den. Admission is generally free (exceptions are noted below), and there is normally a diminutive dancefloor to justify the pricier-than-average drinks.

As well as the venues we've listed below, clubs **Medias Puri** (*see p222*) and **Mondo at Sala Cocó** (*see p218*) also have a big gay following.

## Bar Atril

*C/Paloma 9, Los Austrias & La Latina (91 366 23 34). Metro La Latina.* **Open** *9pm-3.30am Fri, Sat; 4pm-2am Sun.* **Map** *p62 F18.*

A gay bar with a relaxed and attitude-free clientele and staff, this is a great place to start the night. Later on, the music (mainly pop plus the usual divas) gets louder, the crowd gets denser, and the flirting gets more outrageous.

## La Boîte

*C/Tetuán 27 (692 263 155, www. boitemadrid.com). Metro Gran Vía.* **Open** *11.30pm-5.30am Thur; 11.30pm-6am Fri-Sun.* **Admission** *€15 (includes one drink).* **Map** *p83 J14.*

You're guaranteed a fun night out at La Boîte, which has a huge dancefloor, a fantastic sound system and a superb line-up of DJs. Plus there are drag queen acts and delectable staff. It's popular with a young mixed crowd, although you'll need to look your spiffiest to get past the bouncers.

## LL Show Bar

*C/Pelayo 11, Chueca (91 523 31 21, www. llshowbar.com). Metro Chueca.* **Open** *8pm-2am daily.* **Map** *p120 K12.*

This minuscule bar is into its third decade, and has become a Chueca classic for its spectacular and outrageously risqué drag queen and stripper performances, which take place nightly. There's also a dark room downstairs.

## RRick's

*C/Clavel 8, Chueca (91 531 91 86). Metro Gran Vía.* **Open** *11pm-5.30am Tue-Thur, Sun, 11pm-6am Fri, Sat.* **Admission** *(incl 1 drink) €8.* **No cards.** **Map** *p120 K13.*

Expensive drinks and an expensive, older crowd are the hallmarks of this friendly late-night alternative to the discos. With hi-NRG beats and camp Spanish hits, it's standing-room only at weekends.

## Exclusively male/hardcore

### Hot

*C/Infantas 9, Chueca (91 522 84 48, www. grupohot.com). Metro Chueca.* **Open** *6pm-3am Mon-Thur, Sun; 6pm-3.30am Fri, Sat.* **Admission** *free.* **No cards.** **Map** *p120 K13.*

Hot, hairy, homo heaven at this fun bear den for hirsute late thirty- and fortysomethings. Things get even hotter downstairs in the darkroom. Two drinks for the price of one, every day until midnight.

## Leather Club

*C/Pelayo 42, Chueca (91 308 14 62, 667 81 88 59). Metro Chueca.* **Open** *8pm-3am daily.* **Admission** *free.* **No cards.** **Map** *p120 L12.*

The name of this big, two-floor hangout is a bit misleading as little leather is in evidence, but the crowd is raunchy and can be found in the large darkroom or lurking in anticipation in the cabins. Check out the individual movie screens over the urinals.

## Lesbian cafés, bars & clubs

All those places for the boys, and barely enough bars to make a decent pub crawl for lesbians – what's a girl to do? Keep her eyes peeled, that's what. Madrid's lesbian scene is growing, but it still has a long way to go before catching up with the gay male *ambiente*. Plaza de Chueca is where you should start off, in any case: half the bars here seems to be owned by lesbians, even though the clientele is mixed.

As well as the following, another venue popular with lesbians is **Café Acuarela** (*see p229*).

## Club 33

*C/Cabeza 33, Lavapiés (91 369 33 02). Metro Antón Martín or Tirso de Molina.* **Open** *midnight-6am Thur-Sat.* **Admission** *€10 (incl 2 drinks).* **Map** *p109 K16.*

Decorated in muted rainbow colours, this welcoming women's disco is one of the clear favourites on the lesbian scene. Men are admitted only in the company of Sapphic sisters.

## Escape

*C/Gravina 13, Chueca (91 532 52 06). Metro Chueca.* **Open** *midnight-6am Fri-Sun.* **Admission** *(incl 1 drink) €10.* **Map** *p120 L12.*

This cavernous dance hall draped in bullfighter red is one of the most popular destinations for women and is filled to the brim with the sexiest *chicas* in the city at weekends. In fact, its popularity has spiralled to the extent that it's now one of the more boisterous clubs around Plaza de Chueca.

## Truco

*C/Gravina 10, Chueca (91 532 89 21). Metro Chueca.* **Open** *9pm-3.30am Fri, Sat; 9pm-3am Sun.* **Map** *p120 L12.*

Truco is often very crowded, usually with a very young and loud crowd. No matter: this high-octane corner joint remains *the* place for gals who are looking for gals in the earlier part of the evening. It is also a stone's throw from Escape (*see above*).

# Performing Arts

*The city in stages, from blockbusters to home-grown operetta*

Madrid's cultural clout has steadily increased in recent years, with the city finally shaking off a reputation for producing stuffy composers, ensembles with limited scope, a lightweight contemporary classical scene and a reactionary public. Credit must go, too, to a city that depends predominantly on public funds to bring in top-class international musicians and ensembles to its worthy concert venues. Madrid's theatre world is a polarised affair. Gran Vía is littered with Broadway and West End hand-me-downs – Spain's fervent passion for the blockbuster musical has not wavered – but little theatres soldier on in the face of local government and city council limits on licences and funds. Still, the fighting spirit of the fringe makes up for the mainstream's old-fashioned outlook. Although to some outsiders the alternative scene here can seem fairly tame, bear in mind that until the late 1980s there was virtually no non-mainstream theatre here at all.

# CLASSICAL MUSIC & OPERA

Traditionally, the scene orbits around three main venues: the modern and austere (and arguably best-quality classical venue in Europe) **Auditorio Nacional de Música**; the grand hosting opera; and the **Teatro de la Zarzuela** for a decent selection of classical concerts (as well as for *zarzuela*, Madrid's traditional operetta art form).

## Information and tickets

Check venue websites for current and future seasons, as well as any last-minute changes or cancellations. You can pick up leaflets from most venues – which is often quicker than trying to get through by phone – or check the *Guía del Ocio*, or a listings supplement such as *La Luna de Metropolí*, which comes out Fridays with the *El Mundo* newspaper. Tickets can usually be purchased over the phone, via the venue website or from **Ticketea** (www.ticketea.com) or **Ticketmaster** (902 150 025, www.ticketmaster.es). Tickets for state-run venues such as the Auditorio Nacional de Música and Teatro de la Zarzuela are sold at the venue box offices, online at www.entradasinaem.es or by phone (902 22 49 49).

## Zarzuela

*Zarzuela* is an ineffable part of *madrileño* culture, though tricky for the outsider to get a grip on. It was Spain's early answer to the Italian opera – shorter and funnier and incorporating elements of theatre, slapstick and dance. Golden Age playwrights Félix Lope de Vega and Pedro Calderón de la Barca were early pioneers of the genre, which was later developed by the likes of Ramón de la Cruz and composer Federico de Chueca and, moving into the 20th century, Amadeo Vives and Jacinto Guerrero. *Zarzuela* is full of local jokes (usually rhyming and rattled off at speed)

### ♥ Best for culture

**Madrid Players pantomime** *p240*
It's behiiiind you.

**Teatro Español** *p239*
Plays both classic and contemporary.

**Teatro Real** *p235*
Breathtakingly ornate opera house.

**Teatro de la Zarzuela** *p234*
Madrid's idiosyncratic opera genre.

and traditional songs with which the public will sing along, so be prepared. Catch it in its home ground of the Teatro de la Zarzuela, in the Centro Cultural de la Villa in July or August, or at a summer open-air performance.

## Concert venues

In addition to the major venues mentioned above, the classical and contemporary music programme at the **Círculo de Bellas Artes** (*see p87*) has broadened immensely over the last decade or so. The **Teatro Español** occasionally holds *zarzuelas* and performances by chamber and symphonic orchestras. A handful of cafés and restaurants around town offer an opera-accompanied dining experience. Try the **Café Viena** (C/Luisa Fernanda 23. Argüelles, 91 539 83 53, www.vienacapellanes.com) for monthly Cenas Líricas (consisting of dinner and a short *zarzuela* or opera performance, all for €38). Also, check out the professional singing waiters at **La Favorita** (*see p176*) and **La Castafiore** (C/Marqués de Monasterio 5, 91 319 42 21, www.lacastafiore.net). Another place to keep an eye on is the **Centro Asturiano** (C/Farmacia 2, 4º, Chueca, 91 532 82 81, www.centroasturianomadrid.es), which runs a cycle called Lunes Musicales with concerts performed by small ensembles on Mondays.

## Auditorio Nacional de Música

*C/Príncipe de Vergara 146, Salamanca (info 91 337 01 40, www.auditorionacional.mcu.es; tickets 902 22 49 49 or 98 567 96 68, www.entradasinaem.es). Metro Cruz del Rayo or Prosperidad.* **Box office** *4-6pm Mon; 10am-5pm Tue-Fri; 11am-1pm Sat. Closed Aug.* **Main season** *Oct-June.* **Tickets** *€7-€55.*

This impressive concert hall has a main 2,000-seat auditorium and a smaller chamber hall, the Sala de Cámara. As well as being home to the OCNE, the Auditorio also hosts the Comunidad de Madrid's orchestra, ORCAM; the Coro Nacional de España (Spanish National Choir), and the Joven Orquesta Nacional de España (JONDE, worth checking out for their youth and enthusiasm). In addition, ensembles such as

> **In the know**
> **Unfashionably late**
>
> A word of advice if you're attending classical concerts in Madrid – make sure you get there early. The stereotypical Spanish tardiness is not a trait shared by classical music-lovers.

**Teatro Real**

the Universidad Politécnica de Madrid invite orchestras to accompany the university's choir, performing on selected Friday and Saturday evenings at 10.30pm. But the finest concerts are those by invited international orchestras – which are, happily enough, something the Spanish state likes to invest its music budget in. The best seasons are the Grandes Intérpretes and Ibermúsica. Look out, too, for organ recitals. Tickets for the Auditorio usually go on sale about a fortnight before performances, and can be hard to get hold of. Tickets are generally cheaper for Sunday morning concerts.

### Conde Duque
*C/Conde Duque 11, Malasaña (91 318 44 50, www.condeduquemadrid.es). Metro Ventura Rodríguez or Plaza de España. **Concerts** Sept-June. **Tickets** free-€20. **Map** p120 F10.*

The Conde Duque cultural centre programmes a wide range of events, including music festivals such as its summer Concerts de Estío cycle, which features everything from flamenco to classical music. Chamber concerts, often with feature performers from prestigious international orchestras and choirs, are also held here. Most events are affordable, and some are free.

### Real Academia de las Bellas Artes de San Fernando
*C/Alcalá 13, Sol & Gran Vía (91 524 08 64, www.realacademiabellasartessanfernando. com). Metro Sevilla or Sol. **Concerts** Sept-June noon Sat. **Tickets** free. **Map** p83 K14.*

This beautiful building right in the heart of Madrid is a must for a handsome concert

experience. It hosts regular concerts (at least twice a month), including some performed by the Madrid Conservatory's Baroque orchestra. Concerts are free, but seating is limited, so arrive early.

### Teatro Monumental
*C/Atocha 65, Huertas & Santa Ana (91 429 12 81, www.rtve.es/orquesta-coro). Metro Antón Martín. **Map** p95 L16.*

Located in slightly seedy Antón Martín, the Monumental has more character than most, but is functional rather than beautiful. Its main purpose is to record broadcast concerts by the RTVE Orchestra and Choir – consequently it may not have the glitz of the Teatro Real, but it does have excellent acoustics and high-quality performances. The principal diet here is concerts, with a side order of opera and *zarzuela*. Closed for an indefinite period at the time of writing, it is undergoing renovation, but the RTVE Orchestra is set to return for a ten-year period once these are completed.

### ♥ Teatro Real
*Plaza de Isabel II, Los Austrias (information 902 24 48 48, box office 91 516 06 60, www. teatro-real.com). Metro Opera. **Box office** 9.15am-8pm Mon-Fri (10am-8pm Sat performance days). Visits 9.30am-3.30pm daily (with audioguide); 10am-1pm (guided tours). **Main season** Sept-July. **Tickets** Ballet €20-€180. Opera €20-€449. Visits €7/€6 reductions (with audioguide); €7/€6 reductions (guided tours). **Map** p62 G14.*

Shaped like a compressed oval, the interior of the city's opera house is breathtakingly ornate compared with its sombre façade, and it's one of the most technologically advanced

# Music Beyond Madrid

*Head out of the capital for these charming classical festivals*

Concert programmers in and around Madrid have woken up to the charms of the region, taking music out of the theatres and lighting up monasteries, palaces and gardens. What could be more inviting than a soirée of Rachmaninoff, Fauré and Schumann in one of the cool churches of the Sierra when the temperature is in the forties in Madrid?

The **Clásicos en Verano** (www.madrid. org/clasicosenverano) concerts may not feature the greatest musicians, but the range is broad. Come July and August, it seems every nook and cranny, and every old church and town hall around Madrid, is filled with the sweet sounds of piano concertos, percussion groups, choirs, wind ensembles, string quartets, accompanied poetry and medieval music by local groups. The apparently random programming has led to Bach and Handel arias being performed at the San Andrés church in Rascafría, while in nearby Alameda del Valle young men climbed stepladders to read names and numbers from the phone book as if they were poetry.

Not only are these concerts widespread and plentiful (there are about 80 of them in 51 different towns), they're also free. Pass by a tourist information office or the Consejería de

Cultura y Deportes on C/Alcalá 31 to pick up a full programme. Some of the more striking venues include the **Castillo in Manzanares el Real** (see p186) and the **Iglesia de los Arroyos** in El Escorial (see p184).

Care for a turn around the charming gardens of the Aranjuez Palace (see p191) while being serenaded by *zarambeques*, *folías*, *marionas*, *fandangos* and *pasacalles*? The **Música Antigua Aranjuez** festival (www.musicaantiguaaranjuez.net) keeps the music alive in the place that inspired Joaquín Rodrigo's haunting *Concierto de Aranjuez*, with sounds from much earlier in the palace's history. At weekends during the months of May and June, the palace hosts concerts of medieval, Renaissance and Baroque music played on original instruments from the period. Many of the composers featured do not enjoy wide exposure today, although they were well known in their day. Concerts are held inside the palace (in the chapel and the Sala de Teatro), as well as in the palace grounds. The much-loved guided 'musical walks' feature pauses for concerts along the way. Tickets are around €20 for concerts or musical walks, and can be bought from Ticketea (902 044 226, www.ticketea.com).

---

in Europe. Productions are impressive – with complicated revolving sets and attention to detail in costumes and props – and enjoy funding from some of Spain's biggest companies, as well as the Comunidad de Madrid. Projection screens at either side of the stage show the full action, though this doesn't quite compensate for the lack of vision at the far ends of the top galleries (the *tribunas* and part of the *anfiteatro*). There's also a screen above the stage showing Spanish surtitles for non-Spanish operas. The acoustics are so good that the quality of sound is practically the same everywhere in the hall.

The annual Festival de Verano runs alongside the theatre's regular programme in June and July but offers a more orchestra- and dance-orientated programme, as well as children's shows (tickets for these events are much cheaper and easier to obtain). Guided tours run daily: you can choose the self-guided tour with an audioguide, or a guided tour that takes visitors through the main dressing room and auditoria. Tours last 50 minutes, and a minimum of ten people are required for a guided tour to take place (call 91 516 06 96 for all tour enquiries/

bookings). There is no minimum for the tour with an audioguide.

Performances usually begin at 8pm, or 6pm on Sundays, with ballet and family opera matinées at noon. Tickets go on sale approximately ten days before the première and standby tickets are available on the day. With the cheapest tickets, for rows F and G, vision is seriously restricted; check the website for a detailed plan.

### ♥ Teatro de la Zarzuela
*C/Jovellanos 4, Sol & Gran Vía (box office 98 567 96 68, 902 22 49 49 teatrodelazarzuela. mcu.es). Metro Banco de España.* **Box office** *noon-8pm Mon-Fri; 2.30-8pm Sat, Sun.* **Main season** *Sept-July.* **Tickets** *€5-€50.* **Map** *p83 L14.*

The Teatro de la Zarzuela, which served as an opera house for many years before the Teatro Real's renovation, is now principally devoted to its raison d'être – staging *zarzuela*, home-grown Spanish operetta. Despite *zarzuela*'s uncool image and lack of credibility among serious music-lovers, it retains considerable popularity, drawing decent audiences for its frequent performances. Accompanying the Teatro's packed *zarzuela* programme

Teatro de la Zarzuela

are dance performances (often put on by the Ballet Nacional), concerts, plays, conferences and family-orientated shows. The annual Ciclo del Lied, which pays tribute to the lesser-known 19th-century German song form, has an excellent reputation.

## Cultural institutions

Institutions such as the **British Council** (www.britishcouncil.org/spain), the **Institut Français** (www.institutfrancais.es/madrid), the **Istituto Italiano di Cultura** (www. iicmadrid.esteri.it) and the **Goethe Institut** (www.goethe.de/ins/es/mad/esindex.htm) are also worth checking for classical music concerts and related activities.

### Fundación Canal

*C/Mateo Inurria 2, Chamartín (91 545 15 01, www.fundacioncanal.com). Metro Plaza de Castilla. **Concert times vary.** **Main season** Oct-June.*

Set up by Madrid's water company, Canal de Isabel II, this foundation has become active in all areas of the arts during the last few years, programming occasionally excellent exhibitions and concerts throughout the year. The foundation's music programming has included seasons of chamber music performed by musicians from the Orquesta de la Comunidad de Madrid.

### Fundación Carlos Amberes

*C/Claudio Coello 99, Salamanca (91 435 22 01, www.fcamberes.org). Metro Serrano. **Main season** Sept-July. **Map** p155 P9.*

The Carlos Amberes Foundation dates back to 1594, when it was founded by a Flemish benefactor. Today, as well as exhibitions and conferences, it hosts concerts including chamber music, jazz and much in between. These are held most weeks, both in its rather dingy basement and sometimes upstairs in a converted church, which is pretty but has

poor acoustics. The programme tends to focus on the music of the Low Countries.

### Fundación Juan March

*C/Castelló 77, Salamanca (91 435 42 40, www.march.es). Metro Núñez de Balboa. **Main season** Oct-June. **Map** p155 Q9.*

Set up in 1955, this charitable foundation and hive of musical, artistic and scientific activity was one of few such organisations in Spain for a good many years. These days the Fundación Juan March remains a key player on Madrid's classical scene, putting on around 150-200 free concerts per year. These usually consist of soloists or chamber ensembles, and take place on Wednesday evenings from 7.30pm (the most popular slot, featuring better-known professional musicians and broadcast on Radio Nacional), themed cycles on Fridays at 8pm, as well as some Saturdays and Sundays at noon featuring performances ranging from jazz and classical to world music. Sundays are usually dedicated to young, up-and-coming musicians. The concert hall seats 300. When it fills up a second hall with a big screen is opened, and then the bar. The programme is pretty flexible as it doesn't depend on ticket sales, though there's a slant towards Spanish composers. Take in some good art exhibitions while you're there.

## Orchestras & ensembles

### Orquesta y Coro de la Comunidad de Madrid (ORCAM)

*www.orcam.org.*

Madrid's state-funded regional orchestra is one of the city's most highly regarded. It provides accompaniment for the shows at the Teatro de la Zarzuela, but also performs at the Auditorio Nacional. The orchestra's artistic director, Victor Pablo Pérez, provides a programme of mainly Spanish composers.

### Orquesta & Coro Nacionales de España (OCNE)

*ocne.mcu.es.*

A certain element of instability has hounded Spain's national orchestra and choir over the years, with numerous strikes carried out by the state-employed members when asked to practise at home outside their set paid hours. They take to the stage every weekend at the Auditorio Nacional, occasionally performing world premières of contemporary pieces. Félix Alcaraz is the current artistic director of the orchestra and choir, and is attempting to renovate programme content with a particular emphasis on Spanish composers, both traditional and contemporary, as well as making the concerts more accessible to young musicians and a broader audience.

### Orquesta y Coro de RTVE

*www.rtve.es/rtve/orquesta-coro*

The orchestra and choir of Spain's national state-run television and radio stations (Radio Televisión España) was originally founded for broadcasting purposes. Its home is in the **Teatro Monumental** (*see p235*), although this is currently being remodelled and there is no date for the completion of works.

### Orquesta Sinfónica de Madrid (OSM)

*www.osm.es*

The *orquesta titular* of the Teatro Real and oldest existing symphonic ensemble in Spain has a reputation within classical music circles for proposing odd, irregular seasonal programmes. Recent years have looked more stable, however, with a proposed series of chamber concerts, *zarzuelas* and symphonic concerts. At the Teatro Real, the major operas are also usually complemented by related concerts put on by the orchestra and performed in a concert space in one of the upstairs rooms. As well as all the top Spanish conductors, the OSM has also worked with international greats such as Peter Haag, Pinchas Steinberg and Kurt Sanderling.

## THEATRE

Look beyond the heavyweights, such as the **Teatro Español** and the **Teatro María Guerrero**, and you'll find that Madrid has an active fringe scene, with the key players being the **Teatro del Barrio** and **Cuarta Pared**, the oldest of the *salas alternativas*. Other theatres to look for include **Teatro Cofidis Alcázar** (C/Alcalá 20, 91 532 06 16, www.teatrocofidis. com), **Teatro Caser Calderón** (C/Atocha 18, 91 429 40 85 teatrocalderon.com), and **Teatro**

**Lara** (Corredera Baja de San Pablo 15, 91 523 90 27, www.teatrolara.com) for family entertainment along with other shows.

## Mainstream theatres

### Sala Mirador

*C/Doctor Fourquet 31, Lavapiés (box office 91 539 57 67, information 91 528 95 04 95, www.lamirador.com). Metro Atocha or Lavapiés.* **Box office** *1hr before performance Thur-Sun. Closed Aug.* **Tickets** *€8-€18.* **Map** *p109 L18.*

Doubling as a theatre/dance school and performance space, the Sala Mirador is home to the Centro de Nuevos Creadores (Centre of New Creators). It is also the site of the long-running *La Katarsis del Tomatazo*, performed every Saturday night at 10.30pm. The audience are given tomatoes as they enter, which they can use to express their feelings on this singing and dancing cabaret.

### Teatro Alfil

*C/Pez 10, Malasaña (box office 91 521 58 27, information 91 521 45 41, teatroalfil. com). Metro Callao or Noviciado.* **Box office** *1hr before performance Tue-Sun.* **Tickets** *€20-€24.* **Map** *p120 J12.*

Madrid's renegade theatre, the Alfil has been threatened with closure in previous years, but has battled on and produces increasingly radical plays – both *The Vagina Monologues* and *Puppetry of the Penis* have been staged here.

### Teatro de la Abadía

*C/Fernández de los Ríos 42, Chamberí (box office 91 448 16 27, information 91 448 11 81, www.teatroabadia.com). Metro Quevedo.* **Box office** *5-9pm Tue-Sat; 5-8pm Sun. Closed Aug.* **Tickets** *€14-€24; Tue/ Wed/Thur reductions.*

Housed inside an abandoned church, the award-winning Abadía dabbles in music and dance as well as theatre. It participates in the **Festival de Otoño a Primavera** (*see p205*) and Madrid en Danza festivals, and brings unusual one-offs to the regular schedule.

### Teatro de la Comédia

*C/Príncipe 14, Huertas & Santa Ana (91 532 79 27, teatroclasico.mcu.es; tickets 902 22 49 49, www.entradasinaem.es). Metro Sol.* **Box office** *11am-3pm Mon; 2.30pm-until start of performance Tue-Sun. Closed Aug.* **Tickets** *€3-€25.* **Map** *p95 K15.*

The late 19th-century Teatro de la Comédia was closed for years, but finally reopened in 2015 after an expensive expansion and modernisation project that, among other things, added a new 100-seater theatre, the Tirso de Molina. Home to the Compañía Nacional de Teatro Clásico, the theatre stages classical productions of works by Spanish Golden Age greats, performed by the Compañía Nacional, as well as by a number of invited companies. Occasionally, plays by Molière, Shakespeare and the like are included in the programme.

### ❤ Teatro Español

*C/Príncipe 25, Huertas & Santa Ana (box office 91 360 14 84, information 91 318 47 00, www. teatroespanol.es). Metro Sevilla or Sol.* **Box office** *11.30am-1.30pm, 5-7pm Tue-Sat; 11.30am-1.30pm, 5-6pm Sun (same-day tickets available until start of performance).* **Tickets** *€5-€22.* **Map** *p95 K15.*

This grand theatre on Plaza Santa Ana dates back to 1745, but that doesn't mean it's old-fashioned – in fact, it has enjoyed some fairly radical programming in recent years. The 2017-18 season included productions of Euripides' *Trojan Women*, Nelly Arcan's *La fureur de ce que je pense,* and Luis Buñuel's *El Ángel Exterminador.*

### Teatro Fernán Gómez Centro de Arte

*Jardines del Descubrimiento, Plaza de Colón, Salamanca (91 486 25 40, www. teatrofernangomez.es). Metro Serrano.* **Box office** *11am-1.30pm, 5-7pm Tue-Sun.* **Tickets** *€10-€18.* **Map** *p155 O11.*

The theatre in the city's purpose-built cultural centre shows an eclectic mix of concerts, opera, *zarzuela,* cinema, drama and dance. There are also jazz performances, workshops and children's puppet shows.

### Teatro Fernando de Rojas

*C/Alcalá 42, Sol & Gran Vía (91 360 54 00, www. circulobellasartes.com). Metro Banco de España or Sevilla.* **Box office** *5.30-9pm Tue-Sun. Closed Aug.* **Tickets** *vary. No cards.* **Map** *p83 L14.*

Housed in the **Círculo de Bellas Artes** (*see p87*), and not to be confused with the unconnected Teatro de Bellas Artes next door, the Fernando de Rojas stages three or four works a season, mixing contemporary and traditional, Spanish and international.

### Teatro La Latina

*Plaza de la Cebada 2, La Latina (box office 91 188 08 30, information 91 365 28 35, www.teatro lalatina.es). Metro La Latina or Tirso de Molina.* **Box office** *5-8pm Tue; 11am-1.30pm, 5pm until performance Wed-Sat; 11am-1.30pm, 4pm until performance Sun.* **Tickets** *€15-€49.* **Map** *p62 G17.*

Previously known for its homespun comic theatre (plenty of star names in farcical situations and lots of banging of doors), this comfortable venue has undergone a slight shift of image in recent years. Although the programme now consists mainly of high-quality drama, the theatre also sometimes hosts less high-brow productions.

### Teatro María Guerrero

*C/Tamayo y Baus 4, Chueca (information 91 310 15 00, cdn.mcu.es; tickets 902 22 49 49, www.entradasinaem.es). Metro Colón.* **Box office** *noon-8.30pm Mon-Fri; 2.30-8.30pm Sat, Sun.* **Tickets** *€6-€25.* **Map** *p120 M12.*

This beautiful late 19th-century theatre is home to the state-run Centro Dramático Nacional (CDN), and has retained much of its red velvet plushness after comprehensive renovations. The 2017-18 season ran the gamut from Lorca's *Blood Wedding* to the Colectivo Fango's *FOMO (Fear Of Missing Out).*

### Teatro Nuevo Apolo

*Plaza de Tirso de Molina 1, Rastro & Lavapiés (information 91 855 4162, www. summmusic.com). Metro Tirso de Molina.* **Box office** *11.30am-1.30pm, 5.30-8pm Tue; 11.30am-1.30pm, 5pm-until start of performance Wed-Sun.* **Tickets** *€12-€40.* **Map** *p109 J16.*

This grand old theatre first opened almost a century ago. Its programme largely features musicals, classic ballet (*The Nutcracker, Swan Lake*) and musical extravaganzas such

Teatro Español

# Spoken Word

*Check out Madrid's English-language productions*

Even hardened theatre buffs are daunted by a show in a language they don't understand and, of course, almost all Madrid theatre is staged in Spanish. English-speaking visitors might get lucky, though, and happen on a touring production during the **Festival de Otoño a Primavera** (see p205). The RSC has visited in recent years, and Cheek by Jowl presented their production of *Pericles, Prince of Tyre* at the Teatro María Guerrero in the 2017-2018 season. But, best of all, English-language shows are on offer a few times a year courtesy of two local amateur groups, the Madrid Players and La Madrilera.

It would be easy to dismiss the former as a bunch of expat ham-drams and frustrated thesps, but they firmly believe there is no such thing as an 'amateur performance' – especially for paying audiences. The **Madrid Players** (www.madridplayers.org), with about 100 members of various nationalities, have been going for more than 50 years and now regularly perform in some of Madrid's better-known fringe venues. The staple earner, however, is the colourful, uproarious Christmas panto, which most years attracts total audiences of more than 2,000, many of them Spaniards.

Serious drama also has its place: recent seasons have seen performances of Alan Ayckbourn, Samuel Beckett, Thornton Wilder, Michael Christofer, Chekhov and Shakespeare. Some members have worked professionally, others have not, but enthusiasm and sheer hard work ensure high standards. This fact has not been lost on the media; the group has featured several times in major daily newspapers and has even made the national news on more than one occasion. It's worth pointing out that the idea of panto doesn't exist in Spain, and what local viewers make of a painted dame and several blokes in tights is anybody's guess.

Malasaña-based cultural association **La Madrilera** (www.lamadrilera.com) is a less formalised affair, but also puts on productions in English (as well as Spanish), and runs acting courses.

---

as *Forever* (a show about Michael Jackson), along with concerts by the likes of Macy Gray, Maceo Parker and Carla Bruni.

## Teatro Valle-Inclán
*Plaza de Lavapiés s/n, Rastro & Lavapiés (91 505 88 01, cdn.mcu.es; tickets 902 22 49 49, www.entradasinaem.es). Metro Lavapiés. **Open** Box office noon-8.30pm Mon-Fri; 2.30-8.30pm Sat, Sun. **Tickets** €6-€25. **Map** p109 K18.*

The Valle-Inclán is the Centro Dramático Nacional's second venue after the María Guerrero. The main theatre, with 510 seats, is equipped with the latest technology and offers a programme of contemporary Spanish playwrights, as well as works by authors such as Pirandello, Ibsen and Jean Genet. In the adjoining Sala Franciso Nieva, which seats 150, you're more likely to find works by newer writers.

## Teatros del Canal
*C/Cea Bermúdez 1, Chamberí (91 308 99 50, www.teatroscanal.com). Metro Canal. **Box office** 2.30-9pm daily. **Tickets** €12.50-€25.*

Consisting of three theatres – the Sala Roja (Red Room), the Sala Verde (Green Room) and the Sala Negra (Black Room) – the Teatros del Canal performing arts centre, which opened in 2009, is a flashy avant-garde building with advanced audio-visual technology and impressive interiors. The centre also houses the Centro Danza Canal (CDC) dance school. It hosts a range of performances in a variety of genres, including theatre, opera, dance and *zarzuela*.

---

## Fringe/alternative spaces

The **Teatro de las Aguas** (C/Aguas 8, 91 425 93 29, www.teatrodelasaguas.com) occasionally has productions in English. Small, more alternative spaces include **DT Espacio Escénico** (C/Reina 9, 91 521 71 55, dtespacioescenico.com) for theatre, cabaret and dance productions on gay themes; and **Lagrada** (C/Ercilla 20, 91 517 96 98, www. teatrolagrada.com) for kitchen sink dramas and contemporary plays.

### Cuarta Pared
*C/Ercilla 17, south of the centre (91 517 23 17, www.cuartapared.es). Metro Embajadores. **Box office** 1hr before performance Thur-Sun. Closed Aug. **Tickets** €14; €11 reductions. Children's shows €9; €7 reductions.*

Cuarta Pared plays a crucial role in training and production. The resident company turns out some excellent work, and it also hosts visiting productions, is a major dance venue and stages acclaimed children's theatre.

### El Montacargas

*C/Antillón 19, Puerta del Ángel, south of the centre (91 526 11 73, www. teatroelmontacargas.com). Metro Puerta del Ángel. **Box office** 30mins before show Thur-Sun. **Tickets** €12; €9 reductions. Children's shows €8. No cards.*

The programming here favours contemporary Spanish work, but it also hosts the Clown Festival in September.

### Teatro del Barrio

*C/Zurita 20, Lavapiés (91 084 36 92, www. teatrodelbarrio.com). Metro Antón Martín or Lavapiés. **Box office** 1hr before show. **Tickets** €8-€13. No cards. **Map** p109 K17.*

Formerly known as the Sala Triángulo, one of the best independent theatres in Madrid, this was taken over by a local cooperative and turned into a popular neighbourhood cultural hub. As well as theatre performances, it also hosts children's shows, talks, concerts and workshops.

### Teatro Pradillo

*C/Pradillo 12, Chamartín (91 416 90 11, www. teatropradillo.com). Metro Concha Espina. **Box office** 30mins before performance. **Tickets** €8-10. No cards.*

This fantastically intimate theatre, with just 120 seats, runs a varied programme throughout the year. A particular strength is dance – the Pradillo gave well-known dancers Manuel Liñan and Daniel Doña their big breaks – while another strong point is children's theatre, and in particular puppet shows.

## DANCE

Three major companies are based in Madrid: the contemporary, but far from radical, **Compañía Nacional de Danza**; the state **Ballet Nacional de España**, which specialises in Spanish styles of dance; and **Victor Ullate Ballet – Comunidad de Madrid**.

As ever, contemporary dance teeters on an economic knife-edge, but spaces such as the **Teatro Pradillo** (*see p241*) continue to show good work. Among the main contemporary dance companies are **Provisional Danza** (www.provisionaldanza. com), one of the pioneers of contemporary dance in Spain since 1987, led by renowned choreographer Carmen Werner. The **Centro Danza Canal** (CDC) dance school and the Víctor Ullate Ballet – Comunidad de Madrid

company are based in the **Teatros del Canal** performing arts centre (*see p240*). It's also worth noting that the **Teatro Real** (*see p235*) often stages dance productions, notably with the Ballet Nacional de España and the Compañía Nacional de Danza.

▶ *For flamenco performances, see p227.*

## Dance classes

If you take more than a passive interest in flamenco, you might want to try classes. Below are some of the more established dance centres.

### Estudios Amor de Dios

*C/Santa Isabel 5, 1°, Lavapiés (91 360 04 34, www.facebook.com/amordediosflamenco). Metro Antón Martín. **Open** varies (call for details). **Map** p109 L17.*

The world's most famous flamenco school is now nearly 70 years old. It sits (or rather stamps) above the Antón Martín indoor market building.

### El Horno

*C/Esgrima 11, Lavapiés (91 527 57 01, www.centroelhorno.com). Metro Tirso de Molina. **Open** 10am-11pm Mon-Fri; 10am-7pm Sat. **Map** p109 J17.*

El Horno has a flamenco and *sevillana* leaning (but also offers classes from martial arts to singing).

## SEASONS AND FESTIVALS

The **Festival de Otoño a Primavera** (*see p205*) is the biggest event for theatre, dance and puppetry, attracting major international names and sometimes putting on shows in English. The summer **Veranos de la Villa** (*see p204*) offers even more outdoor performances, or for a trip out of town, don't miss the **Festival Internacional de Teatro Clásico** (call 91 521 07 20 or visit festivaldealmagro.com for details) in Almagro every July. The event pays tribute to Lope de Vega, Molière, Shakespeare et al with plays, workshops and street performances. FITEC, the **Festival Internacional de Teatro de Calle** (91 601 83 23, festivalfitec.com), features street art, music, theatre and dance in the Getafe suburb. The **Madrid en Danza** festival, held for three weeks in November and December, is one of the most prestigious Spanish dance events, and attracts outstanding national and international performers.

# Understand

Puerta de Alcalá

# History

*From shanty town to cosmopolitan capital*

Around 100 years after Madrid had become capital of the Spanish Empire on the whim of Philip II, an attempt was made to construct an ancient past for it, and writers developed the story of its descent from a Roman city called Mantua Carpetana. Though there were Roman towns nearby at Alcalá de Henares (Complutum) and Toledo (Toletum), and Roman villas along the valley of the Manzanares river, there is no real evidence that there was ever a local Mantua, or that any of these settlements was the origin of modern Madrid. The story of Mantua Carpetana, however, served to obscure the insignificance of Madrid before Philip II moved his court here in 1561, and, above all, the embarrassing fact that it was founded by Muslims: specifically, in about 860 AD, during the reign of Mohammed I, fifth Emir of Córdoba.

## Arabian sights

Following their eruption into the Iberian peninsula in 711, the Arab armies did not occupy the inhospitable lands north of the Sierra de Guadarrama, but established a frontier more or less along the old Roman road linking Mérida, Toledo and Saragossa. The original *qasr* (a word absorbed into Spanish as Alcázar) or fortress of Madrid was one of a string of watchtowers built north of this line in the ninth century, as Christian raids into Al-Andalus became more frequent. The rocky crag on which it stood, where the Palacio Real is today, was ideal for the purpose, since it had a view of the main tracks south from the Guadarrama. It also had excellent water, from underground streams within the rock. Madrid's original Arabic name, Mayrit or Magerit, means 'place of many springs'.

## Madrid's original Arabic name, Mayrit or Magerit, means 'place of many springs'

Mayrit became more than just a fortress, with an outer citadel, the eastern wall of which ran along the modern C/Factor, and a wider town or *medina* bounded by the Plaza de la Villa and C/Segovia. A section of wall, the Muralla Árabe on Cuesta de la Vega, and the remains next to the Palacio Real are the only remnants of Muslim Madrid visible in the modern city. Both citadel and *medina* consisted of a mass of narrow alleys, like the old quarters of North African cities today.

Mayrit was attacked by Christian armies in 932 and 1047, and in the 970s was used by the great minister of Córdoba, Al-Mansur, as a base for his celebrated 100 campaigns against the north. By the 11th century, it had a population of around 7,000.

Muralla Árabe

## Christian conquest

In the 11th century, the Caliphate of Córdoba disintegrated into a mass of petty princedoms called *taifas*, and Mayrit became part of the Emirate of Toledo. In 1086, Alfonso VI of Castile took advantage of this situation to conquer Toledo, and with it Madrid. The town's main mosque became the church of Santa María de la Almudena, which would survive until the 19th century. For many years, however, Madrid would remain on the front line. In 1109, it was again besieged, by a Moorish army that camped below the Alcázar in the place since known as Campo del Moro (Field of the Moor). A new wall was built, enclosing the area between the Alcázar and Plaza Isabel II, Plaza San Miguel and Plaza Humilladero.

Christian Madrid was a very rural town, and most of the population who worked did so on the land. Madrid did acquire large religious houses, notably the Friary of San Francisco, where the church of San Francisco el Grande still stands, supposedly founded by St Francis of Assisi in 1217. But it was still not entirely Christian. Many Muslims, known as Mudéjares, had stayed in the conquered areas, retaining their own laws and religion, and were prized by the Castilian monarchs for their skills as builders and masons; their work can still be seen today in the towers of San Nicolás de los Servitas and San Pedro el Viejo. In Madrid they were confined to the area known as the Morería. Medieval Madrid also had a smaller Jewish population, concentrated outside the walls in Lavapiés.

Madrid did finally begin to play more of a role in the affairs of Castile in the 14th century. In 1309, the Cortes, or parliament, met here for the first time. Medieval Castile did not have a fixed capital, but instead the Court followed the king around the country. In the 14th and 15th centuries Castile was dogged by a series of social revolts and civil wars between monarchs, the nobility and rival claimants from the royal family. Against this backdrop, Madrid began to gain popularity as a royal residence, a country retreat more than a centre of power.

Political instability did not prevent substantial economic progress in 15th-century Castile, with Madrid becoming a reasonably prosperous trading centre for the first time. Trade outgrew the old market in Plaza de la Villa, and in the 1460s an area east of the 12th-century wall was built up as a ramshackle new market square, the origin of the Plaza Mayor. A new town wall was built, not for defence but so that taxes could be levied on people living in the new parts of the town. Its eastern entrance was a new gate, the Puerta del Sol.

Madrid retained a degree of royal favour and continued its modest growth, and at the end of the Middle Ages had a population of around 10,000-12,000.

On 11 May 1561, the small-time aristocrats who ran the town of Madrid received a letter from their king, Philip II, warning that he, the entire royal household and all their hundreds of hangers-on would shortly be coming to stay.

## Capital idea

Philip II (1556-98) was the fundamental figure in Madrid's history. He was a deeply pious, shy, austere man. His father had travelled incessantly about his many dominions, and led his armies into battle. Philip, in contrast, ruled his inheritance from behind a desk, as a kind of king-bureaucrat, sometimes dealing with over 400 documents a day. This extraordinary exercise in paperwork naturally required a permanent base.

Why Philip chose a town without a cathedral, college or printing press as capital remains unclear. The fact that Madrid was near the centre of the Iberian peninsula probably appealed to him, as he was fascinated by geometry and Renaissance ideas of a king as the 'centre' of the state, but his choice made no economic sense at all, since it gave Spain the only major European capital not on a navigable river. Madrid – which for centuries would normally be referred to in Spain as 'La Corte', the Court, never as a city in its own right, which indeed it wasn't – would be a capital of the monarchy's own creation, a pure expression of royal power.

Having established his ideal capital, Philip did little to build or plan it. He had extended the Alcázar when he was still crown prince, then his attention shifted to El Escorial, where he increasingly spent his time. Royal piety was demonstrated by the endowment of new houses for religious orders, such as the Descalzas Reales. Philip II founded 17 convents and monasteries in Madrid, Philip III 14 and Philip IV another 17, and they would cover a third of the city until the 19th century. A wider city wall was put up in 1566, and the Puente de Segovia in the 1580s. Philip's favourite architect, Juan de Herrera, planned the rebuilding of the Plaza Mayor, but the only part that was built during his reign was the Casa de la Panadería in 1590.

The establishment of the Court and aristocracy – the great centres of consumption and patronage – in Madrid made it a magnet for people from all over Spain and abroad. The population went from under 20,000 in 1561 to 55,000 in 1584 and close to 85,000 by 1600. Building did not keep up with the influx, and a law decreed that in any house of more than one storey, the upper floor could be requisitioned to house members of the Court. In response, people simply put up houses with only one floor, and much of the new Madrid grew as a mass of shabby, low buildings.

This improvised capital did not impress foreign visitors. Lambert Wyts, a Flemish aristocrat who arrived in 1571, said that it was 'the foulest and filthiest town in Spain'. Thick mud made it impossible to ride a horse down the main streets in winter until a few cobbles were put down in the 1580s. There were no drains of any kind, and the streets were full of waste thrown out of the houses every night, producing an 'unbearable stench'.

Madrid had taken on a characteristic that would stay with it to this day – that it was a city of outsiders, in which at least 50 per cent of the population was from somewhere else. Another trait for which Madrid would be repeatedly condemned was that it was a city that consumed but did not produce anything. The trades that did develop in Madrid – shoe-making, carpentry, jewellery-making, fan-making, lace-working – were overwhelmingly to service the Court and aristocracy.

## The Court adjourns

The greatest success of Philip II's reign was the defeat of the Turkish fleet in the Battle of Lepanto in Greece in 1571. In 1580, he became king of Portugal and appeared to be at the height of his strength. However, suspensions of payment on his debts were becoming frequent, and in the 1560s a rebellion broke out in the Netherlands that would develop into a morass into which Spanish armies and wealth would disappear. Philip's dispute with England – leading to the Armada catastrophe – and interventions in France's religious wars were as costly.

As the number of unresolved problems mounted, a gnawing frustration spread through Castilian society, and scapegoats were sought. The former Muslims, nominally converted in 1502, were put under increasing pressure and then expelled from Spain in 1609, and the Inquisition – if not the all-pervading force of Protestant caricature – gained great powers to investigate deviations from Catholic orthodoxy.

Philip II died in 1598 at El Escorial, aged 71. His son Philip III (1598-1621) and grandson Philip IV (1621-65) had neither the intelligence, confidence nor motivation to carry on with the awesome burden of work he'd set as an example. Philip III began the practice of ruling through a favourite, or *valido*, in his case the Duke of Lerma. Spain's impoverished state, aggravated by a devastating plague in 1599, was impossible to ignore, and Lerma responded by making peace with England and the Dutch.

He also committed the ultimate injury to Madrid by moving the Court to Valladolid, in 1601. The stated reason was that this would revive the economy of northern Castile, although Lerma stood to benefit personally. He also argued that Madrid was so overrun with undesirables that it had become intolerable. The monarchy's purpose-built capital was out of control and it would be best to write it off and start again.

Within a few months Madrid was so deserted 'it appeared as if the Moors or the English had sacked and burnt it'. By 1605, the population had fallen back to just 26,000, little more than before Philip II's arrival in 1561. However, the Valladolid experiment did not work, and it became evident that Madrid had acquired a momentum that was difficult to ignore. In 1606, the Court returned amid huge rejoicing, and only a year later the population was already back to 70,000.

## Pomp and circumstance

It was after Madrid's definitive establishment as capital, with Philip III's brief declaration *Sólo Madrid es Corte* (Only Madrid is the Court), that more was at last done to give it the look of a grand city. Plaza Mayor was finally completed in 1619, followed by the Ayuntamiento, or city hall, and the Buen Retiro palace. The aristocracy, too, began to build palaces around the city once they were assured they wouldn't have to move on again, and Madrid acquired several much more elaborate Baroque churches.

**The Plaza Mayor was the great arena of Habsburg Madrid; holding a third of the city's population at that time, it was used for state ceremonies, bullfights, executions and fiestas**

The Plaza Mayor was the great arena of Habsburg Madrid. Able to hold a third of the city's population at that time, it was the venue for state ceremonies, bullfights, executions, *autos-da-fé* (the ritual condemnation of heretics), mock battles, circus acts and carnival *fiestas*, as well as functioning as a market square.

Habsburg Madrid functioned rather like a giant theatre, a great backdrop against which the monarchy could display itself to its subjects and to the world. On either side were royal estates, which determined the shape of the city left in the middle and its peculiar north–south pattern of growth. Several times a year royal processions took place, with stops for various ceremonies in the Plaza Mayor and high masses in various churches. For the occasion, buildings were covered in garlands, and temporary arches were erected along the route with extravagant decorations extolling the virtues of the dynasty. As the Spanish monarchy slid towards economic collapse the lavishness of these ceremonies only increased, maintaining an illusion of power and opulence.

Away from this ceremonial route, the Habsburgs built few squares and no grand avenues, and old Madrid continued to develop along the tangled street plan it retains today. Even so, the opulence of the Court – and the poverty outside the capital – still attracted more people into the city, and in about 1630 Madrid reached its maximum size under the Habsburgs, with possibly as many as 170,000 inhabitants. In 1656, it was given its fifth and final wall, roughly surrounding the area now considered 'old Madrid', which would set the limits of the city for the next 200 years.

## The price of war

For many years the centre of all the Court pomp was King Philip IV. Throughout the 1620s and 1630s, while the Court maintained its image of grandeur, his *valido*, the Count-Duke of Olivares, struggled to maintain the Spanish Empire against threats on every side. In the 1620s, Spain won a series of victories, and for a time it seemed the rot had been stopped. In 1639, though, a Spanish fleet was destroyed by the Dutch, and in 1643 the French crushed the Spanish army at Rocroi in Flanders. Naval defeats made it ever more difficult for Spain to import gold and silver from America. Olivares sought to extend taxation in the non-Castilian dominions of the crown, which led in 1640 to revolts in Portugal and Catalonia. Portugal regained its independence, and the Catalan revolt was only suppressed after a 12-year war.

By mid-century the effects of endless wars on Castile were visible to all, in abandoned villages and social decay. Even Madrid went into decline, so that by 1700 the population had fallen back to about 100,000. In the 1660s, the total collapse of the Spanish Empire seemed an immediate possibility. Castile, the first world power, had been left poorer than many countries it had tried to dominate.

## End of the Habsburg line

In the Court, meanwhile, life became ever more of a baroque melodrama. Of Philip IV's 12 legitimate children by his two wives, only two girls had survived into adulthood – the youngest, the Infanta Margarita, the little princess in Velázquez's *Las Meninas*. In 1661, however, when Philip was already prematurely aged, the queen, Mariana of Austria, had a son.

The new heir, the future King Charles II, was chronically infirm from birth and provided the dynasty with scant consolation. The Habsburgs' marked tendency to ill-health was accentuated by their habit of marrying cousins or nieces. The Habsburg jaw, the growth of which can be followed through family portraits, had in Charles become a real disability. He was unable to eat solid food. Because of this – or, more likely, the endless cures he was subjected to for his many ailments – he suffered uncontrollable diarrhoea, which detracted from the stately dignity of Court ceremonies.

In the meantime, the economy and the government continued to slide. Concern centred again on the need for an heir, and Charles was married off twice, despite a general belief that he was both impotent and sterile. As it became evident that the throne of the Spanish Empire would soon become vacant, the Court was overrun with bizarre intrigues, with different factions and the agents of European powers all waiting for Charles' final demise. In 1695, the French ambassador reported that the king 'appeared to be decomposing', and could barely walk without assistance. Even so, Charles hung on until the age of 38. In 1700, though, with the pathetic last words, *'Me duele todo'* ('It hurts everywhere'), he finally died, and the Spanish Habsburg dynasty came to an end.

## Bourbon Madrid

Philip V (1700–46), first Bourbon king of Spain, secured his throne in 1714, after the 12-year War of the Spanish Succession. He was the grandson of Louis XIV of France and María Teresa, daughter of Philip IV of

**Charles II**

Spain. Castile, abandoning its more usual Francophobia, gave him complete support. The alternative, Archduke Charles of Austria, was supported by Catalonia and the other Aragonese territories, to which he had promised a restoration of their traditional rights. Twice, in 1706 and 1710, Charles' British, Dutch, Portuguese and Catalan army took Madrid, but was unable to hold it.

Once victorious, Philip reformed his new kingdom along the lines laid down by his illustrious grandfather in France. In 1715, the remaining rights of the former Aragonese territories were abolished, so that it is from this date that Spain can formally be said to exist.

A French king brought with him other innovations. Philip V – raised at Versailles – and his Italian second wife Isabella Farnese, were not taken with Madrid or its gloomy Habsburg palaces, and so built their own Franco-Italian villa at La Granja. They were not overly upset when the entire Alcázar burned down in 1734, and a new Palacio Real was commissioned from Italian architects. Philip V and his administrator of Madrid, the Marqués de Vadillo, also funded many buildings by a local architect, Pedro de Ribera.

Reform led to economic recuperation and a recovery in Madrid's population. People still came and went, but the city also acquired a more stable resident population, with a merchant community, and an artisan and working class. Even so, in many ways

# The Majas

*Goya's portraits of the majas are clothed (or otherwise) with intrigue*

In the 18th century, ordinary people in European cities began to look increasingly similar, wearing more or less the same three-cornered hats, breeches and mop-caps. Not so in Madrid, where this was the era of the *majos* and *majas*. A *majo* wore embroidered shirts, a short jacket with a swathe of buttons and a hairnet, and carried a knife. *Majas* wore short, mid-calf skirts with a mass of petticoats, pearl-white stockings, embroidered bodices, intricately braided hairstyles and dramatic lace mantillas. They were drawn from trades such as coach-driving, dressmaking, cigarette-rolling or market trading, and most often came from Lavapiés. *Majas* especially were known for their wit, grace and verbal ferocity. In a capital that was still largely a city of servants, but whose servants were renowned for talking back, they deferred to no one.

They were mostly seen in all their finery at *fiestas* such as the Romería de San Isidro. Goya depicted them often. Also, their cocky elegance led to their style being taken up by the upper classes, so that even *grandes dames* such as the Duchess of Alba would dress up as *majas*, which is what probably gave rise to the story that Goya's nude *maja* and clothed *maja* are portraits of the duchess herself.

This theory has been discredited by scholars in recent years, but still has many subscribers; the woman depicted does bear a startling resemblance to the duchess, and the large bow round her waist also featured in several of Goya's portraits of her. And, yes, it is possibly true that the duchess had an affair with the painter, with whom she holed up for several months on one of her country estates after her husband died. It is unlikely that she would have allowed allow herself to be painted in such a way, though, given her standing in society. Some critics suggest the head was painted on the body later, and this is certainly the visual effect. What is irrefutable, however, is that Goya was obsessed with Alba, and a more probable explanation for the likeness is simply that he tended to project her image on to an idealised form of female beauty. *La maja desnuda (Nude Maja)* and *La maja vestida (Clothed Maja)* are both on display at the Prado.

Nude Maja (c. 1800)

Clothed Maja (c. 1803)

Madrid had changed little. Its main function was still to serve the Court, the ceremonies of which set the calendar. These were as lavish as ever: until the 1770s the amount spent annually by the Crown in Madrid was greater than the entire budget of the Spanish navy.

Fernando VI (1746-59) was a shy but popular king who gave Spain its longest period of peace for more than 200 years. Childless, he was succeeded by his half-brother Charles III (1759-88). Previously King of Naples for 20 years, he too was less than impressed by Madrid. However, more than any of his predecessors he set about improving the city, becoming known as Madrid's Rey-Alcalde or 'King-Mayor'.

## Enlightenment strikes

Charles was fascinated by Enlightenment ideas of progress, science and applied use of reason. No democrat, he sought to bring about rational improvement from the top. Reforms were undertaken in the bureaucracy and armed forces, and to improve trade with Spanish America. He challenged the privileges of the religious orders, and expelled the Jesuits from Spain in 1767 for their refusal to co-operate.

In Madrid, Charles first undertook to do something about the mud in winter, suffocating dust in summer and foul smells at all times – which were noted by every visitor to the city. A 1761 decree banned the dumping of waste in the streets, and Charles' Italian engineer-architect Francesco Sabatini began building sewers and street lighting. A string of major buildings was erected, of which the Casa de Correos in Puerta del Sol and Puerta de Alcalá are the best known. A later queen of Spain remarked that it sometimes seemed as if all the monuments of Madrid had been built by Charles III.

Charles III's grandest project was the Paseo del Prado. He sent scientific expeditions to every corner of his empire, and planned to exhibit the fruits of their varied researches in a natural history museum – which would later become the Museo del Prado – and the adjacent Jardín Botánico.

Reform and improved trade did create a feeling of well-being in late 18th-century Madrid. Nevertheless, Spain was still a very feudal society, and the real economy remained backward and frail. And, in an absolute monarchy, a great deal depended on each monarch. Charles IV (1788-1808) had none of his father's energy or intelligence. Also, he chose as his minister the corrupt Manuel Godoy. After the French Revolution, Spain joined other monarchies in attacking the new regime; in 1795, however, Godoy made peace and then an alliance with France, leading to an unpopular war with Britain. Then, in 1808, when Godoy was vacillating over changing sides once again, he was forestalled by anti-French riots that proclaimed Charles IV's son Fernando as king in his place. Napoleon sent troops to Madrid, assuming this decrepit state would be as easy to conquer as any other. It was not to be, at least not initially, and the consequences were horrific (*see p252* The Third of May).

Once victory was his, Napoleon made his brother, Joseph Bonaparte, king of Spain. In Madrid he tried in a well-meaning fashion to make improvements, among them some squares for which the city has since been very grateful, notably the Plaza de Oriente and the Plaza Santa Ana. However, this did nothing to overcome the animosity around him. In 1812, the Duke of Wellington and his army arrived to take the city, in a battle that destroyed much of the Retiro palace. The French were finally driven out of Spain in 1813. As well as the fighting itself, the year 1812 brought with it a catastrophic famine, which in Madrid killed over 30,000 people.

The shock of this upheaval initiated a period of instability that continued until 1874 – in fact, it could be said that the instability only really ended with the death of Franco in 1975. Spain withdrew into its own problems, with one conflict after another between conservatives, reformists, revolutionaries and other factions. Each struggled to impose its model on the state and create a political system that could accommodate, or hold back, the pressures for modernisation and some form of democracy.

In 1812, parliament had met in Cádiz and given Spain its first constitution. Yet when Fernando VII (1808-33) returned from French captivity in 1814, his only thought was to cancel the constitution and return to the methods of his ancestors. His absolute rule, though, was incapable of responding to the bankruptcy of the country. The regime was also struggling to hold on to its American colonies, which were by then in complete rebellion. In 1820, a liberal revolt in the army forced Fernando to reinstate the constitution. He was saved three years later, ironically by a French army, sent to restore monarchical rule. Meanwhile, defeat at Ayacucho in Peru (1824) left Spain with only Cuba, Santo Domingo and Puerto Rico of its former American empire.

In 1830, Fernando VII's wife María Cristina gave birth to a daughter, soon to be Queen Isabel II (1833-68). Previously, the most reactionary sectors of the aristocracy, the Church and other ultra-conservative groups had aligned themselves behind the king's brother Don Carlos. When Fernando died in 1833, Carlos demanded the throne, launching what became known as the Carlist Wars. In order to defend her daughter's rights, María Cristina, as regent, had no choice but to look for support from liberals, and so was obliged to promise some form of constitutional rule.

## Old romantics

For the next 40 years Spanish politics were a see-saw, as conservative and liberal factions vied for power, while the Carlists, off the spectrum for most people in Madrid, occasionally threatened at the gates. Madrid was the great centre for aspiring politicians, and the problems of Spain were discussed endlessly in its salons and new cafés, which multiplied around this time. This was the era of Romanticism, and writers such as the journalist Larra and poet José Espronceda were heavily involved in politics. Similarly, many of the politicians of the day were also writers.

# The Third of May

*Goya's extraordinary painting of the reality of war*

More than 200 years old, this remains one of the world's most modern paintings. It marked a complete transformation in the portrayal of war. Previously, with very few exceptions, war paintings had presented war as a noble contest, glorifying heroic deeds and celebrating kings and commanders – a prime example, Velázquez's *Las Lanzas*, hangs near Goya's work in the Prado.

In Goya's war images, in contrast – whether the *Tres de Mayo* or the *Desastres de la Guerra* – there is no glory, only misery, brutality and chaos. Death, mutilation and casual savagery are more prominent than victories. There are no generals or famous heroes, only faces in the crowd. There is heroism – again anonymous – but it seems wild, desperate, ultimately futile. It is this searingly honest, unblinking sense of the truth and horror of violence that makes the *Tres de Mayo* so permanently contemporary.

The events portrayed were very real. On 2 May 1808, Madrid awoke to learn that Napoleon had kidnapped the Spanish royal family, and that French troops were taking over the country. The French expected little resistance beyond skirmishes and some manageable grumbling. Instead, uncoordinated Spanish army units and, above all, the people of Madrid, fought the invaders street by street, using knives or their bare hands. As the day wore on, the French gradually won control of Madrid, and in the early morning of 3 May – enraged that they had had to fight so hard against a mere street mob, rather than real soldiers – they set out to teach the city a lesson. Captured 'insurgents' were disposed of in mass executions on the hill of Príncipe Pío, which is now at the southern end of the Parque del Oeste.

Goya painted his *Dos de Mayo*, of the struggle in the Puerta del Sol, and *Tres de Mayo* in 1814, just after the French had been driven out of Spain. How much personal observation went into them is an unanswered question. Goya was in Madrid during those days, and one of his gardeners later claimed the artist had watched the executions through a telescope. However, this is impossible to confirm.

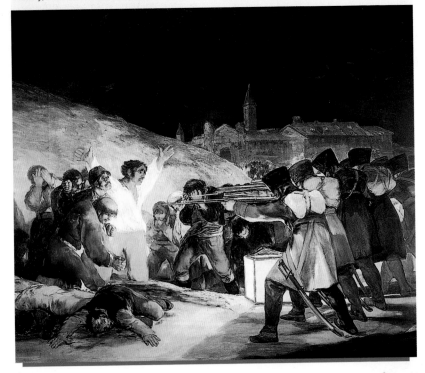

Much of the time, though, these reformers were shepherds in search of a flock, for there were no true political parties. The only way a faction could hope to gain power was with the support of a general with troops at his disposal.

This political instability did not mean that life in Madrid was chaotic. Visitors in the early 1830s found a small, sleepy, shabby city, which seemed sunk in the past. Convents and palaces still occupied nearly half its area. It was around this time that Spain acquired its romantic aura. A growing number of foreigners visited, drawn by Spain's timeless, exotic qualities. One was the French writer Prosper Mérimée, who in 1845 wrote his novel *Carmen*, later put to music by Bizet, who himself never visited Spain at all.

## Visitors in the early 1830s found a small, sleepy, shabby city, which seemed sunk in the past

### Expansion and turmoil

The 1830s, however, also saw the single most important change in Madrid during the 19th century. In 1836, the liberal minister Mendizábal took advantage of the church's sympathy for Carlism to introduce his Desamortización or Disentailment law, which dissolved most of Spain's monasteries. In Madrid, the church lost over 1,000 properties. Most were demolished remarkably quickly, and an enormous area thus became available for sale and new building.

Some urban reformers saw this as an opportunity to build broad, airy avenues, following the always-cited example of Paris. Some major projects were undertaken, the most important being the rebuilding of the Puerta del Sol in 1854-62. However, most of the local traders who benefited from Desamortización lacked the capital to contemplate grand projects, and built separate blocks without ever challenging the established, disorderly street plan. The districts of old Madrid took on the appearance they have largely kept until today, with great numbers of tenement blocks. They allowed Madrid to grow considerably in population, without going outside its still-standing wall of 1656.

A few factories had appeared in the city, but for the most part the Industrial Revolution was passing Madrid by.

Constitutional governments expanded the administration, and the ambitions of the middle class were focused on obtaining official posts rather than on business ventures. Two more major changes arrived in the 1850s. In 1851, Madrid got its first railway, to Aranjuez, followed by a line running to the Mediterranean. Railways would transform Madrid's relationship with the rest of the country, opening up a realistic possibility of it fulfilling an economic function. Equally important was the completion of the Canal de Isabel II, bringing water from the Guadarrama, in 1858. Madrid's water supply, still part-based on Moorish water courses, had been inadequate for years. The canal removed a crippling obstruction to the city's growth.

Madrid's population was by this time over 300,000. Steps were finally taken for it to break out of its old walls, and in 1860 a plan by Carlos María de Castro was approved for the *ensanche* (extension) of Madrid, in an orderly grid pattern to the north and east. However, as with earlier rebuilding, the plan came up against the chronic lack of large-scale local investors. The only major development undertaken quickly was the section of C/Serrano bought up by the flamboyant speculator the Marqués de Salamanca, whose name was given to the whole district.

Meanwhile, the political situation was deteriorating once again, after a long period of conservative rule that began in 1856. Isabel II had become deeply unpopular, surrounded by an aura of sleaze and scandal. In September 1868, yet another military revolt deposed the government and, this time, the queen as well.

There followed six years of turmoil. The provisional government invited an Italian prince, Amadeo of Savoy, to become king of a truly constitutional monarchy. However, in December 1870, General Prim, strongman of the new regime, was assassinated. Carlist revolts broke out in some parts of the country, while on the left new, more radical groups began to appear. At the end of 1868, a meeting in Madrid addressed by Giuseppe Fanelli, an Italian associate of Russian revolutionary Mikhail Bakunin, led to the founding of the first anarchist group in Spain. The Cortes itself was riven by factions, and Amadeo decided to give up the struggle and return to Italy.

On 12 February 1873, Spain became a republic. Rightist resistance became stronger than ever, while many towns were taken over by left-wing juntas, who declared them autonomous 'cantons', horrifying conservative opinion. To keep control, republican governments relied increasingly heavily on the army. This proved fatal, and on 3 January 1874 the army commander in Madrid, General Pavía, marched into the Cortes, sent all its members home, and installed a military dictatorship.

## The Bourbons return

At the end of 1874, the army decided to restore the Bourbon dynasty, in the shape of Alfonso XII (1874-85), son of Isabel II. The architect of the Restoration regime, however, was a civilian politician, Antonio Cánovas del Castillo. He established the system of *turno pacífico*, or peaceful alternation in power (thus avoiding social tensions), between a Conservative Party, led by himself, and a Liberal Party, which was made up of former progressives. The control of these 'dynastic parties' over the political system was secured by election-rigging and occasional repression.

In the late 1870s, the wealthy of Madrid set out on a building boom. They finally overcame their reluctance to leave the old city, and the Salamanca area became the new centre of fashionable life. Most of the district's new apartment blocks had lifts, first seen in Madrid in 1874. In earlier blocks upper floors had been let cheaply, so that rich and poor had often continued to live side by side. With lifts, however, a top floor could be as desirable as a first, and this kind of class mixing faded.

Government and official bodies, too, undertook a huge round of new building. The Banco de España, the Bolsa and the main railway stations are all creations of the 1880s. Madrid meanwhile acquired a larger professional middle class; it also attracted intellectuals from around the country.

At the same time, Madrid was receiving an influx of poor migrants from rural Spain, with over 200,000 new arrivals between 1874 and 1900. Economic growth was reflected in the appearance of yet more small workshops rather than factories. There were also many with next to no work, and the 1880s saw the beginning of a housing crisis, with the growth of shanty towns around the outskirts of the city.

## The empire strikes back

Just before the end of the century, however, the preconceptions on which Spanish political life had been based received a huge blow. The Restoration regime presented itself as having returned the country to stability and some prestige in the world. However, in the 1890s Spain was involved in colonial wars against nationalists in the Philippines and Cuba. In 1898, the government allowed itself to be manoeuvred into a disastrous war with the United States. In a few weeks, almost the entire Spanish navy was sunk, and Spain lost virtually all its remaining overseas territories. Known simply as 'The Disaster', this was a devastating blow to Spain's self-confidence. The regime itself was revealed as decrepit and incompetent, based on a feeble economy. Among intellectuals, the situation sparked off an intense round of self-examination and discussion of Spain's relationship with the very concept of modernity. The problems of the regime were not due to the country being backward, however. Rather, they spiralled out of control because after 1900 the country entered an unprecedented period of change.

## City without limits

Sudden economic expansion was set off by three main factors. One, paradoxically, was the loss of the colonies, which led to large amounts of capital being brought back to the country. Most important was World War I, which provided opportunities for neutral Spain in the supply of goods to the Allied powers. Then, during the worldwide boom of the 1920s, Spain benefited hugely from foreign investment.

Within a few years, Spain had one of the fastest rates of urbanisation in the world. The economic upheaval caused by the world war led to runaway inflation, spurring a huge movement into the cities. Madrid did not grow as rapidly as industrial Barcelona, which had become the largest city in the country. Nevertheless, after taking four centuries to reach half a million, it doubled its population again in just 30 years, to just under a million by 1930. Only 37 per cent of its people had been born in the city.

The most visible manifestation of this growth was a still-larger building boom. Bombastic creations such as the Palacio de Comunicaciones (now called the Palacio de Cibeles) were symptomatic of the expansive mood. Most important was the opening of the Gran Vía in 1910, a project that had first been discussed no less than 25 years previously, and which would transform the heart of the old city with a new grand thoroughfare for entertainment, business and banking. Another fundamental innovation was electricity. The city's trams were electrified in 1898, and the first metro line, between Sol and Cuatro Caminos, opened in 1919. Electricity allowed Madrid, far from any other source of power, finally to experience an industrial take-off in the years after 1910. At the same time, expansion in banking and office work was also reflected in the large number of white-collar workers.

Madrid was also, more than ever, the mecca for intellectuals and professionals from right across the country. This was the background to the enormous vigour of the city's intellectual life at this time, the so-called 'Silver Age' of Spanish literature. From writers of 1898, such as Antonio Machado and Baroja, to the famous poets of the 1927 generation, Rafael Alberti and García Lorca, the city welcomed a succession of literary talent, not to mention painters, historians and scientists. From the 1910s onward, Madrid's cafés were full of talk, forums for discussion multiplied, and a large number of newspapers and magazines were published.

In politics, this urban expansion made it impossible for the 'dynastic parties' to control elections in the way they were able to do in small towns and rural areas. In an attempt to move back towards some form of constitutional rule, the government decided to hold local elections on 12 April 1931. They were not expected to be a referendum on the monarchy. However, when the results came in it was seen that republican candidates had won sweeping majorities in all of Spain's cities.

## The Second Republic

On 14 April 1931, as the results of the local elections became clear, the streets of Spain's cities filled with people. In Madrid, a jubilant mass converged on the Puerta del Sol. It was these exultant crowds in the streets that drove the king to abdicate and spurred republican politicians into action, for they had never expected their opportunity to arrive so soon.

The Second Spanish Republic arrived amid huge optimism, expressing the frustrated hopes of decades. Among the many schemes of its first government, a Republican-Socialist coalition, was a project for Madrid, the Gran Madrid or 'Greater

Madrid' plan, intended to integrate the sprawling new areas around the city's edge. A key part of it was the extension of the Castellana, then blocked by a racecourse above C/Joaquín Costa. The racecourse was demolished, and the Castellana was allowed to snake endlessly northward, forming one of the modern city's most distinctive features. Also completed under the Republic was the last section of the Gran Vía, from Callao to Plaza de España, site of Madrid's best art deco buildings.

Possibilities of further change were to be entangled in the accelerating social crisis that overtook the Republic around this time. The new regime aroused expectations that would have been difficult to live up to at the best of times. Instead, its arrival coincided with the onset of the worldwide depression of the 1930s.

## The polarisation of politics

As unemployment and the gap between rich and poor increased, calls for the end of republican compromise in a second, social, revolution grew, especially from the anarchist CNT and the Communist Party. Even the Socialist Party was radicalised. On the right, similarly, the loudest voices – such as the fascist Falange, founded in 1933 by José Antonio Primo de Rivera, son of the former dictator – demanded authoritarian rule as the only means of preserving social order. The vogue for extremism was fed by the mood of the times, in which Nazism, Italian fascism and Soviet communism appeared as the most dynamic international models.

In 1933, the coalition between Socialists and liberal Republicans broke up. With the left split, elections were won by conservative republicans backed by the CEDA, a parliamentary but authoritarian right-wing

Crowds celebrating election result, 14 April 1931

party. Reform came to a halt. In October 1934, the CEDA demanded to have ministers in the government, and a general strike was called in response. It was strongest in the mining region of Asturias, where it was savagely suppressed by a rising general called Francisco Franco.

Left-wing parties were subjected to a wave of repression that radicalised their supporters further. In new elections in February 1936, however, the left, united once again in the Frente Popular (Popular Front), were victorious. In Madrid, the Front won 54 per cent of the vote.

A liberal-republican government returned to power, with Manuel Azaña as president. By this time, however, the level of polarisation and of sheer hatred in the country was moving out of control. Right-wing politicians called almost openly for the army to save the country. The military had already laid their plans for a coup.

## Revolution and war

On 18 July 1936, the generals made their move, with risings all over Spain, while German and Italian aircraft ferried Franco's colonial army from Spanish Morocco to Andalucia. In Madrid, troops failed to seize the city and barricaded themselves inside the Montaña barracks, the site of which is now in the Parque del Oeste.

The coup was the spark for an explosion of tension. Workers' parties demanded arms. On 20 July, as news came that the army had been defeated in Barcelona and many other cities, the Montaña was stormed and its defenders massacred, despite the efforts of political leaders to prevent it. Among left-wing militants the mood was ecstatic: factories, schools, the transport system and other public services were all taken over, and although the government remained in place, it had little effective power. Ad hoc militias and patrols were the only power on the streets, and, amid the paranoia and hatred that were the other side of revolutionary excitement, summary executions of suspected rightists were common.

Meanwhile, the war still had to be fought. Franco's troops were advancing from Seville preceded by stories of reprisals more terrible than anything done by the 'red terror' in Madrid. The militias seemed powerless to

General Francisco Franco

stop them. Defeat for the Republic seemed inevitable. German planes bombed the city. On 6 November, as Franco's advance guard arrived, the government left for Valencia, a move widely seen as desertion.

## City under siege

Without a government, though, a new resolve was seen in the city. In the southern suburbs, troops were resisted street by street. Women, children and the elderly helped build trenches and barricades. On 9 November 1936, the first foreign volunteers, the International Brigades, arrived, doing wonders for morale. After savage fighting, Franco halted the frontal assault on Madrid later that month.

Madrid saw little more direct fighting. From the Casa de Campo, where the remains of trenches and bunkers still exist, the army settled in to a siege. Attempts to push them back north and south of Madrid were unsuccessful. The city was regularly bombed, and bombarded by artillery, who took their sights from the Gran Vía, 'Howitzer Avenue'.

General Franco, meanwhile, was advancing on other fronts. During 1937, his forces overran the Basque Country and

Asturias, and in March 1938 they reached the Mediterranean near Castellón. In January 1939, they conquered Catalonia. In Madrid, fighting broke out behind Republican lines between the communists, committed to fighting to the end, and groups that wanted to negotiate a settlement with Franco. Those in favour of negotiation won, but Franco had no intention of compromising. On 28 March 1939, the Nationalist army entered the Spanish capital.

## The long dictatorship

Madrid emerged from the Civil War physically and psychologically battered. Hundreds of buildings stood in ruins. Buildings, however, could be rebuilt fairly quickly; healing the damage done to the city's spirit would take decades.

The Madrid of the 1940s was the sombre antithesis of the expansive city of ten years previously. A great many *madrileños* had lost someone close to them, to bombs, bullets, firing squads or prison camps. The black market, rather than art and literature, dominated café conversation, and the figures of earlier years were mostly in exile, or keeping indoors.

# Madrid emerged from the Civil War physically and psychologically battered

HISTORY

The existence of 'two Spains' (right–left, traditional–liberal, rich–poor) was all too apparent. As the victors marched in, they wasted no time in rounding up members (or just suspected sympathisers) of 'enemy' groups, anarchists, Communists, union members and liberals. Some were turned in by neighbours, creating a sordid atmosphere of bitterness and distrust. During the early '40s, while the rest of the world was wrapped up in World War II, thousands were executed in Spain. Others paid the price of defeat by serving as forced labour on fascist landmarks such as the Valle de los Caídos, Franco's victory monument and tomb.

Madrid's loyalty to the Republic almost led to it losing its capital status, as voices were raised calling for a more 'loyal' city to represent the country. Tradition and financial interests bore more weight, however, and the capital stayed put. The Falange, official party of the regime, produced extravagant plans to turn Madrid into a Spanish version of Imperial Rome, but a lack of funding and galloping inflation scotched most of these nouveau-imperialist notions. The economy was in a desperate state, and Spain went through a period of extreme hardship, the *años del hambre* ('hunger years'); many remember not having eaten properly for ten years after 1936. This poverty also led to the phenomenon that would most shape the face of Madrid in the post-war decades: massive immigration from Spain's rural provinces. Madrid grew faster than any other European capital in the 20th century. A 'big village' of just over half a million at the turn of the century, and 950,000 in 1930, it passed the three million mark by 1970.

Most European countries continued to shun the regime, at least in public, but in 1953, as the Cold War intensified, Franco was saved by the US government's 'our son-of-a-bitch' policy in choosing allies. A co-operation treaty gave the regime renewed credibility and cash in exchange for air and sea bases on Spanish soil, and later President Eisenhower flew in to shake the dictator's hand.

For those not devoted to the regime, life under Franco was a matter of keeping one's head down. Football and other forms of escapism played a huge part in people's lives.

The national Stabilisation Plan of 1959 gave the fundamental push to Madrid's development, and brought Spain definitively back into the Western fold. The plan revolutionised the country's economy, and especially that of the Madrid region. In the 1960s, tourism began to pump money into Spain, and Madrid trebled in size to become an industrial powerhouse. Quiet tree-lined boulevards were widened to make way for cars, and elegant Castellana palaces were replaced by glass-sheathed monoliths. Madrid took on much more of the look, and feel, of a big city.

## Life after Franco

The 1960s also saw the revival of opposition to the regime in the shape of labour unrest, student protests, and the rise of the Basque organisation ETA. The oil crisis of 1973 coincided with the assassination by ETA of Franco's prime minister, Admiral Carrero Blanco, when a bomb planted beneath a Madrid street launched his car right over a five-storey building. The regime, already challenged by political opposition, now had to deal with rising unemployment, inflation and a moribund Franco. The transition to democracy had begun.

Franco died in November 1975, closing a parenthesis of nearly 40 years in Spanish history. A new age, uncertain but exciting, dawned. In July 1976, King Juan Carlos, chosen by Franco to succeed him, named a former Falange bureaucrat, Adolfo Suárez, as prime minister. Nobody, however, knew quite what was going to happen. To widespread surprise, Suárez initiated a comprehensive programme of political reform. Clandestine opposition leaders surfaced, parties were legalised and famous exiles began coming home. The first democratic elections since 1936 were held in June 1977, and a constitution was approved in late 1978. Suárez's centrist UCD (Centre-Democratic Union) won the national elections, but local elections in Madrid in 1979 were won by the Socialists, led by Enrique Tierno Galván as Mayor.

The 'other' Spain, however, had not disappeared. In fact, it was starting to feel nervous. Hardcore Francoists were horrified at the thought of socialists and/or communists coming to power. Significantly, many of the 'old guard' still held influential positions in the armed forces, and were not inclined to give them up easily.

On 23 February 1981, democrats' worst nightmares appeared to come true when a Civil Guard colonel called Tejero burst into the Cortes with a squad of men, firing his pistol into the air. A little after midnight, King Juan Carlos appeared on TV and assured the country that the army had sworn him its allegiance and that the coup attempt would fail. The next day, people poured out on to the streets to demonstrate support for freedom and democracy.

The wolf had shown its teeth, but they were not as sharp as had been feared. Moreover, the coup attempt significantly helped to win Felipe González and the Spanish Socialist Workers' Party (PSOE) their landslide victory in the elections of November 1982.

## Social revolution, city renovations

The late 1970s and early '80s saw the arrival of democracy and free speech, the loosening of drug laws and the breakdown of sexual conventions. The compulsorily staid Madrid of earlier years gave way to an anything-goes, vivacious city: an explosion of art, counter-culture and nightlife, creativity and frivolity known as the Movida – very roughly translatable as 'Shift' or 'Movement'.

The Socialists used their control of Madrid's Ayuntamiento – led by the fondly remembered Tierno Galván – to renovate the city's weak infrastructure, with long-overdue facelifts in squares and parks. Mayor Tierno also provided unprecedented support for various progressive causes and for the arts, launching a whole string of new festivals.

# The staid Madrid of earlier years gave way to a vivacious city in the late '70s and early '80s

If Tierno Galván's local administration was happy to be regarded as godfather to the Movida, the national government of Felipe González was more eager still to be seen as leaders of a reborn country. Decades of isolation ended with Spain's entry into the EU in 1986. This had a near-immediate effect on the economy, and in the late '80s the country was the fastest-growing member of the EU. The González governments achieved major improvements in some areas – among them health and the transport system – but also frustrated the expectations of many of their supporters, often giving the impression they believed modernisation would solve all Spain's problems more or less by itself.

The apotheosis of the country's transition was the 'Year of Spain' in 1992, with the Barcelona Olympics, Expo '92 in Seville and, with a somewhat lower profile, Madrid's year as Cultural Capital of Europe. Afterwards, a different mood became apparent. Spain's pre-'92 boom had postponed the effects of the international downturn at the end of the '80s, but it hit Madrid with a vengeance in 1993. Breakneck growth had created its own problems, and land speculation sent property prices spiralling.

Disenchantment with the Socialists and a newly cautious mood that followed the brash overconfidence of the boom years were major factors behind the rise of the re-formed right of the Partido Popular or People's Party (PP). Even before Spain's great year, in 1991, the PSOE had lost control of the Madrid city administration to the PP.

## The popular vote

The 1990s in Spain were markedly different in feel and content from the preceding decade. Led by the deliberately bland José María Aznar, the PP ably connected with the groundswell of discontent provoked by the later years of Socialist administrations. In the 1993 election Felipe González, long the great survivor of Spanish politics, lost his overall majority, but staggered on for another three years by means of a pact with Catalan nationalists. The next time, however, in 1996, the winners were the PP, even though they too still had to rely on pacts with minority parties to be able to form a sustainable government. The PSOE was sent into opposition for the first time in 14 years.

In Madrid, the PP had already made its mark on local life. Having rallied voters by denouncing the sleaze and corruption that overwhelmed the PSOE, and the Socialists' irresponsible – as many saw it – spending of taxpayers' money, the PP felt it had a clear mandate to cut back and balance the books. In Madrid, this meant cuts in budgets for arts festivals, a tightening up on licences for new bars and clubs, and a general attack on the supposed excesses of the nightlife scene.

Despite harsh criticism for its perceived philistine approach to culture, un-liberal stance on issues such as immigration and gay rights, and Francoist origins, the PP won an absolute majority in the 2000 general elections, thanks mainly to its practical approach to the economy and the disarray of the opposition. Its second term in office was a different story, with the 2002 general strike, followed by the sinking of the *Prestige*, Spain's worst-ever ecological disaster. Aznar's flirtation with Bush and Blair led to Spain participating, albeit in a small way, in the Iraq war, against the wishes of 94 per cent of the Spanish people.

The bombings of 11 March 2004, and the subsequent media manipulation, were the last straw. The Socialists, under the mild-mannered José Luis Zapatero, had been carefully rebuilding and were now seen as an alternative. On taking power, Zapatero's government immediately brought the Spanish troops back from Iraq and embarked cautiously but firmly on a programme of modernisation of political structures and society. Steps were taken to redefine the nature of relationships between the autonomous regions and the Spanish state, gender issues were addressed with, among other things, a record number of women in the cabinet, and gay marriages were legalised. First steps were taken on the rocky road to peace in the Basque Country, and in March 2006, ETA declared a 'permanent ceasefire'.

Zapatero won a second term in the 2008 elections. However, with Spain's rate of unemployment rapidly increasing from eight per cent to 20 per cent, the rising cost of living, and the government's wildly unpopular labour and pensions reforms, introduced as part of its austerity drive, the Socialists were to fall from grace.

## A new political order

One of the main casualties of Spain's economic crisis was the old political order. The public discontent over job cuts, corrupt politicians and a dysfunctional democratic system exploded on 15 May 2011 with the occupation of Madrid's Puerta del Sol and the emergence of the 15M movement, aka the *indignados*. This would later coalesce into anti-austerity party Podemos, which – under the guidance of astute ponytailed leader Pablo Iglesias, a former Madrid university lecturer – has stuck an adrenalin shot into the heart of Spanish politics. Along with fellow newcomer Albert Rivera's

Mariano Rajoy

liberal Ciudadanos (Citizens) Party, the leftist group has shaken up the two-party dominance enjoyed by the PP and PSOE since Spain's transition to democracy in the 1970s.

In 2016, after two general elections failed to deliver an outright majority for any of the now four major parties, politicians unused to power sharing spent ten long months struggling to thrash together the deals required to form a government. In the end, an abstention by Socialist deputies allowed PP leader Mariano Rajoy to be elected for a second term as prime minister. But his minority administration faces a tough time taming an unruly house disgusted by his past austerity policies and the seemingly never-ending series of corruption scandals dogging his party. The difficulties of the PP were further compounded in 2017 with the dramatic rise of Catalan nationalism and Rajoy's clumsy handling of the illegal independence referendum. His refusal to enter into dialogue with Catalan premier Carles Puigdemont was widely seen as the reason for the sudden escalation that culminated in the unilateral declaration of Catalan independence in October 2017. Rajoy promptly invoked Article 155, which gave his government direct rule over the region, and called Catalan elections in December. The PP received a pitiful share of the votes, and secessionist parties once again gained a parliamentary (if not a popular) majority. At the time of writing it was unclear whether this would result in negotiation and a taming of nationalist ambitions, or in further elections.

Dodging corruption accusations has also proved something of a challenge for much of Spain's ruling elite. Not even the royal family has escaped unscathed. The trial of King Juan Carlos's youngest daughter, Infanta Cristina, over her husband Iñaki Urdangarin's business dealings (she was acquitted but he was handed a six-year jail sentence) was just one of the scandals that paved the way for the once highly respected monarch's abdication. His successor, his 46-year-old son Felipe, remained largely untainted by the negative press, and since becoming King Felipe VI in June 2014 has been working hard to bolster the monarchy's flagging popularity. Shadows of the past, however, returned to haunt the nation with the authoritarian tone of the televised speech he made two days after the Catalan referendum, in which he accused the Catalan authorities of 'disloyalty' and 'irresponsibility', and made no effort to reconcile his subjects. Republican sentiment swelled in what was already a febrile political atmosphere, and Spain looks to have some complicated times ahead.

# Key Events

*All the Madrid dates that matter*

**c860 AD** Madrid founded during the reign of Emir Mohammed I of Córdoba.

**1085-6** Alfonso VI of Castile conquers Toledo and Madrid.

**1109** Madrid besieged by Moorish army.

**1212** Battle of Navas de Tolosa: decisive defeat of Muslims in Spain.

**1309** First Cortes (parliament) held in Madrid.

**1476** Isabella becomes unchallenged Queen of Castile after battle of Toro.

**1492** Conquest of Granada; expulsion of Jews from Spain; discovery of America.

**1520-1** Madrid joins Comuneros Revolt.

**1547** Birth of Cervantes in Alcalá de Henares.

**1561** Philip II moves the Court to Madrid from Toledo.

**1563-84** Building of El Escorial.

**1566** Beginning of Dutch Revolt.

**1588** Defeat of the Armada against England.

**1599-1600** Plague and famine in Castile.

**1601-6** Court moved to Valldolid.

**1605, 1615** *Don Quixote* published.

**1609** Expulsion of former Muslims from Spain.

**1617-9** Completion of Plaza Mayor.

**1632-40** Buen Retiro Palace built.

**1640** Revolts in Portugal and Catalonia.

**1643** Battle of Rocroi: Spanish army in Flanders decisively defeated by the French.

**1665** Philip IV is succeeded by Charles II, aged four.

**1700** Charles II dies without an heir.

**1702-14** War of the Spanish Succession: Philip V, first Bourbon King of Spain.

**1715** Decree of Nova Planta; Spain created as one state.

**1734** Alcázar of Madrid destroyed by fire.

**1778** Goya moves to Madrid from Aragon.

**1808-12** Madrid under French occupation.

**1812** Cortes in Cádiz agrees first Spanish constitution; disastrous famine in Madrid.

**1810-24** The Latin American Wars of Independence.

**1814** Fernando VII abrogates constitution.

**1820** Military coup begins three years of liberal rule.

**1823** French army restores Fernando VII to full power.

**1833** Carlist Wars begin on death of Fernando VII; constitutional government established in Madrid, with limited powers.

**1836** Main decree on Disentailment of Monasteries.

**1851** The railway to Aranjuez is inaugurated.

**1858** The Canal de Isabel II water system is inaugurated.

**1868** Revolution overthrows Isabel II.

**1871** Amadeo of Savoy becomes king of Spain. First trams in Madrid, drawn by mules.

**1873** Amadeo abdicates; Republic declared.

**1874** January: The Republic becomes a military dictatorship after a coup. December: Alfonso XII is declared king.

**1879** Spanish Socialist Party (PSOE) founded.

**1898** Spanish-American War: a disaster for Spain. Madrid's tramlines electrified.

**1910** Building of Gran Vía initiated.

**1917** General strike in the whole of Spain.

**1919** First Madrid metro line opened.

**1923-1930** Primo de Rivera dictatorship

**1931** Proclamation of Second Republic.

**1934** General Strike is bloodily suppressed in Asturias by General Franco.

**1936** February: elections won by Popular Front. July: military uprising against left-wing government. November: Francoist forces launch assault on Madrid.

**1939** 1 April: Franco declares war over.

**1946-50** UN imposes sanctions on Spain.

**1953** Co-operation treaty with USA.

**1959** Stabilisation Plan opens up the Spanish economy.

**1961** First violent attack by Basque nationalists of ETA.

**1970** Juan Carlos declared as General Franco's successor.

**1975** 20 November: death of Franco.

**1977** 15 June: Spain's first democratic general election.

**1979** April: Enrique Tierno Galván elected Socialist mayor of Madrid.

**1986** 1 January: Spain joins the EEC.

**1991** Partido Popular (PP) takes over Madrid city council.

**2004** 11 March: terrorist attacks kill 192.

**2014** Juan Carlos abdicates; succeeded by his son King Felipe VI.

**2016** PP wins second term after general elections.

**2017** Illegal independence referendum in Catalunya results in Mariano Rajoy imposing direct rule.

# Movida Movies

*Join the counterculture club*

The seasonal skies of Madrid that enthralled Goya and Velázquez have been a similar gift to filmmakers. Many foreign epics of the 1960s were made in the studios on the city's outskirts, including Anthony Mann's *El Cid* (1961) and *The Fall of the Roman Empire* (1964), Nicholas Ray's *King of Kings* (1961) and *55 Days at Peking* (1963), and David Lean's *Dr Zhivago* (1965). Internationally made films to have employed the city and environs include Milos Forman's *Goya's Ghosts* (2006), Paul Greengrass's *The Bourne Ultimatum* (2007) and the Bond film *Quantum of Solace* (2008).

But although Madrid makes the top rank as a location alongside such cities as New York, Paris and Tokyo, it is best understood by Spanish filmmakers, who have captured the skies, architecture and contrasts in several classic and modern masterpieces. The creative force of Spanish cinema was especially intense during the Movida, the cultural, sexual and chemical free-for-all that followed Spain's transition to democracy in the 1970s and early '80s – immortalised in the earliest films of Pedro Almodóvar.

Pedro Almodóvar

## Reel rebellion

The Movida took its name from a Spanish phrase meaning 'to have a business thing happening', which also doubled as slang for 'a drug transaction'. It was partly an ad hoc translation of British punk. Unlike British punk, however, the Movida was not so much a working-class movement as a drug-fuelled middle-class pretence of bohemian rebellion against the society of the past.

Perhaps the most crucial venue for the Movida's cinematic manifestation was the Alphaville (C/Martín de los Heros 14), nowadays known as the **Golem**. This still-thriving cinema opened in 1977 (when Spain's transition to peaceful democracy and public liberty was assured), and immediately established its revolutionary credentials with a week-long festival of Cuban films. Since then, it has continued to feature politically charged cinema, especially of the contemporary German kind. Wim Wenders' *The American Friend* (1977) still holds the record for the longest continuous run, at an impressive 67 weeks. This pales into insignificance, however, alongside the ten years of late-night screenings enjoyed by Almodóvar's *Laberinto de pasiones (Labyrinth of Passion*, 1982).

## Almodóvar's early days

*Laberinto de pasiones* is a melodramatic, absurdist farce about a nymphomaniac called Sexilia (Cecilia Roth), a gay Islamic

A LOVE STORY....WITH STRINGS ATTACHED!

A FILM BY ALMODOVAR

MIRAMAX FILMS ...... EL DESEO S.A. ....... ALMODÓVAR
TIE ME UP! TIE ME DOWN!
VICTORIA ABRIL ANTONIO BANDERAS LOLES LEÓN ...... FRANCISCO RABAL

DUE TO THE EXPLICIT NATURE OF THIS FILM NO ONE UNDER 18 WILL BE ADMITTED       MIRAMAX

> **Unlike British punk, the Movida was not so much a working-class movement as a drug-fuelled middle-class pretence of bohemian rebellion**

terrorist named Sadec (Antonio Banderas) and the son of the exiled Shah of Iran (Imanol Arias). Gobsmacked by the film's outrageousness, most international critics failed to notice the romanticism and compassion that Almodóvar clearly felt for those who had so recently been marginalised from Spanish society.

The Movida was also documented in the magazine *La Luna*, in Francisco Umbral's long-running column in *El País* and in TV programmes. There were also alternative music and variety shows presented by Paloma Chamorro and Almodóvar's earliest muse, actress Carmen Maura.

Maura starred with the punk diva Alaska in *Pepi, Luci, Bom y otras chicas del montón (Pepi, Luci, Bom*, 1980), which was two years in the making on a £20,000 budget raised by Almodóvar from his friends. In this scatological melodrama of female solidarity, Pepi (Maura) and Bom (Alaska) seek to liberate the masochistic Luci (Eva Siva) from her marriage to a policeman who respects her too much to beat her. Luci becomes a groupie for a band of degenerates, which provokes her jealous husband into beating her senseless, thereby resulting in a happy ending. The perverse yet romantic logic of the film was a faithful reflection of its time and audience, many of whom featured in the scenes set in the legendary Rock-Ola nightclub and other venues of the Movida, such as the Alphaville.

## The fall-out

Almodóvar's humour became gradually darker and darker in his later films, when disillusionment with democracy and the repercussions from the drug-fuelled and sex-motivated excesses of the Movida soiled the carefree mood. By the time of *¡Átame! (Tie Me Up! Tie Me Down!*, 1989), the director was seeking to reconcile his wayward characters with the more conventional elements of Spain, such as the family unit and fidelity, because the human cost of the Movida in terms of drug abuse and AIDS was by then so apparent. Drugs had been the main spur to the fantasy nightlife, but by

¿Qué he hecho yo para merecer esto? (*What Have I Done to Deserve This?*, 1984) the drug-dealing son of glue-sniffing housewife Gloria (Carmen Maura) is warning her not to graduate to hard drugs; and in *¡Átame!*, although the psychopathic Ricky (Antonio Banderas) kidnaps ex-junkie porn star Marina (Victoria Abril), he shows great concern for her returning need. Indeed, a prime motor of the plot of *Todo sobre mi madre* (*All About My Mother*, 1999) is the effort of the female collective to rescue one of their ilk from her addiction, and there is clearly something desperately retrospective about the wish-fulfilment ending of this film, which culminates in the miraculous birth of a child whose immune system holds a cure for AIDS.

## Remains of the days

Sadly, the Rock-Ola nightclub (C/Padre Xifré 5, Avenida de América), which featured in *Laberinto de pasiones*, is now a supermarket. Several of the most iconic venues of the Movida have also gone, such as the Carolina discotheque (C/Bravo Murillo 202), which became a clothes shop. Nevertheless, the erstwhile Alphaville, now known as **Golem** (*see p264*) and the clubs **El Penta** (C/Palma 4), **La Vía Láctea** (C/Velarde 18), both in Malasaña, and **El Sol** (C/Jardines 3 , just off Gran Vía) remain.

**La Bobia** bar on the edge of the Rastro (C/San Millán 3), where the opening sequence of *Laberinto* was filmed, is still standing, but now houses a rather dull Asturian cider house. A leisurely walking tour could start from here, after which you could move on up to the **Plaza Mayor**, where Otto and Ana so narrowly miss each other in Julio Medem's *Los amantes del Círculo Polar* (*Lovers of the Arctic Circle*, 1998), and on to the **Plaza de España**, where Sofía and Jota collide in Medem's

La ardilla roja (*Red Squirrel*, 1993). From here, you can either head up the raucous **Gran Vía**, so miraculously deserted in Alejandro Amenábar's *Abre los ojos* (*Open Your Eyes*, 1997), or head into the side streets surrounding the Ópera district, where Matías meets his cousin Violeta in Fernando Trueba's *Ópera prima* (*First Effort*, 1980). Either route should get you to Callao in time for an aperitivo beneath the hoarding of the **FNAC** superstore (C/Preciados 28), which hosted the advertising for Leo's novel in Almodóvar's *La flor de mi secreto* (*The Flower of My Secret*, 1995), before a stroll to the Sevilla metro station where Antonio, the rogue ETA terrorist, shoots a cop in Imanol Uribe's *Días contados* (*Running Out of Time*, 1994). Enjoy lunch in one of the bars on the Plaza de Colón, close to the **Teatro María Guerrero** (*see p239*) where Becky (Marisa Paredes) performed 'Piensa en mí' in Almodóvar's *Tacones lejanos* (*High Heels*, 1991). Then consider an afternoon shopping in chic Chueca, where Almodóvar filmed *La ley del deseo* (*Law of Desire*, 1987).

Whatever others might have you believe, the Movida is now long gone, being uniquely of its time and therefore rightly defunct. You can still go from bar to bar in Madrid, check out a gig at El Sol, catch something avant-garde at the former Alphaville, and pretend along with many avid tourists that the Movida is still happening. But don't be fooled – Almodóvar turns 70 in 2019 and, like the director himself, this extraordinary period in Madrid's cultural history is best revisited through his early films.

# Almodóvar's humour became gradually darker and darker in his later films

Law of Desire (Pedro Almodóvar, 1987)

# Architecture

*The making of Madrid*

Madrid's past, turbulent and grand in equal measure, is barely apparent from the capital's architecture. The city walls stayed up until the 1860s – longer than in most European cities – meaning that Madrid was forced to build on top of itself, replacing existing constructions at such a rate that by the late 19th century it was a surprisingly modern city.

Its history is, however, reflected in a highly individual, eccentric mixture of architectural styles. To a greater or lesser degree, traces of most of Madrid's past epochs and their influences – Moorish, Flemish, Italian, French and American – are to be found. A truly *madrileño* architectural identity is elusive, but the city can claim one, typically unusual, style as its own – neo-Mudéjar. Madrid also has many unique monuments.

The urban planning boom of the past decade, which saw building works blocking up squares and closing off streets for years, slowed with the recession, delaying projects such as the high-profile Campus of Justice. But its legacy is some hugely impressive new architecture (CaixaForum, Matadero Madrid) and a host of revitalised, more pedestrian-friendly public spaces.

Cineteca, Matadero Madrid *p178*

## In the beginning

The first town wall was built by the Moors, and a segment of it (the **Muralla Árabe**) can be found on Cuesta de la Vega, near the Almudena cathedral. For centuries after their 're-conquest', Madrid and most of Castile continued to have large populations of Muslims living under Christian rule, the Mudéjares. The Castilian monarchs were greatly in thrall to their superior building skills, especially in bricklaying and tiling, and throughout the Middle Ages many of the country's important buildings incorporated techniques and styles that had originated in Muslim Andalucia. Hallmarks of the Mudéjar style are Moorish arches and intricate geometric patterns in brickwork, as seen on the 12th-century tower of Madrid's oldest surviving church, **San Nicolás de los Servitas** (*see p67*), built by Arab craftsmen (the body was later rebuilt). Madrid's other Mudéjar tower, on **San Pedro el Viejo** (*see p76*), was built 200 years later. Other medieval buildings in Madrid, such as the 15th-century **Torre de los Lujanes** (*see p64*) in Plaza de la Villa, were much plainer in style, reflecting the town's humble status before 1561.

## Capital gains

Capital status, gained briefly in 1561 and definitively from 1606, transformed Madrid and its architecture. As royal seat, 'the Court', the tastes of successive rulers were especially important. Philip II's favourite architect, Juan de Herrera, was the first to leave a stamp on the city. He and his royal master had little idea of urban planning, but their major constructions – the **Puente de Segovia** (1584), the first stages of the Plaza Mayor, and the widening of calles Atocha and Segovia – gave Madrid a shape that lasts to this day.

**El Escorial** (*see p184*), designed by Herrera and Juan Bautista de Toledo, firmly established the 'Herreran' or 'Court' style – austere, rigid and typically employing grey slate for rooftops and the ubiquitous pointed turrets – that became near-obligatory for major buildings in Madrid until the end of the Habsburg era in 1700, despite changes in fashion elsewhere in Europe. Now a symbol of the 'Madrid of the Austrias', it is also known as Castilian Baroque, but few of its features are especially 'Castilian': the slate pinnacles came from Flanders, which appealed to the Flemish-born Charles V.

Herrera's chief disciple, Juan Gómez de Mora, modified his master's legacy with a lighter and less monolithic style. He oversaw the completion of the **Plaza Mayor** (*see p68*) in 1619 – his original plan is still recognisable in the slate spires, high-pitched roofs and dormer windows – and the 1630 **Casa de la Villa**, the City Hall. Gómez was also structurally innovative, as seen in the massive cellars and housing blocks along Cava San Miguel, which back on to and complete the Plaza Mayor. Because of the abrupt drop in the level of the land, he had to build up to eight storeys high for these blocks to meet the rest of the square, making

Casa de la Villa

# Underneath the Arches

*The Moorish origins of Madrid's very own architectural style*

Around 1870, an architectural style emerged in Madrid that the city can claim as its own: neo-Mudéjar. The first example was the new bullring to replace the plain 18th-century one that stood near Puerta de Alcalá. In the revivalist atmosphere of the 19th century, architects Ricardo Rodríguez Ayuso and Lorenzo Alvarez Capra decided not to look to Gothic or Egyptian traditions for inspiration, but searched instead for something to revive that was closer to home. They opted for the styles and superb bricklaying techniques that had been employed by the Muslim Mudéjar master builders of medieval Castile.

Neo-Mudéjar uniquely incorporated Moorish horseshoe arches, interlaced brickwork and arabesque tiling, together with a modern use of glass and cast iron. The 1870s bullring no longer stands, but the style became near-obligatory for *plazas de toros* throughout Spain, and Madrid's next ring at **Las Ventas**

(*see p159*), completed in 1934, sports many neo-Mudéjar features. The style was extended to other buildings too. Perhaps the best example in Madrid is the **Escuelas Aguirre**, also by Ayuso and Alvarez Capra, at the intersection of Calles Alcalá and O'Donnell on the north side of the Retiro. Its outstanding feature is a slim minaret-style tower, with a glass and iron lookout-gallery.

Another splendid Arab-inspired tower is the giant spire of the **Santa Cruz** church at the top of C/Atocha (no.6), built in 1899-1902. And the city's **Matadero Madrid** cultural centre (*see p178*) is a revamped neo-Mudéjar series of buildings that once housed the city abattoir. But the style was also used for more everyday buildings, as in the block of flats at C/Barquillo 21 in Chueca, which displays a façade combining diamond-pattern brickwork, neo-Moorish plaster details and ironwork balconies.

Las Ventas bullring

them Madrid's tallest buildings until the 20th century.

His great rival in Madrid was Gian Battista Crescenzi, an Italian who adopted the 'Court style' – with some Italian flourishes – to please his Spanish masters. Both architects probably worked, at different times, on the **Palacio de Santa Cruz** (*see p62*) near the Plaza Mayor, which was built in 1629-43 and is nowadays home to the Foreign Ministry. It shows clear Italian Baroque influences, with a façade much more richly shaped than anything Herrera would have tried. Crescenzi also undertook the largest single building scheme of Habsburg Madrid, the **Palacio del Buen Retiro**, parts of which have survived.

Though the Habsburgs commissioned much that was noble and even palatial, 17th-century visitors to Madrid still saw haphazard growth, chaos and dirt rather than a city fit to be capital of the first worldwide empire. Much building was unimpressive owing to the rickety economy, which meant bricks and mortar were favoured over expensive stone.

## Bourbon renewal

The expiry of the Spanish Habsburgs with King Charles II in 1700 was followed by war and the arrival of the Bourbons, under Philip V. The new dynasty endeavoured to embellish and dignify Madrid. The Bourbons were French, and Philip V's second wife, Isabella Farnese,

Conde Duque *p130*

was Italian, and these two influences would long predominate in the dynasty's architectural tastes. Nevertheless, Philip V's administrator in Madrid, the Marqués de Vadillo, commissioned a local architect, Pedro de Ribera, for many projects, among them the 1722 **Hospice** (now the Museo de Historia, *see p123*), the **Cuartel Conde Duque** barracks (now the Centro Cultural Conde Duque), the **Puente de Toledo** and many churches. Ribera's buildings, while following the Herreran tradition, feature exuberant Baroque façades centred on elaborately carved entrance porticoes. Many Ribera entrances still survive on buildings that have since been rebuilt, as in the 1734 **Palace of the Dukes of Santoña** at C/ Huertas 3, now occupied by the Cámara de Comercio.

The influence of French and Italian architects was more apparent elsewhere in 18th-century Madrid. After the old grey-spired **Alcázar** burnt down in 1734, Philip V commissioned a new **Palacio Real** (*see p66*) from a group of mainly Italian architects led by Filippo Juvarra and Giambattista Sacchetti. Responsible for many projects was Charles III's 'chief engineer', Francesco Sabatini. The great exponents of the sober, 'pure' neoclassicism of the later years of Charles III's reign, though, were Spaniards: Ventura Rodríguez, who had also worked on the Palacio Real, and Juan de Villanueva, architect of the **Museo del Prado** (*see p144*) and the **Real Observatorio Nacional** (*see p152*). Like the greatest project of the king's reign, the Paseo del Prado – of which these buildings were part – they clearly reflect Enlightenment ideals of architecture and urban planning.

## Rise and sprawl

Joseph Bonaparte's brief reign (1808-13) saw the first demolition of monasteries and convents, to be replaced by squares such as Plaza Santa Ana. Generally, though, the first half of the 19th century brought architectural stagnation to Madrid. After the great clearance of monasteries began in the 1830s, many of the buildings that replaced them were simple apartment and tenement blocks, such as the *corralas* (*see p108*). Public buildings of this time, such as the 1840s **Cortes** or the **Teatro Real** (*see p235*), were often conservative and neoclassical in style.

Greater changes came to Madrid after 1860, with the demolition of the walls and Carlos María de Castro's plan for the city's extension or *ensanche*. Areas covered by the plan are easy to spot on a map by their grid street pattern. Chief among them is **Salamanca**, still the most self-consciously grand *barrio* of the *ensanche*. Its wealthiest residents built in an eclectic mix of styles; some of their opulent mansions still stand on calles Velázquez and Serrano. Other *ensanche* districts – like Chamberí and Argüelles – show rational urban layout, wide thoroughfares and regular-sized blocks.

Public buildings of the first years of the Bourbon Restoration were as eclectic as Salamanca mansions. Madrid's own revivalist style, neo-Mudéjar (*see p269* Underneath the Arches), was used for official buildings, bullrings, churches, homes and factories. In contrast, one of the most extraordinary constructions of the time, Ricardo Velázquez's **Ministerio de Agricultura** in Atocha, is a remarkable combination of Castilian brickwork and extravagant, French Beaux Arts-style sculpted decoration. This was also the great period of cast-iron architecture in Madrid, with fine structures such as the city markets and the **Estación de Atocha** (*see p149*).

Art nouveau (called *modernismo* in Spain), so characteristic of early 20th-century Barcelona, aroused little interest in Madrid, but there are some examples. The **Sociedad General de Autores** (1902), by Jose Grasés Riera, is the best known, but the **Casa Pérez Villamil** at Plaza Matute 6, off C/Huertas, is also impressive.

## Cutting a swathe

As the *ensanche* progressed and Madrid's economy boomed from the 1900s to the 1920s, the city's architects looked for inspiration forwards and backwards in time, and both inside and outside Spain. The **Gran Vía** (*see p84*), which celebrated its centenary in 2010, was born of this thinking. An all-modern thoroughfare through Madrid's old centre, the Gran Vía destroyed 14 old streets, becoming grander and more eccentric as it progressed. Writer Francisco Umbral claims it recalls New York or Chicago, but its first building of any standing, the stunning, ornately domed 1905 **Edificio Metrópolis**, shows French inspiration. No.24 is neo-Renaissance, the 1930s **Palacio de la Música** cinema (no.35) has distinctly Baroque touches, and the 1929 **Telefónica** building (on the corner of C/Fuencarral) is a New York skyscraper in miniature. The 1930 apartment block at Gran Vía 60 is a classic of *madrileño* cosmopolitanism by Carlos Fernández Shaw, who in 1927 also built a futuristic petrol station where C/Alberto Aguilera meets Vallehermoso. Also working at this time was the very original Antonio Palacios, main architect of the **Palacio de Cibeles** (1904-

18) and the more subtle **Círculo de Bellas Artes** (*see p87*).

During its brief existence, the Spanish Republic further encouraged rationalist, rather self-consciously modern architecture, as in the earliest parts of the **Nuevos Ministerios** (*see p154*). Art deco was in vogue, as in office blocks such as the **Capitol** building on Gran Vía (corner of C/ Jacometrezo) or the curious model housing district of **El Viso**.

Civil war and the arrival of the Franco regime brought much destruction, and had an immediate impact on architecture. Falangist architectural thinking was dominated by nostalgia for a glorious past, and so Madrid acquired monster constructions that looked straight back to imperial Spain's Golden Age, combined with ideas from German and Italian Fascist architecture. The results were often grandiose, bombastic and, probably unwittingly, kitsch. The foremost example is the **Ministerio del Aire** (*see p166*), at the top of C/Princesa. In Plaza de España is the manically colossal **Edificio España** (*see p32*), the work of brothers Joaquín and José María Otamendi, completed in 1953. Conceived along American lines to be a 'small city' in one huge block, with shops, offices, a hotel and apartments, the building acquired all sorts of neo-Herreran decorative touches outside. It has lain derelict for many years, but is to be turned into an upmarket hotel as part of a plan to revamp the square (*see p32* Squaring Up).

Edificio España

By the 1950s, the regime's ideological enthusiasms were fading, although it still sought to impress. Built with no pretence at neo-Baroque or anything similar is the tacky 32-floor 1957 **Torre de Madrid** on Plaza de España. These years, though, also saw the beginnings of real modernity in Madrid, most notably with Francisco Cabrero and Rafael Aburto's **Casa Sindical** at Paseo del Prado 18-20, built in 1948-49 for the Francoist labour unions and now the Health Ministry. Until the 1960s, the floundering Spanish economy still limited the scope for building. When it did improve, Madrid opened up to international influences, but many of its newest buildings were dreary apartment blocks, built for a rapidly growing population.

## Back to the future

As Spanish society and the economy opened up with the rebirth of democracy in the late 1970s, one effect of Francoist retro-obsessions was that Spanish architects – and the public – felt little inclination to look back with nostalgia or add neoclassical fronts to new buildings, and welcomed modernity with gusto. The most influential contemporary architects in Madrid have been Alejandro de la Sota and Francisco Sáenz de Oíza, both active since the 1950s, and Sáenz's gifted and original protégé Rafael Moneo.

An important factor in construction during the 1980s was the Socialist takeover of the city council in 1979, and the government in 1982. Mayor Tierno Galván's Ayuntamiento was committed to the regeneration of public spaces, and so facilitated the emergence of one of the characteristic features of modern Madrid – daringly imaginative 'grand revamps'

of long-decrepit historic buildings. An outstanding example is the **Estación de Atocha** (*see p149*), a run-down, filthy 1880s cast-iron railway terminal that Moneo transformed into a multi-purpose space. The **Reina Sofía** and **Thyssen** museums (*see p112 and p96*) were also rebuilt, and the Centro Cultural Conde Duque was created out of Ribera's 1720s barracks.

Outside the public domain, the most vigorous contributions to Madrid since the mid 1980s have been the skyscrapers that line the upper Paseo de la Castellana: the superb white 1988 **Torre Picasso** (*see p154*) by Minoru Yamasaki and the spectacular leaning towers of the **Puerta de Europa** (*see p154*) at Plaza Castilla. With Madrid's expansion, building has taken place on the city's edge, such as the **Feria de Madrid** complex, Manuel Delgado and Fernando Vasco's **Estadio Wanda Metropolitano** (a dramatic structure in the form of a tilted oval plate; *see p169*), and Richard Rogers' huge **Barajas airport** terminal with its undulating Chinese bamboo-insulated roofs, which opened in 2006.

The past decade has also seen some exciting new projects, including Moneo's Prado extension (2007), Herzog & de Meuron's **CaixaForum** (*see p273* Power to the People), the remodelling of the old city abattoir for **Matadero Madrid** (*see p178*) and Lord Foster's **Torre Caja Madrid** skyscraper (2009). Projects currently in the pipeline include a grand, green overhaul of **Plaza de España** (*see p84*), which will include a new esplanade to link it with Gran Vía (see p32, Squaring Up), and a Norman Foster-led refurbishment of the Salón de Reinos (Hall of Realms) extension to the **Prado Museum** (*see p144*). This will see the creation of a huge atrium, and add 2,500 square metres (26,900 square feet) of exhibition space.

Estación de Atocha

# 💜 CaixaForum Madrid

*Paseo del Prado 36 (91 330 73 00, obrasocial. lacaixa.es). Metro Atocha. **Open** 10am-8pm daily. **Admission** €4. **Map** p95 M17.*

Already one of the city's landmarks, the CaixaForum is Madrid's stunning avant-garde cultural centre on the Paseo del Prado, designed by Herzog & de Meuron and completed in 2008. The building was the result of a six-year conversion of the 1899 Mediodía Electrical Power Station, one of the few examples of industrial architecture in central Madrid. By virtue of its location, CaixaForum can be considered a new addition to the 'Paseo del Arte', sitting as it does between the Prado, Reina Sofía and Thyssen, the museums on the Paseo del Prado.

The centre holds a wide range of art exhibitions, film screenings, concerts and educational programmes, and has become one of Madrid's most-visited attractions – as much for its awe-inspiring appearance as for the cultural attractions within. The arts centre's name comes from sponsorship by Catalan savings bank 'La Caixa', whose Obra Social Fundacíon 'La Caixa' operates community and welfare projects in Spain and abroad.

The building is striking for its rusted metal appearance and its apparent defiance of the laws of gravity, with the front part of the structure appearing to float off the ground. Its adjacent 24m (79ft) 'vertical garden', designed in conjunction with French botanist Patrick Blanc, complements the building's intense red and is now one of Madrid's most photographed spots. Herzog has stated that the aim of the garden is to provide a connection with the botanical gardens opposite, and the leafy landscape of the Paseo del Prado.

The only material from the original Mediodía power station that the architects were able to use was the building's brick shell, which needed to be fully restored and secured with cast iron. The extraneous parts of the building were removed with surgical precision – including the stone base, the removal of which opened up the new public square in front of the building, while simultaneously providing a sheltered space where summertime visitors can cool off.

ARCHITECTURE

Plan

Plaza de Matute, Huertas

# Accommodation

For a compact city, Madrid has an unusually large number of hotels. In fact, so many new properties have opened in the past few years that some locals believe there are too many, in the centre at least. For visitors, of course, this can only be a good thing. Intense competition means higher standards of accommodation and service, even in lower-priced places. In particular, the difference between budget and mid-range hotels is becoming increasingly marginal, with the newer *pensiones* now offering en suite bathrooms in most rooms. And, across all price brackets, staff are friendlier and keener to help than ever before.

### Stars, prices and discounts

Star ratings are somewhat arbitrary in Spain, and the difference between four- and five-star hotels can be hard to spot. Moderate hotels have not been the city's strong point, but this is beginning to change thanks to chains such as **Room Mate** and **Petit Palace**.

Due to trade fairs and conferences, prices tend to be highest in January, when some hotels require minimum stays of two to three nights. Conversely, there are great deals to be had in the summer months. Note that the cheapest online rate is often non-refundable.

### Where to stay

Although Madrid is pretty small for a capital city, its accommodation is spread over a wide area, so it's good to have an idea of what you want before you book.

**Sol** and **Gran Vía** are the best areas for mid-range accommodation right in the thick of things, and, though undoubtedly touristy, are home to a clutch of decent bars and restaurants, and are

**There are great deals to be had in Madrid in the summer months**

**In the know**
**Price categories**

We have included a selection of the best hotels in the city in each pricing category. Categories are based on the cost of a double room in spring.

| | |
|---|---|
| **Luxury** | over €200 |
| **Expensive** | €150-€200 |
| **Moderate** | €100-€150 |
| **Budget** | up to €100 |

great for shopping. Heading north from here, **Malasaña** has a choice of good budget *pensiones*, particularly along C/Palma, and an increasing number of boutique hotels. Bordering Malasaña to the east, gay-friendly **Chueca** is home to some fine one-off properties. Both areas, especially Malasaña, offer a real neighbourhood vibe.

South of Chueca, lively **Huertas** and **Santa Ana** are great districts for cheap *pensiones* and boutique hotels. On the edge of here, the Paseo del Prado has a variety of budget accommodation right on the doorstep of the big three art museums. Upmarket areas include **Retiro** and **Los Austrias**. Although on opposite sides of town (Retiro, with its famous park, is in the east, while history-imbued Los Austrias is in the west), both are home to Madrid's old money, and are peaceful – though bars and restaurants can be expensive.

Just north of the Parque del Retiro, around the chic shopping street C/Serrano, is **Salamanca**. If you feel at home among the smart, wealthy set, you'll blend in well here. Business travellers should head for **Chamberí**, north of the centre, and, further north still, to **Chamartín**, both of which are convenient for the airport.

**The Paseo del Prado has a variety of budget accommodation right on the doorstep of the big three art museums**

**Iberostar Las Letras Gran Vía** *p280*

## Luxury

### Gran Meliá Palacio de los Duques

*Cuesta de Santo Domingo 5-7, Sol & Gran Vía (91 541 67 00, www. melia.com). Metro Ópera or Santo Domingo.* **Map** *p83 G13.*
One of Madrid's most glamorous hotels was built on the site of a convent and 19th-century palace and designed in homage to Velázquez. There are two excellent restaurants – the Montmartre bistro and the upmarket Dos Cielos, which overlooks a pretty garden – and a spa with sauna, but the hotel's crowning glory is the rooftop sundeck, with small pool, jacuzzi and panoramic views.

### Hotel Orfila

*C/Orfila 6, Chamberí (91 702 77 70, www.hotelorfila.com). Metro Alonso Martínez or Colón.* **Map** *pull-out M10.*
This small mansion in a tranquil residential area has been transformed into an elegant five-star hotel. Built in the 1880s as a private home for an artistic family, the Orfila also contained a theatre and a literary salon during the 1920s. Thankfully, the hotel has held on to its 19th-century decor, not to mention its façade, carriage entrance and dramatic main stairway. Bedrooms are wonderfully quiet. The elegant restaurant looks on to the lovely garden patio.

### Hotel Único

*C/Claudio Coello 67, Salamanca (91 781 01 73, www.unico hotelmadrid.com). Metro Serrano.* **Map** *p155 P10.*
The Hotel Único achieves the perfect blend of modern and classic. It's housed in a graceful 19th-century Salamanca building with slick black-and-white chequered tiles and upholstered chairs in the public areas, impressive staircases that are perfect for making a grand entrance, and mod cons throughout. The 44 spacious rooms and suites are comfortable and well designed, with huge comfy beds, wooden floors, muted tones and patterns and slick bathrooms. The Michelin-starred restaurant is another plus.

### ME Madrid Reina Victoria

*Plaza Santa Ana 14, Santa Ana (91 701 60 00, www.melia.com). Metro Antón Martin.* **Map** *p95 K15.*
This grand old hotel has had a spectacular revamp and caters to a glamorous set. Rooms are smallish, with unimaginably comfortable beds, lighting systems that require a manual but are great once you figure them out, good-quality Apivita toiletries and complimentary tea and coffee. Get a room overlooking the lovely Plaza Santa Ana if you can. The rooftop restaurant has amazing views of the city, but has recently been enclosed by glass panels thanks to the volume favoured by the DJs who play here nightly.

### Only You Boutique Madrid

*C/Barquillo 21, Chueca (91 005 22 22, www.onlyyouhotels.com). Metro Chueca.* **Map** *p120 M12.*
Spain's best-loved designer, Lázaro Rosa-Violán, was behind the maximalist interiors at Only You, where you'll find a riot of styles in the eclectic decor. The lifts alone have launched a thousand Instagram shots with their Chinese-tiled façade and faux bookshelves inside. Rooms, too, are luxuriously kitted out with studded navy blue leather headboards, plush carpets and animal-print bathrobes.

### The Principal Madrid Hotel

*C/Marqués de Valdeiglesias 1, Chueca (91 521 87 43, www. theprincipalmadridhotel.com). Metro Banco de España or Sevilla.* **Map** *p120 L13.*
The cognoscenti love The Principal for its speakeasy feel (from an almost anonymous street entrance, a lift whisks you up to the top-floor reception), buzzy rooftop cocktail bar and sundeck, and luxurious touches from Gilbert & Soames toiletries to the complimentary pastries available all day in the bar. Ask for a room overlooking the stunning Metropolis building.

Other upmarket places include **Hotel Urban** (www.hotelurban. com), with ancient figurines and artworks in the rooms and in the painfully hip public spaces, and **Hotel Wellington** (www.hotel-wellington.com), a graceful place with chandeliers and marble just a stone's throw from Salamanca, the city's most expensive shopping area.

## Expensive

### Círculo Gran Vía Hotel

*Gran Vía 24 (91 521 03 00, www. marriott.com). Metro Gran Vía.* **Map** *p83 K13.*
From the hotel's common areas, it's easy to stray into the frenetic and glitzy world of Madrid's casino, with which the Círculo shares a building, but the calm zen room interiors are a world apart. The feel is Scandinavian, with modern beechwood furniture and sinuously curved wing chairs and headboards. On the corner of Gran Vía and C/ Hortaleza, the hotel is right in the heart of things, but the soundproofing is such that a good night's sleep is guaranteed.

### Dear Hotel

*Gran Vía 80 (91 412 32 00, www. dearhotelmadrid.com). Metro Plaza de España.* **Map** *p83 G12.*
The Dear was ahead of the curve when it opened in what was then the unloved area at the end of Gran Vía, which is now undergoing an ambitious facelift, with a raft of new openings. The hotel is chic, minimalist and excellent value, not least for the view from its small rooftop pool and restaurant/breakfast room. This takes in the whole of the city, but most spectacularly the vast Casa de Campo park, which stretches out to the west.

### Hotel Casual Madrid del Teatro

*C/Echegaray 1, Santa Ana (91 429 95 51, casualhoteles.com). Metro Sevilla.* **Map** *p95 K15.*
It's rare to find somewhere this much fun at this price level. Rooms carry a theatrical theme, along with complimentary fittings (ruched satin curtains, fringed lampshades) that predate this incarnation of the hotel but fit right in. If you can, get the corner room with terrace and a bathtub. Breakfast and other

facilities are sparse, but the Mi-Fi gadget (free to use for guests) is useful for getting online around town.

## Hotel Emperador

*Gran Vía 53 (91 547 28 00, www. emperadorhotel.com). Metro Santo Domingo.* **Map** *p83 G12.*
While the traffic speeds by on the Gran Vía outside, the Emperador has to deal with a flow of groups and tourists that is almost as unrelenting. Decor is rather dreary, and it's not the most exciting hotel, but it does have as its USP a wonderful rooftop swimming pool (which is also open to non-residents for a hefty €45), four times the size of most hotel pools.

## NH Collection Madrid Suecia

*C/Marqués de Casa Riera 4, Gran Vía (91 200 05 70, www.nh-hotels. com). Metro Banco de España.* **Map** *p83 L14.*
In common with most NH hotels, the Suecia is done up in simple pastel tones, without too many frills, but is smart, comfortable and well thought out. Tea- and coffee-making facilities in the rooms come as standard, and staff are particularly attentive to any requests you might have. The rooftop bar is one of Madrid's loveliest, and in the basement is the seductive speakeasy-style cocktail bar, aptly named Hemingway.

## Urso Hotel

*C/Mejía Lequerica 8, Malasaña (91 444 44 58, www.hotelurso. com). Metro Alonso Martínez or Tribunal.* **Map** *p120 L10.*
A luxury boutique with smart but understated rooms, the better to showcase the glorious lobby – a cleverly designed space of mirrors and Chinois wallpaper. There is a spa and indoor pool, and downstairs, behind another wall of mirrors, is the wonderful Media Ración restaurant. Breakfast is a sumptuous affair served in a beautifully wallpaper space on the first floor, and the price of a room includes two tickets to the Prado museum.

Other options include the **Hotel Villa Real** (www.hotelvillareal.

com), offering elegant rooms, marble bathrooms and Roman mosaics, and **Iberostar Las Letras Gran Vía** (www. hoteldelasletras.com), with literary quotations strewn across its colourful walls.

---

Moderate

## Hotel Abalu

*C/Pez 19, Malasaña (91 521 44 92, www.hotelabalu.com). Metro Noviciado.* **Map** *p120 H12.*
The Abalu is near the Gran Vía and metro, but its extravagant interior design pulls in as many visitors as its location does. Rooms range from restrained to gloriously over the top; the staff are generally friendly although sometimes hard to pin down.

## Hotel Sercotel Gran Conde Duque

*Plaza Conde del Valle Suchil 5, Chamberí (91 447 70 00, www. sercotelhoteles.com). Metro San Bernardo.* **Map** *pull-out G9.*
A quiet, out-of-the-way hotel with front rooms facing a pretty, leafy *plaza*. Rooms are tastefully kitted out with yellow and green upholstery, while the belle époque salon downstairs serves afternoon tea. Beds are king-size and one room, 315, has a waterbed. Previous guests have included Celia Cruz and Marcel Marceau, and Pedro Almodóvar has been spotted in the bar. Guests can use the gym on the other side of the square.

## Palacio de Tepa

*C/San Sebastian 2, Santa Ana (91 389 64 90, www.nh-collection. com). Metro Sol.* **Map** *p95 K15.*
The NH group prides itself on comfort and customer service, and the five-star Palacio de Tepa is no exception. A sombre palette of creams and browns guides the modern decor, and won't frighten the horses, but it's the little touches that make the place, such as the ground-floor sitting room with complimentary tea, coffee, mineral water and newspapers. Original features of the 1808 building, with a façade by Juan de Villanueva, have been respected, and superior rooms are under the eaves, with wooden ceilings. Like

the suites, these have Nespresso machines.

## Petit Palace Ópera

*C/Arenal 16, Los Austrias (91 564 43 55, www.petitpalaceopera. com). Metro Sol.* **Map** *p83 H14.*
Fans of chintz should steer well clear, but the good-value Petit Palace chain of hotels is perfect for techno fiends on a budget. The Ópera's compact but sleekly designed rooms come with iPads and Mi-Fi devices free for guests to borrow, with Mi-Fi giving you online access around town. Bikes are also offered and the hotel is particularly family-friendly, with gifts for the little ones.

## Posada del León de Oro

*C/Cava Baja 12, La Latina (91 119 14 94, www.posadadelleondeoro. com). Metro La Latina or Tirso de Molino.* **Map** *p62 G16.*
A converted 19th-century coaching inn, the León de Oro has a somewhat stark approach to modern design, but is comfortable and friendly, with decent-sized beds and underfloor heating. Its 17 rooms sit around a central atrium, their minimal lines softened by wooden beams and bold splashes of colour.

---

**In the know**
## Hostales

Note that a *hostal*, which is also known as a *pensión*, is closer in meaning to 'guesthouse' than 'hostel'. Not all *hostales* have someone on the door 24 hours a day, so check how to get back in at night. These places tend to be family-run affairs, and while some owners speak English, any effort on your part to attempt a few words of Spanish will be well received. It's also worth noting that many *hostales* and *pensiones* are located up several flights of stairs in old buildings without a lift. If this is likely to be a problem, check before you book.

### Room Mate Oscar

*Plaza Pedro Zerolo 12, Chueca (91 701 11 73, room-matehotels.com). Metro Chueca or Gran Vía.* **Map** *p120 K13.*

Room Mate Oscar oozes affordable chic, from the ergonomic white plastic chairs to the smart bathrooms. The staff are as welcoming and easy on the eye as the spacious rooms, and the location in one of Chueca's main squares is unbeatable. The huge roof terrace – which comes complete with a bar and swimming pool – is a big plus, and a prime hangout on the city's gay scene.

Other mid-range hotels include **Room Mate Alicia** (room-matehotels.com), another hit from this classy but reasonably priced chain (*see above*) and **The Hat** (thehatmadrid.com), which is right in the heart of things in Los Austrias and has a rooftop bar.

---

### Budget
### Hostal Benamar

*C/San Mateo 20, 2ª, Chueca (91 308 00 92, www.hostalbenamar. es). Metro Alonso Martínez or Tribunal.* **Map** *p120 K11.*

Well situated between Chueca and Alonso Martínez, this *hostal* can be divided into two different parts. The friendly owners promote the renovated section, which has marble floors, modern en suite bathrooms and computers in every room. The other section is older but clean, with shared bathrooms.

### Hostal Gala

*C/Costanilla de los Ángeles 15, Sol (91 541 96 92, www.hostalgala. com). Metro Santo Domingo.* **Map** *p83 G13.*

This well-located boutique *hostal* on a quiet but central street is run by a very friendly couple. Rooms are comfortable and tasteful, with wooden floors, air-conditioning, retro-modern wallpaper and spacious bathrooms with power showers. Some rooms have balconies, while the superior double has a lounge area.

### Hostal Oriente

*C/Arenal 23, Sol (91 548 03 14, www.hostaloriente.es). Metro Ópera.* **Map** *p83 G14.*

Right on the doorstep of the opera house, and just a short walk from Sol, the comfortable Oriente is in an excellent location. The rooms are stylish – particularly for this price range – and pristine, and have compact bathrooms and TVs. The friendly staff are a further draw.

### Hostal Riesco

*C/Correo 2, 3ª, Sol (91 522 26 92, www.hostal-riesco.com). Metro Sol.* **No cards.** **Map** *p83 J15.*

The Riesco is a *hostal* that feels more like a hotel, with its balconied façade, stucco ceilings and chintzy curtains. All rooms come with en suite bathrooms, and the location is hard to beat – it's rare to find such good-value accommodation so close to Sol and the Plaza Mayor.

### Hostal Sil & Serranos

*C/Fuencarral 95, Malasaña (91 448 89 72, www.silserranos. com). Metro Bilbao.* **Map** *p120 J10.*

Clean and smartly decorated, these *hostales* are well located for night-time revelling – indeed, rooms looking out on to C/ Fuencarral will bear witness to the *madrileño* enthusiasm for partying. Although interior rooms are a little darker, the noise is minimal and the price slightly lower. All rooms have air-conditioning, small bathrooms and digital TV, and the properties are run by a fun couple.

### Lapepa Chic B&B

*Plaza de las Cortes 4, 7ª, Huertas (mobile 648 474 742, lapepa-bnb. com). Metro Banco de España.* **Map** *p95 M15.*

A cheerful B&B with an unbeatable location between the major art museums and the bars of Santa Ana. All 14 rooms are pristine, en suite, and decorated in red and white. Breakfast is included and available until noon.

Other affordable options include **Hostal Triana** (www. hostaltriana.com), a traditional, good-value *hostal* with sparklingly clean rooms, and **Hostal Atocha Almudena Martín** (hostalatocha.es ), a very friendly *hostal* offering air-conditioned rooms with en suite bathrooms and decent showers.

Room Mate Alicia

# Getting Around

## ARRIVING & LEAVING

### By air

**Barajas Airport**
*91 321 10 00, 902 404 704.*
Madrid's airport is 14km (9 miles)
north-east of the city on the A2
motorway. With the addition
of terminal T4 a further 6km
(4 miles) away, the airport is
now used by around 50 million
passengers per year. All airlines
that are members of the Oneworld
network (including BA, Iberia and
American Airlines) share T4 for
national and international flights.
All other traffic is distributed
between the 3 older terminals.
All terminals are linked by
shuttle buses.

There are 24hr exchange
facilities in T1: those in T3 and
T4 are open 6.30am-10.30pm. All
terminals have ATM machines,
and there are tourist offices in T1,
T2 and T4.

### Airport buses

The city council's **express
airport bus** (no.203) runs a
24/7 service (every 16-18mins
in the day and 35mins at night).
The easily identifiable yellow
buses – which run between T1,
T2, T4 and, in town, O'Donnell,
Cibeles and Atocha – take around
40mins and the journey costs €5.
Note that Cibeles is the first/last
stop between 11.30pm and 6am.
Timetables are available at www.
emtmadrid.es.

**Aerocity** (902 151 654, www.
aerocity.com) provides shuttle
services between the airport
and city hotels. Handy for small
groups and cheaper than taking
several taxis. Prices vary (€20-
€40) depending on group size.

**Local buses** (91 406 88 10,
www.emtmadrid.es) 200 and 204
run between the public transport

hub on the Avda de América and
T1, T2 and T4. A single ticket
costs €1.50.

### Metro

The metro is another cheap
way to get to central Madrid,
though there is a €3 supplement
for journeys to the airport, so a
regular journey will cost between
€4.50 and €5. Bear in mind that
the Aeropuerto metro station is
between T2 and T3, which means
that if, as is very likely, you arrive
at T1, you have a 10-15min walk
to get there. From T4, take the
shuttle to T2 (allow 20mins in
total). From the airport it's 4 stops
on metro line 8 (pink) and 12mins
to Nuevos Ministerios. From here
it's around 15mins to the centre of
Madrid. You can save money by
buying a Metrobús ticket at the
airport station.

### Taxis

Taxi fares to central Madrid are
set at €30, or €20 if the distance
is less than 10km (6 miles) from
the airport, including a €5.50
airport supplement (no luggage
supplement). There are lots of
taxis at Barajas, but ignore drivers
who approach you inside the
building; use ones at the ranks
outside the terminal. For more on
taxis, *see p284.*

### Train

The RENFE *cercanías* line from
the airport will take you from T4
to Atocha in 25mins (€2.60).

### By bus

Almost all international and long-
distance coach services to Madrid
terminate at the Estación Sur de
Autobuses, C/Méndez Álvaro (info
91 468 42 00, 5.30am-1am, www.
estacionautobusesmadrid.com).
It's next to metro (line 6) and

*cercanía* (local train lines C5, C7
and C10) stations, both also called
Méndez Álvaro. Bus 148 also runs
from there to the centre (Plaza del
Callao and Plaza de España). Taxi
fares from the bus station carry a
€3 supplement.

### By train

The Spanish state railway
company RENFE has 2 main
stations in Madrid. Trains from
France, Catalonia and northern
Spain arrive at **Chamartín**, on
the north side of the city, some
distance from the centre. High-
speed AVE trains from Andalucía,
Barcelona and Valencia, express
services from Lisbon and trains
from southern and eastern Spain
arrive at **Atocha**, at the southern
end of the Paseo del Prado. There
are exchange facilities at both
stations, and a tourist office at
Chamartín. Atocha is also the
main hub of RENFE's local rail
lines (*cercanías*) for the Madrid
area (*see p284*).

Metro line 10 is the fastest from
Chamartín to the city centre, and
Atocha RENFE (the train station;
not the same metro as Atocha)
is 4 metro stops from Sol on line
1. A taxi fare to the centre from
Chamartín should be around
€14, including a €3 station
supplement. There are extra
supplements at night and on Sun
(15¢ per km). The same need for
caution with cabs at the airport
(*see left*) applies to drivers touting
for fares at main rail stations. For
more information on all Madrid
local rail services, *see p284.*

**RENFE** *91 32 03 20, www.renfe.
com.* **Open** 24hrs daily.

**Estación de Atocha** *Glorieta
del Emperador Carlos V. Metro
Atocha Renfe. **Map** pull-out N18.*

**Estación de Chamartín** *C/ Agustín de Foxá, Chamartín. Metro Chamartín.*

## PUBLIC TRANSPORT

To really get to know Madrid, it's best to explore on foot. Most of the main attractions are within walking distance of one another, and for orientation purposes think of Puerta del Sol as the centre. Street numbers in Madrid all run outwards from Sol. Public transport is cheap and efficient – both bus and metro will get you where you want to go within 30mins, although it's best to avoid the buses during rush hour. Note: all transport and taxi fares are subject to revision in Jan.

For transport outside Madrid, *see p182* In the know. For transport for disabled travellers, *see p287*.

### Fares & tickets

Madrid's fare structure is based on a €1.50 minimum, valid for up to 5 stops, and then 10¢ for each stop thereafter (excluding Barajas Airport, which carries a €3 supplement) within the capital, no matter how long the journey. On the metro you can change any number of times as long as you don't leave a station. The exceptions are trips to the stations Rivas Urbanizaciones, Rivas Vaciamadrid, La Poveda and Arganda del Rey (all Line 9), and all stations beyond Puerta del Sur on the Metro Sur line, which circles the southern suburbs.

However, it's easier and more economical to buy a ticket for 10 journeys (*billete de diez/Metrobús*), which can be used on the bus and metro, available at all metro stations and some *estancos* and *kioskos*, but not on the buses. You can share the ticket between 2 or more people and keep it for as long as you like (or until the prices go up). The current price of a Metrobús is €12.20.

On the metro, you simply insert the ticket into the machine at the gate that leads through to the platform, which cancels one unit for each trip – remember to collect it afterwards – and will reject expired tickets. There is no

checking or collection of tickets at station exits. On buses, the Metrobús should be inserted arrow downwards into the blue and yellow machine just behind the driver.

### Abonos – season tickets

If you're planning to stay much longer than a fortnight, a 30-day season ticket (*Abono 30 días*) is a good idea. Unlike the Metrobús, it is valid for *cercanías* trains as well as the metro and city buses, allowing you to use it on some trips out of town. Your first *abono* is available only from *estancos*, and must be obtained with an identity card or passport. You'll need 2 passport photos and must fill in a brief form. Subsequently, you can buy tickets to revalidate the card from metro stations and EMT kiosks as well as *estancos*.

Unless you are intending to travel a lot outside the city, Zone A should cover everywhere you need to go. A standard 1-mth Zone A *abono* currently costs €54.60, and there are substantial reductions for young people and for over-65s. It can be used on the buses to the airport, for which *see p282*.

### Metro

The metro is the quickest and simplest means of travelling to most parts of the city. Each of its 13 lines (including the Metrosur and Ramal lines) is identified by a number and a colour on maps and at stations. The metro is open 6am-2am daily. Tickets are available at all stations from coin-operated machines and staffed ticket booths. Trains run every 3-6mins on weekdays, and every 10-15mins after 11pm and on Sun. The metro can get packed in rush hours (7.30-9.30am, 1-2.30pm, 7.30-9pm).

**Metro information** *Sol metro station, Sol & Gran Vía (91 779 63 99, www.metromadrid.es). Metro Sol.* **Open** *7am-10pm Mon-Fri; 10am-10pm Sat-Sun.*
This customer service point provides information and sells transport tickets, tourist passes and season tickets.

### Buses

Run by **Empresa Municipal de Transportes (EMT)**. *See p283* for information about fares and tickets.

Most run about 6am-11.30pm daily, with buses every 10-15mins (more often on more popular routes). Night buses then take over. You board buses at the front, and get off via the middle or rear doors. The fare is the same for each journey (€1.50), however far you go. Officially, there is a limit to how much luggage you can take on city buses, and trying to board with luggage during rush hours is almost impossible. Drivers are not obliged to give you the change for anything larger than a €20 note, nor will they allow you to travel for free. But they must write down your contact details for the bus company to send you the change later on.

For tourist buses, *see p182*.

### Night buses

Between midnight and around 5am there are 27 night routes in operation – N1 to N27 (N27 goes out to the airport) – called Búho (Owl) buses. All begin from Plaza de Cibeles and run out to the suburbs, and are numbered in a clockwise sequence. Although the metro closes at nights, at the weekends special buses, called Metro Búho, cover the routes of the 11 central metro lines (L1-L11). The buses alight at the bus stop nearest to each metro station. The timetable for each line varies, but generally the buses run from 12.45am until 5.45am. L1-L11 buses run every 15-20mins. There are 3 buses that cover the L12 Metrosur route, which connects Alcorcón, Leganés, Getafe, Fuenlabrada and Móstoles. The L12 buses run every 30mins, from 1.15am to 5.30am.

**EMT Information** *C/Cerro de la Plata 4, Retiro (91 406 88 10, www.emtmadrid.es). Metro Pacífico.* **Open** *8am-2pm Mon-Fri; telephone information line open 7am-9pm daily.*

### Cercanías/local trains

The highly efficient *cercanías* or local network of railways of the Madrid area has been expanding in recent years in order to link the suburbs with the centre more directly. It consists of 10 lines converging on Atocha, several of which connect with metro lines along their routes.

As well as the suburbs, *cercanías* trains are useful for trips to Guadarrama and towns near Madrid such as Aranjuez or El Escorial. Also, line C-7 effectively forms a circle line within Madrid that is quicker than the metro for some journeys, and the RENFE line between Chamartín and Atocha is the fastest link between the 2 main stations. *Cercanías* lines run from 5-6am to 11pm-midnight daily, with trains on most lines about every 10-30mins. Fares vary with distance, but the lines are included in the monthly season ticket. For a map of the *cercanías* network, *see pull-out map.*

### TAXIS

Madrid taxis are white, with a diagonal red stripe on the front doors. The city has more than 15,000 taxis, so they are rarely hard to find, except late at night at the weekend or on days when it's raining heavily. When a taxi is free there is a '*Libre*' (free) sign behind the windscreen, and a green light on the roof. If there is also a sign with the name of a district in red, it means the driver is on the way home, and is not obliged to take you anywhere that isn't near that particular route. There are taxi ranks, marked by a blue sign with a white T, throughout the centre of Madrid. At the airport and rail and bus stations, it's always best to take a taxi from the official ranks; within the city, however, those in the know flag cabs down in the street, thereby avoiding the risk both of scams, and of station supplements. To avoid being swindled by a non-official taxi, make sure the driver has their licence number visible on the front and a meter, and always ask for the approximate fare before getting in.

### Fares

Official fare rates and supplements are shown inside each cab (in English and Spanish), on the right-hand sun visor and/or the rear windows. The minimum fare is €2.40-€2.90 (depending on the day/time), which is what the meter should show when you first set off. The higher rate applies at night (9pm-7am) and on Sun and public holidays, and there are extra supplements for trips starting from the bus and train stations (€3) and to and from the trade fair complex (€3). There are set fares between Madrid and the airport: €20 if travelling within 10km of the airport, or €30 between the airport and the city centre. Also, the fare rate is higher for journeys to suburban towns in the outer tariff zone (zone B). Drivers are not officially required to carry more than €20 in change, and some accept credit cards.

### Receipts & complaints

To get a receipt, ask for '*un recibo, por favor*'. If you think you've been overcharged or have any other complaint, insist the receipt is made out in full, with details of the journey and the driver's signature, NIF number and licence plate, and the date. Make a note of the taxi number, displayed on a plaque on the dashboard. Take or send the receipt, keeping a copy, with a complaints form to the city taxi office at the address below. The form is included in the Taxi Information leaflet available from tourist offices.

**Oficina Municipal del Taxi** *C/ Albarracín 31 3ª, Eastern suburbs (91 480 46 23). Metro García Noblejas.* **Open** *8.30am-2pm Mon-Fri.*

### Phone cabs

You can call for a cab from any of the companies listed below. Operators will rarely speak much English, so if you aren't at a specific address give the name of the street and a restaurant or bar that makes a suitable place to wait, or position yourself near a street corner and say, for example, 'San Agustín, *esquina* Prado' (San Agustín, corner of Prado). The operator will also ask you

your name. Phone cabs start the meter from the point when a call is answered. Some cabs will take credit cards.

**Radio-Taxi Asociación Gremial** *91 447 32 32, www. radiotaxigremial.com.*

**Radio-Taxi Independiente** *91 405 12 13, www. radiotaxindependiente.com.*

**Radioteléfono Taxi** *91 547 82 00, www.radiotelefono-taxi.com.*

**Teletaxi** *91 371 21 31.*

### CYCLING

Cycling in Madrid used to be a terrifying prospect, but things have changed considerably over the last few years. The city-run **BiciMad** (www.bicimad. com) bike-sharing scheme was introduced in 2014, and the number of bike lanes has steadily expanded since then. Cycling is still a challenge – many streets are steep, and local drivers are still learning to share the roads with cyclists – but the city is now relatively bike-friendly. Bikes are a great idea for trips to the larger city parks (Retiro, Casa de Campo) and especially the Madrid Sierras. Bikes can be taken free of charge on some *cercanías* lines and on the metro at weekends. Cycle hire shops often ask that you leave proof of identity (take a photocopy to avoid having to leave your passport) as well as a cash deposit. There are an increasing number of companies and associations in Madrid that are dedicated to cycling, including **Pedalibre** (www. pedalibre.org) and **Ciclos Otero** (www.oterociclos.es).

### DRIVING

Thanks to traffic jams, driving in the city is rarely a quick way of getting anywhere, and finding a parking space is another headache.

### Signs & terms

*cede el paso* – give way
*usted no tiene la prioridad* – you don't have the right of way
*único sentido* – one way

*cambio de sentido* – indicates a junction that allows you to change direction
*recuerde* – remember
*cinturón de seguridad* – seat belt
*ronda de circunnavegación* – ring road.

## Car & motorbike hire

Car hire can be pricey, so shop around; there are often good weekend deals. Most companies have a minimum age limit (usually 21, sometimes 25) and require you to have had a licence for over a year. You will also need a credit card (as opposed to a debit card), or leave a big cash deposit (sometimes up to €500). Check if IVA (VAT) and unlimited mileage are included. All the companies listed require you to take out a *seguro franquicia* – a fixed amount you have to pay in the event of an accident or any damage caused to the vehicle, and which is put on your credit card when you take the car (usually around half the hire cost – it is only charged if you return the vehicle damaged).

**Avis** *Estación de Chamartín, C/ Agustín de Foxá 25, Chamartín (902 090 343, www.avis.es). Metro Plaza de Castilla.* **Open** *8am-9pm Mon-Fri; 8am-2pm Sat, Sun.*

**BlaferMotos** *C/Clara del Rey 17, Chamartín (91 413 00 47, www. blafermotos.com). Metro Alfonso XIII.* **Open** *8.30am-6.30pm Mon-Fri; 10am-1.30pm Sat.* Motorcycle specialists.

**Easycar** *Barajas Airport (www. easycar.com).*

**Enterprise** *Plaza de España car park (1st floor) (91 542 50 15, www. enterprise.es). Metro Plaza de España.* **Open** *8.30am-7.30pm Mon-Fri; 9am-1pm Sat.*

**Europcar** *Paseo de la Castellana 193 (91 555 99 30, www.europcar. com). Metro Plaza de Castilla.* **Open** *8am-7pm Mon-Fri; 9am-2pm Sat.*

**PlanCar** *C/Mauricio Legendre 3, Chamartín (91 530 92 69, www. plancar.com). Metro Chamartín.*

**Open** *9am-2pm, 4.30-8pm Mon-Fri; 9am-2pm Sat.*

▶ *See the Avis, Enterprise and Europcar websites for other locations throughout the city.*

### Breakdown services

If you are planning to take a car to Spain it's advisable to join a motoring organisation such as the AA or RAC, which have reciprocal arrangements with their Spanish equivalent, RACE.

**RACE (Real Automóvil Club de España)** *Assistance 900 112 222, info 900 100 992, www.race.es.* The RACE has English-speaking staff and will send immediate 24hr breakdown assistance. Repairs are carried out on the spot when possible; if not, your vehicle will be towed to the nearest suitable garage. Members of affiliated organisations abroad are not charged for call-outs, but non-members pay around €115 (on-the-spot membership) for the basic breakdown service.

### Legal requirements

For driving laws and regulations (in Spanish) see the Ministry of Interior's website (www.dgt.es).

### Parking

For car-owning *madrileños* parking is a daily trauma. The city police (Policía Municipal) give out tickets readily (many locals never pay them). Be careful not to park in front of doorways with the sign '*vado permanente*', indicating an entry with 24hr right of access. The SER (Servicio de Estacionamiento Regulado) system applies (*see below*) to the whole city centre. Residents park for free if they have an annual sticker.

**SER** Non-residents must pay to park in zones painted in blue or green from 9am to 9pm Mon-Fri and 9am to 3pm Sat (9am-3pm Mon-Sat in Aug). These hours will be extended until midnight from 2018. Pay-and-display machines are located

on pavements. Maximum validity of tickets is 2hrs in blue zones and 1hr in green, after which a new card must be used, and the car parked in a new spot. Cars parked in the SER zone without a card can be towed away (*see right*). In the blue areas, tickets cost €2.75 for 2hrs, €8.20 for 4hrs (maximum stay of 4hrs) and in the green areas, €2.35 for 1hr, €4.70 for 2hrs (maximum stay of 2hrs). All streets in this zone that have no additional restrictions posted are SER parking areas.

**Central car parks** *Plaza de las Cortes, Plaza Santa Ana, C/ Sevilla, Plaza Jacinto Benavente, Plaza Mayor, Plaza Descalzas, C/Tudescos, Plaza de España.* **Open** *24hrs daily. Rates €1.25 for 30mins; €3.45 for 90mins, €8.90 for 3hrs; €31.25 for 12 to 24hrs (the maximum).*

There are some 50 municipal car parks around Madrid, indicated by a white 'P'-on-blue sign. It's especially advisable to use a car park if your car has foreign plates. Car parks have disabled access. See also www.madridmovilidad.es for more details.

**Towed vehicles** *Information 91 406 88 10 (operator 7am-9pm Mon-Fri; other times, automated service), www.emtmadrid.es/ EMTGruas.*

**Main pounds** *Plaza Colón. Metro Colón.* **Map** *pull-out map N11. C/Velázquez 87. Metro Nuñez de Balboa.* **Map** *pull-out map Q8.* **Open** *24hrs daily.*

If your car seems to have been towed away, call the central number and quote your number plate to be told which pound it has gone to, or go to the website and input your licence plate number. It will cost €147.55 to recover your car. You'll have to pay €1.85 per hr for the first 10hrs, timed from the moment it was towed away. For each complete extra day in the pound it's €19.20. You can also locate your car by entering your registration plate number on the website. Bring your ID and all car papers when you pick it up.

# Resources A-Z

## Travel Advice

For up-to-date information on travel to a specific country – including the latest on safety and security, health issues, local laws and customs – contact your home country government's department of foreign affairs. Most have websites with useful advice for would-be travellers.

**AUSTRALIA**
www.smartraveller.gov.au

**CANADA**
www.voyage.gc.ca

**NEW ZEALAND**
www.safetravel.govt.nz

**REPUBLIC OF IRELAND**
foreignaffairs.gov.ie

**UK**
www.fco.gov.uk/travel

**USA**
www.state.gov/travel

## ACCIDENT & EMERGENCY

**Emergency numbers**

**Emergency services** *112*.
Police, fire or ambulance.

**A&E departments**
In a medical emergency go to the casualty department (*urgencias*) of any of the city's major hospitals (*see below*). All are open 24hrs daily; Clínico or Gregorio Marañón are most central. If you are an EU citizen with no EHIC (*see p288*) or insurance, you can still be seen at any casualty department (pay on the spot and get reimbursed back home by presenting the invoices and medical reports). In a non-emergency, pharmacists are very well informed. Call 112 for an ambulance. For more information *see p288* Health.

**Hospital Clínico San Carlos** *C/ Profesor Martín Lagos, Moncloa (91 330 30 00). Metro Moncloa.*
To get to the Accident and Emergency Department, enter from C/Isaac Peral, which is off Plaza de Cristo Rey.

**Hospital General Gregorio Marañón** *C/Doctor Esquerdo 44-46, Salamanca (91 586 80 00, www.hggm.es). Metro O'Donnell.*

**Hospital Universitario La Paz** *Paseo de la Castellana 261,*
*Chamartín (91 727 70 00, www. madrid.org/hospitallapaz). Metro Begoña.*
The hospital is in Plaza Castilla to the north of the city.

## ADDRESSES

Individual flats in apartment blocks have traditionally been identified by the abbreviations z '*izq*' (*izquierda*, left) or '*dcha*' (*derecha*, right) after the floor number (C/Prado 221, 5ª dcha) and occasionally '*int*' (interior, inward facing) or '*ext*' (exterior); in newer buildings they may be shown more simply (C/Prado 223, 4B). A building with no street number (usually huge places like stations or hospitals) has *s/n* (*sin número*) after the street.

## AGE RESTRICTIONS

**Buying/drinking alcohol** 18
**Driving** 18
**Smoking** 18
**Sex** 16

## ATTITUDE & ETIQUETTE

Some of the stereotypes are true. It's all much more vivacious than at home, and certainly more vocal. It's normal to say 'Hola' to all strangers, even when you're in a lift. Despite appearances, Spaniards have a highly developed queuing culture. People don't always bother standing in line, but they generally know when it is their turn. Common practice is to ask when you first arrive, to no one in particular, '¿Quién da la vez?' or '¿Quién es el último/la última?' ('Who's last?'); see who nods, and follow on after them. Say '*yo*' (me) to the next person who asks.

Packed rush-hour metro trains are common, so *madrileños* have a set way of alighting from them. Rather than just push past people, only to find they are also getting off, it's usual to ask those in front: '¿Va a salir?' ('Are you getting off?'). If they are not, watch in wonder as a path opens up before you.

## CLIMATE

The climate of Madrid has justly been described as 'nine months of winter (*invierno*) and three months of hell (*infierno*)'. Many people can't cope with the summer heat, others love it. Winter in Madrid can be very cold, although there's often bright, crisp sunshine and most rain falls in autumn and spring. Spring is unpredictable – February can often be freakishly warm, while in April, rain is likely. Summer temperatures range from hot to unbearably hot, although it's a dry heat with little humidity. In July and August it doesn't really cool down at night, making partying in the street great fun, but sleeping less so. Traditionally there's a mass exodus in August. Autumn weather is usually bright and warm and it's often possible to eat and drink outside well into October. *See also p287* Local Weather.

## CONSUMER RIGHTS

If you have a complaint, ask for an official complaint form (*hoja de reclamación*), which most businesses, shops, bars and so on are obliged to have available for customers. Fill out the form, leaving the colour copy with the business. Then take this, and any receipts or other relevant paperwork, to the official consumer office, listed below.

**Oficina Municipal de Información al Consumidor** *C/ Príncipe de Vergara 142, Chamartín (91 529 82 10/010). Metro Cruz del Rayo. Open 9-11am Mon-Fri.*

The official centre for consumer advice and complaint follow-up. You will need to make an appointment first.

## CUSTOMS

Customs declarations are not usually necessary if you arrive from another EU country and are carrying legal goods for personal use. Guidelines for quantities accepted as being for personal use include:

• up to 800 cigarettes, 400 small cigars, 200 cigars or 1kg of loose tobacco
• 10 litres of spirits (more than 22% alcohol), 20 litres of fortified wine or alcoholic drinks with less than 22% of alcohol, 90 litres of wine (less than 22%) or 110 litres of beer.

Coming from a non-EU country or the Canary Islands, you can bring:

• 200 cigarettes or 100 small cigars or 50 regular cigars or 250g (8.82oz) of tobacco
• 1 litre of spirits (more than 22% alcohol), 2 litres of any other alcoholic drink with less than 22% alcohol, 4 litres of wine or 16 litres of beer
• personal goods with to a value of €430.

Visitors are also allowed to carry up to €10,000 in cash without having to declare it. Non-EU residents can reclaim the VAT (IVA) on certain large purchases when they leave Spain. For details, *see p291.*

## DISABLED

Madrid is still not a city that disabled people, especially wheelchair users, will find it very easy to get around. However, the situation is steadily improving

as new buildings are constructed with accessibility in mind and old ones are gradually adapted: technically all public buildings should have been made accessible by law, although in practice a great deal still remains to be done. Access to public transport is improving: all buses are wheelchair accessible, along with all the interchange ('*intercambiador*') stations. The Madrid metro website (www.metromadrid.es) lists all the accessible stations.

There is an excellent guide, *Accessible Tourism Guide to Madrid*, which is published by the Ayuntamiento (city council) in collaboration with the disabled association FAMMA. Information is available from the FAMMA office at C/Galileo 69 (91 593 35 50, www.famma.org), and can also be accessed via the city council website (www.esmadrid.com; click on 'Plan your trip' then 'Accessibility').

### Transport

**Buses** There are seats reserved for people with mobility problems behind the driver on most of the city's buses. All buses

are now the *piso bajo* (low floor) type, with low doors and spaces for wheelchairs.

**Metro** All new metro stations have been built with access in mind, which means that those on newer lines (Line 8 to the airport, Line 7 to Pitis, all the interchange stations such as Méndez Alvaro and Puerto del Sol) have good lifts. However, older stations in the city centre generally have a lot of steps, and, although you may get on at a station with a lift, it may turn out to be impossible to get off at your destination. The metro map in this guide (*see pull-out map*) and the free maps available at metro stations indicate stations with lifts, or you can check the Madrid Metro website (www.madridmetro.es).

**RENFE & cercanías** Of the mainline rail stations, Atocha, Chamartín, Nuevos Ministerios and Príncipe Pío all have good access. *Cercanías* trains have very limited access but some newer stations, including all the city's interchanges (such as Puerta del Sol, Méndez Alvaro, Moncloa and Plaza Castilla), have lifts connecting metro, train and bus stations.

# Local Weather

Average temperatures and monthly rainfall in Madrid

| | High (°C/°F) | Low (°C/°F) | Rainfall (mm/in) |
|---|---|---|---|
| January | 9 / 48 | 2 / 36 | 39 / 1.5 |
| February | 11 / 52 | 2 / 36 | 34/ 1.3 |
| March | 15 / 59 | 5 / 41 | 43 / 1.7 |
| April | 18 / 64 | 7 / 45 | 48 / 1.9 |
| May | 21 / 70 | 10 / 50 | 47 / 1.8 |
| June | 27 / 81 | 15 / 59 | 27 / 1.0 |
| July | 31 / 88 | 17 / 63 | 11 / 0.4 |
| August | 30 / 86 | 17 / 63 | 15 / 0.6 |
| September | 25 / 77 | 14 / 57 | 32 / 1.2 |
| October | 19 / 66 | 10 / 50 | 53 / 2.0 |
| November | 13 / 55 | 5 / 41 | 47 / 1.8 |
| December | 9 / 48 | 2 / 36 | 48 / 1.9 |

**Taxis** Special taxis adapted for wheelchairs can be called through **Eurotaxi** (91 547 82 00) and **Teletaxi** (91 371 21 31, www. tele-taxi.es). Make it clear you want an adapted model (ask for a Eurotaxi). The number of such taxis in Madrid is still very limited and the waiting time can be as long as half an hour. Fares are the same as for standard cabs, but the meter is started as soon as a request is received, so the cost can be quite high.

## Wheelchair-friendly museums & galleries

Most of the city's museums and cultural centres are now wheelchair-friendly – see the PDF *Accessible Tourism Guide to Madrid* on www.esmadrid.com (click on 'Plan your trip' then 'Accessibility') for the full list.

## DRUGS

Many people smoke cannabis fairly openly in Spain, but possession or consumption in public is illegal. In private the law is contradictory: smoking is OK but you can be nabbed for possession or distribution. Enforcement is often not the highest of police priorities, but you could theoretically receive a fine and, in extreme cases, get sent to prison. Smoking in bars is also prohibited. Cocaine is common in Spain as well but if you're caught in possession of this or any other Class A drug, you are looking at a hefty fine, and possibly a long prison sentence.

## ELECTRICITY

The standard current in Spain is 220V, but a few old buildings in Madrid still have 125V circuits, so it's a good idea to check before using electrical equipment in older hotels. Plugs are all of the two-round-pin type. The 220V current works fine with British 240V products, with a plug adaptor. With US 110V appliances you will need a current transformer as well as an adaptor.

# EMBASSIES & CONSULATES

For a full list look in the local phone book under *embajadas*. Lots of embassies are at the Torre Espacio at Paseo de la Castellana 259.

**American Embassy** *C/Serrano 75, Salamanca (91 587 22 00, es.usembassy.gov). Metro Rubén Darío.* **Open** *Phoneline 24hrs daily. Office 8.30am-5.30pm Mon-Fri.*

**Australian Embassy** *24th floor, Torre Espacio, Paseo de la Castellana 259D, Northern suburbs (91 353 66 00/visas +44 (0)207 420 3690, www.spain. embassy.gov.au). Metro Begoña.* **Open** *8.30am-1.30pm, 2-4.30pm (visas 9am-noon) Mon-Fri.*

**British Embassy** *Torre Espacio, Paseo de la Castellana 259D, Northern suburbs (91 714 63 00, www.gov.uk). Metro Begoña.* **Open** *8.30am-5pm Mon-Fri.*

**British Consulate** *Torre Espacio, Paseo de la Castellana 259D, Northern suburbs (91 714 63 00). Metro Begoña.* **Open** *Phoneline 8am-4pm. Office 8.30am-1.30pm Mon-Fri.*

**Canadian Embassy** *Torre Espacio, Paseo de la Castellana 259D, Northern suburbs (91 382 84 00, www. canadainternational.gc.ca/spain-espagne). Metro Begoña.* **Open** *Consular services 9am-12.30pm Mon-Fri. Emergency services 8.30am-1pm, 2-5.30pm Mon-Thur; 8.30am-2.30pm Fri. Other services Sept-July 8.30am-2pm, 3-5.30pm Mon-Thur; 8.30am-2.30pm Fri. Aug 8.30am-2.30pm Mon-Fri.* Emergency number for citizens (reverse charge calls accepted) is 00 613 996 8885.

**Irish Embassy** *Paseo de la Castellana 46 4º, Salamanca (91 436 40 93/visas 91 431 97 84, www.irlanda.es). Metro Rubén Darío.* **Open** *Passports phoneline 9.30am-1pm. Passports office 10am-2pm Mon-Fri. Visas phoneline 9.30-11am. Visas office 11.30am-1pm Mon, Wed.* **Map** *pull-out O8.*

**New Zealand Embassy** *C/Pinar 7 3º, Chamberí (91 523 02 26, www. nzembassy.com/spain). Metro Gregorio Marañón.* **Open** *Sept-June 9am-2pm, 3-5.30pm Mon-Fri. July-Aug 8.30am-1.30pm, 2-4.30pm.*

## HEALTH

EU nationals are entitled to free basic medical attention if they have the European Health Insurance Card (EHIC). Travellers from the British Isles should apply for one online at www.gov.uk (providing name, date of birth, and NHS or NI number) at least ten days before leaving home. If you don't have one but can get one sent or faxed within a few days, you will be exempt from charges. Citizens of certain other countries that have a special agreement with Spain, among them several Latin American states, can also have access to free care. These arrangements won't cover all eventualities, so always take out private health insurance; *see p289* Insurance.

Madrid's tap water is good and safe to drink. There are occasional water shortages in summer, and signs posted in hotels urge guests to avoid wasting water. If you want tap rather than bottled water in a restaurant specify that you want *agua del grifo.*

### AIDS/HIV

Advice is available on freephone 900 11 10 00 (10am-8pm Mon-Fri; 9.30am-2.30pm Sat, Sun).

**Centro Sanitario Sandoval** *C/ Sandoval 7, Chamberí (91 445 23 28, www.madrid.org). Metro Bilbao or San Bernardo.* **Open** *8.45am-noon Mon-Fri.* **Map** *pull-out J9.*
An official clinic that carries out free, confidential HIV tests.

### Contraception & women's health

Condoms (*profilácticos, condones* or *preservativos*) are available from most pharmacies, as well as vending machines and supermarkets. Pharmacies also sell other forms of contraception including pills (la píldora), which can be bought without a prescription, as can the morning-after pill (la píldora del día siguente), but some health centres will dispense it free themselves.

**Asociación de Mujeres para la Salud** *Avda Alfonso XIII 118, Chamartín (91 519 56 78, www. mujeresparalasalud.org). Metro Colombia.* **Open** *9am-2pm, 4-8pm Mon-Fri. Closed Aug.*
A feminist medical association offering free advice and counselling.

### Dentists

Dentistry is not covered by EU reciprocal agreements, so private rates will apply to any treatment.

**Clínica Dental Cisne** *C/ Magallanes 18 1ª, Chamberí (91 446 32 21, www.clinica dentalcisne.com). Metro Quevedo.* **Open** *9am-1pm, 3-7pm Mon-Thur; 9am-3pm Fri. Closed Aug.* **Map** *pull-out H8.*
British dentist Dr Ian Daniel is based at this clinic in Chamberí. Hours may vary during the summer, and the clinic sometimes closes in Aug.

### Doctors

*Centros de salud* are local health centres with a few doctors and various specialised clinics. Waiting times can be long and consultations brief, but if necessary you will be referred to a hospital. Usually open 8am-9pm Mon-Fri. These are some of the most central:

**Centro de Salud Alameda** *C/ Alameda 5, Huertas & Santa Ana (91 420 38 02). Metro Atocha.* **Map** *p95 M16.*

**Centro de Salud Argüelles** *C/ Quintana 11, Argüelles (91 559 48 98). Metro Argüelles.* **Map** *pull-out D10.*

**Centro de Salud Las Cortes** *C/ San Jerónimo 32, Huertas & Santa Ana (91 369 04 91). Metro Sevilla.* **Map** *p95 K14.*

### Hospitals
*See p286 Accident & emergency.*

### Opticians

**+ Visión Puerta del Sol** *C/Puerta del Sol 14, (91 701 49 80). Metro Sol.* **Open** *10am-9pm Mon-Sat; 11am-3pm, 4-8pm Sun.* **Map** *p83 J14.*
Book an appointment online at this central optician.

### Pharmacies
Pharmacies (*farmacias*) are signalled by large, green, usually flashing crosses. Those within the official system of the College of Pharmacies are normally open 9.30am-2pm, 5-8pm Mon-Sat. At other times a duty rota operates. Every pharmacy has a list of the College's *farmacias de guardia* (duty pharmacies) for that day posted outside the door, with the nearest ones highlighted (many now show them using a computerised, push-button panel). Duty pharmacies are also listed in local newspapers, and information is available on the 010 phoneline (*see p295*) and at www.cofm.es. At night, duty pharmacies may look closed; knock on the shutters to be served.

There are many pharmacies open 24hrs daily in Madrid.

### Private healthcare

**Unidad Médica Anglo-Americana** *C/Conde de Aranda 1-1º izq, Salamanca (91 435 18 23, www.unidadmedica.com). Metro Retiro.* **Open** *Sept-July 9am-8pm Mon-Fri; 10am-1pm Sat. Aug 10am-5pm Mon-Fri; 10am-1pm Sat.* Offers full range of services, including dentistry. Will make house/hotel calls.

### ID

Foreigners are meant to carry an ID card or a passport with them at all times, and are in theory subject to a fine for not doing so – in practice, you're more likely to get a warning. If you don't want to carry it around with you, it's a good idea to carry a photocopy or a driver's licence instead; technically, it's not legal but it's usually acceptable. ID is needed to check into a hotel, hire a car

and – very occasionally – when you pay with a card in shops.

### INSURANCE
EU nationals are entitled to use the Spanish state health service, provided they have a European Health Insurance Card (*see p288* Health), which must be applied for well in advance of travel. This will cover you for emergencies, but for short-term visitors it's often simpler to avoid dealing with the state bureaucracy and take out private travel insurance before departure, particularly as this will also cover you for stolen or lost cash or valuables.

Some non-EU countries have reciprocal healthcare agreements with Spain, but again, for most travellers it will be best to take out private travel insurance before arriving.

### LEFT LUGGAGE

**Barajas airport** *Terminals T1 & T4 (information 91 746 60 65).* **Open** *24hrs daily.* **Rates** *€10 for 2-24hrs.*

**RENFE train stations** **Open** *Chamartín 7am-11pm daily. Atocha 5.30am-10.20pm daily.* **Rates** *from €3.10-€5.20 depending on locker size.*

### LGBT

**COGAM** *C/Puebla 9, Malasaña & Conde Duque (91 523 00 70, www. cogam.es). Metro Gran Vía.* **Open** *5-9pm Mon-Fri; 6-9pm Sat.* **Map** *p120 J12.*
The largest gay and lesbian organisation in Madrid, COGAM is one of the main organisers of Gay Pride and campaigns on various issues. The on-site café is a great place to chill and find out what's new on the scene.

**Fundación Triángulo** *C/Melendez Valdés 52 1ªD, Chamberí (91 593 05 40, www.fundaciontriangulo. es). Metro Argüelles.* **Open** *10am-2pm, 4-8pm Mon-Fri. Closed Aug.* **Map** *pull-out E8.*

A gay cultural organisation that campaigns on equality issues. It also runs a helpline (91 593 05 40, same times as above) and offers legal help, health advice and AIDS prevention programmes.

## LIBRARIES

Madrid has a great number of municipal public libraries, but few are in the centre of the city and, not surprisingly, they generally have limited selections of books in English. For a full list of libraries, check 'bibliotecas' in the local *Páginas Amarillas (Yellow Pages)*, call 010 or visit www.madrid.org/bibliotecaspublicas.

**Biblioteca Nacional** *Paseo de Recoletos 20, Salamanca (91 580 78 00, www.bne.es). Metro Colón. **Open** 9am-9pm Mon-Fri; 9am-2pm Sat. **Map** p141 O12.*
Spain's national library has early books and manuscripts on display (in the Museo del Libro), and is also the home of the Hemeroteca Nacional, the national newspaper library. To use the library you can apply online for a card that lasts three years.

**Biblioteca Pedro Salinas** *Glorieta de la Puerta de Toledo 1, La Latina (91 366 54 07). Metro Puerta de Toledo. **Open** 9am-9pm Mon-Fri. **Map** p62 F18.*
The most attractive and convenient of Madrid's public libraries. Books can be taken out on loan.

**British Council** *Paseo del General Martínez Campos 31, Chamberí (91 337 35 01, www.britishcouncil. es). Metro Iglesia. **Open** 9am-8.30pm Mon-Fri; 9am-6pm Sat. **Membership** €40 (3mths), €125 (1 year).*
The best place for English-language books in Madrid, the library in the British Council study centre has a massive selection of books and DVDs in English, as well as internet access and daily newspapers. Memberships for three months or 1 year are available.

**Hemeroteca Municipal** *C/Conde Duque 9-11, Conde Duque (91 588 57 71, bibliotecas.madrid.es). Metro Noviciado. **Open** Oct-mid June 9am-9pm Mon-Fri. Mid June-end July, Sept 9am-8pm*

*Mon-Fri. Aug 9am-2pm Mon-Fri. **Map** p120 G10.*
If you just have to track down that essential piece of information, the city newspaper library in the Centro Conde Duque is the place to do it. You need a researcher's card to get in, for which you must provide a copy of your passport and two ID photos.

## LOST PROPERTY

### Airport & rail stations
If you lose something before check-in at Barajas Airport, report the loss to the Aviación Civil office (AENA) in the relevant terminal, or call the lost property office on 91 393 61 19 (for T1 7am-8pm or for T4 7am-10pm). If you think you've mislaid anything on the RENFE rail network, look for the Atención al Viajero desk or Jefe de Estación office at the main station nearest to where your property went astray. The Centros de Viajes in the Chamartín and Atocha train stations are the official lost property centres for the municipal train network. Call 902 24 02 02 for both and ask for the Centro de Viaje or information on *objetos perdidos*.

**EMT (city buses)** *C/Cerro de la Plata 4, Salamanca (91 406 88 10, www.emtmadrid.es). Metro Pacífico. **Open** 8am-2pm Mon-Fri. Phone lines 7am-9pm daily.*
The lost property office for items that have been lost on Madrid's city or airport buses.

**Oficina de Objetos Perdidos (Madrid City Council)** *Paseo del Molino 7, south of the centre (91 527 95 90, www.madrid. es). Metro Legazpi. **Open** 8.30am-2pm Mon-Fri.*
This office mainly receives articles found on the metro, buses, trains, at the airport or in taxis, but if you're lucky, something lost in the street may turn up here.

## MEDIA

### Newspapers
Spanish newspapers may come in tabloid size, but they are far from light-hearted, preferring

heavy political commentary. Sensationalist, celeb-dominated stories are reserved for the *prensa de corazón* (press of the heart), such as *¡Hola!, Diez Minutos* or *¡Qué me dices!*. Free daily papers *Metro, 20 Minutos*, the gossipy *¡Qué!* and *Latino*, aimed at the South American market, are handed out outside some central metro stations.

### ABC
*ABC*'s journalists have the highest professional reputation. The favoured newspaper of the right.

### Marca & As
Sports-only (in fact, mostly football-only) papers. *Marca* is usually the country's bestselling daily paper.

### El Mundo
This centrist, populist paper made its name by unearthing many corruption scandals under the Socialists during the 1990s. Published on a Fri, '*La Luna de Metrópoli*' supplement is good for listings and information on the cultural agenda.

### El País
*El País* has long been the established paper of record, but a change in editorial direction in recent years means it is now seen as yet another mouthpiece of the government, though it does carry excellent daily information on Madrid, with the '*Tentaciones*' supplement on the last Sat of the month a great source for music and popular culture.

### La Razón
Right-wing and sensationalist daily, with much of its editorial coming from *ABC*.

### English-language
Foreign newspapers are on sale in **FNAC** (*see p49*), all **VIPS** stores (*see p91*) and at most kiosks around Sol, Gran Vía, C/Alcalá and the Castellana.

### Listings & classifieds
Local papers carry daily film and theatre listings, and the Fri supplement of *El Mundo* ('*La Luna de Metrópoli*') gives fuller information, reviews and so on.

**Guía del Ocio** *www.guiadelocio. com.*
A weekly listings magazine with cinema, arts, entertainment, concerts, nightlife and restaurant listings, and a good galleries section. It's handy, but can be inaccurate.

### Music & style mags
*Rockdelux*, the Spanish version of *Rolling Stone*, and *Popular 1*, dedicated to heavy metal music, are mainly sold in kiosks or music shops and at festivals. Look out for free mags such as *Mondo Sonoro*.

### Radio
The Spanish are avid radio fans; you'll hear radios blaring out in bars, cafés, buses and taxis.
**Radio Nacional de España** stations to listen for include **Radio 2** (96.5 FM, classical music) and **Radio 3** (93.2 FM, an excellent and eclectic mix of rock and world music). There are dozens of other local stations. One specific English-language programme to look out for is Radio Círculo's *Madrid Live* on for 30mins on Wed at 8pm (repeated on Thur at 8.30pm), which can be found on 100.4FM. Produced and presented by radio journalist Ann Bateson, it focuses on the city's arts, entertainment and social scene.

### Television
The emphasis of Spanish television is on mass entertainment, with an endless diet of tacky game shows, talk shows, really bad imported *telenovelas* (soaps) from South America and badly dubbed American movies. Just about the only redeeming feature is the news, although **La2** ('La Dos') does show some good documentaries and late-night films. **Telemadrid** is Madrid's own TV station, which is good for the megahit movie on Sun nights, but bad for political bias.

## MONEY

Spain's currency is the euro. Each euro is made up of 100 *céntimos*. One thing to remember is that the British/US practice on decimal points and commas is reversed (so 1.000 euros means one thousand euros, while 1,00 euro is one euro). There are banknotes for €5, €10, €20, €50, €100, €200 and €500, in different colours and designs. Due to the increasing circulation of counterfeit notes, smaller businesses may be reluctant to accept anything larger than €50.

### Banks & currency exchanges
Obtaining money through ATMs with a debit or credit card is the easiest option, despite the fees often charged. Banks (*bancos*) and savings banks (*cajas de ahorros*) readily accept cash and travellers' cheques (you must show your passport). Commission rates vary, and it's worth shopping around before changing money (although banks usually give the best rates); also, given the rates charged by Spanish banks, it's often cheaper to get money from an ATM with a credit or debit card rather than with travellers' cheques.

There are a few small bureaux de change (*cambio*) around the Puerta del Sol. Exchange rates are usually worse than in banks.

**Bank hours** Banks and savings banks normally open 8am-2pm Mon-Fri. From Oct to May many branches also open 9am-1pm on Sat. Hours vary a little between different banks, and some have branches that stay open until around 5pm a day a week (usually Thur). Savings banks often open late on Thur afternoons, but are less likely to open on Sat. Banks are closed on public holidays.

**Out-of-hours banking** Outside normal hours you can change money at the airport (terminals T1, T2 and T4, open 24hrs daily), at main train stations (Atocha, 7.30am-10pm daily), in El Corte Inglés (*see p48*), in hotels and at private *cambios*.

### Credit & debit cards
Major credit and charge cards are accepted in most hotels, shops, restaurants and other places (metro ticket machines and pay-and-display parking machines, for instance). American Express cards are less frequently accepted than MasterCard and Visa. Many debit cards from other European countries may also be accepted. You can withdraw cash with major cards from ATMs and banks will also advance cash against a credit card.

**Lost/stolen cards**
All lines have English-speaking staff and are open 24hrs daily. Maestro does not have a Spanish helpline.

**American Express** *freephone 902 375 637.*

**Diners Club** *902 401 112.*

**Mastercard** *freephone 900 971 231.*

**Visa** *900 991 124.*

### Tax
The standard rate for sales tax (IVA) is 21%; this drops to 10% in hotels and restaurants, and 4% on some books. IVA may or may not be included in listed prices – if it's not, the expression *'IVA no incluido'* (sales tax not included) should appear after the price. Beware of this when getting quotes on more expensive items. In shops displaying a 'Tax-Free Shopping' sticker, non-EU residents can reclaim tax on large purchases (*see p50*).

## OPENING HOURS

Eating, drinking and shopping all happen late in Madrid. The siesta has faded to a myth, but *madrileños* do operate to a distinctive schedule. Most shops open from 10am-2pm, and 5-5.30pm to 8-8.30pm Mon-Sat, although many stay closed on Sat afternoons. Food markets open earlier, around 8am. In July and, especially, in Aug most shops and services (such as the post office and government offices) close in the afternoon. Aug is also the time when most shops, bars and restaurants close for their annual holidays (from 2wks up to the whole month). Major stores and malls are open from 10am-9pm Mon-Sat without a break (for the vexed question of Sun shopping, see p50). Big supermarkets (Al Campo, Carrefour) open from 10am-10pm Mon-Sat and the first Sun of each month.

*Madrileños* still eat, drink, go out and stay out later than their neighbours in virtually every other European country. Most restaurants are open 1.30-2pm to 4pm, and 9pm-midnight, and many close on Sun nights and Mon, and for at least part of Aug. Many businesses finish at 3pm in the summer. Most museums (state ones) close one day a week, usually Mon.

## POLICE

Spain has several police forces. In Madrid the most important are the local **Policía Municipal**, in navy and pale blue, and the **Policía Nacional**, in darker blue and white uniforms (or all-blue combat gear). Each force has its own responsibilities, although they overlap. Municipales are principally concerned with traffic and parking problems and local regulations. The force with primary responsibility for dealing with crime are the Nacionales. The **Guardia Civil**, in green, are responsible, among other things, for policing inter-city highways, and customs.

### Reporting a crime

If you are robbed or attacked, report the incident as soon as possible at the nearest Policía Nacional station (*comisaría*) or dial 902 102 112 (9am-9pm daily). You can make statements over the phone if the crime doesn't involve violence or if the perpetrator hasn't been identified. You'll still have to go to the *comisaría* within 72hrs to sign the statement, but you'll be able to skip some queues.

In the centre near Plaza de España, the 24hr **SATE de Madrid** (C/Leganitos 19, Sol & Gran Vía, information 060, station 91 548 85 37) is the main station for foreigners in Madrid. Other police stations in the city centre include **Chamberí** (C/Rafael Calvo 33), **Huertas/ Retiro** (C/Huertas 76-78) and **Salamanca** (C/Príncipe de Asturias 8). All are open 24hrs

daily. You will be asked to make an official statement (*denuncia*). It is extremely unlikely that anything you have lost will ever be recovered, but you will need the *denuncia* in order to make an insurance claim. Very few police officers speak any English.

## POSTAL SERVICES

If you just need normal-rate stamps (*sellos*), it's easier to buy them in an *estanco* (*see right*). Post offices now have automatic stamp dispensing machines (with a weighing system) but they do not always work.

Letters and postcards up to 20g cost 55¢ within Spain, 1.35¢ to the rest of Europe, and 1.45¢ to the rest of the world; prices normally rise on 1 Jan. Note that you will pay more for 'irregular' shaped envelopes (basically, not rectangular). Cards and letters to other European countries usually arrive in three to four days, those to North America in about a week. Normal post boxes are yellow with two horizontal red stripes. There are also a few special red post boxes for urgent mail, with hourly collections. For more information on postal services, call 902 197 197 or see www.correos.es.

**Oficina Principal de Correos en Madrid** *Paseo del Prado 1, Retiro (91 523 06 94, www.correos. es). Metro Banco de España.* **Open** *8.30am-9.30pm Mon-Fri; 8.30am-2pm Sat.* **Map** *p141 N14.*

The central post office offers all manner of postal services. Faxes can be sent and received at all post offices, but rates are expensive, so use a private fax bureau. Not all services are available at all times. For express post, say you want to send a '*carta urgente*'. **Other locations** El Corte Inglés, C/Preciados 1-4, Sol & Gran Vía; Carrera de San Francisco 13, La Latina; C/Mejía Lequerica 7, Chueca; C/Jorge Juan 20, Salamanca; Terminal 1 in the airport.

### Estancos

The main role of the tobacco shop or *estanco* (look for a brown

and yellow sign with the word '*tabacos*') is, of course, to supply tobacco-related products. But they also sell stamps, phone cards and Metrobús and monthly *abono* tickets. *Estancos* are the only places to obtain official money vouchers (*papel de estado*), needed for dealings with Spanish bureaucracy.

### Poste restante

Poste restante letters should be addressed to Lista de Correos, 28000 Madrid, Spain. To collect, go to the main post office (*see left*); you'll need to bring your passport when coming to claim your mail.

## PUBLIC HOLIDAYS

The city is great fun during *fiestas*. On public holidays (*fiestas*), virtually all shops, banks and offices, and some bars and restaurants, are closed. There is a near-normal public transport service, though, except on Christmas Day and New Year's Day, and many museums do remain open, albeit with Sun hours operating. When a holiday falls on a Tue or Thur it's a common practice for people to take the day before or after the weekend off as well, in a long weekend called a *puente* (bridge). Many places are also closed for the whole of Easter Week. For the city's festivals, *see pxxx*. The usual official holidays are:

**New Year's Day/Año Nuevo** *1 Jan*

**Three Kings/ Reyes Magos** *6 Jan*

**Good Friday/Viernes Santo**

**May (Labour) Day/Fiesta del Trabajo** *1 May*

**Madrid Day/Día de la Comunidad de Madrid** *2 May*

**San Isidro** *15 May*

**Virgen de la Paloma** *15 Aug*

**Discovery of America/Día de la Hispanidad** *12 Oct*

**All Saints' Day/Todos los Santos** *1 Nov*

**Virgen de la Almudena** *9 Nov*

**Constitution Day/Día de la Constitución** *6 Dec*

**Immaculate Conception/La Inmaculada** *8 Dec*

**Christmas Day/Navidad** *25 Dec*

## RELIGION

### Anglican

**St George's (British Embassy Church)** *C/Núñez de Balboa 43, Salamanca (91 576 51 09, www. stgeorges madrid.com). Metro Velázquez.* **Open** *Office 10am-1pm Tue, Thur-Fri. Services See the website for times.* **Map** *p155 Q10.*

### Catholic (in English)

**Our Lady of Mercy** *C/Jose Vasconcelos 5, Chamartín (91 733 94 09, www.ourladyofmercy. info). Metro Chamartín.* **English Mass** *11am Sun.*
No shortage of Spanish Masses, but this is the Catholic church for the English-speaking parish of Madrid.

### Jewish

**Sinagoga de Madrid** *C/Balmes 3, Eastern suburbs (91 591 31 31). Metro Iglesia.* **Open** *9am-7.30pm Mon-Thur; 9am-1.30pm Fri; 10am-1.30pm Sun. Call for prayer times.*

### Muslim

**Centro Cultural Islámico de Madrid** *C/Salvador de Madariaga 4, Eastern suburbs (91 326 26 10, www.centro-islamico.es). Metro Barrio de la Concepción.* **Open** *10am-8pm Mon-Thur, Sat, Sun; noon-4pm Fri.*

## SAFETY & SECURITY

As in most major cities, street crime is a problem in Madrid and tourists are often targeted. One plus point is that pickpocketing and bag-snatching are more likely than any violent crime. Places to be especially on your guard are the Puerta del Sol, Gran Vía, the Plaza Mayor, the Plaza Santa Ana and, above all, the Rastro and Retiro park; watch out, too, on the metro. The area

around the junction of Gran Vía and C/Montera is a centre of street prostitution, and can feel uncomfortable at night. Recently, the Lavapiés district has acquired a reputation for street crime, which has developed alongside growing racial tension in the area, with robberies often attributed to young, homeless North African illegal immigrants, even though most thefts reported by *Time Out* readers and local media seem to involve teenage eastern European girls.

Street criminals prey very deliberately on the unwary, and their chances of success can be limited greatly by taking the following simple precautions.

• When sitting in a café, especially at an outside table, never leave a bag or coat on the ground, on the back of a chair or anywhere you cannot see it clearly. If in doubt, keep it on your lap.
• Give the impression of knowing what's going on around you, and – without getting paranoid – be alert and watch out to see if you are being followed.
• Wear shoulder bags pulled to the front, not at your back, especially in the underground. Keep the bag closed and a hand on top of it.
• Avoid pulling out large notes to pay for things, especially in the street at night; try not to get large notes when changing money.
• Be aware that street thieves often work in pairs or groups; if someone hassles you for money or to buy something, or pulls out a map and asks for directions, keep walking, as this can be a ruse to distract you so that the thief's 'partner' can get at your bag. This is often done pretty crudely, and so is not hard to recognise.
• Be extremely careful when you withdraw money from ATMs. Don't let anyone distract your attention while putting in your PIN code.
• Beware of fake policemen: if someone asks to see your ID, ask to see their identification first.

## SMOKING

Many Spaniards are keen smokers, but Spain's tough anti-smoking laws mean that smoking is now banned in enclosed public places. This includes all restaurants, though there has been a marked increase in permit applications for open-air terraces as a result. Some hotels still have smoking rooms, but there will only be a handful.

## STUDY

Foreign students from the EU staying more than 90 days require a residency permit (*Tarjeta de Residencia Para la Realización de Estudios*); non-EU students may also need a visa.

### Language classes

**Carpe Diem** *C/Montera 34, 4° -12, Sol & Gran Vía (91 522 31 22, www. carpemadrid.com). Metro Gran Vía.* **Map** *p83 K13.*
A young, funky Spanish-language academy, with small groups and enthusiastic teachers.

**International House** *C/Zurbano 8, Chamberí (91 319 72 24, www. ihmadrid.com). Metro Alonso Martínez.* **Open** *9am-10pm Mon-Fri; 8am-3pm Sat.* **Map** *pull-out M10.*
International House offers Spanish courses at all levels. **Other locations** throughout the city.

**Universidad Complutense de Madrid** *Secretaría del Centro Complutense para la Enseñanza del Español, Facultad de Filología, Edificio A, Plaza Menéndez Pelayo s/n, Ciudad Universitaria (91 394 53 25, www. ucm.es). Open Office Sept-June 10am-1pm, 3-6pm Mon-Fri. July 10am-1pm Mon-Fri. Closed Aug.*
Three-month Spanish courses for foreigners are held during the academic year. Higher-level students can study linguistics, literature and culture; there are also intensive language courses.

### Universities

**Erasmus, Socrates & Lingua programmes** *Information in the UK: British Council, 0161-957*

7755, www.britishcouncil.org/
study-work-create/opportunity/
study-abroad.

The Erasmus student-exchange
scheme helps students move
freely between EU member
states. To be eligible you must
be studying at an exchange
institution. Prospective students
should contact their college's
Erasmus co-ordinator.

**Universidad de Alcalá de
Henares** C/Escritorios, 4, Alcalá
de Henares (91 881 23 78, www.
alcalingua.com). **Open** Office
9am-7pm Mon-Fri.
Offers Spanish courses for
foreigners all year. Intensive
month-long courses are offered
between June and Sept and cost
€720 for language-only courses
or €900 for language and culture
courses.

**Universidad Autónoma de
Madrid** Ciudad Universitaria de
Cantoblanco, Ctra de Colmenar
km15 (91 497 3699, www.uam.
es/studyabroad). **Open** Office
9am-2pm, 3-5pm Mon-Thur;
9am-1.30pm Fri.
The UAM now competes in
prestige with the Complutense.

**Universidad Carlos III** C/Madrid
126, Getafe (91 624 60 00, 91 624
95 00, www.uc3m.es). **Open** Office
9am-2pm, 4-6pm Mon-Thur;
9am-2pm Fri. Closed Aug.
One of Madrid's newest
universities, with campuses
in Getafe, Leganés, Puerta de
Toledo and Colmenarejo.

**Universidad Complutense
de Madrid** Avda de Séneca 2,
Moncloa (91 452 04 00, www.ucm.
es). **Open** Office 9am-2pm, 4-6pm
Mon-Thur; 9am-2pm Fri.
The prestigious Complutense is
Madrid's main university, and
the largest and oldest in Spain.

## TELEPHONES

### Dialling & codes
Normal Spanish phone numbers
have nine digits; the area
code (91 in the Madrid area)
must be dialled with all calls,
both local and long-distance.
Spanish mobile phone numbers
usually begin with 6 and, very
occasionally, 7. Numbers starting
900 are freephone lines, while

other 90 numbers are special-rate
services. Those starting with 80
are high-rate lines and can only
be called from within Spain.

To call abroad, dial 00 followed
by the country code, then the
area code (omitting the first zero
in UK numbers) and number.
To call Madrid from abroad, dial
the international code (00 in
the UK, 001 from the USA), then
34 for Spain. Country codes are
as follows:

**Australia** 61.

**Canada** 1.

**Irish Republic** 353.

**New Zealand** 64.

**United Kingdom** 44.

**USA** 1.

### Mobile phones
Mobile phones, or móvil, calls are
paid for either through direct
debit or by using prepaid phones,
topped up with vouchers. Most
mobiles from other European
countries can be used in Spain,
but you may need to set this up
before leaving home. You may be
charged international roaming
rates even when making a local
call, and you will be charged
for incoming calls. Not all US
handsets are GSM-compatible;
check with your service provider
before you leave.

If you're staying more than
a few weeks, it may work out
cheaper to buy a pay-as-you-go
package when you arrive or
buy a local SIM card for your
own phone.

### Phone centres
Phone centres (locutorios) offer
cheap international calls, and are
full of small booths where you
can sit down and pay at the end.
Find them particularly around
Lavapiés, Huertas and Malasaña.
Often other services – internet,
currency exchange, money
transfer – are also available.

### Operator services & useful
phone numbers
Usually, operators will only
speak Spanish, though most

international operators speak
basic English.

**National directory
enquiries** 11888 (Yellow Pages,
free on www.paginasamarillas.
com), among others

**International directory enquiries
& operator** 11825

**National operator for reverse
charge calls** 1409

**International operator for
reverse charge calls** 1408

**Telephone faults service** 1002

## TIME

Spain is on CET (Central
European Time), 1hr ahead of
Greenwich Mean Time, 6hrs
ahead of US EST (Eastern
Standard Time) and 9hrs ahead
of PST (Pacific Standard Time).
Daylight saving time runs
concurrently with the UK.

## TIPPING

There are no rules for tipping
and in general Spaniards tip very
little. It's usual to leave 5%-10%
in restaurants, unless the service
has been bad. People sometimes
leave a little change in bars. In
taxis, tipping is not standard,
but many people round up to the
nearest 50¢. It's usual to tip hotel
porters.

## TOILETS

Public toilets are rare, although
there are some with an attendant
in the Retiro, by the lake; at
Chamartín and Atocha stations;
and in the Paseo del Prado.
However, proprietors usually
don't mind if you pop into a bar
or café (better, though, if you
ask first), and big stores such
as El Corte Inglés or fast-food
restaurants are a good bet.

Toilets are known as servicios,
aseos, baños or lavabos. In bars
and restaurants, the ladies'
is generally denoted by a D
(damas), and occasionally by an
M (mujeres) or S (señoras) on the
door, while the men's mostly say
H (hombres) or C (caballeros).

## TOURIST INFORMATION

The Centros de Turismo run by the city council, and the tourist office run by the regional authority (Comunidad de Madrid) provide similar basic information on Madrid and the surrounding region, plus free maps. The city also runs a phone information line for locals, 010 (*see right*), that can be useful to visitors. Tourist offices do not make hotel bookings but can advise on vacancies.

Full information on what's on is in local papers, listings magazines and local English-language magazines (*see p290*). For useful websites, *see p297*. *See also p58*.

### Centro de Turismo de Madrid
*Plaza Mayor 27, Los Austrias (91 578 78 10, www. esmadrid.com). Metro Ópera. Open 9.30am-9.30pm daily. Map p62 H15.*
This is the largest tourist information office in the city.

Smaller *puntos de información turística* are located at: the Plaza de Cibeles; Plaza del Prado at Plaza Neptune; Atocha, next to the Reina Sofía Museum; the Plaza de Callao; Paseo Recoletas; Paseo de la Castellana next to the Santiago Bernabéu Stadium; and at Barajas Airport Terminals 2 & 4. There's also a Foreign Tourist Assistance Service (SATE) at the police station (Comisaría) at C/ Leganitos 19.

### Oficinas de Turismo de la Comunidad de Madrid
*C/ Duque de Medinaceli 2, Huertas (91 429 49 51, 902 10 00 07, turismomadrid.es). Metro Banco de España. Open 8am-8pm Mon-Sat; 9am-2pm Sun. Map p95 L15.*
**Other locations** Atocha train station, Barajas Airport Terminals 1 & 4.

### Summer information officers
During July and Aug pairs of young information guides, in bright yellow and blue uniforms, are sent to roam the central area ready to answer enquiries in a courageous variety of languages (8am-8pm daily). They also staff information stands at Puerta del Sol, Plaza del Callao, Plaza Mayor, by the Palacio Real and by the Prado.

### 010 phoneline
*Open 8am-10pm Mon-Sat; 10am-9pm Sun.*
A city-run information line that will answer enquiries of any kind on Madrid, and particularly on events promoted by the city council. Calls are accepted in French and English. To access the line from outside Madrid, call 91 529 82 10.

## VISAS & IMMIGRATION

UK and Irish nationals will need a valid passport to enter Spain. Due to the Schengen Agreement, most other EU citizens, as well as Icelandic and Norwegian nationals, need only a national ID card.

Visas are not needed by US, Canadian, Australian or New Zealand citizens who are arriving for stays of up to 90 days. Citizens of South Africa and other countries do need a visa to enter Spain; approach Spanish consulates in your home country for information (see embassy. goabroad.com). Visa regulations do changes, so check before leaving home.

## WEIGHTS & MEASURES

Spain uses metric weights, distances and measurements.

## WORK

There are a huge number of foreigners living and working in Madrid. The majority of those from the EU are teaching English. To get a job in one of the academies with better pay and conditions, it's advisable to have a relevant qualification such as TEFL. Private classes are also available, but bear in mind that work often dries up over the summer and holiday periods.

### EU citizens
EU citizens living in Spain for more than three months need a resident's card (*tarjeta de residencia*), as well as ID or a passport from their own country.

### Non-EU citizens
While in Spain on a tourist visa you are not legally allowed to work, though many do. Those wanting a work permit officially need to be made a job offer while still in their home country. It can take time and applications aren't always successful. If you do get lucky, you can apply for Spanish residency at a Spanish consulate in your home country.

# Further Reference

## BOOKS

### Art & architecture

**Hugh Broughton** *Madrid: Guide to Recent Architecture (Ellipsis London, 1997)*. The capital's architecture analysed for a lay audience.

**Jonathan Brown** *Velázquez: Painter and Courtier (Yale University Press, 1986)*. The most comprehensive study in English.

**JH Elliott & Jonathan Brown** *A Palace for a King: The Buen Retiro and the Court of Philip IV (Yale University Press, 1980)*. A vivid reconstruction of the life, culture and spectacle of the Habsburg court, and the grandest of Madrid's palaces.

**Robert Hughes** *Goya (Harvill Press, 2001)*. A dynamic biography of Madrid's favourite son.

**Michael Jacobs** *Madrid Observed (Pallas Athene Arts, 1996)*. A lively survey by one of the best foreign writers on Spain. A good walking companion.

### Context & culture

**Phil Ball** *Morbo (WSC Books, 2011)*. A fascinating history of Spanish football, with a good section on Real Madrid.

**JH Elliott** *Imperial Spain, 1469-1716 (Penguin 2002)*. The standard history.

**RA Fletcher** *Moorish Spain (W&N 2001)*. Varied account of a little-known period in European history.

**Ronald Fraser** *Blood of Spain (Pimlico 1994)*. An oral history of the Spanish Civil War, the most vivid and human account of Spain's great crisis.

**John Hooper** *The New Spaniards (Penguin 2006)*. The best survey of post-1975 Spain, updated to cover changes in the 1990s.

**Juan Lalaguna** *A Traveller's History of Spain (Interlink 2001)*. A handy introduction to the country.

**Paul Preston** *Franco (Suma de Letras 2017); Comrades! (Fontana Press 2011); Doves of War (HarperCollins 2010)*. Exhaustive portraits of the key players on both sides of the Spanish Civil War. The same author's *The Spanish Civil War* is a good concise account of the war.

**Hugh Thomas, ed** *Madrid, A Traveller's Companion (InterLink Books 2005)*. A great anthology of writing on Madrid from the Middle Ages to the 1930s, by the likes of Casanova, Pérez Galdós and the Duke of Wellington.

**Giles Tremlett** *Ghosts of Spain: Travels through a Country's Hidden Past (Faber & Faber 2012)*. An essential read if you're interested in Spain's history and culture over the past century.

### Food & drink

**Sam and Sam Clark** *Moro (Ebury Press 2003)*. The best modern cookbook in English for reproducing the tastes of Spain.

**Alan Davidson** *Mediterranean Seafood (Prospect Books, 2012)*. An excellent reference guide, with illustrations, to Spain's fishy delights.

### Literature

**Pedro Almodóvar** *Patty Diphusa Stories and Other Writings (Faber & Faber 1993)*. Frothy, disposable, but full of the sparky, sexy atmosphere of the Madrid of La Movida.

**Camilo José Cela** *The Hive (Dalkey Archive Press 2001)*. Nobel Prizewinner Cela's sardonic masterpiece on Madrid in the aftermath of the Civil War.

**Miguel de Cervantes** *Don Quixote (Vintage Classics 2005)*. The Golden Age classic, and still an entertaining read. Now available in an excellent and lively translation by Edith Grossman.

**Benito Pérez Galdós** *Fortunata and Jacinta (CreateSpace Independent Publishing Platform 2017)*. The masterwork of Spain's great 19th-century realist novelist, a story of love and class of great depth set amid the political conflicts of 1860s Madrid. If you like *War and Peace*, you'll like this.

**Antonio Múñoz** *Molina Prince of Shadows (Quartet Books 1993)*. A psychological thriller based on the legacy of the recent past in modern Madrid.

**Tim Parfitt** *A Load of Bull: An Englishman's Adventures in Madrid (Pan 2007)*. An entertaining memoir on *madrileños* and their customs.

**Benjamin Prado** *Not Only Fire (Faber & Faber 2003)*. Examination of post-Civil War inter-generational relationships.

**Arturo Pérez Reverte** *The Fencing Master (Vintage 1999); The Flanders Panel (Vintage 1997); The Club Dumas (also published as The Dumas Club; Harcourt Brace 1997)*. Elegant, unconventional mystery novels by one of the most lauded of current Spanish writers.

**CJ Sansom** *Winter in Madrid (Pan 2016)*. An insightful portrait of life in Madrid following the Spanish Civil War.

## MUSIC

**Plácido Domingo** *Romanzas de Zarzuelas*. One of his several recordings of lush tunes from the *zarzuelas* that have played a big part in the recent revival of Madrid's own comic operas.

**El Gran Lapofsky** *Spain is Different*. A fantastic selection of Latin, bossa, nu-jazz and funk-infused tracks – some otherwise unavailable rarities – interspersed with skits from Spaniards telling us just why Spain is different.

**Ray Heredia** *Quien no corre, vuela*. One of the most original *nuevo flamenco* performers.

**Los Jóvenes Flamencos** Several CDs in this series, bringing together all the best *nuevo flamenco* artists of the last 20 years, have been issued by the Nuevos Medios label.

**Carmen Linares** *Antología*. Classic flamenco themes sung by one of the best younger *cantaoras*.

**Corazón Loco** *40 Joyas del Pop Español*. Excellent intro to the perky, occasionally daft and sometimes pretty cool soundtrack of modern Madrid.

**Paco de Lucía** Luzía, or any of the many recordings by the greatest of modern flamenco guitarists.

## WEBSITES

**www.ctm-madrid.es** Madrid transport information.

**www.esmadrid.com** Useful website with information on all visitor attractions.

**www.lecool.com** Weekly round-up of the quirkiest, coolest events.

**www.madrid.es** The Madrid council's functional website, with some information in English.

**www.madrid.org** Equivalent site of the regional body: information on local services, in Spanish only.

**www.renfe.es** Spanish Railways' site, with online booking.

**www.timeout.com/Madrid** Online listings and reviews.

## APPS

**Map of Madrid Offline** Useful, free street maps that won't incur roaming charges.

**Metro de Madrid Oficial** Interactive metro map.

**Madrid Map & Walking Tours** DIY walking routes.

**EMT Madrid** Useful for anyone favouring the bus system.

**Mercamad** Information on the hours, stalls and so on, of 46 Madrid markets.

▶ *For a list of Madrid films, see p213 Essential Madrid Films; for more Madrid music, see p220 Essential Madrid Albums.*

# Spanish Vocabulary

Like other Latin languages, Spanish has different familiar and polite forms of the second person (you). Many young people now use the familiar *tú* form most of the time; for foreigners, thought it can be advisable to use the more polite *usted* with people you do not know, and certainly with anyone over the age of 60. In the phrases listed here all verbs are given in the *usted* form. For help in making your way through menus, *see p38* and *p42*.

## Pronunciation

· **c** before an **i** or an **e** and **z** are like **th** in **th**in

· **c** in all other cases is as in **c**at

· **g** before an **i** or an **e** and **j** are pronounced with a guttural **h**-sound that doesn't exist in English – like **ch** in Scottish 'lo**ch**', but much harder

· **g** in all other cases is as in **g**et

· **h** at the beginning of a word is normally silent

· **ll** is pronounced like a **y**

· **ñ** is like **ny** in ca**ny**on

· a single **r** at the beginning of a word and **rr** elsewhere are heavily rolled

· **v** is more like an English **b**

· In words ending with a vowel, **n** or **s**, the penultimate syllable is stressed: eg *barato*, *viven*.

· In words ending with any other consonant, the last syllable is stressed: eg *exterior*, *universidad*

· An accent marks the stressed syllable in words that depart from these rules: eg *estación*, *tónica*

## Basics

· **please** *por favor*; **thank you (very much)** *(muchas) gracias*; **very good/great/OK** *muy bien*; **you're welcome** *de nada*

· **hello** *hola*; **hello** (when answering the phone) *hola, diga*

· **goodbye/see you later** *adiós/ hasta luego*

· **excuse me/sorry** *perdón*; **excuse me, please** *oiga* (the standard way to attract attention, politely; literally, 'hear me')

· **OK/fine/that's enough** (to a waiter) *vale*

· **open** *abierto*; **closed** *cerrado*

· **entrance** *entrada*; **exit** *salida*

· **very** *muy*; **and** *y*; **or** *o*; **with** *con*; **without** *sin*; **enough** *bastante*

## More expressions

· **good morning/good day** *buenos días*; **good afternoon/ good evening** *buenas tardes*; **good evening** (after dark)/**good night** *buenas noches*

· **do you speak English?** *¿habla inglés?*; **I'm sorry, I don't speak Spanish** *lo siento, no hablo castellano*; **I don't understand** *no lo entiendo*; **speak more slowly, please** *hable más despacio, por favor*; **wait a moment** *espere un momento*; **how do you say that in Spanish?** *¿Cómo se dice eso en castellano?*

· **what's your name?** *¿cómo se llama?* **my name is...** *me llamo...*

· **Sir/Mr** *señor (Sr)*; **Madam/Mrs** *señora (Sra)*; **Miss** *señorita (Srta)*

· **where is...?** *¿dónde está...?*; **why?** *¿por qué?*; **who?** *¿quién?*; **when?** *¿cuándo?*; **what?** *¿qué?*; **where?** *¿dónde?*; **how?** *¿cómo?*; **who is it?** *¿quién es?*; **is/are there any...?** *¿hay...?*

· **what time does it open/close?** *¿a qué hora abre/cierra?*

· **pull** *tirar*; **push** *empujar*

· **I would like** *quiero*; **how many would you like?** *¿cuántos quiere?*; **how much is it?** *¿cuánto vale?*

· **price** *precio*; **free** *gratis*; **discount** *descuento*; **do you have any change?** *¿tiene cambio?*

· **I don't want** *no quiero*; **I like** *me gusta*; **I don't like** *no me gusta*

· **good** *bueno/a*; **bad** *malo/a*; **well/badly** *bien/mal*; **small** *pequeño/a*; **big** *gran, grande*; **expensive** *caro/a*; **cheap** *barato/a*; **hot** (food, drink) *caliente*; **cold** *frío/a*

· **bank** *banco*; **to rent** *alquilar*; **(for) rent, rental** (en) *alquiler*; **post office** *correos*; **stamp** *sello*; **postcard** *postal*; **toilet** *el baño, el servicio, el lavabo*

· **airport** *aeropuerto*; **rail station** *estación de ferrocarril/ estación de RENFE* (Spanish railways); **metro station** *estación de metro*; **car** *coche*; **bus** *autobús*; **train** *tren*; **bus stop** *parada de autobus*; **the next stop** *la próxima parade*

· **a ticket** *un billete*; **return** *de ida y vuelta*

· **excuse me, do you know the way to...?** *¿oiga, señor/señora, sabe cómo llegar a...?*

· **left** *izquierda*; **right** *derecha*

· **here** *aquí*; **there** *allí*; **straight on** *recto*; **near** *cerca*; **far** *lejos*; **at the corner** *a la esquina*; **as far as** *hasta*; **towards** *hacia*; **it is far?** *¿está lejos?*

## Time

· **now** *ahora*; **later** *más tarde*

· **yesterday** *ayer*; **today** *hoy*; **tomorrow** *mañana*; **tomorrow morning** *mañana por la mañana*

· **morning** *la mañana*; **midday** *mediodía*; **afternoon/evening** *la tarde*; **night** *la noche*

· **at what time...?** *¿a qué hora...?* **in an hour** *en una hora*; **at 2** *a las dos*

## Numbers

**0** *cero*; **1** *un, uno, una*; **2** *dos*; **3** *tres*; **4** *cuatro*; **5** *cinco*; **6** *seis*; **7** *siete*; **8** *ocho*; **9** *nueve*; **10** *diez*; **11** *once*; **12** *doce*; **13** *trece*; **14** *catorce*; **15** *quince*; **16** *dieciséis*; **17** *diecisiete*; **18** *dieciocho*; **19** *diecinueve*; **20** *veinte*; **21** *veintiuno*; **22** *veintidós*; **30** *treinta*; **40** *cuarenta*; **50** *cincuenta*; **60** *sesenta*; **70** *setenta*; **80** *ochenta*; **90** *noventa*; **100** *cien*; **200** *doscientos*; **1,000** *mil*; **1,000,000** *un millón*

## Dates & seasons

· **Monday** *lunes*; **Tuesday** *martes*; **Wednesday** *miércoles*; **Thursday** *jueves*; **Friday** *viernes*; **Saturday** *sábado*; **Sunday** *domingo*

· **January** *enero*; **February** *febrero*; **March** *marzo*; **April** *abril*; **May** *mayo*; **June** *junio*; **July** *julio*; **August** *agosto*; **September** *septiembre*; **October** *octubre*; **November** *noviembre*; **December** *diciembre*

· **spring** *primavera*; **summer** *verano*; **autumn** *otoño*; **winter** *invierno*

# Index

INDEX

PICTURE CREDITS

# Credits

**Crimson credits**
**Editor** Sally Davies
**Assistant Editor** Jo Williams
**Listings Editor** Mary-Ann Gallagher
**Proofreader** Rosamund Sales
**Layouts** Patrick Dawson,
Emilie Crabb, Mihaela Botezatu
**Cartography** Gail Armstrong, John Scott

**Series Editor** Sophie Blacksell Jones
**Production Manager** Kate Michell
**Design** Mytton Williams

**Chairman** David Lester
**Managing Director** Andy Riddle

**Advertising** Media Sales House
**Marketing** Lyndsey Mayhew
**Sales** Joel James

## Authors

This guide was written and researched by Sally Davies, with contributions from Robert Elms, Nick Funnell, Mary-Ann Gallagher, Harvey Holtom, Simon Hunter, Michael Jacobs, Anna Norman, Nick Rider and Rob Stone.

## Acknowledgements

The editor would like to thank contributors to previous editions of *Time Out Madrid*, whose work formed the basis of this guide. The editor would also like to thank Sonia Alonso, Annie Bennett, James Blick, Aida Casamayor, Alana Fogarty, Vera de Frutos, Pilar Gimeno, Fabian González, Simon Hunter, Botoa Lefe, Jordi Luque, Concha Marcos, Andrea Martín, Myriam Martín, Yoly Martín, Kate McWilliams, Tess O'Donovan, Paul Richardson, Carlota Sartorius Freschet and Ben Serio for their inestimable help in compiling this edition.

## Photography credits
**Front cover** Getty Images/iStockphoto.
**Back cover** left: Florentino Ar G/Shutterstock.com; centre: Alexandre Arocas/Shutterstock.com; right: La Taberna Antonio Sanchez.
**Interior Photography credits**, see p303.

**Publishing information**
Time Out Madrid City Guide 10th edition
© TIME OUT ENGLAND LIMITED 2018
April 2018

ISBN 978 1 780592 62 6
CIP DATA: A catalogue record for this book is available from the British Library

Published by Crimson Publishing
21d Charles Street, Bath, BA1 1HX (01225 584 950, www.crimsonpublishing.co.uk) on behalf of Time Out England.

Distributed by Grantham Book Services
Distributed in the US and Canada by Publishers Group West (1-510-809-3700)

Printed by Replika Press, India.